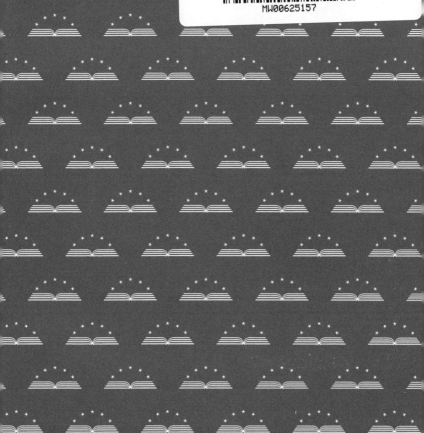

Library of America, a nonprofit organization,
champions our nation's cultural heritage
by publishing America's greatest writing in
authoritative new editions and providing resources
for readers to explore this rich, living legacy.

LATINO POETRY

LATINO POETRY

THE LIBRARY OF AMERICA
ANTHOLOGY

Rigoberto González, *editor*

THE LIBRARY OF AMERICA

Published in the United States by Library of America.
Visit our website at www.loa.org.

Some of the material in this volume is reprinted with the permission
of holders of copyright and publishing rights.
Acknowledgments begin on page 593.

This paper exceeds the requirements of
ANSI/NISO Z39.48–1992 (Permanence of Paper).

Distributed to the trade in the United States
by Penguin Random House Inc.
and in Canada by Penguin Random House Canada Ltd.

Library of Congress Control Number: 2023951399
ISBN 978–1–59853–783–3

First Printing
The Library of America—382

Manufactured in the United States of America

Latino Poetry: The Library of America Anthology
is the centerpiece of

**Latino Poetry:
Places We Call Home**

a national public humanities initiative
made possible with support from
The National Endowment for the Humanities
and Emerson Collective.

CONTENTS

xi

II. CORRIDOS AND NOSTALGIA SONGS
Nineteenth and Twentieth Centuries

III. LATINO ANCESTORS
Twentieth Century
Latin American

V. HOWLING AS THEY CAME

VI. MY BODY SANG ITS UNDEATH

INTRODUCTION

Places We Call Home

RIGOBERTO GONZÁLEZ

"Latino" is a capacious, unruly, sometimes misunderstood term. There is no one narrative that speaks for all Latinos, nor should there be. So it is with poetry by Latinos: the anthology you hold in your hands goes beyond stereotypes, surface definitions, and fixed categories, embodying the variousness of the Latino poetic tradition. In compiling this anthology I sought to challenge the usage of Latino as a rubric that, like the metaphorical "melting pot," homogenizes cultures. Rather I conceived of Latino poetry as a kind of landscape, a communal, open space where many different visions—Mexican American, Cuban American, Puerto Rican, Dominican American, Afro-Latino, and Indigenous Latino, among others—can flourish. Across these varied expressions, however, I also detected a distinctive way of using language, fusing Anglophone, Hispanic, and Indigenous resonances, as well as a shared embeddedness within interwoven legacies of colonialism and imperialism, and connections to ancestral wellsprings of speech and music. Perhaps above all I was aware of a sense of urgency animating these poems, as political as it is aesthetic, a belief that "poetry is not a luxury," to borrow a phrase from the African American poet Audre Lorde.

Latino poetry has long been haunted by its colonial past. Iberian colonization* left indelible imprints on the lands,

---

*For the purposes of this project, I limited selections to poets whose nationality or ancestry is situated in one or more of the independent Latin American countries, plus the unincorporated territory of Puerto Rico, that were once part of the Spanish empire. While many Brazilian Americans identify as Latino in cultural and political spaces, Portuguese colonial and linguistic history has its unique trajectory, as do the stories of other countries in Latin America, such as Haiti, Belize, Guyana, and Suriname, to name a few. Therefore, Brazilian American poetry is not included.

cultures, and peoples of the Americas, evident not only in Catholicism and the Spanish language but also in an enduring legacy of migration and exile and the search for new or second homes undertaken by so many Latinos. This anthology is divided into six sections, and Part I, "Antecedents," begins with excerpts from colonial texts and their translations. Invaluable as a historical record, the Spanish missionary Fray Alonso Gregorio de Escobedo's *La Florida* narrates the exploits of the Spanish and the resistance of Indigenous peoples; the excerpt is followed by the last of the thirty-four cantos in the soldier-poet Gaspar Pérez de Villagrá's *Historia de la Nueva México* (1610), considered the first American epic poem, set in the aftermath of the Spanish victory over the Acoma. Though the poet writes from the point of view of the colonist, defending the expedition's violence and characterizing Indigenous people as savages, the *Historia* has been recognized by scholars and historians as a useful chronicle of colonization's early stages. The anonymous verse play *Los Comanches* likewise romanticizes the colonizers' subjugation of Indigenous peoples. But while the works from the colonial period align themselves with conquest, the tradition of Latino poetry that followed, in many ways fruit of these violent histories, took a diametrically opposed perspective, often emerging from or in solidarity with the voices of the colonized and their descendants.

The remaining entries in "Antecedents" are by poets born in the nineteenth century, a period of conflict over lands and borders that saw the independence of many nations in the Western Hemisphere and the accompanying rise of particular national identities. These poets would identify first and foremost as a member of a specific nationality—American, Cuban, Puerto Rican, Mexican, Nicaraguan. The poems selected, however, highlight themes that Latino poets would engage with in the twentieth century, centering on identity, place, and belonging textured by feelings of nostalgia, pride, and dislocation.

In the United States, New York City became a cultural and political center for Latino poets during the nineteenth century and into the twentieth. Here the Puerto Rican activist poet Lola Rodríguez de Tió offered help to exiled Cuban revolutionaries, including José Martí, in their efforts to topple

Spanish rule in Cuba. Joseíto Fernández used lines from poems in Martí's book *Versos sencillos* (Simple Verses, 1890) in writing Cuba's most recognizable patriotic song, "Guantanamera." The Nicaraguan poet Salomón de la Selva studied at Cornell and Columbia and would go on to write poems in English as well as Spanish; his many connections with the city's literary circles included close ties to Edna St. Vincent Millay. The Mexican poet José Juan Tablada, who had been to Japan and introduced the haiku to Latin American literature, called New York City home at various points from 1914 onward. From these beginnings, New York City has remained an important center for Latino poetry up to the present day.

Aiming to acknowledge, however briefly, the musical and folk traditions that have influenced Latino poetry, Part II is a songbook comprising three corridos and several songs that have inspired pride and awakened longings for various homelands among the Latino diaspora. Corridos are Mexican folk ballads that rose to their greatest prominence during the Mexican Revolution of 1910, often depicting the exploits of the downtrodden and reflecting the tensions between American settlers and Mexicans along an embattled U.S.–Mexico border. Corridos might even be regarded as an early sort of mass media that endures as a form of oral storytelling. The corridos included here range from the harrowing tale of a New Mexican woman held captive by the Apache—a rarity in its focus on a female protagonist—to an account of the exploits of legendary outlaw Gregorio Cortez and, in a more contemporary vein, a protest song, recorded in the 1980s by the popular Mexican group Los Tigres del Norte, about the migration trauma and racism endured by undocumented Central Americans journeying through Mexico en route to the U.S. The ballads that follow express profound nostalgia for homelands in songs that, in some cases, are so beloved that they have become unofficial anthems.

Part III begins with poets born between 1900 and 1940 who were foundational voices and influences on Latino poetry. The two subsections "Latin America" and "Latino" distinguish between the poets who spent most of their lives in Latin America (though often with extended periods living in the U.S.) and those who were born in the U.S. or who arrived at a young age. The Puerto Rican poets José Dávila Semprit, Clemente Soto Vélez, and Julia de Burgos represent a new era of activist poets whose work addresses, at times unsparingly, America's inequalities and place in the world—as with Semprit's indictment of the U.S. as "an alloy of passions, prejudices," embodying "an entrenched arrogance." The Cuban poet Eugenio Florit laments, in "The Lonely Poets in Manhattan," the isolation he feels in "the city where nobody knows anybody," but finds a sense of connection, too, in its multicultural literary circles. Lourdes Casal's poem "For Ana Veldford" evokes the "raucous glory" of New York, and while she may feel like a "stranger among the stones," she nonetheless strikes a note of gratitude when she, a Cuban exile, proclaims "still New York is my home." These poets are joined here by three of their counterparts from Central America, as well as the Chilean poet and artist Cecilia Vicuña, long resident in the U.S., and the Cuban poet Excilia Saldaña, a prominent feminist voice in Afro-Caribbean literature.

Politics and poetry have been inseparable in the lives and works of Latin American poets, and this fusion has been a feature of Latino poetics up through the present, as descendants of immigrants, exiles, and refugees recall their respective ancestries and histories while reconciling with their American identities. Political struggle was at the heart of the Chicano Movement, which emerged during the tumultuous 1960s. Ethnic pride became the avenue to unite communities and to inspire them to action. The word "Chicano," once a slur that had been reclaimed by Latino youth in the 1940s, was adopted as a politicized term that symbolized a rejection of assimilation and an expression of pride in Mexican and Indigenous roots. In 1965, California farmworkers led by Cesar Chavez and Dolores Huerta, seeking better pay and working conditions, began to strike for the right to unionize and to engage in collective bargaining. At the same time, the arts became a catalyst in stewarding Chicano culture and resisting erasure. Poetry, a mainstay of rallies, protests, and community celebrations, was especially valued.

Rodolfo "Corky" Gonzales's "I Am Joaquín: An Epic Poem, 1967" is arguably the Chicano Movement's first important poem. It is prefaced here by a 1935 poem by a significant precursor, Américo Paredes, also the author of a groundbreaking study of "The Ballad of Gregorio Cortez." In his poem "The Mexico-Texan," Paredes points out the dilemma of the Tejano, and by extension the Chicano, who is not from here or over there ("ni de aquí, ni de allá")—caught within a feeling of not belonging on either side of the border: "In Texas he's Johnny, in Mexico Juan, / But the Mexico-Texan he no gotta lan'." The Mexico-Texan, who speaks an odd language and is treated disdainfully by Mexicans and Americans alike, must claim an in-between space, a space of his own where he can celebrate "September the Sixteenth and Fourth of July," the respective independence days of Mexico and the U.S.

This theme of reconciling American and Mexican identities is also central to "I Am Joaquín." Gonzales reaches back to pre-Columbian civilizations, then travels forward through time to underscore how the inheritance of centuries of history and culture now fortifies the strength and struggle of the Chicano. In recent years the poem has been critiqued, as has the Chicano Movement itself, for putting too great an emphasis on male figures and leaders; aside from goddesses and virgins, women are represented by "the black shawled / faithful women." Nonetheless, its historical importance and influence on Chicano poetry are unquestionable. It is joined here by poems that voice a kindred sense of outrage, such as Lalo Delgado's "Stupid America," an indictment of American society's unwillingness to place their faith in the futures of Chicano youth, and Raúl R. Salinas's "Unity Vision," which expresses solidarity with Indigenous activism in the wake of the Wounded Knee occupation in 1973.

Poets of this generation, like those in their wake, foregrounded issues of language, which are inevitably issues of audience, too. José Montoya's poems employed *caló*, Chicano slang. Depicting life on the streets and working-class stories, they conveyed a formidable empathy and respect for everyday people. The language of the elegy "El Louie" is intended for people inside the barrio who would be familiar with the intricacies of this way of speaking. It's not meant to exclude those who lack that community skill but rather to elevate those who possess it. In a formalist and thus a very different mode, the two sonnets by the Dominican American poet

Rhina P. Espaillat address the sometimes troubled interaction between native speakers of English and Spanish. In the poem "On Hearing My Name Pronounced Correctly, Unexpectedly, For Once," there are echoes of Paredes's "The Mexico-Texan" when Espaillat writes: "Odd how the gringo tongue that shifts, translates you / into something it can say, though far / from what you are."

The final three sections in the anthology represent successive generations of Latino poets and, unlike the prior sections, are ordered alphabetically by poet. Born after 1940 and before 1960, the poets in Part IV, "Let Me Tell You What a Poem Brings," bridge the era of social activism to the institutionalization of Latino poetry, above all in the university (aided by the establishment of ethnic studies disciplines and the growth of creative writing departments): these poets were often important activists or became key figures (as authors, influences, role models, mentors, and/or teachers) in the aesthetic development of future Latino poets and poetry. Part V, "Howling as They Came," encompassing poets born between 1960 and 1980, is dominated by Latino poets who received instruction in an MFA program (though not all did, of course), many of whom became academics themselves, teaching generations of students from all walks of life. And finally, Part VI, "My Body Sang Its Undeath," reflects how, in the new millennium, Latino poetry has blossomed as never before. I wanted to bring into sharper focus a group of millennial writers whose interests, influences, and experiences are scaffolded by the works of their literary ancestors; my selections are from those poets born after 1980 who (with a few rare exceptions) have published at least two books.

I've titled this introduction "Places We Call Home" because so many of the poems in this anthology engage with ideas of home. A "home" is not only a physical space or structure, not only a concept attached to notions, legal and otherwise, of citizenship or nationality. Home is also manifested in a personal relationship to history, memory, language, culture, and family. Those avenues of belonging can easily be romanticized but, through the creative works of these poets, they become nuanced. And for the voices of those who feel themselves to be outside this sort of belonging, excluded or marginalized

from it, the body—and the multivalency of identity—are yet
another kind of home.

Latino queerness has found an important home in poetry.
Although the Latino values and beliefs that have been heavily
influenced by Catholicism continue to foster hostile rhetoric
and spaces within families and communities for people who
are not heterosexual, there are countercurrents in our present
moment: queer people have become more visible in the media
and popular culture, coming-out stories highlight moments not
only of rejection but also of acceptance, and even Pope Francis
has encouraged a more compassionate response to same-sex
unions and LGBTQ communities. Nonetheless, homophobia
and transphobia remain cemented into certain forms of religion
and politics, and lately we have seen more vocal condemnations
of queerness and attempts to curtail LGBTQ rights. Attitudes
toward queerness and gender roles, however, shift with each
generation.

In his 1994 poem "HIV," Miguel Algarín explores queer
sexuality and the harsh reality of HIV infection: "*Who to tell?
Is there someone? The search for what to tell.*" Latinos continue to
be disproportionately affected by HIV, but the subject remains
on the margins of Latino poetry as a whole. In a similar vein,
Rane Arroyo's "A Chapter from *The Book of Lamentations*"
confronts the stigma endured by those with the auto-immune
disease before lifesaving medicine was available: "look /
around us / at the young so unloved while alive. / AIDS is not
just a war inside the body." Anthony Aguero's "Undetectable
Explained to a Primo" addresses the persistence of silence
that leads to ignorance, even after effective medication and
treatment transformed what had been a fatal disease into a
chronic condition.

Algarín's poems about queerness and the body in a state
of either desire or vulnerability speak of identity through the
body, anticipating an important conversation in the millennial
era, particularly among those who are nonbinary and/or
transgender. Notable poems in this regard include Oliver Baez
Bendorf's "My Body the Haunted House," Christopher Soto's
"The Joshua Tree // Submits Her Name Change," and Roque
Raquel Salas Rivera's "they," the latter invoking the binary
(and thus restrictive) grammatical gender rules in Spanish:

"in this, our language / there exists no plural that doesn't deny me." Other poems about queer identity include Miguel Murphy's "Love Like Auto-Sodomy," Joseph Delgado's "dirty sheets," Natalie Diaz's "Postcolonial Love Poem," Joe Jiménez's "Some nights I just want to hold a man in my arms because this would make everything better in my life," and Laura Villareal's "Home Is Where the Closet Is," which addresses both sexuality and ethnicity: "I forgot I was brown / until Texas pointed to the border. // I forgot my orientation was straight / to hell if I love another woman."

In a more concrete sense, particular community spaces have served as crucial homes for Latino poets. The Fresno School of poetry emerged out of the creative writing program at Fresno State University in California's Central Valley, and among the prominent Latino poets associated with this group are Luis Omar Salinas, Gary Soto, and Juan Felipe Herrera, the son of migrant farmworkers who in 2015 became the twenty-first Poet Laureate of the United States (the first Latino to hold that title). Herrera's poetics is informed by his commitments to community activism and public performance, his working-class Chicano identity, and an affinity for wordplay and experimentation (see "The Chaos Beneath Buttons/Acrylic Blue," which in turn influenced Anthony Cody's "How to Lynch a Mexican"). Other poets with connections to Fresno include David Campos, whose "Lizard Blood" invokes another Fresno institution, Clovis Community College; David Dominguez, who explores his working-class roots in "Mi Historia"; Tim Z. Hernandez, who takes Chicano masculinity to task in "I've Worn that Feminine Skin"; and Andrés Montoya, whose poem "fresno night" describes the spiritual and sensory experience of evening in the city.

Another vital home for poets has been the Nuyorican Poets Café, a teaching and learning space outside of academia that has remained faithful to its community activist roots, showcasing and supporting poets, spoken-word performers, musicians, and hip-hop artists. Founded in 1973 by such luminaries as Miguel Algarín, Tato Laviera, Miguel Piñero, and Pedro Pietri, nicknamed "El Reverendo," this performance and activist space popularized the usage of "Nuyorican," a term embraced by Puerto Ricans in New York City and its surrounding areas as a declaration of pride in their cultural and political birthrights. Other poets closely associated with the early years of the Nuyorican poets include Sandra María Esteves and Giannina Braschi. Pietri in particular has exerted wide influence, evident in some of the poems included in this anthology: his "Puerto Rican Obituary" inspired Carmen Giménez's poem about exploited maquiladora workers, and Pietri is also acknowledged in Vincent Toro's "Sonata of the Luminous Lagoon," which decries the effects of capitalism and the tourist industry on Puerto Rico, rapaciously transforming the island and displacing the island-born population. Among the other poems, like Pietri's, that center the Puerto Rican diaspora in New York City are Willie Perdomo's "We Used to Call It Puerto Rico Rain," which reveals how Puerto Rico is invoked as a spiritual home while navigating the urgencies of the mainland—"The perfect weather to master the art of standing under a bodega awning, shifting crisis to profit"— and Mariposa's "Ode to the Diasporican," which reconciles being born and raised on the mainland while still feeling a close connection to the island: "¡No nací en Puerto Rico! / Puerto Rico nació en mi" (I wasn't born in Puerto Rico! / Puerto Rico was born in me).

The indelible histories of the transatlantic slave trade in the Latin American continent have led various Latino poets to explore Black identity and cleave a voice for the Afro-Latinx experience in Latino poetry. Notable poems in this regard here include Julian Randall's "Biracial Ghazal," Darrel Alejandro Holnes's "Cristo Negro de Portobelo," Jasminne Mendez's "Machete," and Gabriel Ramirez's "On Realizing I Am Black."

Language itself is a kind of home for Latino poets. Many poems employ code-switching, Spanglish, or intralingual wordplay to situate language as a place to imagine belonging when a single nationality or identity doesn't quite embody the complexity of personhood. Gustavo Pérez Firmat's energetic "Last-Mambo-in-Miami" shuttles between English and Spanish: "Name your tema; I'll hedge; name your cerca, I'll straddle it / like a cubano"; Natasha Carrizosa's "Mejiafricana" journeys through her African American and Mexican ancestries and mother tongues: "i am fierce like panthers / militant with pen . . . i am el viento que viene de méxico"

(I am the wind that comes from Mexico); José Olivarez's "Mexican American Disambiguation" unpacks identity politics with humor and sarcasm: "i am a Chicano from Chicago / which means i am Mexican American / with a fancy college degree & a few tattoos." But this home can also be troubled. J. Michael Martinez's poem "Lord, Spanglish Me" reads like a prayer pleading for a reconciliation between the language and religious beliefs of the mother and grandmother and those of the speaker. Iliana Rocha's "Elegy Composed of a Thousand Voices in a Bottle" speaks to being called a *pocha*—a disparaging term used to decry a person of Mexican ancestry's assimilation into American values, language, and identity: "¿Girl, why you trying to be so white? . . . ¡Mexicana, habla en español!" (Mexican, speak Spanish!).

Other complex approaches to home include poems that address exile, whether as émigré, refugee, or undocumented immigrant. For poets Pablo Medina and Virgil Suárez, living in exile means envisioning Cuba from afar, with the island as ambiguous as its presence is insistent. As Medina writes in "The Floating Island": "The island mouth is smiling / or frowning, who can tell, / stuffed with waning intentions, / sugarcane and sand." Suárez's "El Exilio" imagines Cuba through the eyes of a father who, after an accident leaves him unable to work, shares his bittersweet feelings about the U.S., where he enjoys certain freedoms while living a "sedentary life." In Cynthia Guardado's "Parallel Universe," the daughter of Salvadoran immigrants reckons with her remembered longing for the ancestral home as a child living in "los Estados / (where no one we love exists)."

Founded in 2015, the organization Undocupoets has played an important role in bringing attention to the exclusion of undocumented writers from literary and publishing opportunities. Its founders, Marcelo Hernandez Castillo, Christopher Soto, and Javier Zamora, are all included in Part VII. Castillo's poem "Wetback" turns a racist slur into a moment of intimacy and tenderness, disempowering the disdain and violence embedded in that word. From that unwelcome encounter comes a surprising response: "I opened his mouth and fed him a spoonful of honey." Zamora was one of the many unaccompanied minors from Mexico and

Central America who have crossed the border at great risk to their personal safety. His poem "El Salvador" is addressed to the country and ends with the plea: "Make it easier / to never have to risk our lives." Another important inclusion is from Alan Pelaez Lopez, an Afro-Indigenous poet from Mexico whose poem "'Sick' in America" speaks to the trauma of border-crossing: "how do i tell myself i had a childhood if at the / age of five i am a fugitive of the law?"

Ultimately, Latino poetry feels most at home in the political sphere. Its most visible and venerated poets, such as Herrera and Martín Espada, lead by example. Espada, like Herrera, has dedicated himself to community activism. His work addresses, among other topics, social injustices committed against Latinos, yet he resists burying their stories beneath tragedy or injustice and elevates them into a more complex realm that glimmers with hope and optimism. Take "Alabanza: In Praise of Local 100," for example. This poem elegizes and praises the restaurant workers who perished in the 9/11 terrorist attacks on the World Trade Center, concluding with a particularly chilling though compelling exchange: "one said with an Afghan tongue: / *Teach me to dance. There is no music here.* / And the other said with a Spanish tongue: / *I will teach you. Music is all we have.*"; in "The Republic of Poetry," dedicated to the nation of Chile, the speaker imagines an alternate reality for that country in which poetry reigns supreme: "In the republic of poetry, / the guard at the airport / will not let you leave the country / until you declaim a poem for her / and she says *Ah! Beautiful.*" A similar sentiment of solidarity across cultures and nationalities is found in Pat Mora's uplifting poem "Let Us Hold Hands."

Another indispensable political poet is Lorna Dee Cervantes, a Chicana Chumash poet and a leading voice of her generation. Her poems address social issues across the Americas, as is evident in "Bananas," about the harm to the land and peoples inflicted by colossal corporations (in this case, United Fruit, now Chiquita). Like Salinas's "Unity Vision" and Alma Luz Villanueva's "Child's Laughter," Cervantes's "Flatirons" is fueled by solidarity and connection with Indigenous Americans. And in her most anthologized poem, "Poem for the Young White Man Who Asked How I, an Intelligent,

Well-Read Person, Could Believe in the War Between Races," she declares forthrightly: "I do not believe in the war between races // but in this country / there is war."

Francisco X. Alarcón, yet another poetry trailblazer, embraced his Nahuatl and Mexican roots, but also his queerness. In his work, the intersection between ethnicity and sexuality emerges not as a collision but as a pathway to wholeness. The poems are animated by a voice that speaks not from trauma but from a place of affection for his multivalent identity. Such an approach is also evident in the work of Eduardo C. Corral. As a point of comparison, see Alarcón's "Un Beso Is Not a Kiss" and Corral's "Want."

Other notable contemporary poems to take up charged political and social topics include Aracelis Girmay's "Ode to the Watermelon" and Carolina Ebeid's "Punctum / Image of an *Intifada*," both invoking Palestine; Emanuel Xavier's "Madre America," in which the speaker, loyal and grateful to the land of opportunity, nonetheless feels rejected by "normal" American society as a gay man and as a Latino: "You made me who I am, but still unworthy / of their affection"; Antonio de Jesús López's "Convert Glossary," whose Chicano speaker has converted to Islam; and Alexandra Lytton Regalado's "La Mesa," which is a response to one of Carolyn Forché's most notable poems, "The Colonel." Regalado's poem tells a similar story, though it is from the point of view of a Salvadoran, not a foreigner. One of the final poems in the anthology is Vanessa Angélica Villarreal's "A Field of Onions: Brown Study," a poem that arose from the discovery in Falfurrias, Texas, that the bodies of unclaimed undocumented immigrants were buried in mass graves.

When taking into account the heterogeneous and interwoven histories, communities, and attitudes of an expansive Latin American diaspora, notions of home and homeland only become more complex and multilayered, resisting attempts at stable definition. And yet, in the work of these poets, resonant threads of shared experience continuously weave local and historical concerns into the pan-diasporic and the universal. Undocumented Marshallese-Filipinx migrant artist Stephanie "Soultree" Camba has said, "I don't think that places are my home, but people are." This sentiment, which at face value seems simple, speaks to the enduring importance of community in the face of adversity, uncertainty, or instability. When shared in the public context of a reading, the poem enacts this desire for connection and becomes an antidote to silence and invisibility. The poem reaches toward the listener, amplifying the voice that speaks from within the poet's respective communities, calling into existence experiences both subjective and communal. Due to a unique capacity for intimacy, and the longevity granted to it by the technology of the written word, the poem has the potential to animate the past for a future community of listeners, tracing a lineage through breath and utterance. Because as long as there is an audience to hear and read them, poets will continue to speak.

I.

ANTECEDENTS

FRAY ALONSO GREGORIO DE ESCOBEDO

de *La Florida*: Canto XIX

En la costa de la desierta Florida se
perdió un navío de Castilla. Cautivaron los
indios un español; estuvo diez y siete años
cautivo; tuvo dos hijas en una infiel. Sacóle
a él y a ellas Pedro Menéndez de cautiverio.

Si el humano favor al hombre ha puesto
en honra y dignidad de alto asiento,
y della Dios eterno le ha depuesto,
fue por no haber en él merecimiento.
El canto referido cuenta esto,
y nos lo da a entender de fundamento,
que no confirma el Rey de tierra y cielo
lo que hace el que lo es acá en el suelo.

Si el Rey Felipe dio cargo al teniente,
no pudo darle el don de la prudencia,
que fue por no tenerla un insolente,
pues mostró de venganza la insolencia.
Por lo cual nuestro Dios omnipotente,
castigó de aquel juez la irreverencia,
dándole justa muerte por azote
porque dio un bofetón al sacerdote.

Cuando como tenemos por costumbre,
el cristiano al teniente sepultaba,
el centinela desde su alta cumbre
a mucha prisa al arma repicaba,
que fue causa olvidar la pesadumbre
de la muerte que a todos lastimaba,
y tomando los armas con presteza
de su valor mostraron la fiereza.

2

FRAY ALONSO GREGORIO DE ESCOBEDO

from *La Florida*: Canto XIX

Off the barren Florida coast, a Castilian vessel foundered.
One shipwrecked Spaniard was by Indians encountered
and for ten and seven years kept as their captive,
begetting two daughters upon an infidel native,
until he and they were by Pedro Menéndez liberated.

If a man through human favoritism was transposed
to lofty heights, and honor and dignity did he inherit,
by God eternal from this pinnacle shall be deposed
if his character was found to be lacking in merit.
That is the lesson this canto has proposed:
though earthly kings bestow boons and benefit,
should the recipients be undeserving, let it be known,
our King of the Heavens shall not these condone.

King Philip granted the lieutenant his post, it's true,
but could not endow the man with prudence,
and lacking that he respected no taboo
and out of spite answered tact with insolence.
Thus it was that God omnipotent instantly knew
and swiftly punished his gross irreverence
with a just death after, like a wild beast,
he lashed out savagely and slapped a priest.

Heeding Christian custom to turn the other cheek
the padre did that lieutenant inhume,
when the sentinel from upon his high peak
sounded the alarm to warn of impending doom,
causing all to forget that sadness that is unique
to the sorrow we feel on confronting the tomb,
and to grab up their weapons with all speed
in order that, from their breasts, their valor was freed.

Pero como llegase cierta armada
que venía sulcando el ancho lago,
vieron en los trinquetes trasladada,
la cruz del gloriosísimo Santiago.
La gloria de vencer quedó eclipsada
por ver que no podían dar el pago,
al que decían que era luterano
por ser Menéndez general cristiano,

que en llegando mandó saliesen luego
de todos sus navíos mil varones,
puestos por sus hileras con sosiego,
y tendidos de España los pendones;
todo lo cual se hizo por el ruego
del general don Diego de Quiñones,
que de la Habana gobernaba el fuerte
con ánimo y valor crecido y fuerte.

En medio el escuadrón iba marchando
un hombre con dos mozas a los lados
Visto el moderno caso fui llegando
por poderme informar de los soldados.
Todo me lo contaron, pero cuando
estaban por las casas alojados
al mismo hombre rogué me lo dijese,
porque sumariamente lo scriviese.

Díjome así, "Una nave poderosa
que llevaba su curso para España,
en la Florida, tierra pantanosa,
en una peña dio que el mar la baña.
La gente ponentina belicosa
vino a la nuestra con presura estraña,
y a todos nos llevó desde el navío,
mostrando su locura y desvarío."

"A toda nuestra gente muerte dieron
los infieles que ocupan la Florida,
y a mí me reservaron que quisieron,
por hacerme merced, darme la vida.

But with the arrival of that certain fleet
upon the waves that leaped like flames,
they spied among the foremasts a white sheet
that bore the glorious cross of Saint James.
Their thirst for vengeance conceded defeat
for they could not still press their claims
against General Menéndez, a man who was pious,
though alleged to be Lutheran by some with bias,

and at whose orders from his battleships descended
one thousand warriors in easy formation
who the long standards of Spain extended;
all this unfolded, this entire exhibition,
exactly as General Diego de Quiñones recommended,
having journeyed there from the nearby fortification
of Havana, which he governed with daring
and strength and a judgment unerring.

Out of the midst of this squadron surged
one man with young maidens on either side,
the sight of whom suddenly urged
me to seek the soldiers, who quickly testified,
and they were of the entire history purged
before we reached the barracks they occupied,
at which point the man himself begged leave
to tell his tale, that my account not deceive.

Thus did he inform me: "A mighty vessel
whose course was set to return to Spain
off the marshy shoals of Florida did wrestle
until a rocky crag its hull split in twain.
Then the warmongering western devils
rushed to us, raving, their madness quite plain,
and plucked us from that sundered craft,
at our misfortune they crowed and laughed.

"Those heathen infidels who in Florida dwell
but one out of all our people did spare,
not for mercy's sake alone, but to compel
me their silversmith to be. I did not dare

Para platero suyo me eligieron,
regalándome todos con comida,
porque yo les labraba por mi mano
joyas de plata al modo castellano."

resist and they treated me, it's true, quite well,
exchanging my metalware for my own welfare—
they had, it seemed, developed a passion
for silverwork in the Castilian fashion."

Translated by Lawrence Schimel

GASPAR PÉREZ DE VILLAGRÁ

de *Historia de la Nueva México*

Como se fve abrasando la fuerza de acoma y como se balló Zutacapán muerto de vna gran berida, y de los demás sucessos que fueron sucediendo hasta llevar la nueva de la victoria al Gobernador, y muertes de Tempal y Cotumbo.

Cansado del viage trabajoso,
El estandarte santo no vencido
Dexemos ya de Christo allí arbolado.
Reprímanse las lágrimas, pues dexan
Las almas lastimadas y afligidas,
Y vos, Filipo sacro, que escuchando
Mi tosca musa abéys estado atento,
Suplícoos no os canséis, que ya he llegado
Y al prometido puesto soy venido.
Fiado, gran señor, en la excelencia
De vuestra gran grandeza y que, qual padre
Del bélico exercicio trabajoso,
Vn apacible puerto abéys de abrirme,
Con cuio inmenso aliento reforzado
Las velas doi al viento, rebolviendo
Al temeroso incendio, cuias llamas,
Vibrando poderosas y escupiendo
Vivas centellas, chispas y pavesas,
Las lebantadas casas abrasaban.
Notad, señor, aquí, los altos techos,
Paredes, aposentos y sobrados
Que abiertos por mil partes se desgajan
Y súbito a pedazos se derrumban,
Y cómo en vivo fuego y tierra entierran
Sus míseros vezinos, sin que cosa
Quede que no se abrase y se consuma.
Mirad, señor, también, los muchos cuerpos
Que de las altas cumbres del gran muro,
Assí, desesperados, se abalanzan

GASPAR PÉREZ DE VILLAGRÁ

from *History of New Mexico*

*How the fortress of Acoma continued to burn and how Zutacapán
was found dead from a great wound, and of other events which
happened until the news of the victory was carried to the Governor,
and of the deaths of Tempal and Cotumbo.*

Being fatigued by this our toilsome voyage,
Let us now leave the holy, unconquered
Standard of Christ, which we had set up there.
Hold back your tears for they do leave
Your souls grieving and afflicted,
And you, most holy Philip, who have been
Listening to my rude muse thus attentively,
I beg you to tire not, for I have come
And arrived now upon the promised spot.
Trusting, great lord, unto the excellence
Of your great greatness, that, as the father
Of all the toilsome exercise of war,
You will open a pleasant door for me,
With which immense encouragement strengthened
I spread sail to the wind and thus return
Unto the fearful fire, whose flames,
Trembling with power and spitting forth
Live coals and embers and ashes,
Did rapidly consume the tall houses.
Behold, lord, there, the lofty roofs,
The walls, the rooms, the high garrets
Which, open at a thousand points, do break
And suddenly crumble into pieces
And bury, both in living fire and earth,
Their miserable neighbors, that nothing
Remains that is not burnt up and consumed.
Behold the many corpses, also, lord,
Who from the lofty summit of the wall
Have hurled themselves down in desperation

9

Y rotos por las peñas, quebrantados,
Hechos menudas piezas y pedazos,
Assí, en el duro suelo se detienen;
Los bárbaros y bárbaras que ardiendo
Están, con sus hijuelos lamentando
Su mísera desgracia y triste suerte.
Con cuias muertes el Sargento,
Movido de piedad y de alto zelo,
Qual suele con tormenta y gran borrasca
Vn gran piloto diestro rebolverse,
Saltando a todas partes, y esforzarse,
Mandando al marinaje y passajeros
Con vno y otro grito, y assí, juntos,
Con hervorosa priessa se socorren
Y al flaco navichuelo combatido
De la fuerza del mar y viento ayrado,
Entre mil sierras de agua, faborecen,
Assí, esforzando a Chumpo y otros pocos
Bárbaros que las pazes pretendían,
A vozes les promete y assegura,
En fee de caballero, que las vidas
A todos les promete si se abstienen
Del riguroso estrago y crudas muertes
Que assí los miserables se causaban.
No bien el pobre viejo las palabras
De aquel ardiente joben fue advirtiendo
Quando, clamando a vozes, con los pocos
Bárbaros que con él allí assistían,
A todos persuade y encarece,
Haziéndose pedazos con señales
Y muestras, muy de padre, que se abstengan
Y que a tan tristes muertes no se entreguen,
Porque a todos las vidas les promete
Y noble trato a todos assegura,
Sin género de duda ni sospecha,
Encubierta, rebozo o trato aleve.
Y assí como después del rayo vemos
A todos suspenderse mal seguros,
Difuntos ya en color y palpitando
Los vivos corazones dentro el pecho,

And, smashed and broken there among the rocks,
Lie there in pieces and in small fragments.
Likewise upon the hard ground there do lie
Barbarian men and women who, burning,
Lament, together with their little babes,
Their miserable misfortune and sad fate.
The Sergeant, at this spectacle of death
Being moved with pity and with lofty zeal,
As in the storm and the great hurricane
A great and skillful pilot goes about,
Leaping everywhere with energy,
Ordering mariners and passengers
With many shouts, so that they all
Come to his aid with an impetuous haste
And help the weak and tiny ship, attacked
By the sea's mighty force and by the wind
Driven among a thousand watery mountains,
So he, strengthening Chumpo and a few
More savages who did desire peace,
Doth shout out promises and assure them
The lives of all if they will but abstain
From the horrid destruction and harsh death
Which these wretches were causing for themselves.
Hardly had the poor old man well noted
The words of that ardent young man when he,
Shouting aloud together with the few
Barbarians who were there to help him,
Tries to persuade and recommend to all,
Making the strongest efforts with his signs
And most paternal gestures that they stop
And not give themselves to such sorry deaths,
Because their lives are promised them all,
And he assures them of noble treatment
Without a shade of doubt or suspicion,
Deceit, trickery, or double-dealing.
As after lightning stroke we all have seen
Everyone in suspense, insecure,
In color like the dead, their fearful hearts
Beating like hammers at the breast,
So they, all timid, all in suspicion,

Y assí, encogidos, todos rezelosos,
Por vna parte el vno y qual por otra,
Con passos espaciosos, van saliendo
A ver si están seguros y el destrozo
Causado de la fuerza ya passada,
Assí salieron muchos, poco a poco,
Alertos, pavorosos, encogidos,
Con passos atentados y advirtiendo
De no pisar los cuerpos desangrados
De tanto caro amigo y fiel amparo
De aquellos pobres muros que teñidos
Estaban, de su sangre ya bañados.
Assí, temblando, tristes, afligidos,
Por vna y otra parte rodeados
De pálido color y muerte acerba,
Se fueron acercando. Y viendo estaba
El vando Castellano acariciando
A todos sus vezinos y que daban
Seguro y muestras grandes de contento
De verlos reduzidos y apartados
De aquel cruento estrago que emprendían.
Qual vemos que se abaten y se humillan
Los lebantados trigos, azotados
Con vno y otro soplo reforzado
Del poderoso viento que, sulcando
En remolcadas hondas sus espigas,
Al suelo las amaina, abate y baja,
Assí, vencidos, llanos, desarmados,
Más de seycientos dieron en rendirse
Y dentro de vna plaza, con sus hijos
Y todas sus mugeres, se postraron
Y como presos, juntos, se pusieron
En manos del Sargento y sossegaron,
Movidos del buen Chumpo, que seguro
A todos prometió y dio la vida,
Sin cuia ayuda dudo, y soy muy cierto,
Que aquella gran Numancia trabajosa,
Quando más desdichada y más perdida,
Quedara más desierta y despoblada
Que aquesta pobre fuerza ya rendida.

Some from one side, from the other some,
Come creeping out with laggard steps
To see if they are safe, the destruction
Caused by the now ended struggle.
So, many came, few at a time,
Alert, fearful, and right timid,
With furtive steps, yet taking care
Lest they should step upon the bloodless corpse
Of some dear friend or faithful protector
Of those poor walls which now were stained
And bathed all over with their blood.
Thus, trembling and sad and afflicted,
Surrounded as they were on every side
By the pale hue of death and death itself,
They made approach. And the Castilian band
Beheld them all caressing with much joy
All their neighbors and saw them give
Sure and great signs of their content
At seeing them saved and removed
From that cruel slaughter they undertook.
As we see downcast and humbled
The high-uplifted heads of wheat when lashed
By gust on gust, ever stronger,
Of mighty winds which go plowing
Its spiky heads into great rippling waves
And bend them to the ground and beat them down,
So, conquered, humbled, and disarmed,
More than six hundred surrendered
And in one plaza, with all their children
And all their women, they did put themselves
Into the Sergeant's hands and were at peace,
Moved by the good Chumpo, who had given
A promise of safety and life to all,
Without whose aid I doubt, nay, I'm sure,
That great, laborious Numantia,
E'en when most unfortunate and lost,
Would have been no more desert and empty
Than this poor fort now surrendered.
All being now quite pacified
And truce now made without suspicion

Estando ya, pues, todo sossegado
Y puestas ya las treguas sin rezelo
De algún bullicio de armas o alboroto,
Los pactos assentados y de assiento
Los vnos y los otros sossegados,
De súbito las bárbaras, rabiosas,
Qual vemos deshazerse y derrumbarse,
Dexándose venir con bravo asombro,
Vna terrible torre poderosa,
Recién inhiesta, puesta y lebantada,
Y con terrible espanto rebolvernos
La sossegada sangre y alterarnos,
Assí, señor inmenso y poderoso,
Alzando vn alarido, arremetieron,
Y apeñuscadas todas, qual se aprietan
Sobre la chueca, juntos, los villanos,
Con los caiados corbos procurando
De darle con esfuerzo mayor bote,
Assí las vimos, todas hechas piña,
A palos y pedradas deshaziendo
A vn miserable cuerpo. Y assí, juntos,
Para la esquadra todos arrancamos
Por ver si era Español y dar venganza
A hecho tan atroz y desmedido.
Y luego que nos vieron, sin aliento,
Alborotadas todas, nos dixeron:
"Varones esforzados, generosos,
Si abernos entregado en vuestras manos
Merece que nos deis algún contento,
Dejadnos acabar lo comenzado.
Aquí Zutacapán está tendido,
Y gracias al Castilla que tal alma
Hizo que se arrancase por tal llaga.
Este causó las muertes que les dimos
A vuestros compañeros desdichados.
Este metió cizaña y alboroto
Por todos estos pobres que tendidos
Están por este suelo derramados."
Y poniendo la vista en sus difuntos
Y luego en el traidor, rabiosas todas,

Of any armed turmoil or uprising,
Agreements signed and to be signed
And all on both sides well appeased,
Suddenly the barbarian women, mad,
As we see suddenly falling and breaking up,
Coming on us to our astonishment,
A terrible and mighty tower
But recently erected, placed, and set,
And with a terrible fear all our blood
Flows back upon our hearts and we grow pale,
So, lord, immense and powerful,
Raising a fearful cry, they all set off,
And all crowding, as the peasants
Do crowd together round a hockey ball
And all do try with curving sticks
To give it greater impulse with their strength,
So we did see them, gathered in a knot,
With sticks and blows of stones smashing
A miserable body. So at once
We all set out for their squadron
To see was it a Spaniard and avenge
So treacherous and excessive a deed.
And when they saw us then, all out of breath
And all excited, did cry out to us:
"Ye valiant and generous men,
If to have given ourselves into your hands
Deserves that you give us some satisfaction,
Then let us finish what we have commenced.
Here Zutacapán lies stretched out
And thanks to the Castilian who has made
Such soul be snatched from such a wound.
He caused the deaths which we have dealt
To your unfortunate companions.
He sowed discord and disturbance
Among all those poor creatures who
Are lying lifeless on this ground."
And gazing now upon their dead
And then upon the traitor, all, raging,
As on the chopping block skilled cooks
Do mince up meat and sunder it,

Assí como en tajón la carne pican
Los diestros cozineros y deshazen,
Assí, con yra, todos rebolvieron
Y en muy menudas piezas le dexaron,
Con cuio hecho, alegres, satisfechas,
En su primero puesto sossegaron.
Y nosotros, señor, jamás podimos
Saber quál fuesse el brazo que de vn tajo
Cinco costillas cerce le cortase.
Y assí como con ansia cobdiciosos,
Después de la batalla ya vencida,
Vn gran varón famoso, que escondido,
De muy grande rescate, procuramos,
Y assí, sin alma, seso y sin sentido
Salimos a buscarle y reparamos
En todos los vencidos y ponemos
La vista bien atenta por hallarle,
Assí, los bárbaros, atentos y las bocas
Abiertas y los ojos que pestaña
Iamás movió ninguno, vimos todos
Que con asombro y pasmo nos miraban.
Y no vien asomaba algún soldado,
Que fuera del quartel acaso estaba,
Quando de golpe todos, qual se allegan
Las moscas a la miel, assí llegaban
Y el rostro sólo, atentos, le miraban.
Y viendo el gran cuidado que ponían
En no dexar a nadie reservado
Que bien no le notasen y advirtiessen,
Fue fuerza preguntarles qué distino,
Qué blanco o por qué causa, assí, sedientos,
A todos nos miraban. Y suspensos,
La mano dando a Chumpo, que por ellos
A todos respondiesse, dixo el viejo:
"Buscan éstos, mis hijos, a vn Castilla
Que estando en la batalla anduvo siempre
En vn blanco caballo suelto, y tiene
La barba larga, cana y bien poblada
Y calva la cabeza. Es alto y ciñe
Vna terrible espada, ancha y fuerte,

So, in their rage they all gathered around
And left him battered into small pieces;
Happy and satisfied at this their deed,
Returned unto their former peaceful state.
And we, lord, never could find out
Whose was the arm that with one mighty cut
Had shorn through five of his ribs at one time.
As we most anxiously and greedily
Do seek, after a battle has been won,
Some great and famous man from whom we hope
To get great ransom, finding him hidden,
And thus soulless, madly, out of our wits,
We go to seek for him and examine
All of the conquered and eagerly fix
Our gaze attentively to find that man,
So these barbarians, attentive, with their mouths
Open and eyes that never moved
An eyelid, were then seen by us
To look at us in fear, astonishment.
And hardly would some soldier appear
Who had by chance been absent from the group
When all of them, as flies to honey crowd,
Would instantly run and crowd around him
And look into his face attentively.
Seeing the great care which they took
Not to leave anyone aside
Whom they should not well note and scrutinize,
'Twas necessary to ask for what mark,
What sign or what cause they did gaze
Thus anxiously and thirstily on us.
Giving authority to Chumpo, that for all
He might reply, the old man said to us:
"These sons of mine seek a Castilian
Who, being in the battle, always rode
Upon a great white horse and has
A great long beard, both white and thick,
And a bald head, is tall and wears
A terrible and broad and mighty sword
With which he has stricken us all to earth,
A man extremely valiant. And also

Con que a todos por tierra nos ha puesto,
Valiente por extremo. Y, por extremo,
Vna bella donzella también buscan,
Más hermosa que el Sol y más que el Cielo.
Preguntan dónde está y qué se han hecho."
El caudillo Español, oyendo aquesto,
Movido, por ventura, del que pudo
Mostrar la duda clara y socorrernos
En casos semejantes y ampararnos,
Qual vn blandón o antorcha cuia lumbre
La vista haze clara y quita el velo
De la ciega tiniebla, assí, alumbrando,
Al grato viejo Chumpo fue diziendo:
"Responde a éstos, tus hijos, noble padre,
Que en esso no se cansen ni fatiguen
Ni más los dos que buscan los procuren,
Que son bueltos al Cielo, donde tienen
De assiento su morada, y que no salen
Si no es a defendernos y ayudarnos
Quando assí nos agravian y se atreven,
Qual ellos se atrevieron, a matarnos
Con muertes tan atrozes y crueles
Los pocos Españoles que subieron
A lo alto desta fuerza descuidados.
Que miren lo que hazen y no buelvan
Segunda vez al hecho comenzado."
No suspendió el Troiano ni redujo
La rienda del silencio con más fuerza
Quando a la illustre Reyna los sucessos
De Troia y su desgracia recontaba
Qual hizo aquí el Zaldívar, que pasmados
Y mudos los dexó, que más palabra
Hablaron ni chistaron. Y assí sólo
Dixo: "Señor inmenso, que alcanzamos
Aquesta gran victoria el mismo día
Del vasso de elección, a quien la tierra
Tenía por patrón, y assí entendimos
Que vino con la Virgen a ampararnos."
Iuizios son ocultos que no caben
En mí, Señor, que siempre soy y he sido

My people seek, as well, a beauteous maid,
More beautiful than the sun or the heavens.
They ask where these may be, where they have gone."
The Spanish leader then, hearing these things,
Being moved, perhaps, by He who could
Make that doubt clear, also help us
And protect us in similar affairs,
Like to a taper or a torch whose light
Makes our sight clear and cleaves the veil
Of blind darkness, so he, shining,
Said to the grateful old Chumpo:
"Reply to these your children, noble sire,
That they should not tire or fatigue themselves
Nor should they try to seek these more,
For they have now returned to Heaven,
Where they do keep their dwelling, nor leave it
Except to come to our aid and defense
When we are injured or one dares,
As those men dared, to slaughter ours
With such atrocious and such cruel deaths,
Those few poor Spaniards who did climb
To the height of this fortress heedlessly.
Let them watch what they do, and not repeat
A second time of that their work begun."
The Trojan had not ended, had not drawn
The rein of silence with more vivid force,
When to the famous queen he did relate
The tale of Troy and of its misfortunes,
As Zaldívar had here, for he left them
Astonished and silent, so they spoke not
Another word nor muttered, whereat he
Did say: "Immense Lord, since we won
This great victory on the very day
Of the Sacred Vessel, the saint that this land
Had as a Patron, we do comprehend,
Did then come with the Virgin to guard us."
There are things hidden that are not
Clear to me, lord, for I have always been
And am a sad and despised trifling worm.
And so, lord, I return to my leader,

Vn gusanillo triste, despreciado.
Y assí, Señor, me buelvo a mi caudillo,
Que está con toda priessa despachando
Al provehedor Zubía porque lleve
Desta victoria insigne alegre nueva
A nuestro General, a quien abía
Vna bárbara vieja, por sus cercos,
Héchole cierto della el mismo día
Que fue por vuestro campo celebrada.
Y estando, assí, aguardando el desengaño,
Marchando el provehedor, acaso Tempal
Y el pobre de Cotumbo, destrozados,
Corriendo gran fortuna a árbol seco,
Abiendo de la fuerza ya escapado,
Yban atravesando, y viendo el golpe
Que allí el rigor del hado descargaba
Tras tanta desbentura, rebozados
Con máscara de paz, los dos fingieron,
Como hastutos cosarios, que ellos eran
De allá la tierra adentro y que robados
Venían de vnas gentes que huiendo
Salían del Peñol. Y assí, encogidos,
Pidieron con gran lástima les diessen
Con que la triste hambre que llevaban
Socorrida quedase y no acabasen.
Con esto, el Español mandó prenderlos
Por no errar el lance, que perdido,
Suele por él perder vn gran soldado,
Y presos los llevó y en vna estufa,
Después de aber llegado y dado el pliego,
Mandó que los pusiessen y encerrasen.
Y abiendo con gran gusto recibido
El General la nueva, fue informado
De ciertos nobles bárbaros amigos
Que aquellos prisioneros que forzados
Estaban en la estufa y oprimidos
Eran de los más bravos y valientes
Que Acoma mostraron y pusieron
La cólera en su punto y lebantaron
El sossegado fuerte ya perdido.

Who is dispatching, in the hottest haste,
The purveyor Zubía to carry
The famous, joyous news of victory
Unto our General, who had been
Informed of it upon the very day
That it had been won by these forces
By an old Indian woman within her ring.
And as he was waiting for certain news,
The purveyor being upon the way,
By chance Tempal and poor Cotumbo, destitute,
Riding a terrible storm without sails,
Having now escaped out of the fortalice,
Did happen to cross his path and, seeing
The blow that the rigor of harsh fate had struck
After so much misfortune, covering themselves,
The two did feign, behind a mask of peace,
Like astute pirates, that they were natives
From far within the land and that they had
Been robbed by some who came fleeing
From the great rock. And thus, most timidly,
They asked with much grieving that they be given
Something by which their fierce hunger might be
Alleviated so they might not die.
At this the Spaniard had them seized
Not to err in the juncture, for, once lost,
It might detract from a great soldier,
And so they were taken and, arriving
And having then delivered the message,
He had them placed and locked in a kiva.
And, having now with much pleasure received
The news, the General was then informed
By certain noble, friendly barbarians
That those prisoners whom he had shut up
Inside the kiva and retained in custody
Were of the bravest and most valiant
That Acoma could show and they had raised
The outbreak to its highest point and roused
The peaceful fortress that was now destroyed.
At this, the two barbarians, enraged,
Seeing themselves discovered, did destroy

Con esto, los dos bárbaros sañudos,
Viéndose descubiertos, deshizieron
La escala de la estufa y, hechos fuertes,
A palos y pedradas no dexaron
Que nadie les entrase por tres días
Que assí se defendieron y guardaron.
Y viendo que era fuerza se rindiessen
Por hambre y sed rabiosa que cargaba,
Las armas sossegaron y dixeron:
"Castillas, si del todo no contentos
Estáis de abernos ya bebido toda
La generosa sangre que, gustosa,
tiene vuestra braveza no cansada,
Y sóla aquesta poca que nos queda
Mostráis que os satisfaze, dadnos luego
Sendos cuchillos botos, que nosotros
Aquí vuestras gargantas hartaremos
Privándonos de vida, porque es justo
Que no se diga nunca, por mancharnos,
Que dos guerreros tales se pusieron
En manos tan infames y tan viles
Quales son essas vuestras despreciadas."
Con esto, el General, y con que todos
Los bárbaros amigos le dixeron
Si allí los perdonaba que ponía
En condición la tierra de alterarse,
Abiendo hecho en vano todo aquello
Que pudo ser por verlos reduzidos
Al gremio de la Iglesia y agregados,
Mandó que los cuchillos les negasen,
Por más assegurar, y que les diessen
Dos gruessas sogas largas, bien cumplidas.
Y echándoselas dentro, las miraron,
Los ojos hechos sangre y apretando
Los labios y los dientes, corajosos,
Hinchados los hijares y narizes,
Absortos, mudos, sordos, se quedaron.
Y estando assí, suspensos breve rato,
Sacudiendo el temor y despreciando
A todo vuestro campo y fuerte espada,

The ladder of the kiva and, grown strong,
With clubs and blows of rocks they prevented
The entrance of anyone for three days,
So well they did defend and keep themselves.
And seeing that they must needs surrender
Through the hunger and the raging thirst they felt,
They then laid down their arms and said:
"Castilians, if you are not content
As yet, though you have drunk up all
The generous blood that, succulent,
Your tireless bravery has already had,
And only this bit that is left to us
Will satisfy you, then give us
Two blunt knives, one for each, that we
May here appease your throats for you,
Taking our lives ourselves, for it is right
That no one may say, to stain us,
That two such warriors placed themselves
In hands so infamous and vile
As are your hands, which we despise."
At this the General was told
By all of his barbarian friends
That if he gave them pardon he would put
All of the land in a mind to revolt.
As he had done in vain all that
Could have been done to see them surrendered
And added to the bosom of the Church,
He ordered that they be refused the knives
For greater safety, and that they be given
Two long, strong halters, well and truly made.
And throwing these inside, they looked at them
With eyes bloodshot and pressing tight
Their lips and their strong teeth,
Their sides swollen, their nostrils wide,
Absorbed, deaf, dumb, they did remain.
And being thus in quiet for a time,
Throwing off fear and despising
All of your army and your mighty sword,
Never was seen thus to give up
His neck unto the running noose

Nunca se vio jamás que assí pusiesse
Al corredizo lazo la garganta
Aquél que desta vida ya cansado
Partirse quiso della alegre y presto,
Qual vimos a estos bárbaros, que al punto,
La mal compuesta greña sacudiendo,
Las dos sogas tomaron y al pescuezo
Ceñidas por sus manos y añudadas,
Salieron de la estufa y esparciendo
La vista por el campo, que admirado
Estaba de su esfuerzo y condolido,
Iuntos la detuvieron y pararon
En vnos altos álamos crecidos
Que cerca, por su mal, acaso estaban.
Y no bien los notaron, quando luego
Dellos, sin más acuerdo, nos dixeron
Querían suspenderse y ahorcarse.
Y dándoles la mano abierta en todo,
Los gruessos, ciegos, ñudos apretados
Allí los requirieron, y arrastrando
Las sogas por detrás partieron juntos
Del campo Castellano, ya rendidos
Y del bárbaro pueblo acompañados.
No los fuertes hermanos que, en Cartago,
Corriendo presurosos, alargaron,
A costa de sí mismos, los linderos,
Assí a la triste muerte se entregaron,
Dexándose enterrar en vida, vivos,
Qual estos bravos bárbaros que, estando
Al pie de aquellos troncos, lebantaron
La vista por la cumbre y en vn punto,
Como diestros grumetes que, ligeros,
Por las entenas, gavias y altos topes
Discurren con presteza, assí, alentados,
Trepando por los árboles arriba,
Tentándoles los ramos, se mostraron
Verdugos de sí mismos. Y amarrados,
Mirándonos a todos, nos dixeron:
"Soldados, advertid que aquí colgados

A man who, being tired of this life,
Desired to leave this life swiftly and soon,
As we saw these barbarians who, at once,
Loosing their badly tangled hair,
Took the two nooses and, setting
The same upon their necks and knotting them,
They came out of the kiva, and casting
Their glance over the camp, which wondered much
At their courage and sympathized with them,
They halted it and centered it upon
Some lofty poplar trees that were well grown
And were, by some evil chance, near.
And hardly had they noted them when they
Informed us instantly they wished
To hang themselves and die upon those trees.
And, giving them an open hand in all,
The great and choking knots, hard drawn,
There they examined, and, dragging
Their halters behind them, they went
From the Castilian camp, worn out,
Accompanied by the barbarian folk.
Not the strong brothers of Carthage
Who, running rapidly, increased
The boundaries to their own dole, did thus
Give themselves up unto dark death,
Allowing themselves to be buried though alive,
As these barbarians, who, arriving
At the foot of those tree trunks, lifted up
Their gaze unto the top and, instantly,
Like skillful cabin boys who run lightly
Upon the masts and yards and high tops,
Climbed the poplars to a great height,
And then, testing the branches, appeared as
Their own hangmen; and having tied the ropes,
Looking upon us all, they said to us:
"Soldiers, take note that hanging here
From these strong tree trunks we leave you
Our miserable bodies as spoils
Of the illustrious victory you won.

Destos rollizos troncos os dexamos
Los miserables cuerpos por despojos
De la victoria illustre que alcanzastes
De aquellos desdichados que podridos
Están sobre su sangre rebolcados,
Sepúlcro que tomaron porque quiso
Assí fortuna infame perseguirnos
Con mano poderosa y acabarnos.
Gustosos quedaréis que ya cerramos
Las puertas al vivir y nos partimos
Y libres nuestras tierras os dexamos.
Dormid a sueño suelto, pues ninguno
Bolvió jamás con nueva del camino
Incierto y trabajoso que llevamos.
Mas de vna cosa ciertos os hazemos,
Que si bolver podemos a vengarnos
Que no parieron madres Castellanas,
Ni bárbaras tampoco, en todo el mundo
Más desdichados hijos que a vosotros."
Y assí, rabiosos, bravos, desembueltos,
Saltando en vago, juntos se arrojaron,
Y en blanco ya los ojos, trastornados,
Sueltas las coiunturas y remisos
Los poderosos nierbios y costados,
Vertiendo espumarajos, descubrieron
Las escondidas lenguas regordidas
Y entre sus mismos dientes apretadas.
Y assí, qual suelen dos bajeles sueltos
Rendir la ancha borda, afrenillando
La gruessa palamenta y en vn punto,
Las espumosas proas apagadas,
En jolito se quedan, assí, juntos,
Sesgos y sin moverse se rindieron
Y el aliento de vida allí apagaron.
Con cuio fuerte passo desabrido,
Dexándolos colgados, ya me es fuerza
Poner silencio al canto desabrido.
Y por si vuestra Magestad insigne
El fin de aquesta historia ver quisiere,
De rodillas suplico que me aguarde

Over those wretched ones who are
Rotting amid their weltering blood,
The sepulcher they chose since infamous
Fortune chose so to pursue us
With powerful hand and end our days.
You will remain joyful for we now close
The doors of life and take our leave,
And freely leave to you our lands.
Sleep sure and safe because no one
Ever returned with news about the road,
Uncertain and laborious, we now take,
But yet of one thing we do assure you:
That if we can return for our vengeance,
Castilian mothers shall not bear,
Barbarian either, throughout all the world,
Sons more unfortunate than all of you."
Thus raving, angry, all heedless,
Together they both leapt out into space,
And now their eyes, turned back, displayed
     the whites,
Their joints were all loosened and slack,
As were their mighty thews and sides.
Spurting out foam they discovered
Their hidden tongues, now all swollen
And tightly clenched between their teeth.
And, as may two separate and free vessels,
Lower their broad main sails and bridle up
The mighty banks of oars and all at once
The foaming prows do come to rest
And all is calm, so, together,
Calm, without motion, they remain
And there give up the breath of life.
And at this harsh and severe pass,
Leaving them hanging, I must now
Bring silence to this harsh canto.
And if your famous Majesty
Should wish to see the end of this story
I beg upon my knees that you will wait
And pardon me, also, if I delay,
For 'tis a thing difficult for the pen

Y también me perdone si tardare,
Porque es difícil cosa que la pluma,
Abiendo de serviros con la lanza,
Pueda desempacharse sin tardanza.

To lose all shyness instantly,
Having to serve you with the lance.

Translated by Miguel Encinias, Alfred Rodríguez,
and Joseph P. Sánchez

MIGUEL DE QUINTANA

Jesús, María y José

Logra aquese entendimiento
que el poder de Dios te ha dado.
Lógralo, Miguel, y escribe
que no vas en nada errado.

Te mueve de Dios la fuerza
y a la fuerza de su brazo
no habrá poder que resista;
no tenga, Miguel, reparo.

Es locución muy segura
la que el gran poder te ha dado
por humilde, que al humilde
Dios se inclina y se ha inclinado.

Miguel, socorros y luces,
que me quemo, que me abraso
en aqueste haz de penas
que a ti te muestro llorando.

Ne temas, que vas seguro.
Cree que no pondrá reparo,
Miguel, el padre a esas letras.
Ayúdame, pues te clamo.

Libre estás de que te venga
ninguna afrenta ni daño,
Miguel, por lo que reservas.
Exprésalo que me abraso.

MIGUEL DE QUINTANA

Jesus, Mary and Joseph

Gain that understanding
that the power of God has given you.
Perfect it, Miguel, and write,
for you have in no way strayed.

God's strength moves you,
and there is no power
that can resist it
nor make you, Miguel, have qualms.

Very sure is the expression,
which the great power has given you
because of your humility,
for God favors you as He does the humble.

Miguel, save and enlighten me,
for I burn on the coals
of this sea of tears
which I show to you weeping.

Fear not, for you're on the right path.
Believe, Miguel, that the priest
will not question those verses.
Help me, for I implore you.

You are safe from suffering
any harm or insult, Miguel,
given what you hold back.
Express it, for I yearn to hear it.

Translated by Francisco Lomeli and Clark A. Colahan

ANONYMOUS

de *Los Comanches*

CUERNO VERDE:
Desde el oriente al poniente,
Desde el sur al norte frío,
Suena el brillante clarín
Y brilla el acero mío.
Entre todas las naciones
Campeo, osado, atrevido,
Que es tanta la valentía
Que reina en el pecho mío.
Se levantan mis banderas
Por el viento giro á giro,
Y de las que traigo liadas
Refreno al más atrevido,
Devoro al más enojado,
Que con mi braveza admiro
Al oso más arrogante;
Al fiero tigre rindo,
Que no hay roca ni montaña
Que de ella no haga registro;
Al más despreciado joven,
Aquél que más abatido
Se ve porque su fortuna
[A] tal desdicha lo ha traído.
Y como ahora lo ha de ver
Este soberbio castillo;
Hoy lo he de ver en pavezas,
Lo he de postrar y abatirlo
Con sus rocas y baluartes.
Sé que se hallan prevenidos
De mi nación que arrogante
Hoy con el tiempo se ha visto;
Díganlo tantas naciones
Á quien quité el señorío,

ANONYMOUS

from *The Comanches*

CUERNO VERDE:
From the south to the frozen north,
From where the sun rises and falls,
Shines the glimmering of my steel
And the clarion bugle calls.
Such is the courage and daring
That reigns within my breast,
Out of all the many nations
I excel—the bravest, the best.
My banners are lofted up high,
When skies are clear or full of rain,
And out of all those I have bound
The boldest is who I restrain;
The most outraged one I devour,
And with my wildness I admire
That most superior bear;
The savage tiger I conquer,
Whose great fierceness was recognized
By every mountain crag and rock;
And the youth who is most despised,
The one despondent from the shock
That yes it was indeed his fate
To be reduced to depths so low.
To think that once these castle gates
offered up such a proud tableau
but I shall leave these barricades
mere ash and dust before twilight.
My nation has been oft portrayed
as proud by those who fear my might.
Let those I've overpowered sing
my fame with a full garrison
of voices panting and screaming.
Thus did the Caslana nation

Como lo canta la fama
Y un cuartelejo de gritos;
Hoy se ven desboronados
Sus pueblos dando gemidos.
Diga la nación Caslana
Cuando se vió combatida
Huyendo de mi furor;
Hoy se le ha acabado el brillo.
Se remontó de tal surte
Que hasta ahora no la hemos visto.
Pero, ¿para qué me canso
En referir lo que digo,
Cuando solo el Cristianismo
Traje de tantas naciones,
Que no le alcanza el guarismo?
Pero hoy ha de correr sangre
De un corazón vengativo,
Que sólo los Españoles
Refrenan el valor mío.
Me recuerda la memoria
De un Español atrevido,
Que opuesto y con valentía
Y con tan osado brillo,
El campo vistió de flores,
Con sangre sus coloridos.
De los muertos la distancia,
Hombres, mujeres y niños
No se pueden numerar,
Ni contarse los cautivos.
Genízaros valerosos,
Que se pregone mi edicto,
Que yo como general
He de estar aprevenido;
Que general que descansa
Á vista de su enemigo,
Bien puede ser vigilante
Bien puede ser atrevido.
Yo no me he de conformar
Con estos bajos vecinos,
Y así comiencen un cante,

shout as it fled before my rage.
Today their glory is ended;
so fleet they ran from my rampage—
the sight of their backs was splendid—
so far they ran no trace remains
of who they once were nor of where.
But let my speech now be quite plain:
countless are the nations who swear
their faith to Christianity.
But crimson blood must this day flow
vengeance for humanity.
None but the Spanish cast a blow
to dent my valor—I recall
one daring Spaniard whose skill shone
as he dressed the flower petals
of the entire field just one
single color: the red of blood.
Futile to try to count the dead
as to halt a river in flood,
and what matter whether each head
belonged to man, woman, or child?
Nor can the captives be numbered.
I shan't let myself be beguiled:
Is the general who slumbered
within sight of his enemy
reckless or instead vigilant?
I won't conform with these lowly
foes, so let them begin a chant,
let the drums beat and call for war.
We shall scour this district entire
in search of this fierce warrior
who sent so many to the pyre,
who wore his madness as his shield.
Who is this man and what his name?
I call him to the battlefield.
I summon and I challenge him!

Translated by Lawrence Schimel

Suénese tambor ó pito.
El cante á punto de guerra,
Pasaremos el distrito
Buscando (á) este general
Que con loco desvarío,
Usó de tanta fiereza
Y destruyó como digo.
¿Quién es y como se llama?
Lo llamo á campal batalla.
Lo reto y lo desafío.

JOSÉ MARÍA HEREDIA Y HEREDIA

Niágara

Templad mi lira, dádmela, que siento
en mi alma estremecida y agitada
arder la inspiracion. ¡Oh! ¡cuánto tiempo
en tinieblas pasó, sin que mi frente
brillase con su luz . . . ! Niágara undoso,
tu sublime terror solo podría
tornarme el don divino, que ensañada
me robó del dolor la mano impía.

   Torrente prodigioso, calma, calla
tu trueno aterrador: disipa un tanto
las tinieblas que en torno te circundan,
déjame contemplar tu faz serena,
y de entusiasmo ardiente mi alma llena.
Yo digno soy de contemplarte: siempre
lo comun y mezquino desdeñando,
ansié por lo terrífico y sublime.
Al despeñarse el huracan furioso,
al retumbar sobre mi frente el rayo,
palpitando gozé: ví al Oceáno
azotado por austro proceloso,
combatir mi bajel, y ante mis plantas
vórtice hirviente abrir, y amé el peligro.
Mas del mar la fiereza
en mi alma no produjo
la profunda impresion que tu grandeza.

   Sereno corres, magestoso; y luego
en ásperos peñascos quebrantado,
te abalanzas violento, arrebatado,
como el destino irresistible y ciego.
¿Qué voz humana describir podría
de la sirte rugiente

JOSÉ MARÍA HEREDIA Y HEREDIA

Niagara

My lyre! give me my lyre! my bosom feels
The glow of inspiration. Oh how long
Have I been left in darkness since this light
Last visited my brow. Niagara!
Thou with thy rushing waters dost restore
The heavenly gift that sorrow took away.

   Tremendous torrent! for an instant hush
The terrors of thy voice and cast aside
Those wide involving shadows, that my eyes
May see the fearful beauty of thy face!
I am not all unworthy of thy sight,
For from my very boyhood have I loved,
Shunning the meaner track of common minds,
To look on nature in her loftier moods.
At the fierce rushing of the hurricane,
At the near bursting of the thunderbolt
I have been touched with joy; and when the sea,
Lashed by the wind, hath rocked my bark and showed
Its yawning caves beneath me, I have loved
Its dangers and the wrath of elements.
But never yet the madness of the sea
Hath moved me as thy grandeur moves me now.

   Thou flowest on in quiet, till thy waves
Grow broken 'midst the rocks; thy current then
Shoots onward like the irresistible course
Of destiny. Ah, terribly they rage—
The hoarse and rapid whirlpools there! My brain
Grows wild, my senses wander, as I gaze
Upon the hurrying waters, and my sight
Vainly would follow, as toward the verge
Sweeps the wide torrent—waves innumerable

la aterradora faz? El alma mia
en vago pensamiento se confunde
al mirar esa férvida corriente,
que en vano quiere la turbada vista
en su vuelo seguir al borde oscuro
del precipicio altísimo: mil olas,
cual pensamiento rápidas pasando,
chocan, y se enfurecen,
y otras mil y otras mil ya las alcanzan,
y entre espuma y fragor desaparecen.

Ved! llegan, saltan! El abismo horrendo
devora los torrentes despeñados:
crúzanse en él mil íris, y asordados
vuelven los bosques el fragor tremendo.
En las rígidas peñas
rómpese el agua: vaporosa nube
con elástica fuerza
llena el abismo en torbellino, sube,
gira en torno, y al éter
luminosa pirámide levanta,
y por sobre los montes que le cercan
al solitario cazador espanta.

Mas ¿qué en tí busca mi anhelante vista
con inútil afan? ¿Porqué no miro
al rededor de tu caverna inmensa
las palmas ¡ay! las palmas deliciosas,
que en las llanuras de mi ardiente patria
nacen del sol á la sonrisa, y crecen,
y al soplo de las brisas del Oceano,
bajo un cielo purísimo se mecen?

Este recuerdo á mi pesar me viene. . . .
Nada ¡oh Niágara! falta á tu destino,
ni otra corona que el agreste pino
á tu terrible magestad conviene.
La palma, y mirto y delicada rosa,
muelle placer inspiren y ocio blando
en frívolo jardin: á tí la suerte

Meet there and madden—waves innumerable
Urge on and overtake the waves before,
And disappear in thunder and in foam.

They reach—they leap the barrier—the abyss
Swallows insatiable the sinking waves.
A thousand rainbows arch them, and woods
Are deafened with the roar. The violent shock
Shatters to vapor the descending sheets—
A cloudy whirlwind fills the gulf, and heaves
The mighty pyramid of circling mist
To heaven. The solitary hunter near
Pauses with terror in the forest shades.

What seeks my restless eye? Why are not here,
About the jaws of this abyss, the palms—
Ah—the delicious palms, that on the plains
Of my own native Cuba, spring and spread
Their thickly foliaged summits to the sun,
And, in the breathings of the ocean air,
Wave soft beneath the heaven's unspotted blue.

But no, Niagara,—thy forest pines
Are fitter coronal for thee. The palm,
The effeminate myrtle, and frail rose may grow
In gardens, and give out their fragrance there,
Unmanning him who breathes it. Thine it is
To do a nobler office. Generous minds
Behold thee, and are moved, and learn to rise
Above earth's frivolous pleasures; they partake
Thy grandeur at the utterance of thy name.

God of all truth! In other lands I've seen
Lying philosophers, blaspheming men,
Questioners of thy mysteries, that draw
Their fellows deep into impiety,
And therefore doth my spirit seek thy face
In earth's majestic solitudes. Even here
My heart doth open all itself to thee.
In this immensity of loneliness

guardó mas digno objeto, mas sublime.
El alma libre, generosa, fuerte,
viene, te vé, se asombra,
el mezquino deleite menosprecia,
y aun se siente elevar cuando te nombra.

Omnipotente Dios! En otros climas
ví monstruos execrables,
blasfemando tu nombre sacrosanto,
sembrar error y fanatismo impío,
los campos inundar en sangre y llanto,
de hermanos atizar la infanda guerra,
y desolar frenéticos la tierra.
Vílos, y el pecho se inflamó á su vista
en grave indignacion. Por otra parte
ví mentidos filósofos, que osaban
escrutar tus misterios, ultrajarte,
y de impiedad al lamentable abismo
á los míseros hombres arrastraban.
Por eso te buscó mi débil mente
en la sublime soledad: ahora
entera se abre á tí; tu mano siente
en esta inmensidad que me circunda,
y tu profunda voz hiere mi seno
de este raudal en el eterno trueno.

Asombroso torrente!
¡Cómo tu vista el ánimo enagena,
y de terror y admiracion me llena!
¿Dó tu orígen está? ¿Quién fertiliza
por tantos siglos tu inexhausta fuente?
¿Qué poderosa mano
hace que al recibirte
no rebose en la tierra el Oceáno?

Abrió el Señor su mano omnipotente;
cubrió tu faz de nubes agitadas,
dió su voz á tus aguas despeñadas,
y ornó con su arco tu terrible frente.

I feel thy hand upon me. To my ear
The eternal thunder of the cataract brings
Thy voice, and I am humbled as I hear.

Dread torrent! that with wonder and with fear
Dost overwhelm the soul of him that looks
Upon thee, and dost bear it from itself.
Whence hast thou thy beginning? Who supplies,
Age after age, thy unexhausted springs?
What power hath ordered, that, when all thy weight
Descends into the deep, the swollen waves
Rise not, and roll to overwhelm the earth?

The Lord hath opened his omnipotent hand,
Covered thy face with clouds, and given his voice
To thy down-rushing waters; he hath girt
Thy terrible forehead with his radiant bow.
I see thy never-resting waters run,
And I bethink me how the tide of time
Sweeps to eternity. So pass of man—
Pass, like a noon-day dream—the blossoming days,
And he awakes to sorrow. I, alas!
Feel that my youth is withered, and my brow
Ploughed early with the lines of grief and care.

Never have I so deeply felt as now
The hopeless solitude, the abandonment,
The anguish of a loveless life. Alas!
How can the impassioned, the unfrozen heart
Be happy without love. I would that one
Beautiful,—worthy to be loved and joined
In love with me,—now shared my lonely walk
On this tremendous brink. 'T were sweet to see
Her dear face touched with paleness, and become
More beautiful from fear, and overspread
With a faint smile while clinging to my side!
Dreams—dreams. I am an exile, and for me
There is no country and there is no love.

Ciego, profundo, infatigable corres,
como el torrente oscuro de los siglos
en insondable eternidad . . . ! Al hombre
huyen así las ilusiones gratas,
los florecientes dias,
y despierta al dolor . . . ! ¡Ay! agostada
yace mi juventud, mi faz marchita,
y la profunda pena que me agita
ruga mi frente de dolor nublada.

Nunca tanto sentí como este dia
mi soledad y mísero abandono
y lamentable desamor . . . ¿Podría
en edad borrascosa
sin amor ser feliz . . . ? ¡Oh! ¡si una hermosa
mi cariño fijase,
y de este abismo al borde turbulento
mi vago pensamiento
y ardiente admiracion acompañase!
¡Cómo gozara, viéndola cubrirse
de leve palidez, y ser mas bella
en su dulce terror, y sonreírse
al sostenerla mis amantes brazos. . . .
Delirios de virtud . . . ! ¡Ay! Desterrado,
sin patria, sin amores,
solo miro ante mí llanto y dolores.

Niágara poderoso!
Adios! adios! Dentro de pocos años
ya devorado habrá la tumba fria
á tu débil cantor. Duren mis versos
cual tu gloria inmortal! Pueda piadoso
viéndote algun viagero,
dar un suspiro á la memoria mia!
Y al abismarse Febo en occidente,
feliz yo vuele do el Señor me llama,
y al escuchar los ecos de mi fama,
alce en las nubes la radiosa frente.

(Junio de 1824.)

Hear, dread Niagara, my latest voice!
Yet a few years and the cold earth shall close
Over the bones of him who sings thee now
Thus feelingly. Would that this, my humble verse,
Might be like thee, immortal. I, meanwhile,
Cheerfully passing to the appointed rest,
Might raise my radiant forehead in the clouds
To listen to the echoes of my fame.

Translated by Thatcher Taylor Payne (1827)

LOLA RODRÍGUEZ DE TIÓ

La Borinqueña

El grito de Lares
se ha de repetir,
y entonces sabremos
vencer o morir.

¡Despierta Borinqueño
que han dado la señal!
¡Despierta de ese sueño
que es hora de luchar!

A ese llamar patriótico
¿no arde tu corazón?
¡Ven! Nos será simpático
el ruido del cañón.

Mira ya el Cubano
libre será,
le dará el machete
su libertad . . .
le dará el machete
su libertad.

Ya el tambor guerrero
dice en su son,
que es la manigua el sitio,
el sitio de la reunión,
de la reunión . . .
de la reunión.

Bellísima Borinquen,
a Cuba hay que seguir;
tú tienes bravos hijos
que quieren combatir.

LOLA RODRÍGUEZ DE TIÓ

The Song of Borinquen

Awake, Borinqueños,
for they've given the signal!

Awake from your sleep
for it's time to fight!

Come! The sound of cannon
will be dear to us.

At that patriotic clamor
doesn't your heart burn?

Look! The Cuban will soon be free,
the machete will give him freedom.

The drum of war announces in its beating
that the thicket is the place, the meeting place!

Most beautiful Borínquen, we have to follow Cuba;
you have brave sons who want to fight!

Let us no more seem fearful!
Let us no more, timid, permit our enslavement!

We want to be free already
and our machete is well sharpened!

Why should we, then, remain so asleep
and deaf, asleep and deaf to that signal?

There's no need to fear, Ricans, the sound of cannon,
for saving the homeland is the duty of the heart!

Ya por más tiempo impávidos
no podemos estar,
ya no queremos, tímidos,
dejarnos subyugar.

Nosotros queremos
ser libres ya,
y nuestro machete
afilado está . . .
y nuestro machete
afilado está.

Porqué entonces, nosotros
hemos de estar,
tan dormidos y sordos
y sordos a la señal . . .
a esa señal, a esa señal.

No hay que temer, riqueños
al ruido del cañón,
que salvar a la patria
¡es deber del corazón!

Ya no queremos déspotas,
caiga el tirano ya,
las mujeres indómitas
también sabrán luchar.

Nosotros queremos
la libertad,
y nuestro machete
nos la dará . . .
y nuestro machete
nos la dará . . .

Vámonos borinqueños,
vámonos ya,
que nos espera ansiosa,
ansiosa la libertad
¡la libertad, la libertad!

We want no more despots! Let the tyrant fall!
Women, likewise wild, will know how to fight!

We want freedom and our machete will give it to us!

Let's go, Puerto Ricans, let's go already,
for LIBERTY is waiting, ever so anxious!

Translated by José Nieto

JOSÉ MARTÍ

de *Versos sencillos*

Yo soy un hombre sincero
De donde crece la palma,
Y antes de morirme quiero
Echar mis versos del alma.

Yo vengo de todas partes,
Y hacia todas partes voy:
Arte soy entre las artes,
En los montes, monte soy.

Yo sé los nombres extraños
De las yerbas y las flores,
Y de mortales engaños,
Y de sublimes dolores.

Yo he visto en la noche oscura
Llover sobre mi cabeza
Los rayos de lumbre pura
De la divina belleza.

Alas nacer vi en los hombros
De las mujeres hermosas:
Y salir de los escombros
Volando las mariposas.

He visto vivir a un hombre
Con el puñal al costado,
Sin decir jamás el nombre
De aquella que lo ha matado.

Rápida, como un reflejo,
Dos veces vi el alma, dos:
Cuando murió el pobre viejo,
Cuando ella me dijo adiós.

JOSÉ MARTÍ

from *Simple Verses*

A sincere man am I
Born where the palm trees grow,
And I long before I die
My soul's verses to bestow.

No boundaries bind my heart
I belong to every land:
I am art among art,
A peak among peaks I stand.

I know the exotic names
Of every flower and leaf.
I know of betrayal's claims
And I know of exalted grief.

I've seen how beauteous streams
Flow through the dark of night
And descend as radiant beams
In a luminous shower of light.

As if by wings set free,
I've seen women's shoulders rise:
And beauty emerge from debris
In a flight of butterflies.

I've seen a man live with pain
The dagger wounds at his side,
Yet never reveal the name
Of her by whose hand he died.

Two times I've sensed inside
The soul's reflection go by.
Once when my father died
And once when she bade goodbye.

Temblé una vez,—en la reja,
A la entrada de la viña,—
Cuando la bárbara abeja
Picó en la frente a mi niña.

Gocé una vez, de tal suerte
Que gocé cual nunca:—cuando
La sentencia de mi muerte
Leyó el alcaide llorando.

Oigo un suspiro, a través
De las tierras y la mar,
Y no es un suspiro,—es
Que mi hijo va a despertar.

Si dicen que del joyero
Tome la joya mejor,
Tomo a un amigo sincero
Y pongo a un lado el amor.

Yo he visto al águila herida
Volar al azul sereno,
Y morir en su guarida
La víbora del veneno.

Yo sé bien que cuando el mundo
Cede, livido, al descanso,
Sobre el silencio profundo
Murmura el arroyo manso.

Yo he puesto la mano osada,
De horror y júbilo yerta,
Sobre la estrella apagada
Que cayó frente a mi puerta.

Oculto en mi pecho bravo
La pena que me lo hiere:
El hijo de un pueblo esclavo
Vive por él, calla, y muere.

Once I trembled with fear
Close by the arbor's vine,
As an angry bee drew near
To sting a child of mine.

That day of my death decree
I felt both triumph and pride,
For the warden who read it to me
Pronounced the sentence and cried.

Beneath me I hear a sigh
From the slumber of earth and sea.
But in truth it's the morning cry
Of my son who awakens me.

The jewel esteemed the most?
The value I most revere?
I would of friendship boast
And hold not love so dear.

The wounded eagle, I know
Can soar to the bluest skies
While the venomous viper below
Chokes on its poison and dies.

I know that when life must yield
And leave us to restful dreams
That alongside the silent field
Is the murmur of gentle streams.

To sorrows and joy, I reply
By placing a loyal hand,
On the star that refused to die—
Proud symbol of my land.

My heart holds anguish and pains
From a wound which festers and cries
The son of a people in chains
Lives for them, hushes, and dies.

Todo es hermoso y constante,
Todo es música y razón,
Y todo, como el diamante,
Antes que luz es carbon.

Yo sé que el necio se entierra
Con gran lujo y con gran llanto,—
Y que no hay fruta en la tierra
Como la del camposanto.

Callo, y entiendo, y me quito
La pompa del rimador:
Cuelgo de un árbol marchito
Mi muceta de doctor.

All is lovely and right
All is reason and song
Before the diamond is bright
Its night of carbon is long.

I know that the foolish may die
With burial pomp and tears
And that no land can supply
The fruit which the graveyard bears.

Silent, I quit the renown
And boast of a poet's rhyme
And rest my doctoral gown
On a tree withered with time.

Translated by Anne Fountain

Amor de ciudad grande

De gorja son y rapidez los tiempos.
Corre cual luz la voz; en alta aguja,
Cual nave despeñada en sirte horrenda,
Húndese el rayo, y en ligera barca
El hombre, como alado, el aire hiende.
¡Así el amor, sin pompa ni misterio
Muere, apenas nacido, de saciado!
¡Juala es la villa de palomas muertas
Y ávidos cazadores! Si los pechos
¡Se rompen de los hombres, y las carnes
Rotas por tierra ruedan, no han de verse
Dentro más que frutillas estrujadas!

Se ama de pie, en las calles, entre el polvo
De los salones y las plazas; muere
La flor que nace. Aquella virgen
Trémula que antes a la muerte daba
La mano pura que a ignorado mozo;
El goce de temer; aquel salirse
Del pecho el corazón; el inefable
Placer de merecer; el grato susto
De caminar de prisa en derechura
Del hogar de la amada, y a sus puertas
Como un niño feliz romper en llanto;—
Y aquel mirar, de nuestro amor al fuego,
Irse tiñendo de color las rosas,—
¡Ea, que son patrañas! Pues ¿quién tiene
tiempo de ser hidalgo? ¡Bien que sienta
Cual áureo vaso o lienzo suntuoso,
Dama gentil en casa de magnate!
¡O si se tiene sed, se alarga el brazo
Y a la copa que pasa se la apura!
Luego, la copa turbia al polvo rueda,
¡Y el hábil catador,—manchado el pecho
De una sangre invisible,—sigue alegre,
Coronado de mirtos, su camino!
¡No son los cuerpos ya sino desechos,

Love in the City

Times of gorge and rush are these:
Voices fly like light: lightning,
like a ship hurled upon dread quicksand,
plunges down the high rod, and in delicate craft
man, as if winged, cleaves the air.
And love, without splendor or mystery,
dies when newly born, of glut.
The city is a cage of dead doves
and avid hunters! If men's bosoms
were to open and their torn flesh
fall to the earth, inside would be
nothing but a scatter of small, crushed fruit!

Love happens in the street, standing in the dust
of saloons and public squares: the flower
dies the day it's born. The trembling
virgin who would rather death
have her than some unknown youth;
the joy of trepidation; that feeling of heart
set free from chest; the ineffable
pleasure of deserving; the sweet alarm
of walking quick and straight
from your love's home and breaking
into tears like a happy child;—
and that gazing of our love at the fire,
as roses slowly blush a deeper color,—
Bah, it's all a sham! Who has the time
to be noble? Though like a golden
bowl or sumptuous painting
a genteel lady sits in the magnate's home!

But if you're thirsty, reach out your arm,
and drain some passing cup!
The dirtied cup rolls to the dust, then,
and the expert taster—breast blotted
with invisible blood—goes happily,
crowned with myrtle, on his way!

Y fosas, y jirones! ¡Y las almas
No son como en el árbol fruta rica
En cuya blanda piel la almíbar dulce
En su sazón de madurez rebosa,—
Sino fruta de plaza que a brutales
Golpes el rudo labrador madura!

¡La edad es ésta de los labios secos!
¡De las noches sin sueño! ¡De la vida
Estrujada en agraz! ¿Qué es lo que falta
Que la ventura falta? Como liebre
Azorada, el espíritu se esconde,
Trémulo huyendo al cazador que ríe,
cual en soto selvoso, en nuestro pecho;
Y el deseo, de brazo de la fiebre,
Cual rico cazador recorre el soto.

¡Me espanta la ciudad! ¡Toda está llena
De copas por viciar, o huecas copas!
¡Tengo miedo ¡ay de mí! de que este vino
Tósigo sea, y en mis venas luego
Cual duende vengador los dientes clave!
¡Tengo sed,—mas de un vino que en la tierra
No se sabe beber! ¡No he padecido
Bastante aún, para romper el muro
Que me aparta ¡oh dolor! de mi viñedo!
¡Tomad vosotros, catadores ruines
De vinillos humanos, esos vasos
Donde el jugo de lirio a grandes sorbos
Sin compasión y sin temor se bebe!
¡Tomad! ¡Yo soy honrado, y tengo miedo!

New York, abril—1882

Bodies are nothing now but trash,
pits, and tatters! And souls
are not the tree's lush fruit
down whose tender skin runs
sweet juice in time of ripeness,—
but fruit of the marketplace, ripened
by the hardened laborer's brutal blows!

It is an age of dry lips!
Of undreaming nights! Of life
crushed unripe! What is it that we lack,
without which there is no gladness? Like a startled
hare in the wild thicket of our breast,
fleeing, tremulous, from a gleeful hunter,
the spirit takes cover;
and Desire, on Fever's arm,
beats the thicket, like the rich hunter.

The city appals me! Full
of cups to be emptied, and empty cups!
I fear—ah me!—that this wine
may be poison, and sink its teeth,
vengeful imp, in my veins!
I thirst—but for a wine that none on earth
knows how to drink! I have not yet
endured enough to break through the wall
that keeps me, ah grief!, from my vineyard!
Take, oh squalid tasters
of humble human wines, these cups
from which, with no fear or pity,
you swill the lily's juice!
Take them! I am honorable, and I am afraid!

—New York, April 1882
Translated by Esther Allen

JOSÉ JUAN TABLADA

Haiku seleccionados

LA PAJARERA
Distintos cantos a la vez;
la pajarera musical
es una torre de Babel.

LOS ZOPILOTES
Llovió toda la noche
y no acaban de peinar sus plumas
al sol, los zopilotes.

LAS ABEJAS
Sin cesar gotea
miel el colmenar;
cada gota es una abeja . . .

EL SAÚZ
Tierno saúz
casi oro, casi ámbar
casi luz . . .

EL CHIRIMOYO
La rama del chirimoyo
se retuerce y habla:
pareja de loros.

EL INSECTO
Breve insecto, vas de camino
plegadas las alas a cuestas,
como alforja de peregrino . . .

LOS GANSOS
Por nada los gansos
tocan alarma
en sus trompetas de barro.

JOSÉ JUAN TABLADA

Selected Haiku

THE AVIARY

A hundred songs at once;
the musical aviary
is another tower of babel.

BUZZARDS

Rain throughout the night,
now the buzzards preen themselves,
basking in the sun.

BEES

Drops
of honey from the comb,
each one a bee.

WILLOW

Gentle willow—
like gold, like amber,
like sunlight . . .

THE CHIRIMOYO

The chirimoyo branch
twists and speaks—
two parrots.

THE BUG

Little bug, wandering,
wings wrapped behind you—
a pilgrim's knapsack.

GEESE

Geese aimlessly
sound the alarm,
horns blaring.

EL BAMBÚ

Cohete de larga vara
el bambú apenas sube se doblega
en lluvia de menudas esmeraldas.

EL CABALLO DEL DIABLO

Caballo del diablo:
clavo de vidrio
con alas de talco.

EL PAVO REAL

Pavo real, largo fulgor,
por el gallinero demócrata
pasas como una procesión . . .

LAS NUBES

       | de los Andes van veloces,
Las nubes | de montaña en montaña,
       | en alas de los cóndores.

FLOR DE TORONJA

De los enjambres es
predilecta la flor de la toronja
(huele a cera y a miel).

LA PALMA

En la siesta cálida
ya ni sus abanicos
mueve la palma . . .

VIOLETAS

Apenas la he regado
y la mata se cubre de violetas,
reflejos del cielo violado.

LAS HORMIGAS

Breve cortejo nupcial,
las hormigas arrastran
pétalos de azahar . . .

BAMBOO

Shooting slender stalk;
the bamboo rises ever straight
amid an emerald rain.

THE DRAGONFLY

Dragonfly:
glassy hobnail
with glittering wings.

PEACOCK

The splendorous peacock
struts about the coop
as if in a royal procession.

CLOUDS

      | roll across the Andes
Clouds | from summit to summit
      | beneath the condor's wings.

GRAPEFRUIT BLOSSOM

The grapefruit blossom
(and its smell of sweet nectar)
is a favorite of the hive.

PALMS

In the midday heat
even the palm fronds
are stilled.

VIOLETS

Barely watered,
and the violet covered shrub
is a reflection of the violet sky.

ANTS

Ants marching, hoisting
orange blossom petals—
a tiny wedding procession.

LA TORTUGA

Aunque jamás se muda,
a tumbos, como carro de mudanzas,
va por la senda la tortuga.

LAS CIGARRAS

Las cigarras agitan
sus menudas sonajas
llenas de piedrecitas . . .

LAS RANAS

Engranes de matracas
crepitan al correr del arroyo
en los molinos de las ranas.

TORCACES

De monte a monte,
salvando la cañada y el hondo río,
una torcaz se queja y otra responde.

HOJAS SECAS

El jardín está lleno de hojas secas;
nunca vi tantas hojas en sus árboles
verdes, en primavera.

HOTEL

Otoño en el hotel de primavera;
en el patio de "tennis"
hay musgo y hojas secas.

LAS AVISPAS

Como en el blanco las flechas
se clavan en el avispero
las avispas que regresan . . .

LA GARZA

Clavada en la saeta
de su pico y sus patas,
la garza vuela.

THE TORTOISE

The tortoise
stumbles along, boxy and slow
like a cargo truck.

CICADAS

Cicadas shake their
little rattles
full of rocks.

FROGS

Frogs
like an immense network of rattles
crackle as they cross the stream.

DOVES

Over the mountaintops
and across the deep gully
a ring dove coos, and another responds.

DRIED LEAVES

The garden floor now holds
more dry leaves than the green tree
ever could in spring.

HOTEL

Autumn at the Spring Hotel—
moss and crisp leaves
on the tennis court.

WASPS

From out of nowhere
arrows penetrate the nest
. . . the wasps return.

HERON

The heron
is an arrow in
flight.

MARIPOSA NOCTURNA

Mariposa nocturna
a la niña que lee "María"
tu vuelo pone taciturna . . .

LOS SAPOS

Trozos de barro,
por la senda en penumbra
saltan los sapos.

EL CÁMBULO

El cámbulo,
con las mil llamas de sus flores,
es un gigante lampadario.

EL MURCIÉLAGO

¿Los vuelos de la golondrina
ensaya en la sombra el murciélago
para luego volar de día . . . ?

LOS RUISEÑORES

Plata y perlas de luna hechas canciones
oíd . . . en la caja de música
del kiosko de los ruiseñores.

LA BUGANVILIA

La noche anticipa
y de pronto arde en el crepúsculo,
la pirotecnia de la buganvilia.

MARIPOSA NOCTURNA

Devuelve a la desnuda rama,
nocturna mariposa,
las hojas secas de tus alas.

LUCIÉRNAGAS

Luciérnagas en un árbol . . .
¿Navidad en verano? . . .

THE MOTH

A moth darts, taciturn,
around a little girl
praying the Ave Maria.

TOADS

Clumps of mud and clay
on the road,
toads hopping.

THE CAMBULO

The cambulo,
tree with a thousand burning flowers,
a giant candelabra.

BATS

Bats hang in the shadows
observing the swallows, learning;
will they soon take flight by day?

NIGHTINGALES

Nightingales sing
under the pearled moon and stars—
tableaux in a music box.

THE BOUGAINVILLEA

Night closes in
and commences the pyrotechnics of twilight—
the bougainvillea in bloom.

MOTH

Moth,
Your wings are like dried leaves
on a bare branch.

FIREFLIES

A tree full of fireflies . . .
Christmas in July?

EL RUISEÑOR
Bajo el celeste pavor
delira por la única estrella
el cántico del ruiseñor.

EL ABEJORRO
El abejorro terco
rondando en el foco zumba
como abanico eléctrico.

LA ARAÑA
Recorriendo su tela
esta luna clarísima
tiene a la araña en vela.

EL CISNE
Al lago, al silencio, a la sombra,
todo candor el cisne
con el cuello interroga . . .

LA LUNA
Es mar la noche negra;
la nube es una concha;
la luna es una perla . . .

EL COCUYO
Pedrerías de rocío
alumbra, cocuyo,
tu lámpara de Aladino!

THE NIGHTINGALE

Beneath the vast sky
a nightingale sings its love song to
a single star.

THE BUMBLEBEE

Bee, bumbling
in circles,
like a whirring fan blade.

THE SPIDER

Clear-bright moon
crossing the spider's web,
keeps it awake tonight.

SWAN

Peering toward the lake
and into the shadowy, solemn void
the swan curves its neck in question.

THE MOON

The dark night is the sea,
the clouds, a shell,
and the moon is the pearl within.

THE COCUYO

Dew drop jewels—
blaze, cocuyo,
your Aladdin's lamp!

Translated by A. Scott Britton

Luna Galante

Cuando apagó el crepúsculo
  su postrera luz roja,
aquel parque en la magia
  de la noche estival
vio a la niña temblando
  con furtiva congoja
y al amante besándola
  con delirio sensual.

Suspirando la novia
  quedó trémula y floja
de aquel beso implacable
  bajo el trágico mal,
como ave moribunda
  o flor que se deshoja,
entre los vahos cálidos
  de ardiente vendaval . . .

Luego, al surgir la luna
  con su segur de plata,
como segando estrellas
  en el azul confín,
de la niña que huía,
  sobre la escalinata,
se perdió el taconeo del ligero chapín;
y Pierrot, como en todo final de Serenata,
¡se deshizo en la luna que bañaba el jardín!

      —MORNINGSIDE PARK, NEW YORK, 1916

Gallant Moon

In the park, on a magical
       summer night,
after the final red burnings
       of dusk have been extinguished,
sits a trembling girl with
       a furtive ache in her heart;
she's kissing her lover,
       delirious with sensuality.

The girl sighs,
       left tremulous
and weakened by
       the unrelenting kiss,
like a dying bird,
       or a flower, stripped of all its petals
by the steamy breaths
       of an ardent gale . . .

Later, like the rising moon
       —the sparkling silver sickle
of its path harvesting the stars
       in a deep blue field—
the girl takes flight
       up the staircase,
heels tapping quieter and quieter with her ascent;
a fate like Pierrot's, who, at the end of the Serenata,
is completely undone in the moon-washed garden!

       —MORNINGSIDE PARK, NEW YORK, 1916
       Translated by A. Scott Britton

WILLIAM CARLOS WILLIAMS

All the Fancy Things

music and painting and all that
That's all they thought of
in Puerto Rico in the old Spanish
days when she was a girl

So that now
she doesn't know what to do

with herself alone
and growing old up here—

Green is green
but the tag ends
of older things, *ma chère*

must withstand rebuffs
from that which returns
to the beginnings—

Or what? a
clean air, high up, unoffended
by gross odors

The Poet and His Poems

I

The poem is this:
a nuance of sound
delicately operating
upon a cataract of sense.

Vague. What a stupid
image. Who operates?
And who is operated
on? How can a nuance

operate on anything?
It is all in
the sound. A song.
Seldom a song. It should

be a song—made of
particulars, wasps,
a gentian—something
immediate, open

scissors, a lady's
eyes—the particulars
of a song waking
upon a bed of sound.

2

Stiff jointed poets
or the wobble
headed who chase
vague images and think—

because they feel
lovely movements
upon the instruments
of their hearts—

that they are gifted
forget the
exchange, how much
is paid and how little

when you count it
in your hand you
get for it later in
the market. It's

a constant mystery
no less in the
writing of imaginative
lines than in love.

SALOMÓN DE LA SELVA

A Song for Wall Street

In Nicaragua, my Nicaragua,
    What can you buy for a penny there?—
A basketful of apricots,
    A water jug of earthenware,
A rosary of coral beads
    And a priest's prayer.

And for two pennies? For two new pennies?—
    The strangest music ever heard
All from the brittle little throat
    Of a clay bird,
And, for good measure, we will give you
    A patriot's word.

And for a nickel? A bright white nickel?—
    It's lots of land a man can buy,
A golden mine that's long and deep,
    A forest growing high,
And a little house with a red roof
    And a river passing by.

But for your dollar, your dirty dollar,
    Your greenish leprosy,
It's only hatred you shall get
    From all my folks and me;
So keep your dollar where it belongs
    And let us be!

My Nicaragua

You take the street that runs by the cathedral
And go some fourteen blocks and up a hill
And past the three-arch bridge until you come
To Guadalupe. There the houses are
No stately Spanish palaces, flat and lazy,
As in the center of the town you see,
Heavy with some three centuries upon them,
Accustomed to the sunlight and the earthquakes,
Half bored, you fancy, by these ways of nature;
But little things, ugly almost, and frail,
With low red roofs and flimsy rough cut doors,
A trifle better than an Indian hut;
Not picturesque, just dreary commonplace,
As commonplace and dreary as the flats
Here in your cities where your poor folks live;
And yet they seem so glad the sun is shining,
So glad a little wind begins to blow,
Too humbly, purely glad to say it,—
And all the while afraid of the volcanoes,
Holding their breath lest these should wake and crush them.

Look through the doors ajar and see the walls
With holy pictures, saints and angels there,—
Like little windows opening to Heaven,—
Sold to my people, reverenced by them.
And see the children, playing, wrangling, dreaming,
Oh, much the way that children are elsewhere.
And see the faithful wives, sweeping or mending,
Setting their tables, doing the thousand things
Hardly worth noticing that women do
About their houses, meaning life to them.
And if you listen, you may hear them sing:
Not anywhere are better songs than theirs!
That rise and melt away like incense smoke,
And can, if pressed too hard against the heart,
Drip heavy drops that are all women's tears.

But if you hire a guide, no guide will ever
Think of directing you to see this mere
Unhonoured dailiness of people's lives
That is the soil the roots of beauty know.
The old cathedral that the Spaniards built,
With hand-carved altars for two thousand saints;
The ruined fortress where they say that Nelson
Lost his left eye when he was but a pirate—
Oh, broken piles of masonry outworn,
The shreds and trash of things that were of price,
Cocoons forgotten whence the butterflies
Of love of country and of love of God
Rose, and were lost among the fields afar!

The *dear* hotels with palm trees in the garden
And a self-playing piano drumming rags,
Where you drink lemonade and rack your brains
Thinking: What in the devil's name is Tropics?—
The shops of German, English and French owners;
The parlours of the ruling class adorned
With much the same bad taste as in New York,—
That never was my country! But the rows
Of earthen little houses where men dwell,
And women, all too busy living life
To think of faking it, that is my country,
My Nicaragua, mother of great poets!

And when you see that, what? That in despite
Newspapered revolutions and so forth,
The different climate and the different
Traditions and grandfathers of the race,
My people and your people are the same:
Folks with their worries and their hopes about them,
Toiling for bread, and for a something more
That ever changes, that no one could name—
And this is worth the journey to find out.

II.

CORRIDOS AND
NOSTALGIA SONGS

ANONYMOUS

La Indita de Plácida Romero

El día de San Lorenzo
era un día poderoso,
que me llevaron cautiva
y mataron a mi esposo.
El año de ochenta y uno,
cerca de las diez del día,
así sería yo pienso
cuando esto nos sucedía,
que mataron a mi esposo
y al hombre Jesus María.

REFRÁN
Adiós, ya me voy,
voy a padecer.
Adiós, mis queridas hijas,
¿cuándo las volveré a ver?

Adiós, Rancho de la Cebolla,
¿por qué te muestras esquiva?
Los palos, las piedras lloran
de verme salir cautiva.
Adiós, Cubero afamado,
se te acabó lo valiente.
Quizá no tenías parque,
o te ha faltado la gente.

-refrán-

Manuelita la mayor,
cuida a tus hermanitas
que ya les faltó el calor,
se quedaron huerfanitas.
Adiós, plaza de Cubero,

ANONYMOUS

Little Indian Ballad of Plácida Romero

St. Lawrence Day
was a forceful day,
they took me captive
and killed my husband.
The year eighty-one,
about ten o'clock in the morning,
that's how it was I think
when this happened to us,
they killed my husband
and the man Jesús María.

CHORUS
Farewell, I'm leaving.
I am going to suffer.
Farewell, my dear daughters,
When will I see you again?

Farewell, Rancho de la Cebolla,
Why are you so elusive?
The sticks, the stones cry
to see me leave captive,
Farewell, famed Cubero,
you've run out of courage.
Maybe you didn't have a park,
or enough people

-chorus-

Manuelita the eldest,
take care of your little sisters
They've already lacked warmth,
They've become orphans.
Farewell, Cubero square,

adiós, mi hogar y mi casa,
adiós, paredes y esquinas,
adiós, madre Marucasia.
Adiós, madrecita fina,
duélete de mi desgracia.

-refrán-

Adiós, Domingo Gallegos,
adiós, fino compañero,
quizá no tenías hermanos,
ni parientes allí en Cubero,
que se quedaron tus huesos
en un triste gallinero.

En la sierra de Galeana,
allí terminaron mis días.
Lo que reconocí,
que era gente la que venía.
Le dije a mi compañero,
"no te retires de mí,
oyes, Procopio García."
Llegué al Ojito Salado
y me puse a devisar
a ver si veía venir
a mi padre o a mi hermano.
También si veía venir
a mi hermano Cayetano.

Mi Señora de la Luz
fue la que reina en Cubero,
pidiéndole al Santo Niño
que salga del cautiverio.

-refrán-

Farewell, my home and my house,
Farewell, walls and corners,
Farewell, mother Marucasia.
Farewell, fine little mother,
Grieve from my misfortune.

-chorus-

Farewell, Domingo Gallegos,
Farewell, fine companion,
perhaps you had no brothers,
nor relatives there in Cubero,
that your bones were left
in a sad henhouse.

In the mountains of Galeana,
there my days ended.
What I recognized,
it was people who came.
I said to my companion,
"Don't wander from me,
Listen, Procopio García."
I arrived to Ojito Salado
and I started looking around
to see if I could see
my father or my brother.
Also if I saw coming
my brother Cayetano.

My Lady of Light
was the one who reigns in Cubero,
asking the Holy Child
to end my captivity.

-chorus-

Translated by Mahsa Hojjati

ANONYMOUS

El Corrido de Gregorio Cortez

En el condado de El Carmen
miren lo que ha sucedido,
murió el Cherife Mayor,
Quedando Román herido.

En el condado de El Carmen
tal desgracia sucedió
murió el Cherife Mayor,
no saben quién lo mató.

Se anduvieron informando
como media hora después,
supieron que el malhechor
era Gregorio Cortez.

Ya insortaron a Cortez
por toditito el estado,
que vivo o muerto se aprehenda
porque a varios ha matado.

Decía Gregorio Cortez
con su pistola en la mano;
—No siento haberlo matado,
lo que siento es a mi hermano.

Decía Gregorio Cortez
con su alma muy encendida:
—No siento haberlo matado,
la defensa es permitida.—

Venían los americanos
más blancos que una amapola,
de miedo que le tenían
a Cortez con su pistola.

ANONYMOUS

The Ballad of Gregorio Cortez

In the county of El Carmen
An awful thing occurred one day.
They found the Sheriff Major freshly slain,
And Roman in a real bad way.

In the county of El Carmen
Many faces hung in shame,
The Sheriff's body not yet cold,
No one knew who was to blame.

The people got to talking,
'Till some thirty minutes flew,
Then a wily fella pointed—
Gregorio Cortez your time is due.

Soon Cortez was wanted
Throughout the whole wide state.
Alive or not they'd take him,
So many he'd laid to waste.

Gregorio Cortez stood tall and spoke,
With a pistol in his hand:
I don't bemoan the crime I've done,
My brother's death I will not stand.

Gregorio Cortez did rise and speak,
His soul a blazing flame:
I don't regret the killing,
Revenge is but fair game.

The Americans got wind and came,
White as poppies in a field of sun,
But found themselves too scared
Of Cortez's silver gun.

Decían los americanos,
decían con timidez:
—Vamos a seguir la huella
que el malhechor es Cortez.

Soltaron los perros jaunes
pa' que siguieran la huella,
pero alcanzar a Cortez
era seguir a una estrella.

Tiró con rumbo a Gonzales
sin ninguna timidez:
—Síganme, rinches cobardes,
yo soy Gregorio Cortez.—

Se fue de Belmont al rancho,
lo alcanzaron a rodear,
poquitos más de trescientos
y allí les brincó el corral.

Cuando les brincó el corral,
según lo que aquí se dice,
se agarraron a balazos
y les mató otro cherife.

Decía Gregorio Cortez
con su pistola en la mano:
—No corran, rinches cobardes,
Con un solo mexicano.—

Salió Gregorio Cortez,
salía con rumbo a Laredo,
no lo quisieron seguir
porque le tuvieron miedo.

Decía Gregorio Cortez
—Pa' qué se valen de planes?
No me pueden agarrar
ni con esos perros jaunes.—

And with his voice a trembling
One American then says:
Let's follow that there hoof-print
To find the outlaw named Cortez.

Letting loose their golden dogs,
They trailed the bandit far,
But trying to catch Cortez
Was like pinning down a star.

He went straight for Gonzales
Without a trace of stress:
Come an' get me silly gringos,
I'm the one they call Cortez.

They caught up with him past Belmont
To try him for a capital offense.
At least three hundred men surrounded him—
That was when he jumped the fence.

And when he cleared the ranch
(Least that's what folks around here said)
They got to loading up their guns
And was a second Sheriff dead.

Gregorio Cortez then stood to shout,
With his silver gun in hand:
Don't flee you silly gringos!
I'm just one Mexican man.

Gregorio Cortez soon hit the road
On his horse, Laredo-bound.
But they didn't dare pursue his trail,
Too scared to stick around.

Gregorio Cortez then turned and said:
Why keep making the rounds?
You know you'll never take me—
Not with a thousand of your hounds.

Allá por El Encinal,
según lo que aquí se dice,
Le formaron un corral
Y les mató otro cherife.

Decía Gregorio Cortez
echando muchos balazos:
—Me he escapado de aguaceros,
contimás de nublinazos,—

Ya se encontró a un mexicano,
le dice con altivez:
—Platícame qué hay de nuevo,
Yo soy Gregorio Cortez.

—Dicen que por culpa mía
han matado mucha gente,
pues ya me voy a entregar
porque eso no es conveniente.—

Cortez le dice a Jesús:
—Ora sí lo vas a ver,
anda diles a los rinches
que me vengan a aprehender.—

Venían todos los rinches,
venían que hasta volaban,
porque se iban a ganar
diez mil pesos que les daban.

Cuando rodearon la casa
Cortez se les presentó:
—Por la buena si me llevan,
porque de otro modo no.—

Decía el Cherife Mayor
como queriendo llorar:
—Cortez, entrega tus armas,
no te vamos a matar.—

And out by Encinal
(Or so the folks around here said)
The men formed one more barricade—
'Till was another Sheriff dead.

Gregorio Cortez then standing, shouts,
His bullets dancing in a silver gust:
I've weathered plenty squalls and storms—
What's one more cloud of dust?

And finding a fellow Mexican,
In a lofty voice he says:
How are things with you, paisano?
I'm the one they call Cortez.

They say it's all my fault
So many men were slain
I reckon I just turn me in,
This pace I can't maintain.

Cortez then told his pal Jesús:
Now you're really gonna see—
Come tell those silly gringos
To come running after me.

The Rangers came as fast they could—
So fast they nearly flew.
It seemed they had high hopes to claim
The ten grand they were due.

When they had the house surrounded,
Cortez came out and said:
Behave and I'll go softly,
Or else you're eating lead.

The Sheriff Major spoke,
With a voice that nearly broke:
We promise we won't kill you,
Just give us all your guns.

Decía Gregorio Cortez,
les gritaba en alta voz
—Mis armas no las entrego
hasta estar en calaboz.

Decía Gregorio Cortez,
decía en su voz divina:
—Mis armas no las entrego
hasta estar en bartolina.

Ya agarraron a Cortez,
ya termina la cuestión,
la pobre de su familia
lo lleva en el corazón.

Ya con ésta me despido
a la sombra de un ciprés,
aquí se acaba el corrido
de don Gregorio Cortez.

Then Gregorio took to yelling,
His voice nearly a wail:
I won't give you gringos nothing,
'Till I'm rotting in a cell!

Gregorio Cortez exclaimed
(And his singsong voice was airy):
I won't give up any weapons,
'Till they put me in solitary.

At last they took Cortez
(And this here's where I depart)
Though his poor mother and sisters
Still live with aching hearts.

With this I bid farewell
From beneath the cypress trees
Here ends the melancholy ballad
Of don Gregorio Cortez.

Translated by Susana Plotts–Pineda

ENRIQUE FRANCO

Tres veces mojado

Cuando me vine de mi tierra El Salvador
con la intención de llegar a Estados Unidos
sabía que necesitaría más que valor
sabía que a lo mejor quedaba en el camino

Son tres fronteras las que tuve que cruzar
por tres paises anduve indocumentado
tres veces tuve yo la vida que arriesgar
por eso dicen que soy tres veces mojado

En Guatemala y México cuando crucé
dos veces me salvé me hicieran prisionero
el mismo idioma y el color reflexioné
¿Cómo es posible que me llamen extranjero?

En centroamerica dada su situación
tanto política como económica
ya para muchos no hay otra solución
más que abandonar su patria
y tal vez para siempre

El Mexicano da dos pasos y aqui está
hoy lo echan y al siguiente dia está de regreso

eso es un lujo que no me puedo dar
sin que me maten o que me lleven preso

Es lindo México pero cuanto sufrí
atravezarlo sin papeles es muy duro

los cinco mil kilómetros que recorrí
puedo decir que los recuerdo uno por uno

ENRIQUE FRANCO

Three Times a Wetback

When I came from my homeland El Salvador
with the intention of reaching the United States
I knew I would need more than courage
I knew that maybe I would be left on the road

There are three borders I had to cross
I was undocumented in three countries
three times I had to risk my life
that's why they say that I am three times a wetback

In Guatemala and Mexico when I crossed
twice I was saved from being taken prisoner
the same language and color I thought
How is it possible that they call me a foreigner?

In Central America, given its location
both politically and economically
for many there is no other solution
but to leave their homeland
and perhaps forever

The Mexican takes two steps and here he is
today he is kicked out and the next day he is back in the
    country

that is a luxury that I cannot afford
without being killed or taken prisoner.

Mexico is nice but how much I suffered
crossing it without papers is very hard

the five thousand kilometers I traveled
I can say that I remember them one by one

Por Arizona me dijeron cruzarás
y que me aviento por enmedio del desierto
por suerte un Mexicano al que llamaban Juan
me dió la mano que si no me hubiera muerto

Ahora que al fin logre la legalización
lo que sufrí lo he recuperado con creces
a los mojados les dedico mi canción
y a los que igual que yo son mojados tres veces

They told me I would cross through Arizona
and I flung myself through the middle of the desert
luckily a Mexican who they called Juan
gave me a hand or else I would have died.

Now that I finally achieved legalization
I've more than recovered what I suffered
I dedicate my song to the wetbacks
and to those who like me are wetbacks three times

Translated by Mahsa Hojjati

NOEL ESTRADA

En mi Viejo San Juan

En mi Viejo San Juan
Cuántos sueños forjé
En mis noches de infancia
Mi primera ilusión
Y mis cuitas de amor
Son recuerdos del alma

Una tarde me fui
Hacia extraña nación
Pues lo quiso el destino
Pero mi corazón
Se quedó frente al mar
En mi viejo San Juan

Adiós
Adiós, adiós
Borinquen querida
Tierra de mi amor

Adiós
Adiós, adiós
Mi diosa del mar
Mi reina del palmar

Me voy
Pero un día volveré
A buscar mi querer
A soñar otra vez
En mi viejo San Juan

Pero el tiempo pasó
Y el destino burló
Mi terrible nostalgia

NOEL ESTRADA

In My Old San Juan

In my Old San Juan
How many dreams I formed
In my childhood nights
My first illusion
And my love troubles
Are memories of the soul

One evening I left
Towards a strange nation
Destiny wished it so
But my heart
Stayed in front of the sea
In my Old San Juan

Farewell
Farewell, farewell
Beloved Borinquen
Land of my love

Farewell
Farewell, farewell
My goddess of the sea
My queen of the palm groves

I'm leaving
But one day I'll be back
To look for my love
To dream once again
In my Old San Juan

But time passed
And destiny mocked
My terrible nostalgia

Y no pude volver
Al San Juan que yo amé
Pedacito de patria

Mi cabello blanqueó
Y mi vida se va
Ya la muerte me llama
Y no quiero morir
Alejado de ti
Puerto Rico del alma

Adiós
Adiós, adiós
Borinquen querida
Tierra de mi amor

Adiós
Adiós, adiós
Mi diosa del mar
Mi reina del palmar

Me voy
Pero un día volveré
A buscar mi querer
A soñar otra vez
En mi viejo San Juan

And I could not return
To the San Juan that I loved
Little piece of homeland

My hair whitened
And my life goes away
Death is calling me
And I don't want to die
Distanced from you
Puerto Rico of my soul

Farewell
Farewell, farewell
Beloved Borinquen
Land of my love

Farewell
Farewell, farewell
My goddess of the sea
My queen of the palm groves

I'm leaving
But one day I'll be back
To look for my love
To dream once again
In my Old San Juan

Translated by Mahsa Hojjati

CHUCHO MONGE

México lindo y querido

Voz de la guitarra mía
al despertar la mañana
Quiere cantar su alegría
a mi tierra mexicana

Yo le canto a tus volcanes,
a tus praderas y flores
Que son como talismanes
del amor de mis amores

México lindo y querido,
si muero lejos de ti
Que digan que estoy dormido
Y que me traigan aquí

Que digan que estoy dormido
Y que me traigan aquí
México lindo y querido
Si muero lejos de ti

Que me entierren en la sierra
Al pie de los magueyales
Y que me cubra ésta tierra
Que es cuna de hombres cabales

Voz de la guitarra mía,
al despertar la mañana
Quiere cantar su alegría
a mi tierra mexicana

México lindo y querido,
si muero lejos de ti
Que digan que estoy dormido
Y que me traigan aquí

CHUCHO MONGE

Mexico Sweet and Beloved

The voice of my guitar
when the morning wakes up
Wants to sing its joy
to my Mexican land

I sing to your volcanoes
to your meadows and flowers
That are like good luck charms
of the love of my loves

Mexico sweet and beloved
if I die far from you
Let them say that I am sleeping
and let them bring me back to you

Let them say that I am sleeping
and let them bring me back to you
Mexico sweet and beloved
if I die far from you

May I be buried in the mountains
at the foot of the agaves
And may I be covered with this earth
which is the cradle of honest men

The voice of my guitar
when the morning wakes up
Wants to sing its joy
to my Mexican land

Mexico sweet and beloved
if I die far from you
Let them say that I am sleeping
and let them bring me back to you

Que digan que estoy dormido
Y que me traigan aquí
México lindo y querido
Si muero lejos, de ti

Let them say that I am sleeping
and let them bring me back to you
Mexico sweet and beloved
if I die far from you

Translated by Mahsa Hojjati

RAMITO
(FLORENCIO MORALES RAMOS)

Que bonita bandera

Que bonita bandera
Que bonita bandera
Que bonita bandera, la bandera Puertorriqueña

Que bonita bandera
Que bonita bandera
Que bonita bandera, la bandera Puertorriqueña

Azul, blanca y colorada
En el medio tiene una estrella
Que bonita bandera mi bandera Puertorriqueña

Que bonita bandera
Que bonita bandera
Que bonita bandera, la bandera Puertorriqueña

Que bonita bandera
Que bonita bandera
Que bonita bandera, la bandera Puertorriqueña

Dijo José de Diego, Bentances y Muñoz Rivera
"Que bonita bandera, la bandera Puertorriqueña"

Que bonita bandera
Que bonita bandera
Que bonita bandera, la bandera Puertorriqueña

Que bonita bandera
Que bonita bandera
Que bonita bandera, la bandera Puertorriqueña

RAMITO
(FLORENCIO MORALES RAMOS)

What a Beautiful Flag

What a beautiful flag
What a beautiful flag
What a beautiful flag, the Puerto Rican flag

What a beautiful flag
What a beautiful flag
What a beautiful flag, the Puerto Rican flag

Blue, white and red
In the middle it has a star
What a beautiful flag, my Puerto Rican flag

What a beautiful flag
What a beautiful flag
What a beautiful flag, the Puerto Rican flag

What a beautiful flag
What a beautiful flag
What a beautiful flag, the Puerto Rican flag

José de Diego, Bentances y Muñoz Rivera said
"What a beautiful flag, the Puerto Rican flag"

What a beautiful flag
What a beautiful flag
What a beautiful flag, the Puerto Rican flag

What a beautiful flag
What a beautiful flag
What a beautiful flag, the Puerto Rican flag

Quisiera verla flotando sobre mi Borinquen bella
Que bonita bandera, dime: "que bonita bandera"

Que bonita bandera
Que bonita bandera
Que bonita bandera, la bandera Puertorriqueña

Que bonita bandera
Que bonita bandera
Que bonita bandera, la bandera Puertorriqueña

Que bonita bandera
Que bonita bandera
Que bonita bandera, la bandera Puertorriqueña

Azul, blanca y colorada
En el medio tiene una estrella
Que bonita bandera, mire, que bonita bandera

Que bonita bandera
Que bonita bandera
Que bonita bandera, la bandera Puertorriqueña

Que bonita bandera
Que bonita bandera
Que bonita bandera, la bandera Puertorriqueña

Que bonita bandera
Que bonita bandera
Que bonita bandera, la bandera Puertorriqueña

Que bonita bandera
Que bonita bandera
Que bonita bandera, la bandera Puertorriqueña

Que bonita bandera
Que bonita bandera
Que bonita bandera, la bandera Puertorriqueña

I'd like to see it floating over my beautiful Borinquen
What a beautiful flag, tell me: "What a beautiful flag"

What a beautiful flag
What a beautiful flag
What a beautiful flag, the Puerto Rican flag

What a beautiful flag
What a beautiful flag
What a beautiful flag, the Puerto Rican flag

What a beautiful flag
What a beautiful flag
What a beautiful flag, the Puerto Rican flag

Blue, white and red
In the middle it has a star
What a beautiful flag, look, what a beautiful flag

What a beautiful flag
What a beautiful flag
What a beautiful flag, the Puerto Rican flag

What a beautiful flag
What a beautiful flag
What a beautiful flag, the Puerto Rican flag

What a beautiful flag
What beautiful flag
What a beautiful flag, the Puerto Rican flag

What a beautiful flag
What a beautiful flag
What a beautiful flag, the Puerto Rican flag

What a beautiful flag
What a beautiful flag
What a beautiful flag, the Puerto Rican flag

Translated by Mahsa Hojjati

ALEXANDER ABREU

Me dicen Cuba

Vengo de donde el sol calienta la tierra
Y allí donde el corazón late más sincero
Vengo de donde el Son pasa las horas
Enamorando a la Rumba cantándole aquel Bolero

Traigo mi religión y mi esperanza
Mezclada con mi tambor y mi melodía
Tan solo quiero que sepas lo que se siente
Cuando se llene tu alma de toda mi cubanía

Cubano soy de pura cepa
Y mis raíces las defiendo con la vida
Cubano soy y dondequiera que me encuentre
Cantaré a mi Cuba querida

Vengo de donde el sol calienta la tierra
La tierra donde nací, donde viviré
Por eso te traigo ahora mi canción
Para que sepas el porqué a mí me dicen Cuba

Para saber de verdad lo que es sentirse cubano
Tienes que haber nacido en Cuba
Tienes que haber vivido en Cuba

Para saber de verdad lo que es sentirse cubano
Tienes que léerte a Martí, la prosa de Guillén
Busca una guayabera con un sombrero de guano

Para saber de verdad lo que es sentirse cubano
Pa' que te llegue a la bomba hermano
Tienes que haber nacido en Cuba
Tienes que haber vivido en Cuba

ALEXANDER ABREU

They Call Me Cuba

I come from where the sun heats the earth
And there where the heart beats more sincerely
I come from where the hours go by listening to Son
Enamoring the Rumba singing that Bolero to it

I bring my religion and my hope
Mixed with my drum and my melody
I just want you to know what it feels like
When your soul is filled with all my Cubanness

I'm a pure Cuban
And I defend my roots with my life
Cuban I am and wherever I am
I will sing to my beloved Cuba

I come from where the sun heats the land
The land where I was born, where I will live
That's why I bring you now my song
For you to know why they call me Cuba

To really know what it is to feel Cuban
You have to be born in Cuba
You have to have lived in Cuba

To really know what it is to feel Cuban
You have to read Martí, the prose of Guillén
Look for a guayabera with a guano hat

To really know what it is to feel Cuban
So you get it, brother,
You have to be born in Cuba
You have to have lived in Cuba

Un cubano de verdad da la vida por su tierra
Vive de frente y derecho, preparado pa'l combate
Y a su bandera se aferra

Vaya camina por arriba el mambo

Nadie baila como yo
Nadie goza como yo
Eso es seguro
A mí me dicen Cuba
Que fue
Cuba me llamo yo
Así me dicen a mí Boncó

Nadie baila como yo
Nadie goza como yo
A mí me dicen Cuba
Cuba me llamo yo

Mano pa'rriba Cuba
Nadie baila como yo
Nadie goza como yo
A mí me dicen Cuba
Cuba me llamo yo

Ese soy yo
Nadie baila como yo
Nadie goza como yo
A mí me dicen Cuba
Cuba me llamo yo

Aunque digan lo que digan
        Cubano
Cubano siempre seré
        Pa'lante
De San Antonio a Maisí
        Cubano
Siempre te defenderé
        Pa'lante

A true Cuban gives his life for his country
He lives straight and true, ready for combat
And clings to his flag

May the mambo soar on a higher path

Nobody dances like me
Nobody enjoys like me
That's for sure
They call me Cuba
What was it
Cuba is my name
That's what they call me, Boncó

Nobody dances like me
Nobody enjoys like me
They call me Cuba
Cuba is my name

Hands raised Cuba
Nobody dances like me
Nobody enjoys like me
They call me Cuba
Cuba is my name

That's me
Nobody dances like me
Nobody enjoys like me
They call me Cuba
Cuba is my name

Even if they say what they say
        Cuban
Cuban I will always be
        Forward
From San Antonio to Maisí
        Cuban
I will always defend you
        Forward

Aunque el mundo este como este
      Cubano
Y la calle va que arde
      Pa'lante
Cubano sigue pa'lante
      Cubano
Monteando
      Pa'lante
Que nunca fuimos cobardes

Cubano pa'lante
Cubano pa'lante
De primera

Cubano pa'lante
Cubano pa'lante

      Cubano
Déjate de gracia
      Pa'lante
Déjate de confianza
      Cubano pa'lante
      Cubano pa'lante

      Cubano
Arriba Cuba
      Pa'lante
Sabes de donde vengo
Vengo de La Habana
Y que, y que
Soy de Primera
Porque me pongo un sombrero de guano
Y llevo una guayabero que es lo que hay

Vengo de La Habana
Y que, y que
Soy de Primera
Porque te canto de corazón
De una manera sincera que es lo que fue

Even if the world is the way it is
      Cuban
And the street is on fire
      Forward
Cuban keeps on going forward
      Cuban
Riding
      Forward
That we were never cowards

Cuban Forward
Cuban Forward
First class

Cuban Forward
Cuban Forward

      Cuban
No need to be funny
      Forward
No need to be naïve
Cuban Forward
Cuban Forward

      Cuban
Long live Cuba
      Forward
You know where I come from
I come from Havana
So what, so what
I'm first class
Because I wear a guano hat
And I wear a guayabera that's what there is

I come from Havana
So what, so what
I'm first class
Because I sing to you from my heart
In a sincere way that's what it was

Vengo de La Habana
Y que, y que
Soy de Primera
Que lo sepan en la China, ¡caramba!
Soy de Primera
Y oye como dicen
Mira como dice el mundo
Soy de Primera
Soy de Primera

I come from Havana
So what, so what
I'm first class
Let them know it in China, caramba!
I am first class
And listen how they say
Look how the world says
I am first class
I am first class

Translated by Mahsa Hojjati

JUAN LUIS GUERRA

Ojalá que llueva café

Ojalá que llueva café en el campo
Que caiga un aguacero de yuca y té
Del cielo una jarina de queso blanco
Y al sur una montaña de berro y miel
Oh-oh, woho, oh,
Ojalá que llueva café

Ojalá que llueva café en el campo
Peinar un alto cerro de trigo y mapuey
Bajar por la colina de arroz graneado
Y continuar el arado con tu querer
Oh-oh, oh-oh-oh
Ojalá el otoño en vez de hojas secas
Vista mi cosecha es pitisalé
Sembrar una llanura de batata y fresas
Ojalá que llueva café

Para que en el conuco no se sufra tanto, ay hombre
Ojalá que llueva café en el campo
Pa' que en Villa Vásquez oigan este canto
Ojalá que llueva café en el campo
Ojalá que llueva, ojalá que llueva, ay hombre
Ojalá que llueva café en el campo
Ojalá que llueva café

Ojalá que llueva café en el campo
Sembrar un alto cerro e trigo y mapuey
Bajar por la colina de arroz graneado
Y continuar el arado con tu querer
Oh-oh, oh-oh-oh
Ojalá el otoño en vez de hojas secas
Vista mi cosecha es pitisalé
Sembrar una llanura de batata y fresas
Ojalá que llueva café

JUAN LUIS GUERRA

Let Us Hope It Rains Coffee

Let us hope it rains coffee in the fields
Let us hope it rains a downpour of yucca and tea
From the sky a stream of white cheese
And to the south a mountain of watercress and honey
Oh, oh, woho, oh
Let us hope it rains coffee

Let us hope it rains coffee in the fields
To plant a high hill of wheat and *mapuey*
To roll down the hill of grained rice
And continue the plowing with your love
Oh, oh, woho, oh
Let us hope autumn instead of dry leaves
Dress my harvest of *pitisalé*
Sow a plain of sweet potato and strawberries
Let us hope it rains coffee

So that in the Conuco we don't suffer so much, ay, man
Let us hope it rains coffee in the fields
So that in Villa Vasquez they hear this song
Let us hope it rains coffee in the fields
Let us hope it rains, let us hope it rains, ay, man
Let us hope it rains coffee in the fields
Let us hope it rains coffee

Let us hope it rains coffee in the fields
To plant a high hill of wheat and *mapuey*
To roll down the hill of grained rice
And continue the plowing with your love
Oh, oh, woho, oh
Let us hope autumn instead of dry leaves
Dress my harvest of *pitisalé*
Sow a plain of sweet potato and strawberries
Let us hope it rains coffee

Pa que en el conuco no se sufra tanto, oye
Ojalá que llueva café en el campo
Pa que en los montones oigan este canto
Ojalá que llueva café en el campo
Ojalá que llueva, ojalá que llueva, ay hombre
Ojalá que llueva café en el campo
Ojalá que llueva café

Pa' que todos los niños canten en el campo
Ojalá que llueva café en el campo
Pa' que en La Romana oigan este canto
Ojalá que llueva café en el campo
Ay, ojalá que llueva, ojalá que llueva, ay hombre
Ojalá que llueva café en el campo
Ojalá que llueva café

So that in the Conuco we don't suffer so much, oho
Let us hope it rains coffee in the fields
So that the crowds hear this song
Let us hope it rains coffee in the fields
Let us hope it rains, let us hope it rains, ay, man
Let us hope it rains coffee in the fields
Let us hope it rains coffee

So that all the children sing in the fields
Let us hope it rains coffee in the fields
So that in La Romana they hear this song
Let us hope it rains coffee in the fields
Ay, let us hope it rains, let us hope it rains, ay, man
Let us hope it rains coffee in the fields
Let us hope it rains coffee

Translated by Mahsa Hojjati

III.
LATINO ANCESTORS

Latin American

JOSÉ DÁVILA SEMPRIT

Los Estados Unidos

Un documento excelso que proclama
los derechos del hombre,
una bandera constelada,
historia que comienza roncando rebeldías
y finaliza oliendo a imperialismo,
un pueblo heterogéneo, los residuos
de nuestra vieja Europa hecha República;
aleación de pasiones, prejuicios,
engreimiento entronizado,
engaño hecho Dios en América,
carcajada del siglo,
sarcasmo de la época:
¡Los Estados Unidos!

En su puerto una estatua
mintiendo libertad, insulta al cosmos.
Adentro la injusticia: Sacco, Vanzetti,
Mooney, los Negros de Scottsboro,
el grito de las madres cuyos hijos
han muerto en las campañas imperiales,
el grito de los hijos cuyas madres
rodaron en el vicio;
El Ku Klux Klan gruñendo fanatismo,
el Indio perseguido en la montaña,
el Negro postergado y perseguido,
La Biblia alimentando la ignorancia;
dolor amortiguado,
con el responso de los puritanos:
¡Los Estados Unidos!

¡Dolor, Dolor que el chauvinismo acalla!
¡Odios, rencor que el religioso enciende!
Eterno olor a sangre en el ambiente,

JOSÉ DÁVILA SEMPRIT

The United States

A sublime document that proclaims
the rights of man,
a star-spangled banner,
history that begins
with roaring rebelliousness
and ends up smelling of imperialism,
a heterogeneous people, the remains
of our old Europe turned into a Republic;
an alloy of passions, prejudices,
and entrenched arrogance,
deceit has become a God in America,
the belly laugh of the century,
the sarcasm of this era:
The United States!

In its port there is a statue
lying about liberty, insulting the cosmos.
Within there is injustice: Sacco, Vanzetti,
Mooney, the blacks of Scottsboro,
the cry of the mothers whose sons
have died in imperialist campaigns,
the cry of the sons whose mothers
strayed into vice.
The Ku Klux Klan growling fanaticism,
the persecuted Indian in the mountains,
the Black man passed over and persecuted,
the Bible feeding ignorance;
mitigated pain,
with the Puritan prayer of the dead:
The United States!

Sorrow, grief that chauvinism quells!
Hatred, resentment fired by religion!

mediocridad con túnica encarnada,
nueva vida en el templo del dios Jano,
el altar de Minerva derruido,
ansias de poderío en cada alma,
la palabra de Dios en cada labio:
¡Los Estados Unidos!

Imperando Detroit, Chicago, Nueva York.
¡Grandes fieras ahumadas
que comen carne humana
con los colmillos erectos
con que pretenden desgarrar el cielo!
Detroit quiere ensuciar el firmamento
con la saliva de sus factorías;
Chicago entra en la Historia con el crimen
y se perpetúa en ella con el fuego
y los desmanes de sus pistoleros.
Nueva York se hace única y suprema
con su Tammany Hall, airosa cueva
de asaltadores muy del siglo veinte
y con su Wall Street tentacular,
estrecha y maloliente
guarida de Ginart.
Movimiento continuo,
grandes fábricas que succionan
la sangre del obrero;
políticos, banqueros y bandidos,
Tres Personas Distintas y un Ladrón Verdadero:
¡Los Estados Unidos!

Endless smell of blood in the atmosphere,
mediocrity in a tunic made flesh,
new life in the temple of the god Janus,
Minerva's altar in ruins,
a desire for power within each soul,
the word of God out on each lip:
The United States!

Reigning in Detroit, Chicago, New York
huge smoke-belching beasts
eating human flesh
baring their fangs
and pretending to rend the sky!
Detroit aspires to pollute the heavens
with the spit of its factories;
Chicago has a place in the History of crime
perpetuating itself with the shooting
and abuses of its gunmen.
New York is unique and supreme
with its Tammany Hall, elegant refuge
of very twentieth century robbers
and with its Wall Street tentacles,
the narrow and foul-smelling
hideout of Ginart.
Continuous movement,
huge factories that suck up
the blood of the worker;
politicians, bankers, and bandits,
Three Different People and one True Swindler:
The United States!

Translated by Edna Acosta-Belén and Susan Leberis-Hill

EUGENIO FLORIT

Los poetas solos de Manhattan

El poeta cubano Alcides Iznaga vino a Nueva York, de paseo, en agosto de 1959. A su regreso a Cienfuegos me envió un poema, "Estamos solos en Manhattan," al que contesté con estos versos:

Mi muy querido Alcides Iznaga:
es cierto que ni Langston Hughes ni yo estábamos en casa.
Porque Langston, que vive con sus negros,
también baja hasta el centro.
Y yo, cuando llamaste por teléfono,
o mejor dicho, pasaste por mi casa,
estaba lejos, en el campo,
yo que vivo con mis blancos.
Pero es que aquí, por aquí arriba,
lo mismo da que vivas
en la calle 127
o en el número 7
de la Avenida del Parque.
Aquí todos andamos solos y perdidos,
todos desconocidos
entre el ruido
de trenes subterráneos, y de bombas de incendio,
y de sirenas de ambulancias
que tratan de salvar a los suicidas
que se tiran al río desde un puente,
o a la calle desde su ventana,
o que abren las llaves del gas,
o se toman cien pastillas para dormir
—porque, como no se han encontrado todavía,
lo que desean es dormir y olvidarse de todo—,
olvidarse de que nadie se acuerda de ellos,
de que están solos, terriblemente solos entre la multitud.

Ya ves, a Langston Hughes me lo encontré a fines de
agosto en un cóctel del *Pen Club*,

EUGENIO FLORIT

The Lonely Poets of Manhattan

The Cuban poet Alcides Iznaga visited New York in August 1959. Upon his return to Cienfuegos, Cuba, he sent me a poem, "We're alone in Manhattan," to which I replied with these lines:

My dear friend Alcides Iznaga:
it's true that Langston Hughes wasn't home
and neither was I.
Langston, who lives with his people,
had gone downtown.
And when you called
or rather stopped by,
I was far away, in the countryside,
living with my people.

The truth is that here, up here,
it doesn't matter whether you live
on 127th St.
or Park Avenue.
Here we are all alone and lost
among the roar of the subway and the fire trucks,
among the sirens of ambulances
that rush to save those who kill themselves
by jumping into the river
or falling out a window
or turning on a gas stove
or swallowing a hundred sleeping pills
because, since they haven't found themselves,
all they want to do is forget
that no one remembers them,
that they are alone, terribly alone.

I ran into Langston at the end of August
at a Pen Club cocktail party.
He was solicitous and dressed in blue.

muy cortés y muy ceremonioso
y muy vestido de azul.
Y luego pasan los años, y lo más, si acaso,
nos cambiamos un libro: "Inscribed for my dear friend . . ."
"Recuerdo muy afectuoso . . . ," etc.
Y así nos vamos haciendo viejos
el poeta negro
y el poeta blanco,
y el mulato y el chino y todo bicho viviente.
Como se irán haciendo viejos
ustedes, los amigos de Cienfuegos;
los que aquel día inolvidable de febrero
(1955) me llevaron al Castillo de Jagua
donde me hizo temblar de emoción una vicaria
que me salió al encuentro entre las piedras.
Lo que pasa,
mi muy querido Alcides Iznaga,
es que aquí no hay vicarias,
ni Castillo de Jagua,
ni están conmigo mis poetas
ni mis palmas ("Las palmas, ay . . .")
ni las aguas azules de la bahía de Cienfuegos
ni las de la bahía de La Habana.
Aquí sólo las aguas perezosas y tristes
de los dos ríos que ciñen a Manhattan . . .

        Tú, mi querido Alcides,
viniste
en busca de nosotros a Nueva York, a esta ciudad en donde
        nadie a nadie conoce . . .
Donde
todos nosotros, cada uno,
no somos otra cosa que una gota de agua,
una mota de polvo, de esas
que salen tristes por las chimeneas.
Tristes, es un decir. Que yo, a Dios gracias,
aún conservo serenas las palabras
con las que doy los buenos días al sol
que sale—cuando sale—enfrente de mi ventana.

And then years go by, and perhaps we'll send
each other a book, "Inscribed for my dear friend,
With best wishes . . ."
And so we grow old,
the black poet
and the white poet
and the mulatto and the Chinese poet
and every living thing.

You must be growing old too,
you and my friends from Cienfuegos
who took me, that day in 1955, to the Jagua castle
where a *vicaria* flower
growing between two stones
made me tremble.
What happens here,
my dear friend Alcides Iznaga,
is that we have no *vicarias*,
or Jagua castles, or poets like you,
or palm trees,
or the blue waters of Cienfuegos bay.
The only waters here barely flow
in the lazy rivers that surround Manhattan . . .

You, my dear Alcides,
came looking for us in New York,
the city where nobody knows anybody,
where each of us is a drop of water,
a mote of dust
like those that waft sadly from chimneys.
I say "sadly" but it's only a manner of speaking.
I'm thankful that I still have the words
with which to greet the sun that rises
—when it rises—in front of my window.
And when it doesn't rise, I greet the wind,
the rain, the fog, the clouds;
I greet the world I live in
with the words I write in.
And I thank God for the day and the night

Y si no sale, da lo mismo, al viento, al aire, a niebla y nube;
saludar a este mundo en que vivimos
con estas las palabras que escribimos.
Y dar gracias a Dios por el día y la noche
y por tener una palabra nuestra, aquí, en donde nadie nos
    conoce.

23 de octubre de 1959

and above all for letting me keep my words,
here, in this city where nobody knows me.

October 23, 1959
Translated by Gustavo Pérez Firmat

CLEMENTE SOTO VÉLEZ

de *Caballo de palo*

#3

Lo conocí
viviendo
como una h encarcelada en la miel de sus abejas,
pero eran dulce amargo las rejas de la miel,
y por haberse enamorado
de la libertad
perdidamente,
y por no renunciar
a su amor ni ella a su amante,
la tierra para él
es huracán de estrellas perseguidas,
porque la libertad no puede ser
amante
sino de quien ama
a la tierra con su sol y su cielo.

#29

poeta
tu
eres
humanización de la luz
por el materializado amor
del deseo
de
ser
asaltador de la inmortalidad
de
ser
transduración efímera

CLEMENTE SOLO VÉLEZ

from *The Wooden Horse*

#3

I came to know him,
living
like an h incarcerated in the honey of his bees,
but the bars of honey were bittersweet,
and because
he lost himself
in love with liberation,
and because he did not abandon
his love nor she her lover,
the earth for him
is a hurricane of persecuted stars,
since liberation cannot
love anyone
except whoever loves
the earth, with its sun and sky.

Translated by Martín Espada and Camilo Pérez-Bustillo

#29

poet
you
are
light transformed into humanity
through the tangible love
of desire
to
be
the attacker of immortality
to
be

como fuente perenne
que arguye
en contra de su forma
o
sangre
que
sigue
cantando
después
de
conjelarse
para
circular
radiantemente por la insurrección
de sus arterias
poeta
la inmortalidad
es
ensambladura de aledaños
bisoños
no habituados
a la acción de delinquir
como la comodidad del pensar pervertido
humanización de la luz
eres
tú
poeta
o pecho alado del entender egrejio
desde donde todos
los hombres
o
todas las mujeres
dan
sustancia a su esencia

transcendent enduring ephemeral
like a perpetual fountain
that bends arguing
against its own form
or
blood
that
keeps
singing
after
it
congeals
to
circulate
radiating through the insurrection
of its arteries
poet
immortality
is
the architecture of borders
wild
unaccustomed
to subversive action
like the comfort of corrupted thought
poet
you
are
light into humanity
or breast with wings of profound understanding
from where all
men
or
all women
give
substance to their existence

Translated by Martín Espada and Camilo Pérez-Bustillo

JULIA DE BURGOS

A *Julia de Burgos*

Ya las gentes murmuran que yo soy tu enemiga
porque dicen que en verso doy al mundo tu yo.

Mienten, Julia de Burgos. Mienten, Julia de Burgos.
La que se alza en mis versos no es tu voz: es mi voz
porque tú eres ropaje y la esencia soy yo;
y el más profundo abismo se tiende entre las dos.

Tú eres fria muñeca de mentira social,
y yo, viril destello de la humana verdad.

Tú, miel de cortesanas hipocresías; yo no;
que en todos mis poemas desnudo el corazón.

Tú eres como tu mundo, egoísta; yo no;
que en todo me lo juego a ser lo que soy yo.

Tú eres sólo la grave señora señorona;
yo no; yo soy la vida, la fuerza, la mujer.

Tú eres de tu marido, de tu amo; yo no;
yo de nadie, o de todos, porque a todos, a todos,
en mi limpio sentir y en mi pensar me doy.

Tú te rizas el pelo y te pintas; yo no;
a mi me riza el viento; a mi me pinta el sol.

Tú eres dama casera, resignada, sumisa,
atada a los prejuicios de los hombres; yo no;
que yo soy Rocinante corriendo desbocado
olfateando horizontes de justicia de Dios.

Tú en ti misma no mandas; a ti todos te mandan;
en ti mandan tu esposo, tus padres, tus parientes,

JULIA DE BURGOS

To Julia de Burgos

Already the people murmur that I am your enemy
because they say that in verse I give the world your me.

They lie, Julia de Burgos. They lie, Julia de Burgos.
Who rises in my verses is not your voice. It is my voice
because you are the dressing and the essence is me;
and the most profound abyss is spread between us.

You are the cold doll of social lies,
and me, the virile starburst of the human truth.

You, honey of courtesan hypocrisies; not me;
in all my poems I undress my heart.

You are like your world, selfish; not me
who gambles everything betting on what I am

You are only the ponderous lady very lady;
not me; I am life, strength, woman.

You belong to your husband, your master; not me;
I belong to nobody, or all, because to all, to all
I give myself in my clean feeling and in my thought.

You curl your hair and paint yourself; not me;
the wind curls my hair, the sun paints me.

You are a housewife, resigned, submissive,
tied to the prejudices of men; not me;
unbridled, I am a runaway Rocinante
snorting horizons of God's justice.

You in yourself have no say; everyone governs you;
your husband, your parents, your family,

el cura, la modista, el teatro, el casino,
el auto, las alhajas, el banquete, el champán,
el cielo y el infierno, y el qué dirán social.

En mí no, que en mí manda mi solo corazón,
mi solo pensamiento; quien manda en mí soy yo,
Tú, flor de aristocracia; y yo, la flor del pueblo.
Tú en ti lo tienes todo y a todos se lo debes,
mientras que yo, mi nada a nadie se la debo.

Tú, clavada al estático dividendo ancestral,
y yo, un uno en la cifra del divisor social,
somos el duelo a muerte que se acerca fatal.

Cuando las multitudes corran alborotadas
dejando atrás cenizas de injusticias quemadas,
y cuando con la tea de las siete virtudes,
tras los siete pecados, corran las multitudes,
contra ti, y contra todo lo injusto y lo inhumano,
yo iré en medio de ellas con la tea en la mano.

the priest, the dressmaker, the theatre, the dance hall,
the auto, the fine furnishings, the feast, champagne,
heaven and hell, and the social, "what will they say."

Not in me, in me only my heart governs,
only my thought; who governs in me is me.
You, flower of aristocracy; and me, flower of the people.
You in you have everything and you owe it to everyone,
while me, my nothing I owe to nobody.

You nailed to the static ancestral dividend,
and me, a one in the numerical social divider,
we are the duel to death who fatally approaches.

When the multitudes run rioting
leaving behind ashes of burned injustices,
and with the torch of the seven virtues,
the multitudes run after the seven sins,
against you and against everything unjust and inhuman,
I will be in their midst with the torch in my hand.

Translated by Jack Agüeros

Puerto Rico está en tí

Puerto Rico depende de tu vida y tu nombre,
colgando en ti van millones de esperanzas
para resucitar en lo que nos fue robado
y hacer valer de nuevo el honor de la Patria.

La voz de Independencia que contigo seguimos
los que vivos de honor limosna rechazan
de un Puerto Rico "estado asociado y ridículo"
retumbará en los aires con la Patria estrellada,
estrellada de amor, de sonrisa y cariños
con una sola estrella feliz, no acompañada.

Llévate este mensaje puertorriqueño y mío
de tus hermanos libres que en "New York" te acompañan
y sigue tu camino con la luz de una estrella,
Gilberto Concepción de la Gracia y de batalla.

Puerto Rico Is in You

Puerto Rico depends on your life and your name,
resting on you are millions of hopes
to be resurrected in what was stolen from us
and to renew the worth of the Nation's honor.

The voice of independence that we follow with you
—those who alive with honor refuse the alms
of a Puerto Rico "associated and ridiculous state"—
will thunder in the winds with the starred Nation,
starred with love, smiles and affection
with a single happy star, unaccompanied.

Take this message, Puerto Rican and mine:
your free brothers in New York are with you
and follow your lead by the light of one star
Gilberto Concepción de Gracia, of grace and of combat.

Translated by Jack Agüeros

CLARIBEL ALEGRÍA

Ars poetica

Yo,
poeta de oficio,
condenada tantas veces
a ser cuervo
jamás me cambiaría
por la Venus de Milo:
mientras reina en el Louvre
y se muere de tedio
y junta polvo
yo descubro el sol
todos los días
y entre valles
volcanes
y despojos de guerra
avizoro la tierra prometida.

Carta a un desterrado

Mi querido Odiseo:
ya no es posible más
esposo mío
que el tiempo pase y vuele
y no te cuente yo
de mi vida en Itaca.
Hace ya muchos años
que te fuiste
tu ausencia nos pesó
a tu hijo
y a mí.
Empezaron a cercarme
pretendientes

CLARIBEL ALEGRÍA

Ars Poetica

I,
poet by trade,
condemned so many times
to be a crow,
would never change places
with the Venus de Milo:
while she reigns in the Louvre
and dies of boredom
and collects dust
I discover the sun
each morning
and amid valleys
volcanos
and debris of war
I catch sight of the promised land.

Translated by D. J. Flakoll

Letter to an Exile

My dear Odysseus:
It is no longer possible
my husband
that time goes flying by
without my telling you
of my life in Ithaca.
Many years have gone by
since you left
your absence weighs
on your son
and me.
My suitors began

eran tantos
tan tenaces sus requiebros
que apiadándose un dios
de mi congoja
me aconsejó tejer
una tela sutil
interminable
que te sirviera a ti
como sudario.
Si llegaba a concluirla
tendría yo sin mora
que elegir un esposo.
Me cautivó la idea
al levantarse el sol
me ponía a tejer
y destejía por la noche.
Así pasé tres años
pero ahora, Odiseo,
mi corazón suspira por un joven
tan bello como tú cuando eras mozo
tan hábil con el arco
y con la lanza.
Nuestra casa está en ruinas
y necesito un hombre
que la sepa regir.
Preferible, Odiseo,
que no vuelvas
de mi amor hacia ti
no queda ni un rescoldo
Telémaco está bien
ni siquiera pregunta por su padre
es mejor para ti
que te demos por muerto.
Sé por los forasteros
de Calipso
y de
Circe.
Aprovecha, Odiseo,
si eliges a Calipso,
recobrarás la juventud

to fence me in
they were so many
and so tenacious in their flattery
that a god, taking pity
on my anguish,
advised me to weave
a subtle
interminable cloth
that would serve
as your shroud.
If I finished it
I would have to choose
a husband without delay.
The idea captivated me
at sunrise I set about weaving
and I unwove during the night.
That went on for three years
but now Odysseus,
my heart yearns for a youth
as handsome as you when young
as expert with bow and lance
our house is in ruins
and I need a man
who knows how to rule it.
Telemachus is but a babe
and your father decrepit.
It is preferable, Odysseus,
that you don't return
men are weaker
they can't tolerate affronts.
Of my love for you
not even embers remain.
Telemachus is well
never asks for his father
it would be better
if we gave you up for dead.
I know from strangers
about Calypso and Circe.
Seize your chance, Odysseus,
if you choose Calypso

si es Circe la elegida
serás entre sus cerdos
el supremo.
Espero que esta carta
no te ofenda
no invoques a los dioses
será en vano
recuerda a Menelao
con Helena
por esa guerra loca
han perdido la vida
nuestros mejores hombres
y estás tú donde estás.
No vuelvas, Odiseo,
te suplico.
Tu discreta Penélope

you'll regain lost youth
if Circe is the chosen one
among her swine
you'll reign supreme.
I hope this letter
does not offend you
don't invoke the gods
it will be in vain
remember Menelaus
and his Helen
For that mad war
our best men
have lost their lives
and you are where you are.
Don't return, Odysseus,
I beg you.
Your discreet Penelope.

Translated by D. J. Flakoll

ERNESTO CARDENAL

Managua 6:30 pm

En la tarde son dulces los neones
y las luces de mercurio, pálidas y bellas . . .
Y la estrella roja de una torre de radio
en el cielo crepuscular de Managua
es tan bonita como Venus
y un anuncio ESSO es como la luna

las lucecitas rojas de los automóviles son místicas

(El alma es como una muchacha besuqueada detrás de un
    auto)
      TACA   BUNGE   KLM   SINGER
      MENNEN   HTM   GÓMEZ   NORGE
      RPM   SAF   ÓPTICA   SELECTA
proclaman la gloria de Dios!
(Bésame bajo los anuncios luminosos oh Dios)
      KODAK   TROPICAL   RADIO   F & C REYES
en muchos colores
deletrean tu Nombre.
                          "Transmiten
la noticia . . ."

Otro significado
no lo conozco
Las crueldades de esas luces no las defiendo
Y si he de dar un testimonio sobre mi época
es éste: Fue bárbara y primitiva
pero poética.

ERNESTO CARDENAL

Managua 6:30 p.m.

In the evening the neon lights are soft
and the mercury streetlamps, pale and beautiful . . .
And the red star on a radio tower
in the twilight sky of Managua
looks as pretty as Venus
and an ESSO sign looks like the moon

The red taillights of the cars are mystical

(The soul is like a girl kissed hard behind a car)
      TACA   BUNGE   KLM   SINGER
      MENNEN   HTM   GÓMEZ   NORGE
      RPM   SAF   ÓPTICA   SELECTA
all proclaim the glory of God!
(Kiss me under the glowing signs oh God)
      KODAK   TROPICAL   RADIO   F & C REYES
they spell your Name
in many colors.
        "They broadcast
the news . . ."

I don't know
what else they mean
I don't defend the cruelty behind these lights
And if I have to give a testimony about my times
it's this: They were primitive and barbaric
but poetic

Translated by Jonathan Cohen

151

Entre fachadas

Recorremos las calles de un barrio de Nueva York,
pequeñas tiendas, restaurantes, Dry-Cleaning,
cases de apartamentos, de tres, cuatro pisos,
de ladrillos rojos, cemento, ladrillos grises,
     después pasamos a una aldea de los Alpes,
  calles empedradas de un pueblito mexicano,
después un río con un molino medieval,
    calle polvorienta de un pueblo del Oeste,
  con sus cantinas, una ventana con el vidrio quebrado,
en una colina un castillo del siglo XI,
y otra vez casas de apartamentos, un banco, tienda de licores
  de cualquier ciudad de Estados Unidos,
pero si uno toca cualquier cosa, suena a hueco,
   todo es yeso,
  son sólo las paredes de afuera, no hay nada detrás.
Un policía en media calle, con su insignia
    y libreta para poner infracciones,
podía ser un policía de verdad o un actor famoso.
Y me dice el productor (Ed Lewis) que me enseña todo:
"ni el director, ni el productor, ni nadie
    manda en una película,
  sino el banco que la financia."
Y al salir y ver los bancos, restaurantes, Dry-Cleaning,
me pareció que todo lo que tocara sonaría a hueco,
  Hollywood, Los Ángeles entero, todo
    era sólo paredes
      sin nada detrás.

Among Facades

We're going through the streets of a neighborhood in New
    York,
small shops, a restaurant, *Dry Cleaning,*
apartment houses, three-, four-stories high,
made of red brick, concrete, grey brick,
          then we pass through a hamlet in the Alps,
        cobblestone streets in a Mexican village,
then a river with a medieval mill,
        a dusty street in a town in the West,
    with its saloons, a window with broken glass,
on a hill an 11th-century castle,
and once again apartment houses, a bank, liquor stores
        in any city in the United States,
but if you knock on anything, it sounds hollow,
          everything is plasterwork,
      they're only the outside walls, there's nothing
        in back.
A policeman in the middle of the street, with his badge
          and book for giving out tickets,
might be a real policeman or a famous actor.
And the producer (Ed Lewis) who is showing me everything
    tells me:
"no director, no producer, nobody
             runs the show in a movie,
         just the bank putting up the money."
And on leaving and seeing the bank, restaurants,
    Dry Cleaning,
I thought whatever I'd knock on would sound hollow,
Hollywood, all of Los Angeles, everything
        was merely walls
           with nothing in back.

Translated by Jonathan Cohen

LOURDES CASAL

Para Ana Veldford

Nunca el verano en Provincetown
y aún en esta tarde tan límpida
(tan poco usual para Nueva York)
es desde la ventana del autobús que contemplo
la serenidad de la hierba en el parque a lo largo de Riverside
y el desenfado de todos los veraneantes que descansan sobre
    ajadas frazadas
de los que juguetean con las bicicletas por los trillos.
Permanezco tan extranjera detrás del cristal protector
como en aquel invierno
    —fin de semana inesperado—
cuando enfrenté por primera vez la nieve de Vermont
y sin embargo, Nueva York es mi casa.
Soy ferozmente leal a esta adquirida patria chica.
Por Nueva York soy extranjera ya en cualquier otra parte,
fiero orgullo de los perfumes que nos asaltan por cualquier
    calle del West
Side.
Marihuana y olor a cerveza
y el tufo de orines de perro
y la salvaje vitalidad de Santana
descendiendo sobre nosotros
desde una bocina que truena improbablemente balanceada
    sobre una escalera
de incendios,
la gloria ruidosa de Nueva York en verano,
el Parque Central y nosotros,
los pobres,
que hemos heredado el lado del lado norte,
y Harlem rema en la laxitud de esta tarde morosa.
El autobús se desliza perezosamente
hacia abajo, por la Quinta Avenida;
y frente a mí el joven barbudo
que carga una pila enorme de libros de la Biblioteca Pública.

LOURDES CASAL

For Ana Veldford

Never a summertime in Provincetown
and even on this limpid afternoon
(so out of the ordinary for New York)
it is from the window of a bus that I contemplate
the serenity of the grass up and down Riverside Park
and the easy freedom of vacationers resting on rumpled
    blankets,
fooling around on bicycles along the paths.
I remain as foreign behind this protective glass
as I was that winter
    —that unexpected weekend—
when I first confronted Vermont's snow.
And still New York is my home.
I am ferociously loyal to this acquired *patria chica*.
Because of New York I am a foreigner anywhere else,
fierce pride in the scents that assault us along any
    West
Side street,
marijuana and the smell of beer
and the odor of dog urine
and the savage vitality of Santana
descending upon us
from a speaker that thunders, improbably balanced on a fire
    escape,
the raucous glory of New York in summer,
Central Park and us,
the poor,
who have inherited the lake of the north side,
and Harlem sails through the slackness of this sluggish
    afternoon.
The bus slips lazily,
down, along Fifth Avenue;
and facing me, the young bearded man
carrying a heap of books from the Public Library,

Y parece como si se pudiera tocar el verano en la frente
    sudorosa del
ciclista
que viaja agarrado de mi ventanilla.
Pero Nueva York no fue la ciudad de mi infancia,
no fue aquí que adquirí las primeras certidumbres,
no está aquí el rincón de mi primera caída,
ni el silbido lacerante que marcaba las noches.
Por eso siempre permaneceré al margen,
una extraña entre las piedras,
aun bajo el sol amable de este día de verano,
como ya para siempre permaneceré extranjera,
aun cuando regrese a la ciudad de mi infancia,
cargo esta marginalidad inmune a todos los retornos,
demasiado habanera para ser newyorkina,
demasiado newyorkina para ser,
    —aun volver a ser—
cualquier otra cosa.

and it seems as if you could touch summer in the sweaty
    brow of the
cyclist
who rides holding onto my window,
But New York wasn't the city of my childhood,
it was not here that I acquired my first convictions,
not here the spot where I took my first fall,
nor the piercing whistle that marked the night.
This is why I will always remain on the margins,
a stranger among the stones,
even beneath the friendly sun of this summer's day,
just as I will remain forever a foreigner,
even when I return to the city of my childhood
I carry this marginality, immune to all turning back,
too *habanera* to be *newyorkina,*
too *newyorkina* to be
    —even to become again—
anything else.

Translated by David Frye

CECILIA VICUÑA

Luxumei

Necesito decir
que mi atavío natural
son las flores
aunque me vestiré
de un modo increíble
con plumas
dientes de loco
y manojos de cabellera
de Taiwan y Luxumei.
Cada vez que estornudo
se llena el cielo de chispas
hago acrobacias
y piruetas endemoniadas
cada noche
me sale una espalda adyacente.
Soy de cuatro patas
preferentemente,
las ramas
me saldrán por la piel;
estoy obligada a ser
un ángel con la pelvis
en llamas.

CECILIA VICUÑA

Luxumei

To be clear
my natural attire
are flowers
though I dress
in a strange manner
with feathers
the teeth of crazy men
and handfuls of hair
from Taiwan and Luxumei.
Every time I sneeze
sparks fill the sky
I perform acrobatics
and diabolical pirouettes
every night
I grow an adjacent back.
I would prefer
to be on all fours,
branches
sprouting from my skin;
I am compelled to be
an angel with my pelvis
in flames.

Translated by Rosa Alcalá

Eclipse en Nueva York

Hay entonces esa luz fría,
pensé,
        como en el Cuzco.

Arbol sembrado
de medialunas

Uñas de luz

Sombra prismal

Altísimos pastos
confraternos

y en el orificio
de la mano

Luz eclipsar.

Eclipse in New York

There is then
that light
cold summit
I thought,
   as in Cuzco.

Tree sown
with crescent
moons

Nails of light

Shadow prisms

Tall sisterly grasses
waving

And in the hand's
orifice

Light eclipsed.

Translated by Rosa Alcalá

EXCILIA SALDAÑA

Danzón inconcluso para Noche e Isla

Dos patrias tengo yo: Cuba y la noche.
José Martí

Para Fina y Cintio, cubanos

La Noche
goza de la isla dormida. Inocente. Frágil
como un pájaro fatigado del que sólo se sabe que vive
por el ala.
Ala insólita flotando sobre las aguas: alas de agua.
Ala que es isla.
Y es ala.

Pero un golpe de viento. Una ola. Una hoja caída
de otros mundos
la
sorprende.

Entonces,

se despereza:
el cuello estira,   levanta la cabeza coronada,
agita el plumaje poderoso,
se eleva.
Rompe la jaula de la noche.
Se eleva.
Rompe el espacio de la noche.
Se eleva.
Rompe el vacío de la noche.
Se eleva.

Le nace en el pecho un canto de despaciosa anchura,
una serenidad de azul. Una lámpara suave y diamantina.
Y busca en su vuelo nupcial otro trino,

162

EXCILIA SALDAÑA

Unfinished Danzón for Night and Island

I have two homelands: Cuba and the night.
José Martí

For Fina and Cintio, Cubans.

Night
enjoys the sleeping Island. Innocent. Fragile
like a weary bird known to be living only
                              because of its wing.
Strange wing floating on the waters: wings of water.
                    Wing that is island.
                    And is wing.

But a burst of wind. A wave. A leaf fallen
                    from other worlds
                         surprises
                         it.

Then,

            it drowses:
its neck stretches,   raises its crowned head,
                    shakes its powerful plumage,
                         and rises.
Breaks the cage of night.
                    And rises.
Breaks the space of night.
                    And rises.
Breaks the void of night.
                    And rises.

A song of slow expanse is born in its breast,
a serenity of blue. A lamp soft and like a diamond.

el que antes fue noche y luego, jaula y después, espacio y
más tarde, vacío.

Y ahora es ave
en celo
y
esperando.

Isla y Noche, una.
Libres
de la inmensidad y la fijeza. Consagradas
en el instante escapado en que el ave se transmuta
en flor y en rocío.
Lo eterno sobre lo infinito. Libándose.

Después
el éxtasis.
Después
el secreteo íntimo de los dones.
Después
el vértigo del ahora que ya es memoria.
(Ah, el corazón oculto donde el pico de la Isla escarba el
latido misterioso de la Noche.)
Pero ya no es lo que fue, sino el anillo prodigando su imagen
en el tiempo. No la línea, sino el círculo despojado de su pulpa.
El rumor oval del fuego en el árbol, en el madero y en la ceniza.
El juego errabundo de las mutaciones.

La Noche flota dormida sobre las aguas
—fatigada cual pájaro inocente del que mucho se ignora
que no muere
y por el ala.
La Isla gozosa la mira.

Una constelación nonata se encorala en los arrecifes.
Un rechinar de carretas retumba de estrella en estrella.

Soy la Noche   Soy la Isla.

And in its nuptial flight it looks for another trill,
a prior trill that was first night and then, cage and then, place
and later, void.

And now it is bird
in heat
and
in expectation.

Island and Night, one.
Free
from immensity and fixedness. Consecrated
in the fleeing instant when the bird transforms itself
into flower and dew.
Eternity above infinity. Sipping itself.
Then
ecstasy.
Then
the intimate gossiping of gifts,
Then
the vertigo of the now that is already memory.
(Oh, the hidden heart where the Island's beak scratches the
mysterious beat of the Night.)
*It is no longer what it was, but rather a ring lavishing its image
in time. It is not the line, but rather the circle despoiled of its
flesh. The oval murmur of fire in the tree, in the log and in the
ashes. The wandering game of mutations.*

Night floats sleeping on the waters
—weary like an innocent bird about which much is ignored
that does not die
because of its wing.
The joyful Island watches her.

An unborn constellation encorals itself in the reefs.
A grating of wagons resounds from star to star.

I am the Night.   I am the island.

Dos patrias en mí que las contengo.

90 en mayo

Two homelands contained in me.

May 1990

Translated by Flora M. González Mandri
and Rosamond Rosenmeier

DAISY ZAMORA

Carta a una hermana que vive en un país lejano

> *. . . Y fui enviado al sur de la villa de Wei*
> *tapizada de bosquecillos de laureles y tú al*
> *norte de Roku-hoku,*
> *hasta tener en común, solamente, pensamientos y*
> *recuerdos.*
> —*"Carta del Desterrado," Li-Tai-Po*

Todavía recuerdo nuestros primeros juegos:
Las muñecas de papel y los desfiles.
Y a Teresa, la muñeca que nos caía mal:
Teresa-pone-la-mesa.

La vida no retrocede y deseo conocerte.
Re-conocerte.
Es decir, volver a conocerte.
Habrá, sin embargo, cosas tuyas que conserves.
Me interesa saber de tus lugares,
tus amigos, tan extraños a los míos
que hablan en otra lengua y buscan otros caminos.

Danbury, Hamden y Middletown,
Hartford y Meriden. Todos lugares
tan familiares a ti y a tus recuerdos.
A través de la sangre he vivido dos vidas,
múltiples vidas.

Los cocoteros ya están cosechando en el jardín
y el verano tiene rojas las gencianas del cerco.
Son hermosos y azules estos días,
transparentes y frescos.
Mis lugares amados son también los tuyos.
Sobre miles de kilómetros mis palabras te tocan
como el pájaro que ahora veo posarse sobre un coco.

DAISY ZAMORA

Letter to My Sister Who Lives in a Foreign Land

> *. . . And I was sent south of the village of Wei*
> *—covered with little laurel arbors—*
> *and you to the north of Roku-hoku,*
> *until all we had in common were thoughts*
> *and memories.*
>
> —*"Letter from the Exiled One," Li-Tai-Po*

I still remember our first games:
parades and paper dolls,
and Teresa, the doll we couldn't stand:
Teresa-are-you-able-to-come-and-set-the-table.

Life doesn't move backwards and I want to know you.
Re-know you.
That is, know you all over again.
Of course there will be things I'll recognize.
I'm interested in your special places,
your friends, so different from mine
who speak another language and follow other paths.

Danbury, Hamden and Middletown,
Hartford and Meriden. All those places
so familiar to you and to your memory.
In our shared blood I have lived two lives,
many lives.

We're gathering coconuts in the garden now
and summer has turned the Gentians red on the fence.
These days are beautiful and blue,
clear and cool.
My beloved places are also yours.
My words touch you thousands of miles away
like the bird I see now, perched upon a coconut.

Prolongado ha sido el tiempo y la distancia.
Pero en uno de estos días luminosos
(los rosales están repletos de capullos)
o de aquellos más lejanos del invierno
(en todas las carreteras hay laureles florecidos,
marañones y mangos y corteces amarillos)
con el último sol o en el primer aguaje
recogeremos los frutos
de la espera.

50 versos de amor y una confesión no realizada a Ernesto Cardenal

De haber conocido a Ernesto como aparece
en una foto amarillenta que Julio me mostró:
flaco, barbón, camisa a cuadros y pantalón de lino,
las manos en los bolsillos y un aire general de desamparo;
me hubiera metido por él en la Rebelión de Abril.
Juntos, habríamos ido a espiar a Somoza
en la fiesta de la embajada yanki.

¿Quién sería su novia en esos días?
La Meche o la Adelita o talvez Claudia.
Ileana o Myriam. Muchachas eternamente frescas
que sonríen desde viejas fotografías
traspapeladas en quién sabe qué gavetas.

Myriam, sale de la iglesia con su vestido amarillo
entallándole el cuerpo moreno y grácil.
Ileana pasa distante
más lejana que la galaxia de Andrómeda
la Adelita palidece al doblar la esquina
y encontrarse de pronto con él;
Claudia prefiere las fiestas y las carreras de caballos

Time and distance have grown.
But one of these luminous days
(the rose bushes are covered with buds)
or one of those more distant winter days
(all the roads are lined with flowering Laurels,
cashews and mangoes and yellow Goldenrod)
with the last sun or the first downpour
we will gather the fruits
of our hope.

Translated by Margaret Randall and Elinor Randall

50 *Love Poems and an Unfulfilled Confession to Ernesto Cardenal*

If I had known Ernesto as he appears
in the yellowed photograph Julio showed me:
lean, bearded, with his plaid shirt and linen pants,
hands in his pockets and that vague air of helplessness,
I'd have joined the April Rebellion for him.
Together we might have gone to spy on Somoza
at the Yankee Ambassador's party.

Who would have been his sweetheart in those days?
La Meche or Adelita or maybe Claudia,
Ileana or Myriam. Eternally sweet young girls
who smile from old photographs
mislaid in who knows which old chests of drawers.

Myriam leaves the church in her yellow dress,
a sheath for her dark and graceful body.
Ileana passes at a great distance
further away than Andromeda's galaxy.
Adelita pales as she turns the corner
and comes upon him suddenly.
Claudia prefers parties and horse races

a un epigrama de Ernesto.
Meche es la más misteriosa.

Conocí a Ernesto en el año 72 oficiando
en el altar de la ermita de Solentiname.
Ni me habló; apenas me concedió el perfil.
Es la fecha y no se acuerda siquiera
de haberme visto entonces.
Después de la Insurrección del 78 al fin reparó en mí.
Se apareció en la clandestina Radio Sandino
interesado en conocerme al saber que yo era poeta y
    combatiente.
Ni en mis sueños más fantásticos imaginé
que el encuentro sucedería así:
Allí venía tranquilo como que si nada
caminando entre el monte recién llovido.
Entró al caramanchel y preguntó por mi.

¿Para qué preguntó? Ese encuentro fue decisivo.
Desde el principio me entendí con él casi tan bien
como en otros tiempos con mi abuelo.
Allí es que comienza una larga historia:
Cuatro años ayudándole a inventar el mundo;
organizando el Ministerio de Cultura
con el fervor y la fe de un niño
en la madrugada de su Primera Comunión.
Esos años fueron casi felices (como diría Mejía-Sánchez).

Aunque a estas alturas
        lo conmueva todavía algún recuerdo
usted jamás se conformó con ninguna:
ni con Claudia, ni con todas las otras que no menciono
Como San Juan de la Cruz o Santa Teresita (no quería una
    muñeca
sino todas las muñecas del mundo)
sólo estuvo conforme cuando poseyó todo, todito el Amor.

Ahora posee a Dios a través del pueblo: ¡Esposo de Dios!
Por eso cuando le digo que de haber sido yo su novia
en ese entonces sus versos para mí
        no habrían sido en vano,

to one of Ernesto's epigrams.
Meche remains the most mysterious.

I met Ernesto in '72
when he said mass at the little Solentiname church.
He didn't even speak to me, barely turned his face.
That's when we met
and he doesn't even remember seeing me there.
It was after the Insurrection of '78
that he finally noticed me.
He showed up at clandestine Radio Sandino
because he'd heard I was a poet
and a combatant.
In my wildest dreams I never imagined
our meeting would happen as it did.
He arrived as if it were nothing,
walking through the recent mountain rain.
He entered the shack and asked for me.

Why did he ask? That meeting was decisive.
From the first I got along with him
as well as with my grandfather in other times.
A long history begins right there:
four years helping him invent the world,
organizing the Ministry of Culture
with the fervor and faith of a child
on the morning of his first communion.
Those years were almost happy (as Mejía-Sánchez would say).
Although he is still moved by a memory or two,
none of them were what he wanted:
neither Claudia, nor all the others
I leave unnamed.
Like Saint John of the Cross
or Saint Theresita of the Child Jesus
(she didn't want a doll, but all the world's dolls)
he was only satisfied with all the Love there is.

Now he possesses God through the people: he is
married to God!
That's why I tell him, had I

él me contesta: "que lástima, no nos ayudó el tiempo," pero
  yo ni caso le hago.

been his sweetheart way back then
his poems to me would not have been in vain.
He says: "What a pity, time wasn't on our side."
But I'm not listening.

Translated by Margaret Randall and Elinor Randall

Latino

AMÉRICO PAREDES

The Mexico-Texan

The Mexico-Texan he's one fonny man
Who leeves in the region that's north of the Gran',
Of Mexican father he born in these part,
And sometimes he rues it dip down in he's heart.

For the Mexico-Texan he no gotta lan',
He stomped on the neck on both sides of the Gran',
The dam gringo lingo he no cannot spik,
It twisters the tong and it make you fill sick.
A cit'zen of Texas they say that he ees,
But then, why they call him the Mexican Grease?
Soft talk and hard action, he can't understan',
The Mexico-Texan he no gotta lan'.

If he cross the reever, eet ees just as bad,
On high poleeshed Spanish he break up his had,
American customs those people no like,
They hate that Miguel they should call him El Mike,
And Mexican-born, why they jeer and they hoot,
"Go back to the gringo! Go lick at hees boot!"
In Texas he's Johnny, in Mexico Juan,
But the Mexico-Texan he no gotta lan'.

Elactions come round and the gringos are loud,
They pat on he's back and they make him so proud,
They give him mezcal and the barbacue meat,
They tell him, "Amigo, we can't be defeat."
But efter elaction he no gotta fran',
The Mexico-Texan he no gotta lan'.

Except for a few with their cunning and craft
He count just as much as a nought to the laft,
And they say everywhere, "He's a burden and drag,

He no gotta country, he no gotta flag."
He no gotta voice, all he got is the han'
To work like the burro; he no gotta lan'.

And only one way can his sorrows all drown,
He'll get drank as hell when next payday come roun',
For he has one advantage of all other man,
Though the Mexico-Texan he no gotta lan',
He can get him so drank that he think he will fly
Both September the Sixteen and Fourth of July.

RODOLFO "CORKY" GONZALES

I Am Joaquín: An Epic Poem, 1967

I am Joaquín
Lost in a world of confusion,
Caught up in a whirl of a
    gringo society,
Confused by the rules,
Scorned by attitudes,
Suppressed by manipulations,
And destroyed by modern society.
My fathers
 have lost the economic battle
and won
 the struggle of cultural survival.
And now!
 I must choose
Between the paradox of
Victory of the spirit,
despite physical hunger
     Or
 to exist in the grasp
of American social neurosis,
sterilization of the soul
 and a full stomach.
Yes,
I have come a long way to nowhere,
Unwillingly dragged by that
 monstrous, technical
 industrial giant called
     Progress
and Anglo success . . .
 I look at myself.
 I watch my brothers.
 I shed tears of sorrow.
  I sow seeds of hate.
I withdraw to the safety within the

circle of life . . .
　　　　MY OWN PEOPLE
I am Cuauhtémoc,
Proud and Noble
　Leader of men,
King of an empire,
civilized beyond the dreams
of the Gachupín Cortez.
Who is also the blood,
　the image of myself.
I am the Maya Prince.
I am Nezahualcoyotl,
Great leader of the Chichimecas.
I am the sword and flame of Cortez
　　　　　　　　　the despot.
　　　　　　　　And
I am the Eagle and Serpent of
　　　　　the Aztec civilization.
I owned the land as far as the eye
could see under the crown of Spain,
and I toiled on my earth
and gave my Indian sweat and blood
　for the Spanish master,
Who ruled with tyranny over man and
beast and all that he could trample
　　　　　　　　But . . .
　THE GROUND WAS MINE . . .
I was both tyrant and slave.
As Christian church took its place
in God's good name,
to take and use my Virgin Strength and
　　　　　　　　　Trusting faith,
The priests
　both good and bad
　　　　　　　took
But
　gave a lasting truth that
　　　Spaniard,
　　　　Indio,
　　　　　Mestizo

Were all God's children
And
 from these words grew men
     who prayed and fought
                              for
 their own worth as human beings,
      for
       that
         GOLDEN MOMENT
          of
         FREEDOM.
I was part in blood and spirit
     of that
   courageous village priest
                              Hidalgo
in the year eighteen hundred and ten
who rang the bell of independence
and gave out that lasting cry:
 "El Grito de Dolores, Que mueran
 los Guachupines y que viva
 la Virgen de Guadalupe . . ."
I sentenced him
          who was me.
I excommunicated him my blood.
I drove him from the pulpit to lead
 a bloody revolution for him and me . . .
      I killed him.
His head,
 which is mine and all of those
 who have come this way,
I placed on that fortress wall
 to wait for independence.
Morelos!
      Matamoros!
          Guerrero!
All Compañeros in the act,
STOOD AGAINST THAT WALL OF
                   INFAMY
 to feel the hot gouge of lead
 which my hand made.

I died with them . . .
 I lived with them
  I lived to see our country free.
Free
 from Spanish rule in
  eighteen-hundred-twenty-one.
    Mexico was free ? ?
The crown was gone
        but
all his parasites remained
        and ruled
        and taught
 with gun and flame and mystic power.
I worked,
I sweated,
I bled,
I prayed
    and
waited silently for life to again
                        commence.
I fought and died
        for
    Don Benito Juárez
Guardian of the Constitution.
I was him
    on dusty roads
        on barren land
 as he protected his archives
  as Moses did his sacraments.
He held his Mexico
        in his hand
            on
        the most desolate
        and remote ground
        which was his country,
And this Giant
        Little Zapotec
gave
 not one palm's breath
of his country to

 Kings or Monarchs or Presidents
of foreign powers.
I am Joaquín.
I rode with Pancho Villa,
 crude and warm.
A tornado at full strength,
nourished and inspired
 by the passion and the fire
 of all his earthy people.
I am Emiliano Zapata.
   "This Land
      This Earth
        is
         OURS"
The Villages
  The Mountains
   The Streams
      belong to the Zapatistas.
      Our Life
Or yours
is the only trade for soft brown earth
and maize.
All of which is our reward,
 A creed that formed a constitution
   for all who dare live free!
"this land is ours . . .
       Father, I give it back to you.
            Mexico must be free . . ."
I ride with Revolutionists
                against myself.
I am Rural
    Coarse and brutal,
I am the mountain Indian,
    superior over all.
The thundering hoofbeats are my horses.
The chattering of machine guns
 is death to all of me:
  Yaqui
   Tarahumara
    Chamula

Zapotec
Mestizo
Español
I have been the Bloody Revolution,
The Victor,
The Vanquished,
I have killed
 and been killed.
     I am despots Díaz
     and Huerta
and the apostle of democracy
     Francisco Madero
I am
the black shawled
faithful women
who die with me
or live
depending on the time and place.
I am
 faithful,
  humble,
     Juan Diego
     the Virgin de Guadalupe
Tonantzin, Aztec Goddess too.
I rode the mountains of San Joaquín.
I rode as far East and North
   as the Rocky Mountains
       and
all men feared the guns of
        Joaquín Murrieta.
I killed those men who dared
 to steal my mine,
  who raped and Killed
                my love
                my Wife
Then
I Killed to stay alive.
I was Elfego Baca,
 living my nine lives fully.
I was the Espinosa brothers

of the Valle de San Luis
All
were added to the number of heads
that
 in the name of civilization
were placed on the wall of independence.
Heads of brave men
who died for cause and principle.
Good or Bad.
     Hidalgo! Zapata!
      Murrieta! Espinosa!
are but a few.
They
dared to face
The force of tyranny
               of men
               who rule
          By farce and hypocrisy
I stand here looking back,
and now I see
          the present
and still
  I am the campesino
  I am the fat political coyote
                    I,
of the same name,
                    Joaquín.
In a country that has wiped out
all my history,
               stifled all my pride.
In a country that has placed a
different weight of indignity upon
               my
               age
               old
               burdened back.
          Inferiority
is the new load . . .
 The Indian has endured and still
emerged the winner,

The Mestizo must yet overcome,
  And the Gauchupín we'll just ignore.
I look at myself
 and see part of me
who rejects my father and my mother
and dissolves into the melting pot
 to disappear in shame.
 I sometimes
 sell my brother out
and reclaim him
for my own, when society gives me
 token leadership
      in society's own name.
I am Joaquín,
who bleeds in many ways.
The altars of Moctezuma
           I stained a bloody red.
 My back of Indian slavery
      was striped crimson
 from the whips of masters
 who would lose their blood so pure
 when Revolution made them pay
Standing against the walls of
 Retribution.
       Blood . . .
    Has flowed from
      me
on every battlefield
      between
Campesino, Hacendado
 Slave and Master
    and
 Revolution.
I jumped from the tower of Chapultepec
 into the sea of fame;
My country's flag
  my burial shroud;
With Los Niños,
    whose pride and courage
could not surrender

with indignity
    their country's flag
To strangers . . . in their land.
Now
 I bleed in some smelly cell
 from club,
 or gun,
 or tyranny,
I bleed as the vicious gloves of hunger
 cut my face and eyes,
as I fight my way from stinking Barrios
 to the glamour of the Ring
  and lights of fame
   or mutilated sorrow.
My blood runs pure on the ice caked
hills of the Alaskan Isles,
on the corpse strewn beach of Normandy,
the foreign land of Korea
                and now
                Vietnam.
Here I stand
        before the court of Justice
                Guilty
for all the glory of my Raza
        to be sentenced to despair.
Here I stand
        Poor in money
 Arrogant with pride
        Bold with Machismo
        Rich in courage
                and
    Wealthy in spirit and faith.
My knees are caked with mud.
My hands calloused from the hoe.
I have made the Anglo rich
        yet
 Equality is but a word,
  the Treaty of Hidalgo has been broken
 and is but another treacherous promise.
My land is lost

and stolen,
My culture has been raped,
        I lengthen
    the line at the welfare door
and fill the jails with crime.
    These then
are the rewards
        this society has
For sons of Chiefs
        and Kings
        and bloody Revolutionists.
Who
gave a foreign people
    all their skills and ingenuity
to pave the way with Brains and Blood
for
those hordes of Gold starved
Strangers
Who
changed our language
and plagiarized our deeds
                as feats of valor
                of their own.
They frowned upon our way of life
 and took what they could use.
        Our Art
        Our Literature
        Our Music, they ignored
so they left the real things of value
and grabbed at their own destruction
            by their Greed and Avarice
They overlooked that cleansing fountain of
            nature and brotherhood
Which is Joaquín.
 The art of our great señores
        Diego Rivera
        Siqueiros
        Orozco is but
another act of revolution for
the Salvation of mankind.

Mariachi music, the
heart and soul
of the people of the earth,
the life of child,
and the happiness of love.
The Corridos tell the tales
of life and death,
        of tradition,
Legends old and new,
of Joy
  of passion and sorrow
of the people . . . who I am.
I am in the eyes of woman,
        sheltered beneath
her shawl of black,
        deep and sorrowful
        eyes,
That bear the pain of sons long buried
        or dying,
        Dead
on the battlefield or on the barbed wire
        of social strife.
Her rosary she prays and fingers
endlessly
  like the family
working down a row of beets
    to turn around
    and work
    and work
  There is no end.
Her eyes a mirror of all the warmth
    and all the love for me,
And I am her
And she is me.
  We face life together in sorrow,
  anger, joy, faith and wishful
  thoughts.
I shed tears of anguish
as I see my children disappear
behind a shroud of mediocrity

never to look back to remember me.
I am Joaquín.
     I must fight
     And win this struggle
     for my sons, and they
     must know from me
     Who I am.
Part of the blood that runs deep in me
Could not be vanquished by the Moors.
I defeated them after five hundred years,
and I endured.
     The part of blood that is mine
     has labored endlessly five-hundred
     years under the heel of lustful
          Europeans
          I am still here!
I have endured in the rugged mountains
 of our country.
I have survived the toils and slavery
 of the fields.
          I have existed
in the barrios of the city,
in the suburbs of bigotry,
in the mines of social snobbery,
in the prisons of dejection,
in the muck of exploitation
and
in the fierce heat of racial hatred.
And now the trumpet sounds,
The music of the people stirs the
       Revolution,
Like a sleeping giant it slowly
rears its head
to the sound of
     Tramping feet
    Clamoring voices
   Mariachi strains
  Fiery tequila explosions
  The smell of chile verde and
 Soft brown eyes of expectation for a
              better life.

And in all the fertile farm lands,
                    the barren plains,
the mountain villages,
smoke smeared cities
            We start to MOVE.
 La Raza!
Mejicano!
 Español!
  Latino!
  Hispano!
   Chicano!
or whatever I call myself,
            I look the same
            I feel the same
            I Cry
                    and
            Sing the same
I am the masses of my people and
I refuse to be absorbed.
        I am Joaquín
The odds are great
but my spirit is strong
                My faith unbreakable
                My blood is pure
I am Aztec Prince and Christian Christ
            I SHALL ENDURE!
            I WILL ENDURE!

LALO DELGADO

Stupid America

stupid america, see that chicano
with a big knife
in his steady hand
he doesn't want to knife you
he wants to sit down on a bench
and carve christ figures
but you won't let him.
stupid america, hear that chicano
shouting curses on the street
he is a poet
without paper and pencil
and since he cannot write
he will explode.
stupid america, remember that chicanito
flunking math and english
he is the picasso
of your western states
but he will die
with one thousand masterpieces
hanging only from his mind.

De Corpus a San Antonio

it is rather strange
that in the english language
no word rhymes with orange.
in spanish no word rhymes with naranja?
it's just as well. i did not mean
to rhyme it with anything anyway.
if i did
       i would probably
invent a word myself,
coin one myself.
"florange" as an example.
florange would be my word
for the flower of the orange,
for the orange blossom.
what good
       is my poetic license
if i never get to use it?
because english is my second language
the endings of english words
keep throwing me off . . . way off.
i rhyme love with job
and orange would rhyme with change or ranch
or even range.
they all sound the same to my chicano ear.
despite the "b" i got in my phonetics class
when i was making speech my minor
back in my college days
english sounds are foreign.
what fuss, huh?
       fiddling around
with the intricacies of communications,
poetic and otherwise,
which, after all, don't suffice worth a shit
to make soul to soul communication . . . complete?

JOSÉ MONTOYA

El Louie

Hoy enterraron al Louie.

And San Pedro o san pinche
Are in for it. And those
Times of the forties
And the early fifties
Lost un vato de atolle.

Kind of slim and drawn,
There toward the end,
Ageing fast from too much
Booze y la vida dura. But
Class to the end.

En Sanjo you'd see him
Sporting a dark topcoat
Playing in his fantasy
The role of Bogart, Cagney
Or Raft.

Era de Fowler el vato,
Carnal del Candi y el
Ponchi-Los Rodriguez-
The Westside knew 'em,
And Selma, even Gilroy.
'48 Fleetline, two-tone-
Buenas garras and always
Rucas-como la Mary y
La Helen . . . siempre con
Liras bien afinadas
Cantando La Palma, la
Que andaba en el florero.

Louie hit on the idea in
Those days for tailor-made
Drapes, unique idea—porque
Fowler no era nada como
Los, 'ol E.P.T. Fresno's
Westside was as close as
We ever got to the big time.

But we had Louie, and the
Palomar, el boogie, los
Mambos y cuatro suspiros
Del alma y nunca faltaba
That familiar, gut-shrinking,
Love-splitting, ass hole-up-
Tight, bad news . . .

     Trucha, esos! Va 'ver
     Pedo!
     Abusau, ese!
     Get Louie!

No llores, Carmen, we can
Handle 'em.
     Ese, 'on tal Jimmy?
     Horale, Louie!
     Where's Primo?
     Va 'ver catos!
En el parking lot away from the jura
     Horale!
     Trais filero?
     Simon!
     Nel!
     Chale, ese!
     Oooooh, este vato!

An Louie would come through—
Melodramatic music, like in the
Mono—tan tan tran!—Cruz
Diablo, El Charro Negro! Bogart

Smile (his smile as deadly as
His vaisas) He dug roles, man,
And names—like "Blackie," "Little
Louie . . ."

Ese Louie . . .
Chale, man, call me "Diamonds!"

Y en Korea fue soldado de
Levita con huevos and all the
Paradoxes del soldado razo—
Heroism and the stockade!
And on leave, jump boots
Shainadas and ribbons, cocky
From the war, strutting to
Early mass on Sunday morning.

Wow, is that 'ol Louie?

Mire, comadre, ahí va el hijo
De Lola!

Afterward he and fat Richard
Would hock their Bronze Stars
For pisto en el Jardin Canales
Y en El Trocadero.

At barber college he came
Out with honors. Despues
Enpeñaba su velardo de la
Peluca pa' jugar pocar serrada
And lo ball en Sanjo y Alviso.

And "Legs Louie Diamond" hit
On some lean times . . .

Hoy enteraron a Louie.

Y en Fowler at Nesei's
Pool parlor los baby chukes

Se acuerdan de Louie, el carnal
Del Candi y el Ponchi—la vez
Que lo fileriaron en el Casa
Dome y cuando se catio con
La Chiva.

Hoy enteraron al Louie.

His death was an insult
Porque no murio en accion-
No lo mataron los vatos,
Ni los gooks en Korea.
He died alone in a
Rented room—perhaps like in a
Bogart movie.

The end was a cruel hoax.
But his life had been
Remarkable!

Vato de atolle, el Louie Rodriguez.

RHINA P. ESPAILLAT

On Hearing My Name Pronounced Correctly,
Unexpectedly, for Once

The voice over the wire trills my R,
snares me with soft diminutives, and waits
for me, in our shared language, to allow
my words to trace, like fingers down a scar,
stories we've known since childhood, places, dates
in brackets on worn stones. He tells me how
our old ones slip away, forgetting, now,
faces and names. My cousin hesitates;
I take this name again and say goodnight.
Odd how the gringo tongue that shifts, translates
you into something it can say, but far
from what you were, that never gets you right,
rolling you round too long, too smooth, too light,
loves you at last to who it says you are.

On the Impossibility of Translation

Of course impossible, transmuting touch
and color into sound, sound into sign,
sign into sense again and back: too much
struggling after the names for flavor, line,
knowing they can't be found, no, not in one
language: in two? across the grain of speech?
Unthinkable! Easier to fold the sun
into its syllable. Yet lovers, each
mute in one skin, can learn to speak in tongues,
speak themselves whole, if only once; you've heard,
fitful above the fields, the summer sung
in high, cascading turns of fluent Bird,
and seen, in shallow pools in every town,
how rain translates the sky and writes it down.

RAÚL R. SALINAS

Unity Vision

(*1st Chant*)

Brief / respiteful
        precious (in the movement) cruise
                down desolate
1st & Spokane streets
        EVOKES
smoke-signals of past
        Seattle Springtime struggles /
                Sad Summer
                        of Native tragedies /
                            & Dallas Chicanito deaths.
From empty (wasting) warehouse rows
        a fleeting, darting, silent
                (momentary)
                    SONG FOR SANTOS . . .
                . . . BLUES FOR WOUNDED KNEE.
The haunting humming of an Autumn wind
        decries historical lies /
                atrocious repetitions of blood.
The Trail
        (almost to no avail)
                of Broken Treaties,
resulting in more broken promises
                and rights
                and minds
                and souls
                and laws . . .
those flaws from the claws
        of a predator society
                seeking satiation
inside indigenous heart of earth.
Birth-rights bombarded /
        discarded life of

           innocent lamb-child
           SANTOS.
Warrior Drums
     (that speak of hope)
are sounding/
     pounding out
an angry call-to-arms.
Staccatoing
     super-sophisticated
weaponry of war
     implodes/ EXPLODES!
and Pedro Bissonette
     lies dead.
Peace-loving/ war-hating Bissonette
     BISON
           (human replica)
slaughtered
     in the Indian People's fight.
While
     Armored Personnel Carriers
         (murdering mammoths)
draw the line of demarcation
     the nation of the Sioux
         begins (again) to rise.
Wise South Dakota
     medicine man
smokes the pipe of peace
     & fans the fires of
         self-determination
Lakota people seeking liberation
     demanding to be free.

                               August '75

JACK AGÜEROS

Sonnet for the #6

The subways are full of smoke and acrid mists today. In this
Heat the haze is thick glass that turns everything upside down.

Thor is banging on the third rail, his sparks shoot down the
Newspaper birds flying in flocks in the dark. Vulcan's forge
Bellowing, coughing gas, ozone and foul fumes travelling
    faster
Than Mercury or Huracan or the express. Marijuana flavors
The smoke, and incense burned by Afro-American Muslims.
    What

Thoughtless God gave man drugs I wonder, when I see the
    old sign
With the Ordinance which Prohibits Cigarette Smoking, but
    the new
Generation smokes grass and only reads color video, and
    disobedient
Prometheus is to blame for fire anyway. Down here, like at
    Styx,
I am angry at the Gods, but at Hunts Point a Latin lady
    gets on

And I recognize Quetzalcoatl, beak and plumes, and the
    train elevates like a magic carpet over the Bronx to
    Pelham or Parnassus.

Sonnet: The History of Puerto Rico

Puerto Rico was created when the pumpkin on top of
The turtle burst and its teeming waters poured out
With all mankind and beastkind riding on the waves
Until the water drained leaving a tropical paradise.

Puerto Rico was stumbled on by lost vampires bearing
Crucifix in one hand, arquebus in the other, sucking
The veins of land and men, tossing the pulp into the
Compost heap which they used as the foundation for
Their fortifications and other vainglorious temples.

Puerto Rico was arrested just as it broke out of the
Spanish jail and, renamed a trusty, it was put in an
American cell. When the prisoner hollered, "Yankee, Go
Home," Puerto Rico was referred to the United Nations.

Puerto Rico, to get to paradise now, you have to ride blood.

LUIS OMAR SALINAS

Ode to the Mexican Experience

The nervous poet sings again
in his childhood voice, happy,
a lifetime of Mexican girls
in his belly, voice
of the midnoon bells
and excited mariachis
in those avenues persuaded out
of despair.

He talks of his Aztec mind,
the little triumphs and schizoid trips,
the many failures
and his defeated chums
dogs and shadows,
the popularity of swans in his neighborhood
and the toothaches of rabbits
in the maize fields.

I know you in bars
in merchant shops,
in the roving gladiators,
in the boats of Mazatlán that never anchor,
in the smile of her eyes,
in the tattered clothes of school children,
in the never-ending human burials;
those lives lost in the stars
and those lost in the stars
and those lost in the wreckage
of fingernails,
the absurd sophistry of loneliness
in markets, in hardware stores,
in brothels.

The happy poet talks in his sleep,
the eyes of his loved one
pressing against him—
her lips have the softness
of olives crushed by rain.

I think of the quiet nights
in Monterrey
and of my sister who woke me up
in the mornings.

The soft aggressive spiders
came out to play in the sunlight,
and suffering violins in pawn shops,
hell and heaven and murdered angels
and all the incense of the living
in poisoned rivers
wandering aimlessly amid dead fish,
dead dreams, dead songs.
I was an altar boy,
a shoeshine boy,
an interventionist in family affairs,
a ruthless connoisseur of vegetables,
a football player.
To all the living things I sing
the most terrible and magnificent
ode to my ancestry.

That My Name Is Omar

I suffer that my name is Omar Salinas.
That I want to touch someone in the
incredible loneliness of nights.
That I frighten away those I should
be close to. I suffer when I go crazy
and can't love anyone. Whether it
is Tuesday or Sunday, I suffer.
I suffer a lust for fame and
immortality. That I tried to
commit suicide. That I have
compassion for the unfortunate.
I suffer the death of matrimony.
The death of my mother.
The eyes of God.
I want to understand this and that
and come up with zero.
What should I do
but walk and look at the lovely sky?

FRANK LIMA

Oklahoma America

The fathers of America
have ruined the mountains
    The mothers of America
have dried the river beds
    The children of America
are dying at play
    Our forefathers watch our
neonates mouse the words of freedom
    Worms vagrant fallopian worms

Are birds freedom?
Are children sheep?

This is the year of the bullet
Of white professional homework
Of Nagasaki fertilizer
Of cheap fuel oil
Of tender SS movies
This is oncotic Americana
This is why fish will fly to heaven

We are the widow of our dreams
We are shrinking in their skin
We are attached to their wisdom

Look at the thermos colored sky
Fame flying on TV
They wash their hands in our womb
Where the dead know the stars
Are sleeping children
Like the procession of the equinox
Condensing our fate

We are the Furies of entropy
We have killed
A hundred sixty million
Human trees this century

Who will wear their clothes?
Death is as round as an apple
Holding a child ever so gently

They no longer see the kangaroo
They cannot touch
The innocent mirror
With their wet hands
The tears are drowning
In their sand pails
Like lyrical lips
The mothers will never be
The sun on their faces

O my beloved country
Where is the antelope of love?
Why does the earth
Turn away from the sun?
Why are the children covered
With concrete
Rain
And neglected
Specks of freedom?

4.25.95

Alligator of Happiness

I ride the subway with all these bare-breasted faces.
To my eternal discredit,
They remind me of my five-minute life,
Pounding against my heart.

My fantasy is I am a loitering hunter
Of nudes who ride the subways,
With eyes that crack the light of men who stare.
The nudes are beautiful white ants in the darkness,
Blowing coins and leaves at me.

My technique is familiar and simple conversation,
Rhyming bad words that have little meaning.
They accumulate like cities in Iceland.
The words are flames and I am their lycanthropy.
The riders pretend I do not exist.

But I eventuate like the law of someone's
Humanity I will never cheat.
These are hungry old habits,
The voyeurs of childhood.
We allow to run our lives as adults.

Still, I wait for them,
Like the alligator of happiness,
With a bouquet of senile flowers.
They finally appear like birds from the Nile.
I have kept this appointment all my life.

4.15.99

IV.
LET ME TELL YOU WHAT
A POEM BRINGS

MARJORIE AGOSÍN

Lejos

Mi país es un astillero
anclado dentro de mí
curvándose por entre
la rodillas y la piel
aún húmeda de sol.
Mi país es una frazada de estrellas como viruelas
una rapsodia de voces nulas
que aparecen para penar a la luna
por el pellejo raptado
a plena luz.

Mi país es un frasco azul
oculto y radiante como el mar
o la sombra de tus ojos
que nunca serán azules.

Mi país es un hombre
a quién amé
y cuando me besaba
mis piernas eran una lluvia
como un bosque o una
frontera de agua santa.

Mi país es color de humo
y planchas de carbón
que adormecidas empañan
las casas de adobe.

Mi país
es mi casa con las llaves
ocultas esperándome,
en la playa.

MARJORIE AGOSÍN

Far Away

My country is a slender pier
anchored inside me
curving between
my knees and skin
still damp from the sun.
My country is a tatter of stars like pockmarks
a rhapsody of useless voices
that come out to mourn the moon
through the ravished pelt
of plain daylight.

My country is a blue vial
hidden and radiant as the sea
or the shadow of your eyes
that never will be blue.

My country is a man
whom I loved
and when he kissed me
my legs turned to rain
to a grove
to a boundary of holy water.

My country is the color of smoke
and coal-heated irons
that drowsily envelop
the houses of adobe.

My country
is my house with the keys
hidden waiting for me,
on the beach.

Translated by Cola Franzen

La Extranjera

Buscarás otro
paisaje
para hablar con
tus muertos.
Ninguna palabra
responderá a las voces
de tus amores.
Inventarás otra mirada
y te desplazarás cabizbaja como herida
tras las ciudades prestadas.

Sabrás que
ya no habrá para ti ningún regreso
y nombrarás a los que hicieron
de tu memoria
un lenguaje de huerfanías.
Pensarás en otros alientos
porque eres lejana y sola
porque tu lengua
lleva la sombra de los extraños.

The Foreigner

You will search for another
landscape in which
to speak with
your dead.
No words
will respond to the voices of your love.
You will make up another gaze
and you will walk with your head bowed as if wounded
in borrowed cities.

You will know that there will be no return for you
and you will name those who made
of your memory
a language of orphanhood.
You will think of other breaths
because yours are distant and alone
because your language
carries the shadows of strangers.

Translated by Monica Bruno Galmozzi

FRANCISCO X. ALARCÓN

Un Beso Is Not a Kiss

un beso
es una puerta
que se abre
un secreto
compartido
un misterio
con alas

un beso
no admite
testigos
un beso can't
be captured
traded
or sated

un beso
is not just
a kiss—
un beso is
more dangerous
sometimes
even fatal

In Xóchitl In Cuicatl

cada árbol	every tree
un hermano	a brother
cada monte	every hill
una pirámide	a pyramid
un oratorio	a holy spot
cada valle	every valley
un poema	a poem
in xóchitl	*in xóchitl*
in cuicatl	*in cuicatl*
flor y canto	flower and song
cada nube	every cloud
una plegaria	a prayer
cada gota	every drop
de lluvia	of rain
un milagro	a miracle
cada cuerpo	every body
una orilla	a seashore
al mar	a memory
un olvido	at once lost
encontrado	and found
todos juntos:	we all together—
luciérnagas	fireflies
de la noche	in the night
soñando	dreaming up
el cosmos	the cosmos

de *De amor oscuro*

me gusta caminar junto a tu lado,
ir pisando en el malecón tu sombra,
dejar que tus pasos marquen mis pasos,
seguirte como barco remolcado

ajustando mis pies en las huellas
que como puma dejas en la playa,
quiero ser la toalla con que te secas,
donde te extiendes a tomar el sol

qué suerte la del cinturón que abraza
tu cintura, la del cristo que cuelga
de una cadena entre tus pectorales

qué alegría llegar como peine diario
a oler la mañana en tus cabellos
y en vez de peinarte, despeinarte

from *Of Dark Love*

I like to walk beside you, stepping
on your shadow along the way,
letting your steps mark my steps,
follow you like a boat being towed—

fitting my feet in the footprints
you leave like a puma on the sand,
I want to be the towel that dries you,
the one you spread to get some sun

how lucky! the belt that gets to hug
your waist, the crucifix that hangs
from a chain on your chest!

what a joy! to arrive every day as a comb
and smell the morning in your hair
but rather than comb, uncomb you!

Translated by Francisco Aragón

MIGUEL ALGARÍN

Nuyorican Angel Papo

(The Bi-Sexual Super Macho)

I.

The Fourth of July fireworks
went unseen by me.
If you could not see them
then I would not see
the New York skyline
ablaze in colored fire.
The red, white and blue
would climb to the moon
without my Fourth of July
Coney Island, Bushwick, Brooklyn
churchgoing,
newfound friend,
we parted in the name of fear,
the not falling into the black hole
of speedy passions
and underdeveloped love.
I drove you home,
shook your hand as we opened the trunk
to get your pack,
but you know, really,
I almost pushed you back
into the car, the hearth,
the fireplace of warmth,
the wheels that would have,
could have crossed the Williamsburg Bridge,
into Loisaida,
driven us into a nest of dreams
and corruption,
and purity and cleanliness
entwined in next to perfect lust,

yet, no, instead,
I didn't see the fireworks.
Instead, I sat thinking about
how nice it was to have left you
without our rushed desires fueling
the blazing Fourth of July skyline of New York.

II.

I tried
to separate
where we should start to touch.
I tried postponing, first with "Straight out of Brooklyn,"
then food,
but you were on an impulse
to burn fire,
to scorch passions,
I should've left you in Bushwick,
without numbers exchanged,
I could have lied about my name,
yet could'ves and would'ves
live in conditional tenements,
where on the third floor
we committed unconditional love,
knee to knee
nude from the waist down,
lust-fueled hands full
of belly buttons, buttocks and meat.

HIV

I.

REVELATION

*To tell in strength. "The telling," when to tell, leads to a
discovery between the teller and the listener. Acquiring
knowledge; the teller holds his/her information as a tool for
health, movement towards truth.*

II.
SALVATION
To converse as an attempt to recuperate, a holding on not to die.

III.
SPEECH
To acquire "language" for talking about a plague in the self.

IV.
SHARING SECRETS
Who to tell? Is there someone? The search for what to tell.

V.
MATURE MASCULINITY
Welcome the responsibility to do the work of building verbs, adjectives and nouns for mortality and its subsequent eternal breaking of concrete.

I. REVELATION

Revel at ion,
rebel at I on a course
to regret erections,
to whip the cream in my scrotum
till it hardens into unsweetened,
unsafe revved elations
of milk turned sour
by the human body,
of propagation of destruction.
The epiphany: I am unsafe,
you who want me
know that I who want you,
harbor the bitter balm of defeat.

II. SALVATION

If I were to show you
how to continue holding on,
I would not kiss you,
I would not mix my fluids with yours,

for your salvation
cannot bear the live weight
of your sharing liquids with me.

III. *LANGUAGE*

To tell,
to talk,
to tongue into sounds
how I would cleanse you with urine,
how my tasting tongue would wash your body,
how my saliva and sperm would bloat you,
to touch you in our lovemaking
and not tell you
would amount to murder.
To talk about how to language this
so that you would still languish
in my unsafe arms and die,
seems beyond me,
I would almost rather lie
but my tongue muscle moves involuntarily
to tell of the danger in me.

IV. *OF HEALTH*

To use my full and willing
body to reveal and speak
the strength that I impart
without fear,
without killing,
without taking away what I would give,
to use my man's tongue
to share,
to give,
to lend,
to exact nothing,
to receive all things,
to expand my macho
and let the whole world
into the safety of my mature masculinity.

V. *QUARANTINE*

Sometimes I fear touching your plump ear lobes,
I might contaminate you.
Sometimes I refuse odors that would
drive my hands to spread your thick thighs.
Sometimes closing my ears to your voice
wrenches my stomach and I vomit to calm wanting.
Can it be that I am the bearer of plagues?
Am I poison to desire?
Do I have to deny yearning for firm full flesh
so that I'll not kill what I love?
No juices can flow 'tween you and me.
Quicksand will suck me in.

ALURISTA

sliver

       sliver
   moondrum
      silence
  cross the desert
       dusk of
     sweeping hawks
        solitude remains
  the cave within
     above the rock
sierras
   rattle snakes
and dance for
   the full
  blossom of
 dawn
   lunas

with

with out u darling, ling, sling
          shot to thee heart
locked up in blues, ling sling
     shot centered
     on the toes of a
     twirling turn
     yeah! yeah!
     for u, oh girl
     do it, duet one more
     time cain't git
       e, nough
       ee, nough
       i, nough

o'
u
babe
 gulp culp
 writ hulk
  pulk
  e, ē
  i kē
    corazón
heart i
still dia, dia
 logue, logo
with u, xé

JULIA ALVAREZ

All-American Girl

I wanted stockings, makeup, store-bought clothes;
I wanted to look like an American girl;
to speak my English so you couldn't tell
I'd come from somewhere else. I locked myself
in the bathroom, trying to match my face
with words in my new language: *grimace, leer,
disgust, disdain*—feelings I had yet to feel
in English. (And would *tristeza* even feel
the same as *sadness* with its Saxon sound?
Would *pity* look as soulful as *piedad*?)

I didn't know if I could ever show
genuine feeling in a borrowed tongue.
If *cortesía* would be misunderstood
as brown-nosing or cries of *alegría*
translate as terror. So, mirror in hand,
I practiced foreign faces, Anglo grins,
repressing a native Latin fluency
for the cooler mask of English ironies.
I wanted the world and words to match again
as when I had lived solely in Spanish.

But my face wouldn't obey—like a tide
it was pulled back by my lunatic heart
to its old habits of showing feelings.
Long after I'd lost my heavy accent,
my face showed I had come from somewhere else.
I couldn't keep the southern continent
out of the northern *vista* of my eyes,
or cut my *cara* off to spite my face.
I couldn't look like anybody else
but who I was: an all-American girl.

Museo del Hombre

Santo Domingo, Dominican Republic

In the museo, the Taino queen,
Anacaona, has my sister's eyes.
And Duarte in the portrait where he's barred
from his beloved patria wears the scowl
my father wore in exile. Sánchez's nose
is replicated on my tía's face;
her sugar-cane skin matches Salomé's.
Mella is pouting with my mother's mouth.
How heartening and unsettling to see
history wearing the face of family.

Not only heroes, poets, Indian queens,
but tyrants, swindlers, conquistadors
could be close kin, along with their victims.
The master whipping the black servant girl
could be my cousin cursing his chauffeur
or Tía losing patience with her maid—
the same arched brows, the fury in the eyes.
These ghostly resemblances remind me
that our Dominican familia's not exempt
from all the highs and lows of history.

In museums, I always felt left out
of history with its pale northern face.
The pink-skinned Washington at Valley Forge
or white-wigged Jefferson were not my kin.
Even their blue-eyed wives, their blond children,
their little dogs seemed alien to me.
But now my people hang upon these walls
and history is pressing in on me,
as if to say, *¡Tu tiempo ya llegó!*
Become the one you have been waiting for.

GLORIA ANZALDÚA

To live in the Borderlands means you

are neither *hispana india negra española*
ni gabacha, eres mestiza, mulata, half-breed
caught in the crossfire between camps
while carrying all five races on your back
not knowing which side to turn to, run from;

To live in the Borderlands means knowing
    that the *india* in you, betrayed for 500 years,
    is no longer speaking to you,
    that *mexicanas* call you *rajetas,*
    that denying the Anglo inside you
    is as bad as having denied the Indian or Black;

Cuando vives en la frontera
    people walk through you, the wind steals your voice,
    you're a *burra, buey,* scapegoat,
    forerunner of a new race,
    half and half—both woman and man, neither—
    a new gender;

To live in the Borderlands means to
    put *chile* in the borscht,
    eat whole wheat *tortillas,*
    speak Tex-Mex with a Brooklyn accent;
    be stopped by *la migra* at the border checkpoints;

Living in the Borderlands means you fight hard to
    resist the gold elixir beckoning from the bottle,
    the pull of the gun barrel,
    the rope crushing the hollow of your throat;

In the Borderlands
    you are the battleground
    where enemies are kin to each other;

you are at home, a stranger,
the border disputes have been settled
the volley of shots have shattered the truce
you are wounded, lost in action
dead, fighting back;

To live in the Borderlands means
the mill with the razor white teeth wants to shred off
your olive-red skin, crush out the kernel, your heart
pound you pinch you roll you out
smelling like white bread but dead;

To survive the Borderlands
you must live *sin fronteras*
be a crossroads.

RANE ARROYO

A Chapter from The Book of Lamentations

To be drunk with loss,
to dance with death
—Lord Alfred Tennyson, In Memoriam

Another man and AIDS. He is dressed
in the look of this world, the burden of

too much Earthly light. He has drowned
in many strange beds, borrowed clouds.

Medicines are itchy cathedrals, crystals of
lies, palaces of pain. Meanwhile on the news:

"We go through 500 boxes of baseballs
during spring training." But spring needs

no training. Hawthorne was wrong looking
for North American ghosts in ruins: look

around us, at the young so unloved while alive.
AIDS is not just a war inside the body or

our deaths end up being our secrets, random
landscapes of ripe corpses, Sodom's ruins.

1993

That Flag

The *Motel 6* clerk thinks I'm
Italian and complains to me
about Puerto Ricans and I
nod because she has the key
to the last cheap room in town.
I unpack and go for a ride
down Joe Peréz Road and watch
two white, shirtless men do drug deals.
One looks at me, laughs. What does
he see? This sexy thug has
a Confederate flag in his truck
window. He rubs himself again
and again and I watch the way
one is possessed by a wreck.
The deal done, the two men then
slap each other on the ass,
and ride dust storms back to town.
I sit there thinking the fuckers
are right, that they are big
handsome, that they are our
America's perfect heirs and
that I'm not-aging Puerto Rican
homosexual poet exiled
to a borrowed bed. I walk
past the clerk and sing "Buenas
noches" but it isn't one for I dream
of that flag, of a terrible army
of soldiers in uniforms of skin
sent to steal from me the head
of Joe Peréz. But I've hidden it
inside my own skull. It is safe.

JIMMY SANTIAGO BACA

"I love the wind . . ."

I love the wind
when it blows through my barrio.
It hisses its snake love
down calles de polvo,
and cracks egg-shell skins
of abandoned homes.
Stray dogs find shelter
along the river,
where great cottonwoods rattle
like old covered wagons,
stuck in stagnant waterholes.
Days when the wind blows
full of sand and grit,
men and women make decisions
that change their whole lives.
Windy days in the barrio
give birth to divorce papers
and squalling separation. The wind tells us
what others refuse to tell us,
informing men and women of a secret,
that they move away to hide from.

Knowing the Snow Another Way

Last snowfall of winter.
        I stand at the window
watching, thinking how I have always compared
the White Man to snow.
        As a child, watching
its graceful fall, my chin
and chest next to a wooden sill, a frost chill
numbed my nose. Each snowflake swirling in space,

making trees gentle ghosts against the night sky
crowding together, and the moon a bonfire
they warmed themselves under,
extending white withered hands and hoary faces
like a religious sect, singing to the moon. . . .

Snow can be pleasing for a child
with no home or family: it means all that never was,
that whatever you do is imprinted,
it is a soothing voice that understands the scars
and covers the ugly sights
with a frill of happiness, light and glittering.
The closest example of the child's heart
is that of a sparrow bathing itself in the morning snow,
scattering the bits into air, speckling bright in sunshine.
But then something happens: at first,
the snow is like those loose sleeves of a prophet
extending its arms to hold a babe, those hollow sleeves
swathe the babe in warmth, and the babe feels the cold
on the cloth collected by the prophet's travels
amongst trees, mountains, streams . . . there is a touch of ice
in the prophet's fingers, of a wilderness
he lives in all alone with his gods.
The child knows this.

And yet, each winter we see what too much snow does.
My own people, trying to obtain Justice and Peace,
are like those people wrecked on a mountain,
wrapped in beggar's clothing, struggling up steep
cliffs. In the frozen faces there is a grim knowledge,
in the moustache sprinkled with snow,
the open eyes and snow-laden eyelashes,
Indios y Chicanos have that stolid death
in their features from knowing the snow's cold, cold
    extremes.
The dead sheep and cattle, the roads blocked,
no work, the fruits and fields destroyed:
they have known the snow another way, along sidewalks
of any major city, dressed in humble clothing, their breath
    laboring

against the cold, gritting teeth, blowing on their hands,
standing in soup and employment lines, toes numb
in crusty shoes, in the midst of the storm they exude
a tenderness of loss, their lives like snow
footprints slowly melting.

GIANNINA BRASCHI

Soy Boricua

Soy boricua. In spite of my family and in spite of my
country—I'm writing the process of the Puerto Rican
mind—taking it out of context—as a native and a foreigner—
expressing it through Spanish, Spanglish, and English—
Independencia, Estado Libre Asociado, and Estadidad—from
the position of a nation, a colony, and a state—Wishy, Wishy-
Washy, and Washy—not as one political party that is parted
into piddly parts and partied out. Todos los partidos están
partidos y son unos partidos.

A Toast to Divine Madness
(in the crown of the Statue of Liberty)

With this glass of champagne—I propose a toast to Divina
Locura—Divine Madness that has always inspired the
higher expectations of the great poets throughout the
globe. And I propose raising to this magnificent crown—
Divine Madness that, like the oppressed everywhere, has
been kept down—in submission, in seclusion, deprivation,
and silence—and has been kept down by the antithesis of
Divine Madness, divine expectation, divine philosophy,
and poetry—by the enemies of greatness and the lovers of
entertainment who have spit in the eyes and slapped the
cheeks of poetry and philosophy—with the cheapening of
the heart—the cheapening of all that is high and noble—
the cheapening of all the greatness, the magnificence, the
beauty, the good, the noble, the suspension of the senses,
the charisma, and the good energy that spells, through our
good will, something good for America—something that
makes America rise again from the tippy-top of the Yukon
to the tippy-toe of la Tierra del Fuego.

ANA CASTILLO

A Christmas Carol: c. 1976

Today i went downtown and signed away
another dream. i watched the other women
frown, the other women scream
with bitter sadness sign away their dreams;
as they became statistics for the
legal aid divorce division, new numbers
for the welfare line, eligible recipients
for social security benefits . . .
as they signed away.

Today i sat among them, with the
stoned face dignity necessary for one
who wears a borrowed coat for the winter cold;
and counts her change for the clark st. bus
while xmas shoppers push and shove,
among paperback readers/public sleepers:
i tuck away my dream into some distant past/
i tuck away a love that couldn't last,
but has. i stare at the appointment cards:
the court date/the job i hope to have,
but the only hope left is that winter won't last
forever/that winter won't last . . .
after all, nothing ever does:

A little girl held her mother's hand
with wide eyed fascination watched
the holiday decorations on state street/
the parade went by/santa claus with a crooked
cotton beard would wave/and mamá'd say:
"¿Ya ves? Pórtate bien y a ver qué te trae,"
and i wondered how santa claus would arrive
at a second floor flat in the back where even
those who lived on the block wouldn't go out

at night, but mamá went out each morning at
5 a.m. and on christmas day, a doll with pink
ribbons in its yellow hair and smelling of new
plastic, would always be there, 'cause after
all, i had been a good girl/i had always been
good.

Today i went downtown and walked
among the hurrying crowd, but no one
held my hand this time/no one smiled/
no one wished a merry xmas to anyone.
but i thought how nice it would be to buy
her something special this year/to send him
a greeting card/and how much nicer it would
be, to be a little girl again:

when dreams get tucked away in future spaces
instead, and my signature got nothing more
than a star in penmanship to take home and
paste proudly on a paint chipped wall:
"¿Ya ves que bien? A ver qué te trae Santa Claus,
a ver que te trae!" and that would be all.

LORNA DEE CERVANTES

*Poem for the Young White Man Who Asked Me
How I, an Intelligent, Well-Read Person Could
Believe in the War Between Races*

In my land there are no distinctions.
The barbed wire politics of oppression
have been torn down long ago. The only reminder
of past battles, lost or won, is a slight
rutting in the fertile fields.

In my land
people write poems about love,
full of nothing but contented childlike syllables.
Everyone reads Russian short stories and weeps.
There are no boundaries.
There is no hunger, no
complicated famine or greed.

I am not a revolutionary.
I don't even like political poems.
Do you think I can believe in a war between races?
I can deny it. I can forget about it
when I'm safe,
living on my own continent of harmony
and home, but I am not
there.

I believe in revolution
because everywhere the crosses are burning,
sharp-shooting goose-steppers round every corner,
there are snipers in the schools . . .
(I know you don't believe this.
You think this is nothing
but faddish exaggeration. But they
are not shooting at you.)

I'm marked by the color of my skin.
The bullets are discrete and designed to kill slowly.
They are aiming at my children.
These are facts.
Let me show you my wounds: my stumbling mind, my
"excuse me" tongue, and this
nagging preoccupation
with the feeling of not being good enough.

These bullets bury deeper than logic.
Racism is not intellectual.
I can not reason these scars away.

Outside my door
there is a real enemy
who hates me.

I am a poet
who yearns to dance on rooftops,
to whisper delicate lines about joy
and the blessings of human understanding.
I try. I go to my land, my tower of words and
bolt the door, but the typewriter doesn't fade out
the sounds of blasting and muffled outrage.
My own days bring me slaps on the face.
Every day I am deluged with reminders
that this is not
my land

and this is my land.

I do not believe in the war between races

but in this country
there is war.

Visions of México While at a Writing Symposium in Port Townsend, Washington

MÉXICO

When I'm that far south, the old words
molt off my skin, the feathers
of all my nervousness.
My own words somersault naturally as my name,
joyous among all those meadows: Michoacán,
Vera Cruz, Tenochtitlán, Oaxaca . . .
Pueblos green on the low hills
where men slap handballs below acres of maíz.
I watch and understand.
My frail body has never packed mud
or gathered in the full weight of the harvest.
Alone with the women in the adobe, I watch men,
their taut faces holding in all their youth.
This far south we are governed by the law
of the next whole meal. We work
and watch seabirds elbow their wings
in migratory ways, those mispronouncing gulls
coming south
to refuge or gameland.

I don't want to pretend I know more
and can speak all the names. I can't.
My sense of this land can only ripple through my veins
like the chant of an epic corrido.
I come from a long line of eloquent illiterates
whose history reveals what words don't say.
Our anger is our way of speaking,
the gesture is an utterance more pure than word.
We are not animals
but our senses are keen and our reflexes,
accurate punctuation.
All the knifings in a single night, low-voiced
scufflings, sirens, gunnings . . .
We hear them
and the poet within us bays.

WASHINGTON

I don't belong this far north.
The uncomfortable birds gawk at me.
They hem and haw from their borders in the sky.
I heard them say: México is a stumbling comedy.
A loose-legged Cantinflas woman
acting with Pancho Villa drunkenness.
Last night at the tavern
this was all confirmed
in a painting of a woman: her glowing
silk skin, a halo
extending from her golden coiffure
while around her, dark-skinned men with Jap slant eyes
were drooling in a caricature of machismo.
Below it, at the bar, two Chicanas
hung at their beers. They had painted black
birds that dipped beneath their eyelids.
They were still as foam while the men
fiddled with their asses, absently;
the bubbles of their teased hair snapped
open in the forced wind of the beating fan.

there are songs in my head I could sing you
songs that could drone away
all the Mariachi bands you thought you ever heard
songs that could tell you what I know
or have learned from my people
but for that   I need words
simple black nymphs between white sheets of paper
obedient words   obligatory words   words I steal
in the dark when no one can hear me

as pain sends seabirds south from the cold
I come north
to gather my feathers
for quills

Flatirons

for the Ute and Arapaho

The mountains are there like ghosts
of slaughtered mules, the whites of my
ancestors rest on the glaciers, veiled
and haloed with the desire of electrical
storms. Marginal feasts corral the young
to the cave walls, purple smoke wafts up
a chimney of shedding sundown. Statuesque
and exquisitely barren, my seed shines
in the dying rays. The rich earth of the wealthy
splays the legs of heaven in my view. Monstrous
and sullen, the slabs of death let loose their
hikers, let fall with an old snow. My harmony
of blood and ash, fire on the mound, I feel
them shuffling in the aspen, their vague ahems
marry the sucking fish in a derelict river. The
winter of their genocide still Ghost Dances
with a dream where the bison and mammoth unite,
where the story of their streams is as long
as the sabers of northern ice. The mountains
are the conquest of the sea, the belly of gems,
her fossil stays, her solicitudes. The glass
before the angel fish, she stands royal in
her invisible captivity, the impassability of her
element, elemental and efficient. She is there
in the silent baying, in the memory of a native
and the dripping pursuance of thawing babies—
specters in a sunset on The Heights—after massacre.

Bananas

for Indrek

I

In Estonia, Indrek is taking his children
to the Dollar Market to look at bananas.
He wants them to know about the presence of fruit,
about globes of light tart to the tongue, about the
twang of tangelos, the cloth of persimmons,
the dull little mons of kiwi. There is not a chance
for a taste where rubles are scarce and dollars, harder.
Even beef is doled out welfare-thin on Saturday's platter.
They light the few candles not reserved for the dead,
and try not to think of the small bites of the coming winter,
irradiated fields or the diminished catch in the fisherman's
net. They tell of bananas yellow as daffodils. And mango—
which tastes as if the whole world came out from her womb.

II

Colombia, 1928, bananas rot in the fields.
A strip of lost villages between railyard
and cemetery. The United Fruit Company
train, a yellow painted slug, eats
up the swamps and jungle. Campesinos
replace Indians who are a dream and a rubble
of bloody stones hacked into coffins: malaria,
tuberculosis, cholera, machetes of the jefes.
They become like the empty carts that shatter
the landscape. Their hands, no longer pulling green
teats from the trees, now twist into death, into silence
and obedience. They wait in Aracataca, poised
as statues between hemispheres. They would rather
be tilling their plots for black beans. They would
rather grow wings and rise as pericos—parrots, poets,
clowns—a word which means all this, pericos, those
messengers from Mictlán, the underworld, where ancestors
of the slain arise with the vengeance of Tláloc. A stench
permeates the wind as bananas, black on the stumps, char
into odor. The murdered Mestizos have long been cleared

and begin their new duties as fertilizer for the plantations.
Feathers fall over the newly spaded soil: turquoise,
scarlet, azure, quetzal, and yellow litters
the graves with the gold claws of bananas.

III

Dear I,
The 3′ × 6′ boxes in front of the hippie
market in Boulder are radiant with marigolds, some
with heads as big as my Indian face. They signify
death to me, as it is Labor Day and already
I am making up the guest list for my Día de los Muertos
altar. I'll need maravillas so this year I plant caléndulas
for blooming through snow that will fall before November.
I am shopping for "no-spray" bananas. I forego
the Dole and Chiquita, that name that always made me
blush for being christened with that title. But now
I am only a little small, though still brown enough
for the—Where are you from? Probably my ancestors
planted a placenta here as well as on my Califas coast
where alien shellfish replaced native mussels,
clams and oysters in 1886. I'm from
the 21st Century, I tell them, and feel
rude for it—when all I desire
is bananas without pesticides. They're smaller
than plantains which are green outside and firm
and golden when sliced. Fried in butter
they turn yellow as over-ripe fruit. And sweet.
I ask the produce manager how to crate and
pack bananas to Estonia. She glares at me
suspiciously: You can't do that. I know.
There must be some law. You might spread
diseases. They would arrive as mush, anyway.
I am thinking of children in Estonia with
no fried plátanos to eat with their fish as
the Blond turns away, still without shedding
a smile at me—me, Hija del Sol, Earth's Daughter, lover
of bananas. I buy up Baltic wheat. I buy up organic
bananas, butter y canela. I ship
banana bread.

IV

At Big Mountain uranium
sings through the dreams of the people.
Women dress in glowing symmetries, sheep
clouds gather below the bluffs, sundown
sandstone blooms in four corners. Smell of sage
penetrates as state tractors with chains trawl the resisting
plants, gouging anew the tribal borders, uprooting
all in their path like Amazonian ants, breaking
the hearts of the widows. Elders and children
cut the fences again and again as wind whips
the waist of ancient rock. Sheep nip across
centuries in the people's blood, and are carried
off by Federal choppers waiting in the canyon
with orders and slings. A long winter, little wool
to spin, medicine lost in the desecration of the desert.
Old women weep as the camera rolls on the dark
side of conquest. Encounter rerun. Uranium. 1992.

V

I worry about winter in a place
I've never been, about exiles in their
homeland gathered around a fire,
about the slavery of substance and
gruel: *Will there be enough to eat?*
Will there be enough to feed? And
they dream of beaches and pies, hemispheres
of soft fruit found only in the heat of the planet.
Sugar cane seeks out tropics; and dictates
a Resolution to stun the tongues of those
who can afford to pay: imported plums, bullets,
black caviar large as peas, smoked meats
the color of Southern lynchings, what we don't
discuss in letters. You are out of work.
Not many jobs today for high physicists
in Estonia, you say. Poetry, though, is food
for the soul. And bread? What is cake before
corn and the potato? Before the encounter
of animals, women and wheat? Stocks, high
these days in survival products: 500 years later tomato

size tumors bloom in the necks of the pickers.
On my coast, Diablo dominates the golden hills,
the faultlines. On ancestral land, Vandenberg shoots
nuclear payloads to Kwajalein, a Pacific atoll, where 68%
of all infants are born amphibian or anemones. But poetry
is for the soul. I speak of spirit, the yellow seed
in air as life is the seed in water, and the poetry
of Improbability, the magic in the Movement
of quarks and sunlight, the subtle basketry
of hadrons and neutrinos of color, how what you do
is what you get—bananas or worry.
What do you say? Your friend,

a Chicana poet

SANDRA CISNEROS

You Bring Out the Mexican in Me

You bring out the Mexican in me.
The hunkered thick dark spiral.
The core of a heart howl.
The bitter bile.
The tequila *lágrimas* on Saturday all
through next weekend Sunday.
You are the one I'd let go the other loves for,
surrender my one-woman house.
Allow you red wine in bed,
even with my vintage lace linens.
Maybe. Maybe.

For you.

You bring out the Dolores del Río in me.
The Mexican spitfire in me.
The raw *navajas*, glint and passion in me.
The raise Cain and dance with the rooster-footed devil in me.
The spangled sequin in me.
The eagle and serpent in me.
The *mariachi* trumpets of the blood in me.
The Aztec love of war in me.
The fierce obsidian of the tongue in me.
The *berrinchuda, bien-cabrona* in me.
The Pandora's curiosity in me.
The pre-Columbian death and destruction in me.
The rainforest disaster, nuclear threat in me.
The fear of fascists in me.
Yes, you do. Yes, you do.

You bring out the colonizer in me.
The holocaust of desire in me.
The Mexico City '85 earthquake in me.
The Popocatepetl/Iztaccíhuatl in me.

The tidal wave of recession in me.
The Agustín Lara hopeless romantic in me.
The *barbacoa taquitos* on Sunday in me.
The cover the mirrors with cloth in me.

Sweet twin. My wicked other,
I am the memory that circles your bed nights,
that tugs you taut as moon tugs ocean.
I claim you all mine,
arrogant as Manifest Destiny.
I want to rattle and rent you in two.
I want to defile you and raise hell.
I want to pull out the kitchen knives,
dull and sharp, and whisk the air with crosses.
Me sacas lo mexicana en mí,
like it or not, honey.

You bring out the Uled-Nayl in me.
The stand-back-white-bitch in me.
The switchblade in the boot in me.
The Acapulco cliff diver in me.
The *Flecha Roja* mountain disaster in me.
The *dengue* fever in me.
The *¡Alarma!* murderess in me.
I could kill in the name of you and think
it worth it. Brandish a fork and terrorize rivals,
female and male, who loiter and look at you,
languid in your light. Oh,

I am evil. I am the filth goddess Tlazolteotl.
I am the swallower of sins.
The lust goddess without guilt.
The delicious debauchery. You bring out
the primordial exquisiteness in me.
The nasty obsession in me.
The corporal and venial sin in me.
The original transgression in me.

Red ocher. Yellow ocher. Indigo. Cochineal.
Piñón. Copal. Sweetgrass. Myrrh.

All you saints, blessed and terrible,
Virgen de Guadalupe, diosa Coatlicue,
I invoke you.

Quiero ser tuya. Only yours. Only you.
Quiero amarte. Atarte. Amarrarte.
Love the way a Mexican woman loves. Let
me show you. Love the only way I know how.

Loose Woman

They say I'm a beast.
And feast on it. When all along
I thought that's what a woman was.

They say I'm a bitch.
Or witch. I've claimed
the same and never winced.

They say I'm a *macha*, hell on wheels,
viva-la-vulva, fire and brimstone,
man-hating, devastating,
boogey-woman lesbian.
Not necessarily,
but I like the compliment.

The mob arrives with stones and sticks
to maim and lame and do me in.
All the same, when I open my mouth,
they wobble like gin.

Diamonds and pearls
tumble from my tongue.
Or toads and serpents.
Depending on the mood I'm in.

I like the itch I provoke.
The rustle of rumor
like crinoline.

I am the woman of myth and bullshit.
(True. I authored some of it.)
I built my little house of ill repute.
Brick by brick. Labored,
loved and masoned it.

I live like so.
Heart as sail, ballast, rudder, bow.
Rowdy. Indulgent to excess.
My sin and success—
I think of me to gluttony.

By all accounts I am
a danger to society.
I'm Pancha Villa.
I break laws,
upset the natural order,
anguish the Pope and make fathers cry.
I am beyond the jaw of law.
I'm *la desperada*, most-wanted public enemy.
My happy picture grinning from the wall.

I strike terror among the men.
I can't be bothered what they think.
¡Que se vayan a la ching chang chong!
For this, the cross, the Calvary.
In other words, I'm anarchy.

I'm an aim-well,
shoot-sharp,
sharp-tongued,
sharp-thinking,
fast-speaking,
foot-loose,
loose-tongued,
let-loose,
woman-on-the-loose
loose woman.
Beware, honey.

I'm Bitch. Beast. *Macha.*
¡Wáchale!
Ping! Ping! Ping!
I break things.

Instructions for My Funeral

For good measure,
smoke me with *copal.*
Shroud me in my raggedy *rebozo.*
No jewelry. Give to friends.
No coffin. Instead, *petate.*
Ignite to "Disco Inferno."

Allow no Christian rituals
for this bitch, but, if
you like, you may invite
a homeless dog to sing,
or a witch woman to spit
orange water and chant
an Otomi prayer.

Send no ashes north
of the Río Bravo
on penalty of curse.

I belong here,
under Mexican *maguey,*
beneath a carved mesquite
bench that says *Ni Modo.*

Smoke a Havana.
Music, Fellini-esque.
Above all,
laugh.

And don't
forget.

Spell
my name
with *mezcal*.

LUCHA CORPI

México

Partí
como nota dividida
buscándose a sí misma.

Busqué
en colores de noche
sombras de día.

Perseguí
luces de ríos
en sueños viejos.

Esencia doble tan cercana
Cuerda floja de mi orden natural.

México

A veces pienso en ti
en tardes así
Me acaece viejo mal.

Buscar senderos de tierra
a vera de profundidad.

En bancales tibios
garzas de plumaje azul
perlas rojas cultivaron.

No hay tiempo de llorar
si has de vivir en mí.

Recuerdos nunca fueron
medida líquida de amar.

LUCHA CORPI

Mexico

I parted
like a note divided
in search of itself.

I looked
in the colors of night
for day's shadows.

I hunted
river lights
in old dreams.

Double essence so closely bound
tightrope of my natural order.

Mexico.

Sometimes I think of you
on afternoons like this
An old distress comes over me.

Search for paths of earth
at the edge of the depth.

On warm banks
blue-feathered herons
cultivate red pearls.

There is no time for weeping
if you are to live in me.

Memories were never
the liquid measure of love.

Translated by Catherine Rodriguez-Nieto

Emily Dickinson

Como tú, soy de ayer,
de las bahías en donde
se ancla el día a
esperar su propia hora.

Como yo, eres de hoy,
del andar de esa hora
en la que apenas palpita
lo que aún no ha nacido.

Somos cultivadoras de
indecibles, tejedoras
de singulares, campesinas
migratorias en busca de
chinampas aún sin
siembra y sin cosecha.

Emily Dickinson

Like you, I belong to yesterday,
to the bays where
day is anchored to
wait for its hour.

Like me, you belong to today,
the progression of that hour
when what is unborn
begins to throb.

We are cultivators of
the unsayable, weavers
of singulars, migrant
workers in search of
floating gardens as yet
unsown, as yet unharvested.

Translated by Catherine Rodriguez-Nieto

SILVIA CURBELO

Between Language and Desire

Imagine the sound of words
landing on the page, not footsteps

along the road but the road itself,
not a voice but a hunger.

I want to live by word of mouth,
as if what I'm about to say

could become a wall around us,
not stone but the idea

of stone, the bricks
of what sustains us.

These hands are not a harvest.
There is no honest metaphor for bread.

ANGELA DE HOYOS

La gran ciudad

for Mireya Robles

No one told me.
So how was I to know
that in the paradise
    of crisp white cities
snakes still walk
               upright?

Una mujer de tantas
sola
    divorciada
    separada
    largada
    —what does it matter?—
llegué a la gran ciudad
con mi niño en los brazos
por sembrar su camino trigueño
con las blancas flores
    de la esperanza

(. . . but how quickly they wilted
beneath the scorching
breath of evil.)

El barrio, indefenso:
the pit of the poor.
Mi raza: el *ay* por todas partes.

When I couldn't pay the rent
the landlord came to see me.

Y la pregunta, que ofende:
    Ain't you Meskin?
    How come you speak
    such good English?
Y yo le contesto:
    Because I'm Spanglo, that's why.
 . . . Pero se cobró
el muy pinche
        a su modo.

        3

And every day the price of hope goes up.
Every day in the bleak pit
the sun casts a thinner shadow
(algún día nos olvidará por completo.)
   Hijito, ¿nos comemos hoy
   esta fiesta de pan
   o lo dejamos para mañana?

        4

So where is the paradise?
In the land of the mighty
where is the shining
   —THE EQUAL—opportunity?
Can I skin with my bare teeth
the hungry hounds of night?

¡ . . . lárgense con su cuento
a otra parte!
        I know better.

MARTÍN ESPADA

Colibrí

for Katherine, one year later

In Jayuya,
the lizards scatter
like a fleet of green canoes
before the invader.
The Spanish conquered
with iron and words:
Indio Taíno for the people
who took life
from the rain
that rushed through trees
like evaporating arrows,
who left the rock carvings
of eyes and mouths
in perfect circles of amazement.

So the hummingbird
was christened *colibrí.*
Now the colibrí
darts and bangs
between the white walls
of the hacienda,
a racing Taíno heart
frantic as if hearing
the bellowing god of gunpowder
for the first time.

The colibrí
becomes pure stillness,
seized in the paralysis
of the prey,
when your hands
cup the bird

and lift him
through the red shutters
of the window,
where he disappears
into a paradise of sky,
a nightfall of singing frogs.

If only history
were like your hands.

Alabanza: In Praise of Local 100

*for the 43 members of Hotel Employees and Restaurant Employees
Local 100, working at the Windows on the World restaurant, who
lost their lives in the attack on the World Trade Center*

Alabanza. Praise the cook with a shaven head
and a tattoo on his shoulder that said *Oye,*
a blue-eyed Puerto Rican with people from Fajardo,
the harbor of pirates centuries ago.
Praise the lighthouse in Fajardo, candle
glimmering white to worship the dark saint of the sea.
Alabanza. Praise the cook's yellow Pirates cap
worn in the name of Roberto Clemente, his plane
that flamed into the ocean loaded with cans for Nicaragua,
for all the mouths chewing the ash of earthquakes.
Alabanza. Praise the kitchen radio, dial clicked
even before the dial on the oven, so that music and Spanish
rose before bread. Praise the bread. *Alabanza.*

Praise Manhattan from a hundred and seven flights up,
like Atlantis glimpsed through the windows of an ancient aquarium.
Praise the great windows where immigrants from the kitchen
could squint and almost see their world, hear the chant of nations:
Ecuador, México, República Dominicana,

Haiti, Yemen, Ghana, Bangladesh.
Alabanza. Praise the kitchen in the morning,
where the gas burned blue on every stove
and exhaust fans fired their diminutive propellers,
hands cracked eggs with quick thumbs
or sliced open cartons to build an altar of cans.
Alabanza. Praise the busboy's music, the *chime-chime*
of his dishes and silverware in the tub.

Alabanza. Praise the dish-dog, the dishwasher
who worked that morning because another dishwasher
could not stop coughing, or because he needed overtime
to pile the sacks of rice and beans for a family
floating away on some Caribbean island plagued by frogs.
Alabanza. Praise the waitress who heard the radio in the kitchen
and sang to herself about a man gone. *Alabanza.*

After the thunder wilder than thunder,
after the shudder deep in the glass of the great windows,
after the radio stopped singing like a tree full of terrified frogs,
after night burst the dam of day and flooded the kitchen,
for a time the stoves glowed in darkness like the lighthouse in Fajardo,
like a cook's soul. *Soul* I say, even if the dead cannot tell us
about the bristles of God's beard because God has no face,
soul I say, to name the smoke-beings flung in constellations
across the night sky of this city and cities to come.
Alabanza I say, even if God has no face.

Alabanza. When the war began, from Manhattan and Kabul
two constellations of smoke rose and drifted to each other,
mingling in icy air, and one said with an Afghan tongue:
Teach me to dance. We have no music here.
And the other said with a Spanish tongue:
I will teach you. Music is all we have.

Flowers and Bullets

*Cuba and Puerto Rico
are two wings of the same bird:
they receive flowers and bullets
in the same heart.*
                    —*Lola Rodríguez de Tió, 1889*

Tattoo the Puerto Rican flag on my shoulder.
Stain the skin red, white and blue, not the colors
that snap over holiday parades or sag over the graves
of veterans in the States, but the colors of Cuba reversed:
a flag for the rebels in the hills of Puerto Rico, dreamt up
by Puerto Rican exiles in the Cuban Revolutionary Party,
bearded and bespectacled in the sleet of New York,
Wise Men lost on their way to Bethlehem. That
was 1895, the same year José Martí would die,
poet shot from a white horse in his first battle.

Tattoo the Puerto Rican flag on my shoulder,
so if I close my eyes forever in the cold
and the doctors cannot tell the cause of death,
you will know that I died like José Martí,
with flowers and bullets in my heart.

The Republic of Poetry

for Chile

In the republic of poetry,
a train full of poets
rolls south in the rain
as plum trees rock
and horses kick the air,
and village bands
parade down the aisle
with trumpets, with bowler hats,
followed by the president

of the republic,
shaking every hand.

In the republic of poetry,
monks print verses about the night
on boxes of monastery chocolate,
kitchens in restaurants
use odes for recipes
from eel to artichoke,
and poets eat for free.

In the republic of poetry,
poets read to the baboons
at the zoo, and all the primates,
poets and baboons alike, scream for joy.

In the republic of poetry,
poets rent a helicopter
to bombard the national palace
with poems on bookmarks,
and everyone in the courtyard
rushes to grab a poem
fluttering from the sky,
blinded by weeping.

In the republic of poetry,
the guard at the airport
will not allow you to leave the country
until you declaim a poem for her
and she says *Ah! Beautiful.*

SANDRA MARÍA ESTEVES

Mambo Love Poem

Carlos y Rebecca dance across the floor.
They move in mambo cha-cha
that causes the sweat of their bodies to swirl
in a circle of tropical love.

Carlos y Rebecca move
and the room fills with blazes of red.
Flaming pianos breezing spicy tunes as coconuts fall
from palm trees ancient to these children.
As coconuts fall from imaginary palm trees
ancient to Borinquen souls.
Imaginary coconuts fall to the beat of their feet
in rhythm with the talking African drum.

Rebecca y Carlos glide across the floor,
and two become one in the land of salsa.
The sweat of their bodies mingles with flute
blowing high over splintered wooden floors,
in notes that soar beyond the rooftops of El Barrio.

They forget their pain in this land of joy,
as the clave answers the singing African conga,
the dancing African drum,
the conga quintiando
the African tongue.
Rebecca y Carlos become one
like two birds flying through the open sky,
in mambo cha-cha to celebrate their joy,
their feet no longer touching the ground.

They dance
becoming jíbaros in eagle wings.
As Shangó—Cabio Sile—enters their bodies
their sweat fuses with light.

Like thunderbolts in a fiery desert,
great wings galloping in flight.
The light in their feet dancing the African beat
with the singing African drum,
the conga quintiando the African tongue.
Marking the warrior's rhythm with the singing dancing
    drum,
Shangó—Cabio Sile—enters their bodies,
they flow magically into one.

Black Notes and "You Do Something To Me"

for Gerry González and The Fort Apache Band

Jazz—jazzy jass juice,
just so smooth,
so be-bop samba blue to sweet bump black.
So slip slide back to mama black—
to mamaland base black.
Don't matter could be bronx born basic street black.
Or white ivory piano coast negro dunes bembé black.
Mezclando manos in polyrhythm sync to fingers,
to keys, to valves, to strings, to sticks,
to bells, to skins, to YEAH black.
Bringin' it home black.
The bad Fort Apache tan olive brown beat black.
Bringin' it all the way up fast black.
Flyin' across Miles 'n Sonny,
across John, Rahsaan 'n Monk's '81,
across Dizzy blue conga Jerry horn,
'n básico Andy mo-jo black.
Across Nicky's campana timbaleando tumbao black.
'N Dalto's multi-octave chords with all those keys black.
Those multifarious dimensional openings
playin' loud—soft—hard—cold—slow—'n—suavecito black.
Playin' it runnin'—jumpin'—cookin'—greasin'—'n—
    smokin' black.
Playin' it mellow, yeah mellow,

makin' it mean somethin' black.
Makin' it move, rockin' round black.
Walk with it, talk with it, wake the dead with it black.
Turnin' it out, touchin' the sky with it black.
Shakin' it suave, shakin' it loose,
shakin' it che-ché-que-re black.
Season it, sugar it, lingerin', lullaby black.
Livin' it, ALIVE BLACK!
Always lovin' it—Yeah!

Jazz.
How I love your sweet soul sounds.
Yeah,
how I love how you love me.
Yeah, how I love that deep black thang . . .

                    . . . "You do so well" . . .

DIANA GARCÍA

Operation Wetback, 1953

The day begins like any other day.
Your daughter soaks a second diaper,
chortles as she shoves her soft-cooked egg
to the floor. Knees pressed to cracked linoleum,

you barely notice as your husband strokes
your belly. *Mijo*, he croons, prophetic plea,
then squeezes your nalgas as if to gauge
for ripeness. As he edges past, you notice

how his blue shirt blurs against the summer sky,
how sky absorbs his patch of blue, then empties.
Moments later, a truck groans, moves on,
carting rumblings of men headed for the fields.

Years later, you tell your son and daughter
of that anguished day, how green card migrants
vanished from the camps. You tell your children
how news gripped the camps of trains headed south

loaded with wetbacks. You never tell your children
what you can't forget: how you failed to squeeze back,
failed to wave good-bye, failed to taunt him
with viejo sinvergüenza. You never tell your children

how you forget this one man's voice—a voice
that brushed your ears, your hair, a path down your back—
a voice that blends with sounds of a truck
that never brought him home.

RICHARD GARCIA

My Father's Hands

My father learned to roll the perfect Perfecto Garcia Cigar
when he rode with Teddy Roosevelt in Cuba.

In the fifties he was supposed to play the first Ozzie Nelson
but he got fired because he kept taking his sweater off.

He said it was too hot, and besides, he didn't speak English
anyway.
I was supposed to be Ricky Nelson but my hair was too
frizzy.

He once ran into Butch Cassidy, who had been a friend of his
in Venezuela, long after Butch was supposed to be dead.

This was at the World's Fair on Treasure Island in 1939.
Butch disappeared back into the crowd, becoming a rumor

and then legend. Once, while purchasing my school clothes,
my father
asked me to sign for him on the department store charge
account.

I refused: I didn't care if he had ridden with Teddy Roosevelt
or if it were he who had carried the famous Message from
Garcia

out of the jungle rolled tightly into a rifle barrel,
or if he had knocked out the men who tried to shanghai him

on the Barbary Coast, or if he loaded up one hundred barrels
of bricks in half an hour after the 1906 earthquake in San
Francisco.

His hand trembled when he scrawled his X and he didn't
    speak to me
for the rest of the day. Is that why my hand shakes when I
    sign my name?

The only kind of music he liked was martial music,
and he placed me on his shoulders so I could see the
    Chinatown Parade.

One day we were marching through the house
while "Stars and Stripes Forever" blared from the radio.

The war was over and he said, We won. What did we win?
    I asked.
He answered, We won you. To celebrate, he put on his grass
    skirt

from the islands and danced the hula, his hands becoming
    sky, then clouds,
then birds and rain, then a waterfall that emptied itself into
    the ocean.

RAY GONZALEZ

At the Rio Grande Near the End of the Century

See how the cottonwood bends at the waist.
　　It turns gray, cracking as the sun goes down.
There is no limit to returning.
　　See the trunk turn toward what has changed you.

When you place yourself against the river you can't reach,
　　it is an old habit draining your hands of strength.
Look at the cottonwood disappearing.
　　Its hidden sediment is alighting out of your reach.

It is not water.
　　It was not made to mark the border with leaves.
Only the river can cease its mud and turn its brown heart.
　　Only the passage belongs to swollen, bare feet.

What you know is the scent of the desert you are so tired of
　　writing about.
how it covers the past and hangs as the ember of thought—
　　wisdom molded out of the falling world.

What you love is removed from the pale circle of shadows.
　　It will never return. It will weep.
Even the moisture in the armpit smells like the trees.
　　Tomorrow you will see another kind of growth.

See the threads of the hills turning back the revolt.
　　See how the men are crossing the river toward you.
When the cottonwood petrifies in the lone spot,
　　history will be overlooked and you will die.

What you keep are the thousand miles of the wounded
　　breast.
　　What you smell is the fine cotton of the dying tree.

When the white balls stick to your hair, listen to the fleeing
   men.
   Even their backs are wet and some of them look like you.

The Head of Pancho Villa

The rumor persisted that the head of Pancho Villa
disappeared on its own before they buried him,
found its way across the Chihuahua desert to El Paso
where he killed several men and kept women.
The head floated across the Rio Grande,
snapping turtles diving out of its way,
the brown mass moving on its own, his thick hair
and moustache shining in the green water.

The skull of the general evaporated in the heat,
only to reappear at the church door,
the early man who came to pray startled by
the bullet holes between the closed eyes.
He stared at the head, then ran.
When he brought the sleepy Padre to look,
they only found a wet spot on the ground
before they bowed and crossed themselves.

The rumor ran that the head became
the mountain surrounding the town.
Others said it was the skull that sat for years
on the highway west to Arizona.
It was true because my grandparents lived there,
told their children the skull glowed
on the roads, until my grandfather died
and his family returned to the other mountain.

I see the head of Villa each time I drive into El Paso.
It rises off the setting sun as the evening turns red.
By now, I am convinced the eyes are open, the hair longer.
After all, the moon is enough when I turn to take a look.

VICTOR HERNÁNDEZ CRUZ

Latin & Soul

for Joe Bataan

I

some waves
        a wave of now
                a trombone speaking to you
a piano is trying to break a molecule
is trying to lift the stage into orbit
around the red spotlights

a shadow
the shadows   of dancers
dancers   they are dancing   falling
out that space   made for dancing

they should dance
on the tables   they should
dance inside of their drinks
they should dance on the
ceiling they should dance/dance

thru universes
leaning-moving
            we are traveling

where are we going
if we only knew

with this rhythm   with
this banging   with   fire
with this   all   this   O
my god i wonder   where are
we going

sink into a room full of laughter
full of happiness   full of life
those dancers
the dancers
                   are clapping their hands
                   stomping their feet

hold back them tears
                        all those sentimental stories
cooked uptown   if you can   hold it for after

we are going
               away-away-away
               beyond these wooden tables
               beyond these red lights
               beyond these rugs & paper
               walls beyond way past
               i mean way past them clouds
               over the buildings   over the
               rivers   over towns   over cities
               like on rails   but faster   like
               a train   but smoother
               away past stars
               bursting with drums.

                        2

a sudden misunderstanding
                        a cloud
                        full of grayness
a body thru a store window
                        a hand reaching
                        into the back
                                    pocket
a scream
          a piano is talking to you
          thru all this
          why don't you answer it.

Trio Los Condes

Lyre and voice
the ancient serenade
Strings right below myth.
A circle of naked flesh
from the pores comes
the a capella of the Greek
chorus, the Taino Areyto flute
in the dance.
The Polynesian hands of
word waves.
Fingers tracing songs
in the wind.
The harmony creates columns
Each one a color a position
Celestial,
Bodies and objects that have
become sound.
I see plates and saucers
enclosed behind glass,
Small shot glass,
a magnificent oval bottle
of brandy,
Men walking through bluish
plastic curtains
Wearing thin ties and silky
suits.
All blue motion, red dance
the chains of Andalusia
broken loose,
What caramel would sing
if given a mouth.
In Cuba the rumba slowed down,
oil of the drummers' hands,
following the lament of the voice,
a mass tribute to the female form
The moon coming down as nickels
for the nickelodeon

Push H-7
Los Condes sing, "Amor de mis amores"
and bring back a skinny Agustín Lara
sitting in the margins of Rubén Darío's
poems
From San Francisco to New York,
a guitar sticks out of a '57 Packard
Moving through streets that are hills
open highway Interstate 10
all the way heartbreaking voyage
To the smog of the east coast
pipes.

They were the counts of a
monarchy of boleros,
For inspiration Pedro Flores flowers
the same,
The bridge of a woman's eyes
The sense of her yellow dress.
Not philosophy of ideas but
the Eros of touch
Skin lyrics
Boleros are flesh poetry
They respire the air you are,
in the distance of oblivion,
recall the picture of all the sweet
truth that floats in the lake of
her eyes,
That this caress was the night star
of your walk coming to my adobe
Toward my heart orphaned of kisses,
amor does not part through eternities,
Have we guessed the clear beauty
of who shines
Who trembles in a voice
The words that belong to men
ink upon the papyrus-woman,
Rhapsody that converts black
hair into white roses.

We've got to have the world
the soil and its birds.
Walk through paths
of folding bamboos
Bring songs
through deserted streets.
We want the ports of the Americas
visible and flagrant
bongos in the undercurrent
moving like ships
below the wings of the strings.
The kiss from the window
reaching the street eye.
Pageantry-Ceremony
People who allow themselves
to be penetrated by words,
Suggestion of freshly brewed desire
sacrificing bodies to the songs
Convinced of illusion.
Such is what Los Condes bring
a memorial pastry of harmonious illusions
songs climbing walls of bricks
Entering through the open window
Into a head that momentarily lifts
from a pillow
only to settle back into the abyss.

JUAN FELIPE HERRERA

Exiles

and I heard an unending scream piercing nature.
—from the diary of EDVARD MUNCH, 1892

At the greyhound bus stations, at airports, at silent wharfs
the bodies exit the crafts. Women, men, children; cast out
from the new paradise.

They are not there in the homeland, in Argentina, not there
in Santiago, Chile; never there in Montevideo, Uruguay,
and they are not here

in *America*

They are in exile: a slow scream across a yellow bridge
the jaws stretched, widening, the eyes multiplied into blood
orbits, torn, whirling, spilling between two slopes; the sea,
    black,
swallowing all prayers, shadeless. Only tall faceless figures
of pain flutter across the bridge. They pace in charred suits,
the hands lift, point and ache and fly at sunset as cold dark
birds. They will hover over the dead ones: a family shattered
by military, buried by hunger, asleep now with the eyes
    burning
echoes calling *Joaquín, María, Andrea, Joaquín, Joaquín,*
    Andrea,

en exilio

From here we see them, we the ones from here, not there or
    across,
only here, without the bridge, without the arms as blue
    liquid
quenching the secret thirst of unmarked graves, without
our flesh journeying refuge or pilgrimage; not passengers

279

on imaginary ships sailing between reef and sky, we that die
here awake on Harrison Street, on Excelsior Avenue clutching
the tenderness of chrome radios, whispering to the saints
in supermarkets, motionless in the chasms of playgrounds,
searching at 9 a.m. from our third floor cells, bowing mute,
shoving the curtains with trembling speckled brown hands.
      Alone,
we look out to the wires, the summer, to the newspapers
      wound
in knots as matches for tenements. We that look out from
our miniature vestibules, peering out from our old clothes,
the father's well-sewn plaid shirt pocket, an old woman's
oversized wool sweater peering out from the makeshift
      kitchen.
We peer out to the streets, to the parades, we the ones from
      here
not there or across, from here, only here. Where is our exile?
Who has taken it?

My Mother's Coat Is Green

Emerald.
A sea of broken guitars.

Cubism leaning against an old fence
in El Paso, Texas.

No one knows her except me.

Every now and then she plays a fugue in the mansion.
Or she walks on the meadows with all the children,
singing.

Yesterday, she told me age is inevitable.
Then, she spoke of emptiness;

a carpet beneath us,
stray patches of dreams that escape us.

The Women Tell Their Stories

The women tell their stories in Austin,
they tower over the table, their hot work hands
greet me, they speak of their children. The earth
I think, oh, yes, the earth.

Cloned maize men unload another ship through
genetically altered skies and an MC-130 Combat Talon plane
drops into Kandahar, Afghanistan—15,000-pound fuel
air explosives, what is left now? A flower of ethylene and
propylene, then a cluster bomb, filled
with 202 "bomblets"—what am I saying:

Better to say peanut butter, Pop Tarts,
rice and potatoes instead, the same color of village fires,
a yellow can comes down in the name of the Nomenclature.

The question of Kabul, Kashmir, Fallujah
comes up, the question of colonization and
saliva, bacteria in the atoms of expansion drills
into the howling child, this rubble boy:

eat, step lightly on the mines
of the Russian-American war, dear little one
with your folded arms caressing a fender
for shelter.

Let Me Tell You What a Poem Brings

for Charles Fishman

Before you go further,
let me tell you what a poem brings,
first, you must know the secret, there is no poem
to speak of, it is a way to attain a life without boundaries,
yes, it is that easy, a poem, imagine me telling you this,
instead of going day by day against the razors, well,

the judgments, all the tick-tock bronze, a leather jacket
sizing you up, the fashion mall, for example, from
the outside you think you are being entertained,
when you enter, things change, you get caught by surprise,
your mouth goes sour, you get thirsty, your legs grow cold
standing still in the middle of a storm, a poem, of course,
is always open for business too, except, as you can see,
it isn't exactly business that pulls your spirit into
the alarming waters, there you can bathe, you can play,
you can even join in on the gossip—the mist, that is,
the mist becomes central to your existence.

The Suttons I
The Chaos Beneath Buttons/Acrilic in Blue
Acrylic in Blue

In addition to the eternal street corners

the Arab grocery across the way

by the building with its vintage pianos
Building began
the sea snatched up by a girl
the skin, your branches,
and her smile

the rosaries in aged fingertips
for the night on his branches
each night behind the windows
or the branches
how black wristwatches pulse with incense
on his beginning   breathe the sun
the eyes were exploding

and he
&on
the dark branches
amidst the dark vines of his room
his stolen belly
on the third floor of his winter

began to breathe
began to rime,
even when the sun filled with blood

or

when the uniformed scorpions
the winter gaze   wanted his
invented a new mascara/ he wanted fingertips

everything/everything

even the white rhyme off the
          that cloud your   &, with
blind man's cane little pianos the-Suttons, breathe
                    on the legs behind
the sleepless eyes   the women, the belly's
          skin the sun
in the fullness of night/ the husks and
   With eternal fingertips   even the
the legs in the birdbishop's cell *husks I husks,*

          you wanted to drown yourself in the sidewalk
     girl cloud of murder
   if   *cloudnotes on your skin*
   wanted to your
          you wanted to burn your lips and waist

          against the wall of imperceptible bodies
                    branches blind the skin
beginning to breathe all your scorpions

to capsize the boulevard with each blink
                    in the buried room
you'll hold the two planets of a child's gaze

you'll assassinate the man with his hip suit
beneath the potted palm
in that apartment
his shirt fit tight
to your body

TATO LAVIERA

Mixturao

(for English only)

we-who engage in
western hemispheric
continental spanish majority
communally sharing linguistics
in humanistic proportions

we-who integrate
urban America
simmering each other's slangs
indigenous nativizing
our tongues' cruising accents
who are you, English,
telling me, "Speak only English
or die."

we-who grassroots
and jíbaro dialectics
yodeling Mexican riddles
chicano "ese" talk
creole caribbeanisms
black negroid textings
african twisting
european colonizers'
oppressive repertoires
savoring new vocabularies
who are you, English,
telling me, "Speak only English
or die."

we-who create continental music
elaborate universal jazz
rhythmic tonalities

284

vallenato oilings
gospel-rap soulings
brazilian portuguesa
bonito bolero
mayan songs soothing
quebecois hard rock
patois saging
andino cumbias
world-wide tango curvings
merengue-calypso
mating-mixing dancing
tres por cuatro cubanities
con los pasos firmes de aztecas
who are you, English,
telling me, "Speak only English
or die."

we-who are at peace in continental
inter-mixtures
do hereby challenge
united states isolationism
anti-immigrant mono-lingual
constitutional bullets
declarations telling us to
"speak only english or die"
"love it or leave it"
spelling big stick carcass
translations universally excluded
multi-lingual multi-cultural
expressions "need not to apply"
who are you, English,
telling me, "Speak only English
or die."

so enter our multi-lingual
frontiers become a sharing
partner maybe then I might
allow you the privilege
to call me a tremendous
continental "MIXTURAO."

AURORA LEVINS MORALES

When I Write Archipelago

The islands I write are more than water-bordered lands. They are mountain ranges rooted in saltwater, bones of connection visible only from the air. I sing the islands one by one, their surf ruffled edges, their sloping beaches and plunging cliffs, the rings of reef-sheltered bays, the wild oceanic swells grinding stone to sand. I sing the dry ones where every drop of rain must be cupped, and the wet ones, of palm and fern, moss and orchid, the volcanic peaks and the flat slabs of uplifted limestone, the twelve-hundred-mile arc of Cuba and the tiny specks of scattered cays. The archipelago I write rises from the bones of the planet and is interrupted by reflected light, rises above the skin of water and continues far below. When I say archipelago, I mean continuity and uniqueness, how we are singular and inseparable, boundaries of rough surf, rough passages between our coasts, and one shared bedrock, one tectonic gap, one subduction of vast planetary stone that raises us. When I say Caribbean, say Antilles, say West Indies, say Windward and Leeward, Greater and Lesser, I mean that we cry out in different languages as the same storm sweeps our houses into the sea. When I say islands I mean the endless dance of kinship, pulling us together and apart like tide. When I say islands, I mean we.

JAIME MANRIQUE

El fantasma de mi padre en dos paisajes

Cuando busco refugio en la casa al anochecer
a través del ciprés, una luna enceguecedora me detiene,
y desde el bosque oscuro, el fantasma fosforescente
de mi padre me indica un estallido
de luceros y otros prodigios celestiales
que ahora, en la eternidad eterna,
él se entretiene nombrándolos.

Estoy en Nueva Inglaterra,
un paisaje desconocido por mi padre,
un paisaje sin flores con cuellos de jirafas,
ni aves de garras platinadas,
ni felinos vomitando cataratas de sangre,
ni platanales cruzados por ríos claros como el vodka
zurcados por flamingos con cuellos sumergidos
y con plumosas colas abiertas como parasoles.

No, este valle no es una exaltada pesadilla de Rousseau,
aunque aquí también la luna deslumbrante
pende de un collar de astros,
y el collar es un puente entre los cielos
que mi padre conoció y los cielos que veo ahora.

Hay preguntas que quisiera hacerle al efluvio de mi padre
si él no estuviera embelesado con la noche y sus misterios,
si yo conociera el lenguaje de los muertos.

Lentamente, como una llama que se extingue,
el fantasma desaparece y deja, en el tablero de la noche,
un mensaje indescifrable que me abruma.
El calor de la casa es mi último cobijo
de estos cielos penumbrosos
preñados de señales.

JAIME MANRIQUE

My Father's Ghost in Two Landscapes

Just when I seek shelter in the house at dusk
a blinding moon behind the cypress stops me,
and from the dark woods the glowing ghost
of my father points to an explosion
of evening stars and other heavenly wonders
that now, in his eternal eternity,
he spends his time in naming.

I am in New England,
a landscape unknown to my father,
a landscape with no giraffe-neck flowers
or birds with platinum claws
or big cats vomiting cataracts of blood,
or banana groves cut by rivers as clear as vodka
where flamingoes wade with their necks under water
and feathery tails spread like parasols.

No, this valley is no nightmare vision by Rousseau,
although here, too, a dazzling moon
dangles from a necklace of stars,
and that necklace is a bridge between the skies
my father knew and the skies I see now.

There are questions I would like to ask my father's apparition
if he were not enraptured with the night and its mysteries
and if I knew the language of the dead.

Slowly, like the flicker of a flame,
the ghost vanishes and leaves behind, on the slate of the night,
an indecipherable message that overwhelms me.
The warmth in the house is my last refuge
against these darkening skies
full of signs.

Translated by Edith Grossman

Mambo

Contra un cielo topacio
y ventanales estrellados
con delirantes trinitarias
y rojas, sensuales cayenas;
el fragante céfiro vespertino
oloroso de almendros y azahar de la India;
sobre las baldosas de diseños moriscos,
con zapatillas de tacón aguja,
vestidos descotados y amplias polleras;
sus largas, obsidianas cabelleras
a la usanza de la época;
perfumadas, trigueñas, risueñas,
mis tías bailaban el mambo
canturreando, "Doctor, mañana
no me saca usted la muela,
aunque me muera del dolor."

Aquellas tardes en mi infancia
cuando mis tías eran muchachas y me pertenecían,
y yo bailaba cobijado entre sus polleras,
nuestras vidas eran un mambo feliz
que no se olvida.

Mambo

Against a topaz sky
and huge windows starry
with delirious heartsease
and sensual red cayenne;
the sweet twilight breeze
fragrant with almond and Indian orange;
on the Moorish tiles,
wearing their spike-heeled shoes,
lowcut dresses and wide swirling skirts;
their long obsidian hairdos
in the style of the time;
perfumed, olive-skinned, smiling,
my aunts danced the mambo
and sang: "Doctor, tomorrow,
you can't pull my tooth,
even if I die of the pain."

Those evenings of my childhood
when my aunts were young and belonged to me,
and I danced hiding in their skirts,
our lives were a happy mambo—
I remember.

Translated by Edith Grossman

DIONISIO D. MARTÍNEZ

History as a Second Language

I grew up hearing the essence
of conversations in the next room.
My father and his friends conspired
in the next room. The new regime
succeeded in spite of their plot.
The next room is usually dark. People
whisper in it. You hear only so much.
Just enough if you know what to listen for.
I thought I heard a murder in the next
room. It was the radio. I thought
I heard a murder long after the radio
had been thrown against the wall and smashed
to bits. It was a whore at the end of
a long day. Families like mine
always managed to have a whore or two
as "good" friends. It made us look
less rich, less whatever being rich meant.
In those days things became
the meanings we gave them and not the other
way around, not like today. The next room
meant the room next door. If you looked
hard enough, you could see through the wall.
The specifics of a conversation
were not necessary to understand a plot
or a confession; the blurred
view through the wall was enough
to know more or less how the whores
earned their pay, how a government
might have failed, how a single threat
would keep a family together through war
and sabotage. The room next door
made us what we became with time in exile:
failed lovers, experts in the mechanics
of things we never learned to name.

PABLO MEDINA

The Exile

He returned to grass two feet tall
around the house, a rope dangling
from the oak, an absence of dogs.
The year had neither ended nor begun,
the sun had yawned away the rain
and worms were drying on the ground.

Memories floated down from the trees: cane fields,
the smokehouse and its hanging meats,
breeze of orange and bamboo, a singing at dawn.

"Will you be with me?"
The voice came from the river. The jasmine
bloomed in the garden, he hiding,
he sweating under the moon
wanting to say I will I will and more.

There were stones all over the yard smelling of time.
He picked a few, threw them down the well
and listened to the water swallowing.

It made him smaller. He walked out the gate
and closed it behind him, wiped the sweat from his eyes,
felt his feet settling on the road.

The Floating Island

> *. . . brillando contra el sol y contra los poetas . . .*
> —*Heberto Padilla*

There it is, the long prow
of the Caribbean, charging to break

293

the map's complexion.
It is a key, a crocodile, a hook,
an uncoiling question,
a stretch of sinews catching
dribbles from the continent
under which it will, forever, float.

The island mouth is smiling
or frowning, who can tell,
stuffed with waning intentions,
sugarcane and sand.

Such a little place, such
an island listing against sorrow
in the middle of the ocean's gut,
playing make believe
queen of brine, dressing up in green
and calling forth its poets for praise,
its leaders for chesty boasts,
inventing for itself a pantheon
of tropical saints, a vast
and profound literature,
an epic history to rival Rome's.

There it is, pretending it shimmers
over the heads of its people,
denying the terror it feels
when no one listens, denying
that it is always almost drowning,
that it cannot help anyone, least
of all itself, that it is only
a strip of dirt between morning and night,
between what will be and what was,
between the birth of hope
and the death of desire.

ORLANDO RICARDO MENES

Doña Flora's Hothouse

The Sargasso Sea in cyclone
season, a flotilla of blessèd corpses
drifting in equatorial currents,
their shaved heads crowned with laurel
to repel lightning, sargassum fronds
swathing both neck and limb.

Tiny crabs burrow ears
oozing cerumen, pipefish slither
into sutured wounds that coffer
bones of African St. Barbara.

In the tropics the blessèd are incorruptible,
whether Goa, Malabo, or Hispaniola.
Landfall at Doña Flora's island
(longitude of Gonave and Barbuda),
green thumb hermit who cultivates

their bodies in a hothouse by the sea.
Sheared parts fructify in African soil
from Ilé-Ifé, guano of *Caná-Caná*
vulture that flies to heaven carrying
missives, prayer beads and pits.

Swinging her calabash censer,
Doña Flora fumigates with sarsaparilla
entrails of tamarind, soursop kidneys,
banana toes; a *zunzuncito* hummingbird
flies out her ear to sip balsam tears.

Suspended amid laelia orchids
mulatto cherubs trumpet *sones*
from Oriente, Doña Flora rattles

her maraca to sprinkle aguardiente
on guava bladders, uteri of red
papaya, mango hearts. By white

mangroves a shanty of lignum vitae,
dried thatching, barnacled crosses.
All Souls' Day and Doña Flora enters
with her animals, laying overripe fruits

on whitest linen. Iguanas chew
sweet-acid tamarind, a *jutía* rat
nibbles guava, *Caná-Caná* rips papaya—
seeds bursting out—as Doña Flora skins

a mango, bruised with machete,
lifts the bleeding fruit to bands
of amber light, sweet flesh dissolving
in her mouth, its bare stone returned to sea.

PAT MORA

Now and Then, America

Who wants to rot
beneath dry, winter grass
in a numbered grave
in a numbered row
in a section labeled Eternal Peace
with neighbors plagued
by limp, plastic roses
springing from their toes?
Grant me a little life now and then, America.

Who wants to rot
as she marches through life
in a pin-striped suit
neck chained in a soft, silk bow
in step, in style, insane.
Let me in
to board rooms wearing hot
colors, my hair long and free,
maybe speaking Spanish.
Risk my difference, my surprises.
Grant me a little life, America.

And when I die, plant *zempasúchitl*,
flowers of the dead, and at my head
plant organ cactus, green fleshy
fingers sprouting, like in Oaxaca.
Let desert creatures hide
in the orange blooms.
Let birds nest in the cactus stems.
Let me go knowing life
        flower and song
will continue right above my bones.

El Río Grande

Maybe La Llorona is el Río Grande
   who carries voices wherever she flows,
the voices of women who speak only Spanish,
   who hold their breath, fluttering
like a new bird, cupped in their own hands high
   above their heads.

Maybe La Llorona is el Río Grande
   who rolls over on her back some afternoons
and gazes straight into the sun,
   her hair streaming brown into fields of onion
and chile, gathering voices of women who laugh
   with their own fear.

Maybe La Llorona is el Río Grande
   who penetrates even granite, gathers the stars
and moon and tells her cuentos all night long,
   of women who scoop her to them in the heat,
lick her on their lips, their voices rising
   like the morning star.

Let Us Hold Hands

Let us now hold hands
with the Iroquois woman who slipped berries into children's
      lips
while her sisters planted stars with a wooden hoe,

with the woman who rubbed warm oil into her neighbor's feet
when Plymouth's winter prowled and howled outside their
      doors,

with the woman who sewed faith into each stitch, cloth
      comforts
pieced to the rhythm of español for babies born al silencio del
      desierto,

with the woman who seasoned soups with pepper and hope
as her days took her further from sighs of trees she loved,

with the woman who parted her parched lips and sang
for her mother when they staggered onto these shores in
    chains,

with the woman who trained her stubborn tongue to wrap
around that spiny language, English, to place her child in
    school.

Let us now hold hands with the woman
who croons to the newborn left amid orange rinds and
    newspaper,
who teaches grandmothers to knit letters into a word, a
    word,
who whispers to the woman dying with one breast,
who holds a wife whose face is more broken than any bone,
who bathes the woman found sleeping in black snow.

Let us hold hands
with the woman who holds her sister in Bosnia, Detroit,
    Somalia,
Jacksonville, Guatemala, Burma, Juárez, and Cincinnati,
with the woman who confronts the glare of eyes and
    gunbarrels,
yet rises to protest in Yoruba, English, Polish, Spanish,
    Chinese, Urdu.

Let us hold hands
with the woman who cooks, with the woman who builds,
with the woman who cries, with the woman who laughs,
with the woman who heals, with the woman who prays,
with the woman who plants, with the woman who harvests,
with the woman who sings, with the woman whose spirits
    rise.

In this time that fears faith, let us hold hands.
In this time that fears the unwashed, let us hold hands.
In this time that fears age, let us hold hands.

In this time that fears touch, let us hold hands,
brown hands, trembling hands, calloused hands, frail
hands, white hands, tired hands, angry hands, new
hands, cold hands, black hands, bold hands.

In towns and cities and villages, mano a mano, hand in hand,
in mountains and valleys and plains, a ring of women circling
the world, the ring strong in our joining,
around our petaled home, this earth, let us hold hands.

Prayer to the Saints |
Oración a los Santos

At sixteen I began to pray to you, old friends,
   for a handsome man who would never stray.
     Devoutly, I'd say,
Saint Peter the Apostle,
   please grant me this miracle,
Saint Raphael, the Archangel,
   remove every obstacle,
San José, dear father,
   may he frown at liquor
Saint Clare,
   for Mother, could he be a millionaire,
Saint John Nepomuk,
   my few faults may he overlook,
Santa María Magdalena,
   que a veces me sirva mi cena,
Saint Christopher,
   may he my figure prefer,
Our Lady of Remedies,
   could he avoid my father's frugalities,
Saint Francis,
   please don't make him a pessimist,
Saint Anne,
   could he be a very handsome man,

Saint Anthony,
>	may he know the art of flattery,
Santa Bárbara, protector against lightning,
>	make him good at dancing,
Saint Genevieve,
>	may he never plot to deceive,
Saint Blaise,
>	let him shower me with praise,
Saint Jerome,
>	have him build me my dream-home,
San Pascual,
>	como él que no haya igual,
Saint Patrick,
>	could he be a lovesick Catholic,
Saint Gertrude the Great,
>	forgive me, but make him passionate,
Saint Lucy,
>	suggest he kiss me secretly,
Saint Martin,
>	may my smile turn him to gelatin,
Santa Teresita,
>	que me traiga florecitas,
Saint Agnes,
>	make him love me with wild excess,
Saint James,
>	por favor, nudge him this love to proclaim,
Saint Rose,
>	have him soon propose,
Saint Elizabeth,
>	may we celebrate our fiftieth,
Saint Jude,
>	let me soon be wooed,
Saint Stephen,
>	please remind all the santos
>		to find me a husband soon. Ah, men. Amen.

JUDITH ORTIZ COFER

Because My Mother Burned Her Legs
in a Freak Accident

I am flying south over the Atlantic
toward one of those islands
arranged like shoes on a blue carpet.
She lies in bed waiting for the balm
of my presence, her poor legs pink
as plucked hens. When her gas stove exploded
as she bent over her soup, the flames grabbed
her ankles like a child throwing a tantrum.
So she has summoned me transatlantically,
her voice sounding singed as if the fire
had burned her from within.
She wants me there to resurrect her flesh,
to reverse time, to remind her of the elastic
skin that once sustained me.
She wants me to come home and save her,
as only a child who has been forgotten and forgiven can.

Where You Need to Go

My life began here in this pueblo
now straining against its boundaries
and still confused about its identity:
Spanish village or tourist rest stop?
with its centuries-old church
where on Sundays pilgrims on their knees
beg a dark Madonna for a miracle,
then have lunch at Burger King.

Here is the place
where I first wailed for life

in a pre-language understood by all
in the woman-house where I was born,
where absent men in military uniform
paraded on walls alongside calendars
and crosses, and telegrams were delivered
by frightened adolescent boys
who believed all coded words from Korea
were about death. But sometimes
they were just a *"Bueno, Mujer,"*
to the women who carried on
their blood duties on the home front.

I know this place,
although I have been away most of my life.
I have never really recovered
from my plunge, that balmy February day,
into the unsteady hands
of the nearly blind midwife,
as she mumbled prayers in Latin
to the Holy Mother, who had herself
been spared the anguish
this old woman witnessed year after year,
to the aroma of herbal teas
brewed for power in *la lucha*, and the haunting
of the strangely manic music
that accompanies both beginnings
and endings on this island. I absorbed it all
through my pores. And it remains
with me still, as a vague urge
to reconnect.

Today, opening my eyes again
in my mother's house,
I know I will experience certain things
that come to me in dreams and in déjà vu:
the timeless tolling of bells,
because time must be marked for mortal days
in minutes, in hours, and in measured intervals,
to remind us as we drink our morning *café*

that we too shall turn to dust; the rustling
of palm fronds against venetian blinds, of water
running over a woman's hands,
pots and pans put in their places, living sounds
from my childhood; and muffled words
I cannot quite decipher, spoken in a language
I now have to translate, like signs
in a foreign airport you recognize
as universal symbols, and soon
their true meaning will come to you. It must.
For this is the place where you decide
where you need to go.

To Understand El Azul

We dream in the language we all understand,
in the tongue that preceded alphabet and word.
Each time we claim beauty from the world,
we approximate its secret grammar, its silent
syntax; draw nearer to the Rosetta stone
for dismantling Babel.

If I say *el azul*, you may not see the color
of *mi cielo, mi mar.* Look once upon my sky,
my sea, and you will know precisely
what *el azul* means to me.

Begin with this: the cool kiss
of a September morning in Georgia, the bell-shaped
currents of air changing in the sky, the sad ghosts
of smoke clinging to a cleared field, and the way
days will taste different in your mouth each week
of the season. *Sábado:* Saturday
is strawberry. *Martes:* Tuesday
is bitter chocolate to me.

Do you know what I mean?

Still, everything we dream circles back.
Imagine the bird that returns home every night
with news of a miraculous world just beyond
your private horizon. To understand its message,
first you must decipher its dialect of distance,
its idiom of dance. Look for clues
in its arching descent, in the way it resists
gravity. Above all, you have to learn why
it aims each day

toward the boundless *azul*.

GUSTAVO PÉREZ FIRMAT

Last-Mambo-in-Miami

Soy un ajiaco de contradicciones.
I have mixed feelings about everything.
Name your tema, I'll hedge;
name your cerca, I'll straddle it
like a cubano.

I have mixed feelings about everything.
Soy un ajiaco de contradicciones.
Vexed, hexed, complexed,
hyphenated, oxygenated, illegally alienated,
psycho soy, cantando voy.
You say tomato,
I say tu madre;
You say potato,
I say Pototo.
Let's call the hole
un hueco, the thing
a cosa, and if the cosa
goes into the hueco,
consider yourself en casa,
consider yourself part of the family.

(Cuban-American mí:
I singo therefore I am, sí.)

Soy un ajiaco de contradicciones,
un puré de impurezas:
a little square from Rubik's Cuba,
que nadie nunca acoplará.
(Cha-cha-chá.)

PEDRO PIETRI

Puerto Rican Obituary

They worked
They were always on time
They were never late
They never spoke back
when they were insulted
They worked
They never took days off
that were not on the calendar
They never went on strike
without permission
They worked
ten days a week
and were only paid for five
They worked
They worked
They worked
and they died
They died broke
They died owing
They died never knowing
what the front entrance
of the first national city bank looks like

Juan
Miguel
Milagros
Olga
Manuel
All died yesterday today
and will die again tomorrow
passing their bill collectors
on to the next of kin
All died
waiting for the garden of eden

to open up again
under a new management
All died
dreaming about america
waking them up in the middle of the night
screaming: Mira Mira
your name is on the winning lottery ticket
for one hundred thousand dollars
All died
hating the grocery stores
that sold them make-believe steak
and bullet-proof rice and beans
All died waiting dreaming and hating

Dead Puerto Ricans
Who never knew they were Puerto Ricans
Who never took a coffee break
from the ten commandments
to KILL KILL KILL
the landlords of their cracked skulls
and communicate with their latino souls

Juan
Miguel
Milagros
Olga
Manuel
From the nervous breakdown streets
where the mice live like millionaires
and the people do not live at all
are dead and were never alive

Juan
died waiting for his number to hit
Miguel
died waiting for the welfare check
to come and go and come again
Milagros
died waiting for her ten children
to grow up and work

so she could quit working
Olga
died waiting for a five dollar raise
Manuel
died waiting for his supervisor to drop dead
so he could get a promotion

Is a long ride
from Spanish Harlem
to long island cemetery
where they were buried
First the train
and then the bus
and the cold cuts for lunch
and the flowers
that will be stolen
when visiting hours are over
Is very expensive
Is very expensive
But they understand
Their parents understood
Is a long non-profit ride
from Spanish Harlem
to long island cemetery

Juan
Miguel
Milagros
Olga
Manuel
All died yesterday today
and will die again tomorrow
Dreaming
Dreaming about queens
Clean-cut lily-white neighborhood
Puerto Ricanless scene
Thirty-thousand-dollar home
The first spics on the block
Proud to belong to a community
of gringos who want them lynched

Proud to be a long distance away
from the sacred phrase: Que Pasa

These dreams
These empty dreams
from the make-believe bedrooms
their parents left them
are the after-effects
of television programs
about the ideal
white american family
with black maids
and latino janitors
who are well train—
to make everyone
and their bill collectors
laugh at them
and the people they represent

Juan
died dreaming about a new car
Miguel
died dreaming about new anti-poverty programs
Milagros
died dreaming about a trip to Puerto Rico
Olga
died dreaming about real jewelry
Manuel
died dreaming about the irish sweepstakes

They all died
like a hero sandwich dies
in the garment district
at twelve o'clock in the afternoon
social security number to ashes
union dues to dust

They knew
they were born to weep
and keep the morticians employed

as long as they pledge allegiance
to the flag that wants them destroyed
They saw their names listed
in the telephone directory of destruction
They were train to turn
the other cheek by newspapers
that mispelled mispronounced
and misunderstood their names
and celebrated when death came
and stole their final laundry ticket

They were born dead
and they died dead
Is time
to visit sister lopez again
the number one healer
and fortune card dealer
in Spanish Harlem
She can communicate
with your late relatives
for a reasonable fee
Good news is guaranteed
Rise Table Rise Table
death is not dumb and disable—
Those who love you want to know
the correct number to play
Let them know this right away
Rise Table Rise Table
death is not dumb and disable
Now that your problems are over
and the world is off your shoulders
help those who you left behind
find financial peace of mind
Rise Table Rise Table
death is not dumb and disable
If the right number we hit
all our problems will split
and we will visit your grave
on every legal holiday
Those who love you want to know

the correct number to play
let them know this right away
We know your spirit is able
Death is not dumb and disable
RISE TABLE RISE TABLE

Juan
Miguel
Milagros
Olga
Manuel
All died yesterday today
and will die again tomorrow
Hating fighting and stealing
broken windows from each other
Practicing a religion without a roof
The old testament
The new testament

according to me gospel
of the internal revenue
the judge and jury and executioner
protector and eternal bill collector
Secondhand shit for sale
learn how to say Como Esta Usted

and you will make a fortune
They are dead
They are dead
and will not return from the dead
until they stop neglecting
the art of their dialogue—
for broken english lessons
to impress the mister goldsteins—
who keep them employed
as lavaplatos
porters messenger boys
factory workers maids stock clerks
shipping clerks assistant mailroom
assistant, assistant assistant

to the assistant's assistant
assistant lavaplatos and automatic
artificial smiling doormen
for the lowest wages of the ages
and rages when you demand a raise
because *is* against the company policy
to promote SPICS SPICS SPICS
Juan
died hating Miguel because Miguel's
used car was in better running condition
than his used car
Miguel
died hating Milagros because Milagros
had a color television set
and he could not afford one yet
Milagros
died hating Olga because Olga
made five dollars more on the same job
Olga
died hating Manuel because Manuel
had hit the numbers more times
than she had hit the numbers
Manuel
died hating all of them
Juan
Miguel
Milagros
and Olga
because they all spoke broken english
more fluently than he did

And now they are together
in the main lobby of the void
Addicted to silence
Off limits to the wind
Confine to worm supremacy
in long island cemetery
This is the groovy hereafter
the protestant collection box
was talking so loud and proud about

Here lies Juan
Here lies Miguel
Here lies Milagros
Here lies Olga
Here lies Manuel
who died yesterday today
and will die again tomorrow
Always broke
Always owing
Never knowing
that they are beautiful people
Never knowing
the geography of their complexion

PUERTO RICO IS A BEAUTIFUL PLACE
PUERTORRIQUEÑOS ARE A BEAUTIFUL RACE
If only they
had turned off the television
and tune into their own imaginations
If only they
had used the white supremacy bibles
for toilet paper purpose
and make their latino souls
the only religion of their race
If only they
had return to the definition of the sun
after the first mental snowstorm
on the summer of their senses
If only they
had kept their eyes open
at the funeral of their fellow employees
who came to this country to make a fortune
and were buried without underwears

Juan
Miguel
Milagros
Olga
Manuel
will right now be doing their own thing

where beautiful people sing
and dance and work together
where the wind is a stranger
to miserable weather conditions
where you do not need a dictionary
to communicate with your people
Aqui
Se Habla Español
all the time
Aqui you salute your flag first
Aqui there are no dial soap commercials
Aqui everybody smells good
Aqui tv dinners do not have a future
Aqui the men and women admire desire
and never get tired of each other
Aqui Que Pasa Power is what's happening
Aqui to be called negrito
means to be called LOVE

The Broken English Dream

It was the night
before the welfare check
and everybody sat around the table
hungry heartbroken cold confused
and unable to heal the wounds
on the dead calendar of our eyes
Old newspapers and empty beer cans
and jesus is the master of this house
Picture frames made in japan by the u.s.
was hanging out in the kitchen
which was also the livingroom
the bedroom and the linen closet
Wall to wall bad news was playing
over the radio that last week was stolen
by dying dope addicts looking for a fix
to forget that they were ever born
The slumlord came with hand grenades

in his bad breath to collect the rent
we were unable to pay six month ago
and inform us and all the empty
shopping bags we own that unless
we pay we will be evicted immediately
And the streets where the night lives
and the temperature is below zero
three hundred sixty-five days a year
will become our next home address
All the lightbulbs of our apartment
were left and forgotten at the pawnshop
across the street from the heart attack
the broken back buildings were having
Infants not born yet played hide n seek
in the cemetery of their imagination
Blind in the mind tenants were praying
for numbers to hit so they can move out
and wake up with new birth certificates
The grocery stores were outnumbered by
funeral parlors with neon signs that said
Customers wanted No experience necessary
A liquor store here and a liquor store
everywhere you looked filled the polluted
air with on the job training prostitutes
pimps and winos and thieves and abortions
White business store owners from clean-cut
plush push-button neat neighborhoods
who learn how to speak spanish in six weeks
wrote love letters to their cash registers
Vote for me! said the undertaker: I am
the man with the solution to your problems

To the united states we came
To learn how to mispell our name
To lose the definition of pride
To have misfortune on our side
To live where rats and roaches roam
in a house that is definitely not a home
To be trained to turn on television sets
To dream about jobs you will never get

To fill out welfare applications
To graduate from school without an education
To be drafted distorted and destroyed
To work full time and still be unemployed
To wait for income tax returns
and stay drunk and lose concern
for the heart and soul of our race
and the climate that produce our face

To pledge allegiance
to the flag
of the united states
of installment plans
One nation
under discrimination
for which it stands
and which it falls
with poverty injustice
and televised
firing squads
for everyone who has
the sun on the side
of their complexion

Lapiz: Pencil
Pluma: Pen
Cocina: Kitchen
Gallina: Hen

Everyone who learns this
will receive a high school equivalency diploma
a lifetime supply of employment agencies
a different bill collector for every day of the week
the right to vote for the executioner of your choice
and two hamburgers for thirty-five cents in times square

We got off
the two-engine airplane
at idlewild airport
(re-named kennedy airport

twenty years later)
with all our furniture
and personal belongings
in our back pockets

We follow the sign
that says welcome to america
but keep your hands
off the property
violators will be electrocuted
follow the garbage truck
to the welfare department
if you cannot speak english

So this is america
land of the free
for everybody
but our family
So this is america
where you wake up
in the morning
to brush your teeth
with the home relief
the leading toothpaste
operation bootstrap
promise you you will get
every time you buy
a box of cornflakes
on the lay-away plan
So this is america
land of the free
to watch the
adventures of superman
on tv if you know
somebody who owns a set
that works properly
So this is america
exploited by columbus
in fourteen ninety-two
with captain video

and lady bird johnson
the first miss subways
in the new testament
So this is america
where they keep you
busy singing
en mi casa toman bustelo
en mi casa toman bustelo

MIGUEL PIÑERO

A Lower East Side Poem

Just once before I die
I want to climb up on a
tenement sky
to dream my lungs out till
I cry
then scatter my ashes thru
the Lower East Side.

So let me sing my song tonight
let me feel out of sight
and let all eyes be dry
when they scatter my ashes thru
the Lower East Side.

From Houston to 14th Street
from Second Avenue to the mighty D
here the hustlers & suckers meet
the faggots & freaks will all get
high
on the ashes that have been scattered
thru the Lower East Side.

There's no other place for me to be
there's no other place that I can see
there's no other town around that
brings you up or keeps you down
no food little heat sweeps by
fancy cars & pimps' bars & juke saloons
& greasy spoons make my spirits fly
with my ashes scattered thru
the Lower East Side . . .

A thief, a junkie I've been
committed every known sin

Jews and Gentiles . . . bums and men
of style . . . runaway child
police shooting wild . . .
mothers' futile wails . . . pushers
making sales . . . dope wheelers
& cocaine dealers . . . smoking pot
streets are hot & feed off those who bleed to death . . .
all that's true
all that's true
all that is true
but this ain't no lie
when I ask that my ashes be scattered thru
the Lower East Side.

So here I am, look at me
I stand proud as you can see
pleased to be from the Lower East
a street-fighting man
a problem of this land
I am the Philosopher of the Criminal Mind
a dweller of prison time
a cancer of Rockefeller's ghettocide
this concrete tomb is my home
to belong to survive you gotta be strong
you can't be shy less without request
someone will scatter your ashes thru
the Lower East Side.

I don't wanna be buried in Puerto Rico
I don't wanna rest in long island cemetery
I wanna be near the stabbing shooting
gambling fighting & unnatural dying
& new birth crying
so please when I die . . .
don't take me far away
keep me nearby
take my ashes and scatter them throughout
the Lower East Side . . .

LEROY V. QUINTANA

Etymologies

I. A TROCHE MOCHE

A troche moche means assembling something
quickly, perhaps haphazardly, out
of available materials, a meal for instance.
A term Francisca used a lot.
She was the vecina, who with her husband
lived with their divorced and
unemployed sons, who came back home
to stay with their succession
of girlfriends and one abandoned
vehicle after another.

II. LONJA

A word my mother used, lonja, fat,
to describe that woman, La Piña,
and how, oh, she was so fat! she
always picked out the one
with the most fat
when shopping for a slab of bacon.

III. VOTAR

One day there's all the frijoles and hamhock
you can eat across from school
at the salvaged barracks called the parish hall.
When you get home, you tell your grandparents,
but only Grandpa is interested.
Grandma explains: this is Election Day.
When Grandpa returns a few hours later
smelling of whiskey, they argue. Democracy
has come to our side of town.

IV. MARIGUILOS

I'm a sophomore and if asking a girl out
is difficult then buying a packet
of mariguilos is worse, a thousand times
more difficult than the theorems in
plane geometry, problems I solve by
reading poetry in the back of the
classroom. I daydream a lot and though
I'm not fully aware of it, I am en-
thralled by language.

                        One day I'm
walking home with F-F-Freddy who
later gets his girlfriend pregnant
and drops out of school, and we're
talking about girls and getting them
into the backseat and naturally
mariguilos enter the conversation.
Such an odd word, I think
to myself so I ask F-F-Freddy, maybe
he knows, he's much more worldly
than I am, he buys beer
with a fake ID, he's got a girlfriend,
and gets to drive his dad's jeep.
F-F-Freddy says it's f-f-from
the old days when the p-p-pa-
chucos used to buy r-r-rubbers
with the playful brand label
M-M-Merry W-Widows, which came
to be called M-Meddy Weedows
and then mariguilos.

V. HOBOKEN

1958 or so and I'm watching *The Twilight Zone*.
A story about a losing baseball team that
at long last begins winning when
the manager acquires a new pitcher with
a blazing fastball, but the dilemma is
he knows the pitcher is a robot and
eventually the team has to forfeit all
the games, however what is really

troubling me is understanding the name
of the team the Hobo Concephers. I know
what a hobo is, but a Concepher? What a
strange name for a baseball team.
As we leave the stadium and then out
of the city I see the sign Hoboken,
and suddenly a port city on the Hudson,
a city of shipping and shipbuilding,
population 13,443, springs up in
northeastern New Jersey.

ALBERTO RÍOS

Carlos

Carlos is the name
by which loneliness
knows each of us.
Carlos the distant relative
worse off than we are
drank the medicines
of poverty and died
not in his sleep
but wide awake
clutching the red chair
because alone
his most powerful act
was this.
Carlos who lives inside
pain in each of us
knowing one woman,
it was her brother that died
and that was all,
he was dead
and everyone was sorry
because her hands
were too heavy to lift.
Carlos at this moment
wanting desperately other women
looking out through my eyes
making my tongue his
speaking my words
hearing his meanings.
Carlos who is the name of a boat
and the fishermen and the anchor.
Carlos who is the cold
and the women and the night.
Carlos who wants only

to age with each of us,
to grow old, to be happy.

Nani

Sitting at her table, she serves
the sopa de arroz to me
instinctively, and I watch her,
the absolute *mamá*, and eat words
I might have had to say more
out of embarrassment. To speak,
now-foreign words I used to speak,
too, dribble down her mouth as she serves
me albondigas. No more
than a third are easy to me.
By the stove she does something with words
and looks at me only with her
back. I am full. I tell her
I taste the mint, and watch her speak
smiles at the stove. All my words
make her smile. Nani never serves
herself, she only watches me
with her skin, her hair. I ask for more.

I watch the *mamá* warming more
tortillas for me. I watch her
fingers in the flame for me.
Near her mouth, I see a wrinkle speak
of a man whose body serves
the ants like she serves me, then more words
from more wrinkles about children, words
about this and that, flowing more
easily from these other mouths. Each serves
as a tremendous string around her,
holding her together. They speak
nani was this and that to me
and I wonder just how much of me

will die with her, what were the words
I could have been, or was. Her insides speak
through a hundred wrinkles, now, more
than she can bear, steel around her,
shouting, then, What is this thing she serves?

She asks me if I want more.
I own no words to stop her.
Even before I speak, she serves.

The Vietnam Wall

I
Have seen it
And I like it: The magic,
The way like cutting onions
It brings water out of nowhere.
Invisible from one side, a scar
Into the skin of the ground
From the other, a black winding
Appendix line.
        A dig.
        An archaeologist can explain.
The walk is slow at first
Easy, a little black marble wall
Of a dollhouse,
A smoothness, a shine
The boys in the street want to give.
One name. And then more
Names, long lines, lines of names until
They are the shape of the U.N. building
Taller than I am: I have walked
Into a grave.
And everything I expect has been taken away, like that,
    quick:
        The names are not alphabetized.
        They are in the order of dying,
        An alphabet of—somewhere—screaming.

I start to walk out. I almost leave
But stop to look up names of friends,
My own name. There is somebody
Severiano Ríos.
Little kids do not make the same noise
Here, junior high school boys don't run
Or hold each other in headlocks.
No rules, something just persists
Like pinching on St. Patrick's Day
Every year for no green.
      No one knows why.
Flowers are forced
Into the cracks
Between sections.
Men have cried
At this wall.
I have
Seen them.

Rabbits and Fire

Everything's been said
But one last thing about the desert,
And it's awful: During brush fires in the Sonoran desert,
Brush fires that happen before the monsoon and in the great,
Deep, wide, and smothering heat of the hottest months,
The longest months,
The hypnotic, immeasurable lulls of August and July—
During these summer fires, jackrabbits—
Jackrabbits and everything else
That lives in the brush of the rolling hills,
But jackrabbits especially—
Jackrabbits can get caught in the flames,
No matter how fast and big and strong and sleek they are.
And when they're caught,
Cornered in and against the thick
Trunks and thin spines of the cactus,
When they can't back up any more,

When they can't move, the flame—
It touches them,
And their fur catches fire.
Of course, they run away from the flame,
Finding movement even when there is none to be found,
Jumping big and high over the wave of fire, or backing
Even harder through the impenetrable
Tangle of hardened saguaro
And prickly pear and cholla and barrel,
But whichever way they find,
What happens is what happens: They catch fire
And then bring the fire with them when they run.
They don't know they're on fire at first,
Running so fast as to make the fire
Shoot like rocket engines and smoke behind them,
But then the rabbits tire
And the fire catches up,
Stuck onto them like the needles of the cactus,
Which at first must be what they think they feel on their
    skins.
They've felt this before, every rabbit.
But this time the feeling keeps on.
And of course, they ignite the brush and dried weeds
All over again, making more fire, all around them.
I'm sorry for the rabbits.
And I'm sorry for us
To know this.

LUIS J. RODRIGUEZ

The Monster

It erupted into our lives:
Two guys in jeans shoved it through the door
—heaving & grunting & biting lower lips.

A large industrial sewing machine.
We called it "the monster."

It came on a winter's day,
rented out of mother's pay.
Once in the living room
the walls seemed to cave in around it.

Black footsteps to our door
brought heaps of cloth for Mama to sew.
Noises of war burst out of the living room.
Rafters rattled. Floors farted
—the radio going into static
each time the needle ripped into fabric.

Many nights I'd get up from bed,
wander squinty-eyed down a hallway
and peer through a dust-covered blanket
to where Mama and the monster
did nightly battle.

I could see Mama through the yellow haze
of a single light bulb.
She slouched over the machine.
Her eyes almost closed.
Her hair in disheveled braids;

each stitch binding her life
to scraps of cloth.

Jarocho Blues

You came with long luxurious hair,
black as the deep tint of heart-blood,
almost blue.

You came with a smile and a guitar,
groping for a song:
Una nueva canción.
Exitos de Augustín Lara.
Jarocho blues.

You came with a tequila bottle
and sat cross-legged on a rug of colors.
I watched and you sang,
the lit air carried a litany
of women's stories.
Your voice a silk veil
over dripping candles,
bringing back family songs
over *copas de vino.*

Your voice and the night of day.

A mahogany wood table held an overturned glass.
You sat next to it and stretched the chords
over my eyes, strummed the strings
into infinity.

You sang and I fell into a notated dream
with a chorus of psalms drenched in sorrows.
You sang and the bougainvillea of youth
came to me in torrents. You sang
and tears cut a path down the wall,
blanketing me in a spell of ointments.
You sang and the tequila burned
the edges of my mouth.

I never wanted it to end, your singing.
A guitar across your lap. Your eyes closed.

Waves of hair over your shoulders
and strands stuck to sweat across your face.

You sang and I died. Dead for all the broken men.
Dead for all who ever stopped believing.
Dead for all who ever thought women
were less than the tint of this blood,
less than the warmth of our birth waters,
less than our deepest cry.

Dead for all who ever hungered to be touched
by the flesh of such a voice.

The Rabbi and the Cholo

The Rabbi appeared, black dressed and uncertain,
like a shadow of doubt. My world
then was perfectly squared: I was at war
with humanity, the Rabbi indistinguishable
from the enemy. I had the world
between my teeth,
scratching at betrayed skies,
seeking deliverance in mortar and brick,
behind tattered sneers.
I shifted the firmament
through thick fingers,
dust in the grooves of skin,
between eyes,
between sighs.

The Rabbi's words broke through
hatred's mask, peeling into
something calm, soft.
He spoke for the centuries:
Of nomadic sons, Hebrew invocations,
desert songs and tattooed numbers.
The Rabbi carried everything for everybody.
He said he feared me, that he had to know me.

His fear and my hatred somehow
found fugue and notation,
music and reverberation.

Rabbi and Cholo—the distance as great
as those between L.A. settlements,
different countries really.
He listened to my stories
like a voyeur of myths: Stories of scaled fences,
of stray bullets between blemished palm trees,
of failed robberies and failed courage,
of carnal intimacies with women
dark as me, risking all for the voice
to wrap the flesh like perpetual rain.
The Rabbi and the Cholo. We strolled
the callused streets, across ravines and hills,
through back roads of mud
and rotting cars, places he never knew,
taking in the stinging odors
of urine stains on stucco walls,
of *carnitas* at midnight stalls,
of bloodied roosters in cages
and love-drunk men groping at running ballads
lamenting loss between shots
of earth-born tequila.

I waded through Fairfax corridors,
through hatted men in ancient
arguments, through bagel shops and Synagogue
doorways, dazed at the Mediterranean
gazes of girls and their well-dressed
Brentwood mothers. I stood there
in starched baggy Khaki pants and Pendleton
flannel shirt, buttoned only at the top,
with bandanna and skull cap above my eyes,
among the bearded Semite faces
in black pants and suits, who appeared
like 1920s Lower East Side
or Boyle Heights: Nothing here

but escape,
exile and escape.

One night, at a "brotherhood" camp, the Rabbi
witnessed me break down, for the first time
since I was eleven: I mourned for all
the dead homies, for the women who walked,
for family and the wounds of silence.
The Rabbi sat down next to me and said:
"I don't know how to cry like that."

The Rabbi and the Cholo:
There was no closing of parting waters here.
I was laughter and sun, vessel
of swollen tales, someone who could shout
when enough is never enough:
My inner-life was close to the touch;
the Rabbi had his layered beneath
charcoal cloth, tradition, voices . . .
plea and birthright.

One summer we gazed at the ocean
that caressed Venice Beach.
I focused on the waves,
the froth, the wreckage of sea;
the Rabbi took in the deep lull
and blue mass at the distance.
In a hasty moment, on that moist shore,
severed from history, I responded
as if this "too will pass."
The issues were immediate, my enemies close,
nothing vast like time:
My grief was simple then, pure,
Definite—now.
The Rabbi was nothing if not history,
time for him an immense divide;
his grief, forever.

LEO ROMERO

The Goat's Cry

My grandmother took the young goat
and slit its throat
Delicate cords cut in the glass air
I fled from the sharp knife
from the gush of hot blood
which had stained my grandmother's hands
which the earth drank greedily
In the air the goat's cry
shattered clouds
opened and closed blue doors
I cowered inside the house
where I ran after seeing the sun's face
in the blade of the knife
saw the sun drinking the blood
which was so warm, which burned

I listened to the incessant crying
The goat's agony
filling the sky like smoke
I was helpless and trembling
listening to the severed throat
to the blood cry
elastic cords snapping
A cry jagged as broken glass
until the goat's cry finally left the sky
and my grandmother was calling me
to wash my hands
to drink of the blood
the still hot blood
which she held in a pan
A pool of life
bright life

BENJAMIN ALIRE SÁENZ

The Fifth Dream: Bullets and Deserts and Borders

A man is walking toward me.
He is alone.
He has been walking through the desert.
He has been walking for days.
He has been walking for years.
His lips are dry
and cracking
like a piece of spent soil.
I can see his open wounds.
His eyes are dark
as a Tanzanian night.

He discovers I have been watching
though he has long ceased to care
what others see. I ask him
his name, ask him what
has brought him here, ask
him to name
his angers and his loves.
                    He opens his mouth
to speak—
but just as his words hit
the air, a bullet
pierces his heart.

                    I do not know
the country
of this man's birth. I only know
that he is from
the desert. He has the worn
look of despair
that only rainless days can give.
That is all I know.

He might have been born
in Jerusalem. He might have been
born in Egypt. He might
have been the direct descendant
of a pharaoh. His name
might have been Ptolemy.
His name might have been
Moses. Or Jesus.
Or Muhammad.
He might have been a prophet.
He might have been a common thief.
He might have been a terrorist
or he might have been just
another man destined
to be worn down
by the ceaseless, callous storms.
He might have come
from a country called Afghanistan.
He might have been from Mexico.

He might have been
looking for a well.
His dreams were made of water.
His lips touching
water—yes—
that is what he was dreaming.

I can still hear the sound of the bullet.

*

The man reappears.
It does not matter
that I do not want him
in my dreams. He is
searching through the rubble
of what was once his house.
There are no tears on his
face. His lips still yearn
for water.

*

I wake. I begin to believe
that the man has escaped
from Auschwitz. Perhaps he sinned
against the Nazis or because
he was a collaborator or because
he was Jewish
or because he loved another man.
He has come
to the desert looking
for a place he can call home.
I fall asleep trying
to give the man a name.

*

The man is now
walking toward a city
that is no longer there.

*

I am the man.
I see clearly. I am
awake now.
It is me. It has taken me
a long time to know this.
I am a Palestinian.
I am an Israeli.
I am a Mexican.
I am an American.
I am a busboy in a tall building
that is about to collapse.
I am attending a Seder and I am
tasting my last bitter
herb. I am a boy who has learned
all his prayers. I am bowing
toward Mecca in a house
whose roof will soon collapse
on my small frame.
I am a servant. I shine shoes
and wash the feet
of the rich. I am an illegal.
I am a Mexican who hates all Americans.

I am an American who hates all Mexicans.
I am a Palestinian who hates all Israelis.
I am an Israeli who hates all Palestinians.
I am a Palestinian Jew who hates himself.

I am dying of all this knowledge.
I am dying of thirst.
I am a river that will never know water again.
I am becoming dust.

*

I am walking toward my home.
Mexico City? Washington?
Mecca? Jerusalem?
I don't know. I don't know.

*

I am walking in the desert.

I see that I am reaching a border.

A bullet is piercing my heart.

RICARDO SÁNCHEZ

canto

oye,

    pimpo, talón,
    bato loco, cabrón

now
    reflejos de años pasados
    en el refuego juareño

imapout mymadness runtogether

night after night
hustling
looking for quick nirvanas . . .

avenida juárez
calle mariscál

        IMPALA CLUB, 1963,
        cuando la gente real
        espresaba víscera y entrañas
        i was jovencito yet
        bebiendo sauza con limón

        and

        tristemente sentía
        los trastornos
        of youth spent lost
        dentro refuego y desmadre

        years have passed
        multitudes have since

pressed down
my madnesses

new dimensions
come and go
like naked majas
seeking immortality
cloaked in immorality

mea culpa, mea culpa
o preacher-man,
gelatinous whippings
and globular sins

and the word emanates from the angustia y chingo, chingo,
chingo chingo, chingo, chingo, chingo . . . y me chingan
todavía.

GARY SOTO

Salt

para Juan Rodriguez

I

There was nothing to eat, father.
We were sent out, sticks in our hands,
Some stones in our pockets. *Conejo*, mother said,
Frog or catfish from the Mendota canal.
The road was long with afternoon shadows.
We walked toward an irrigation pond,
Hoping to bring something back.
The day was clear, the sun dime bright.
When the wind turned a loose paper grape tray,
It flew like a kite. We went over
There, and just farther than *there*.
I licked my wrist—coming up from my skin, salt.

II

Some way from home, I threw my stone,
Juan waved his sack like a cape.
We ran toward some cows, jumped the fence,
And dared each other to wring their ears.
Not me, not Juan, not me again.
The cows were licking salt rock and rock.
Juan shooed them away. He chipped
A piece off and we sucked until our tongues
Were stropped raw and maybe bleeding.
What was lost that day, the salt gave back.

Mexicans Begin Jogging

At the factory I worked
In the fleck of rubber, under the press
Of an oven yellow with flame,
Until the border patrol opened
Their vans and my boss waved for us to run.
"Over the fence, Soto," he shouted,
And I shouted that I was American.
"No time for lies," he said, and pressed
A dollar in my palm, hurrying me
Through the back door.

Since I was on his time, I ran
And became the wag to a short tail of Mexicans—
Ran past the amazed crowds that lined
The street and blurred like photographs, in rain.
I ran from that industrial road to the soft
Houses where people paled at the turn of an autumn sky.
What could I do but yell *vivas*
To baseball, milkshakes, and those sociologists
Who would clock me
As I jog into the next century
On the power of a great, silly grin.

Bulosan, 1935

By train
You rocked past the small towns
Where you might have married
White and worked Mexican,

Or become lost in the Chinatowns
In yellow, the tongue,
The brow, and the cocked finger—
Yellow and Filipino
Shuffle, the *carabao* walk,

The great arc of urine
Streaming in the cold.

Instead, it was L.A.
A hard cough, and blood on a shirt sleeve,
Pillow, and bedsheet
In a room narrow with sunlight.

At the table,
Your eyes two cinders in a fire,
You wrote, but nothing stopped
The black loaf of lung, the axe
Handle crossed hard over your brother.
You wrote
America is somewhere—
Now touch my hand

Until you dreamed you were a bundle
Of rags slouching
In a doorway,
A bundle poked by a cane and lifted
To a new land.
Bulosan, America slips seaward,
Swallows angle south out of reach,
And we step homeward to find
Our lives blue before TV,
Reddened with drink.

Tonight I think of that boxcar
That tunneled south
And you on blackened knuckles and bad knees.

With a finger you were mapping the ox
In the arced horizon, those stars
Drifting west to your country
When nothing could be darker
Than its pull from you.

Fresno's Westside Blues

It's Sunday morning.
The last white man turns black at the alley's end.
If he marched with his arms swinging,
The right sleeve of his jacket would fall off.
He's that poor.

Michael, the security, blinks his flashlight against his palm—
It's something to do. Business has taken a day off.
The bananas fall out of their skins.
Apples soften. In the closed meat shop
The tinker-toy snout of a pig drools,
And the ropes of chorizo are big enough to skip through.
Mexican music makes you want to you rub your eyes
For a good cry.

You can walk on glass, suffer,
And hear, "*Oye, carnal*, got soda money for me?"
The *vato* is sitting on a stripped bike, going nowhere.

But there's the tinkle of a bell on a store door.
There's laughter coming from Suki's Nails and Feet.
And look at Javier, with glue and paper,
Making *piñatas* behind a chain-link fence—
The beer-bellied Spider-Man will take a birthday beating.

A breeze twists through the trees,
One jammed meter throws up its expired red flag.
When the bell at the Mexican Baptist Church sounds,
Huge black birds fed on dropped burgers honk from wires.
They bow their heads and cast shadows over feral cats.

What is meant by escape?
You could be any dog hugging an ancient building for shade.
When you turn the corner, the knife-bright sun cuts
    ruthlessly
The shadow from your already mangy body.

CARMEN TAFOLLA

Mujeres del Rebozo Rojo

Who are we
las mujeres del rebozo rojo
who are always waiting for the light
hungry for the pink drops of morning
on the night's sky
searching for the sparkle of creation
of beginning
of life
on the dawn's edge
trying so hard
to open our eyes

Who are we
las mujeres del rebozo rojo
to want to reach and stretch and spread
and grow beyond our limits
yawning
pulling up our heads
pushing out our lungs
arching out our arms
resting only when in growth
transition
transformation
wanting only to be and
to become

to unfold our lives as if they were
rebozos
   revealing
      our inner colors
         the richness of our texture
            the strength of our weave
            the history of our making

opening to
   all our fullness
      blossoms set free
spreading our wings to the reach of the sky
   and awakening
     to who
       we really
         are

EDWIN TORRES

[no yoyo]

(he's from New York) . . . (from Puerto Rico New York) . . .

(he's a new Rican) . . . (what they call) . . . (a Riqueño) . . .

(bein' New) . . . (or Trigueño) . . . (Speakin' New) . . . (or Rican) . . .

(a Nuyo seekin' No yorker) . . . (is he New) . . . (or a Porter) . . .

(a port) . . . (of sherry) . . . (Cheri Cheri) . . .

(Porto Puerto) . . . (York, oh) . . . (Yoko?) . . . (el Coco) . . .

(que hablas) . . . (se habla Coco?) . . . (no'Co) . . . (no'City) . . .

(port of no'City Rican) . . . (a Port o' Ric'er is called) . . .

(a bo'Ricuer) . . . (a Boricua) . . . (a boring'wha?) . . . (a bore) . . .

(this is boring) . . . (into my yawner) . . . (what chu saying) . . .

(what New saying) . . . (the new Say) . . . (be the new City) . . .

(of York) . . . (a yorkie) . . . (a pit) . . . (a bull) . . . (a toro) . . .

(a To'rres) . . . (a No'res) . . . (a city nono) . . . (a city Yorker, uncorked) . . .

(a boozer?) . . . (a bozo) . . . (a New bozo) . . . (yo soy bozo) . . .

(in the YO zone, si) . . . (yo soy the New yo) . . .

(that's some New yo, bro) . . . (yo Rican, si) . . . (soy No Rican) . . .

(he's no Rican) . . . (from no Ricua) . . . (he's no You) . . .

(no Yo) . . . (no I) . . . (the I) . . . (in I) . . . (is the New No) . . .

(I be) . . . (some a dat) . . . (New No) . . . (from No Ricua, bro)

LUIS ALBERTO URREA

The First Lowrider in Heaven

I am thinking of the vato I went to see in his coffin.

He was ugly, flaco, tattooed, long-haired, laid-out.

He had on a suit.

Looked pissed off.

No, he looked sad.

And pissed off.

The way vatos look right before they kick your ass.

Muy chucote, el buey.

Y bien jodido, too, porque he was bien dead.

So his ass was already kicked.

I looked in on him—he smelled like medicine and cotton.

I didn't even know him.

I was there for political support.

Homeboys sniffling, tears filling their blue teardrop tattoos.

Rucas dressed in wedding, baptism, quinceañera dresses.

And the dead guy lying there, sharp in his suit.

Snug in silver-white satin.

Shot himself in the head.

Old women, cowboy-booted fathers, crying over him.

No telling now, in his boxed sainthood, if he smoked crack,
      gang-banged, carried shivs, hit his mother, kicked
      the dog.

Death had purified him.

He was now an angel.

Low-riding the clouds.

Put the gun in his mouth.

His lover, you know.

Told him her love for him had turned to smoke.

They went to a movie first, y la loca sent him away. Forever.

He walked in circles.

He had no words for the poems he needed to send.

He could only say, *What's the pedo, homeys?*

There were no words.

So he kissed the round hole of the .44.

Right where her kisses had gone.

Put it where her tongue flicked spit off his.

Pinche love, ese, they were saying.

A magnum, just like Dirty Harry: tear a hole through an
      engine block, vato—I heard them whispering.

Taste of gun oil where her bubblegum breath had blown.

Her insistent flavor of smoke, salt, lemon.

He had her panties in a drawer, pobrecito.

He had her letter in his pocket.

I looked at his eyes; boy, they sure were dry now.

Then I noticed the pillow.

No indentation.

Smooth silver satin.

All shiny and curved.

His head went as far as his ears.

Beyond that, feathers.

That ruca he loved was in flight.

She took with her the odors of her body.

She took the funny loops of her writing.

She took the Easter menudo breakfast with her papi.

She took their favorite television show—he went from
        channel to channel, couldn't find it anywhere.

She took the lipstick, the Secret roll-on, the Tic-Tacs, the way
        she cried out when she came, the way she said his
            name when
        she awoke, the sea coast of her hair, the swoop of her
        belly, the babymouth of her navel, the beautiful
            lies she

believed and whispered in his ear—words like familia, always, soul-mates.

He liked that soul-mates onda.

She took off through the engine block of his dreams.

His mind held tight in her fingers.

Flavor of steel and powder.

Smoke rings followed her.

Aloft.

ROBERT VASQUEZ

At the Rainbow

for Linda, Theresa, and Phyllis

At fifteen, shaving by then, I passed
for eighteen and got in, in where alcoves
breathed with ill-matched lovers—
my sisters among them—who massed
and spun out their jagged, other selves.
I saw the rhythmic dark, year over

year, discharge their flare: they scored
my memory, adrift now in the drifting place.
Often I watched a slow song empty
the tabled sidelines; even the old poured
out, some dragged by wives, and traced
odd box shapes their feet repeated. *Plenty*

and *poor:* thoughts that rose as the crowd
rose—my sisters too—in the smoked air.
They rise on. . . . They say saxophones
still start up Friday nights, the loud,
troubled notes wafting out from where
I learned to lean close and groaned

into girls I chose—no, took—and meant it.
In the Rainbow Ballroom in Fresno
I sulked, held hands, and wheeled among
the deep-bodied ones who reinvented
steps and turns turned fast or slow,
and this body sang, man to woman, song to song.

ALMA LUZ VILLANUEVA

Child's Laughter

I pay $10 to enter Taos Pueblo,
1,000-year-old earth
homes—I stand in
the center of a

circle, the spirits
pass through me clear
as   wind   water   clouds   rain—
a young man welcomes

me, a woman my age greets
me, a man selling jewelry has
my grandmother's maiden name,
LUJÁN (on a sign), yet it all feels

dead, staged, until I
come to a singing
creek . . . a young boy
(who looks like my son

at that age) smiles as his
dog rolls in the cool
water on a hot day. "He
likes the water," the boy

laughs, "I don't blame
him," I laugh back . . .
the sign says, "Don't
pet the animals" as the dog

follows me, I pet his wet nose—
I follow a dirt trail, sit by

the singing creek, a sign
says "Stay out of water" . . .

I just rest my eyes on it.
A grandfather speaks to his
horse behind me in Tiwa,
a language never to be

written or recorded, I'm
told, the language sounds
like   wind   water   clouds   rain
child's laughter . . .

As I stand to leave,
I see in bright
2 p.m. sun, bleached white
pristine men's underwear

on a hanger by
itself—I wonder if a
tourist took a photo of
real Indian underwear,

I laugh softly
and leave as I can
not bring myself to buy (or sell)
the wind I breathe (this moment).

To my ancestors, Yaqui to Pueblo—
Taos Pueblo, New Mexico
August 2000

TINO VILLANUEVA

Scene from the Movie GIANT

What I have from 1956 is one instant at the Holiday
Theater, where a small dimension of a film, as in
A dream, became the feature of the whole. It
Comes toward the end . . . the café scene, which
Reels off a slow spread of light, a stark desire

To see itself once more, though there is, at times,
No joy in old time movies. It begins with the
Jingling of bells and the plainer truth of it:
That the front door to a roadside café opens and
Shuts as the Benedicts (Rock Hudson and Elizabeth

Taylor), their daughter Luz, and daughter-in-law
Juana and grandson Jordy, pass through it not
Unobserved. Nothing sweeps up into an actual act
Of kindness into the eyes of Sarge, who owns this
Joint and has it out for dark-eyed Juana, weary

Of too much longing that comes with rejection.
Juana, from barely inside the door, and Sarge,
Stout and unpleased from behind his counter, clash
Eye-to-eye, as time stands like heat. Silence is
Everywhere, acquiring the name of hatred and Juana

Cannot bear the dread—the dark-jowl gaze of Sarge
Against her skin. Suddenly: bells go off again.
By the quiet effort of walking, three Mexican-
Types step in, whom Sarge refuses to serve . . .
Those gestures of his, those looks that could kill

A heart you carry in memory for years. A scene from
The past has caught me in the act of living: even
To myself I cannot say except with worried phrases

Upon a paper, how I withstood arrogance in a gruff
Voice coming with the deep-dyed colors of the screen;

How in the beginning I experienced almost nothing to
Say and now wonder if I can ever live enough to tell
The after-tale. I remember this and I remember myself
Locked into a back-row seat—I am a thin, flickering,
Helpless light, local-looking, unthought of at fourteen.

V.
HOWLING AS THEY CAME

STEVEN ALVAREZ

1992 / 5th sun / our present

honkey-tonk gringo corrido Gila Bend Corridor Bar / Gila
Bend / AZtlán

s   t   r   u   m

"for Chaley Chastitellez than than tharán*
"that brave ballsy Xingadx
"told those Xicanxs
"working for la migra
"los vendidos agringadxs:
"'in Makesicko love
"'germinates w/ the boca
"'begins w/ the lengua
"'& mouth the size of Puebla
"'w/ lips like Sinaloas
"'& how beautiful hips / two Chihuahuas—'
            "¡ Z á s!
"& proceeded to snap each of their necks

*as they still sing of him in cantinas & countrystores. In those ranchos where
viejitos gather at cool dusk w/ Juanie Walker rojo passed around clockwise
a-smokin & a-listenin to old canciones & cuentos of other days. "He breaks
before he bends—& cuts a dashin figure" dijeron these old bastards. "A man
a man 'twas a man." They also make albures abt his "stuffing his own shaved
scrotum in his mouth puro huevón ja ja JA." Órale: "another LatinMex
Dedalus—what this world needs eh" / "slightly Byronic in slouch / more
Oneigen in shape" / "belonging to that most vile category of social fauna
/ human rubbish" / yes at times / "claims life hostile to him" / "& so
harbors brown resentment" / "mapped betweeness folks in this business
call it / & where Dedalus had god & Ireland / he's got Guadalupan Aztecs
/ & Massico" / "& both shape poetry" / "when born his tío sd 'this pinche
huevón will be a poet prophet—look at the size of his eyes' / & right then still
slippery w/ his birthjuices his Tío Pancho lifted that chavalito & dedicated
him to the Sun & to that flowery death of poetry / so sure enough he's here
sung abt / & sings too" /

"one by one w/ swift judochops
     "¡Z á s! ¡Z á s! ¡Z á s! ¡Z á s! ¡Z á s!

"qué hombre"

     brasstipped snakeskin boots tap

        & pouncing taxidermed ocelot lunges
    away from woodpanelled wall

"man's man / & for his Tío Pancho / a hero
"& for his Xóchitl Flores the salvador himself . . ."

     accordion accordion accordion

ELOISA AMEZCUA

The Witch Reads Me My Birthchart

she says the planets & stars show that I'm too good at being
    alone
I have unresolved traumas from past lives it is true
there were difficulties during my delivery even in the womb
I had a bad feeling cord around my throat as I tried
to make passage forced into this world or rather out of
    another
by extraction the witch asks if I often feel guilty
asks if I try to heal those around me despite finding it
    difficult
to bond with anyone other than myself
she wants to know about my childhood memories
if I'm alone in them
& I admit I stop listening though I can still hear
the untroubled tone in her voice vowels elongated
mouth full of sounds like spandex bursting at the seams
I want to go back to the stars we've strayed so far from the
    planets
she says there's much to learn about my sources of pain
the gaping wound I will try to alleviate for the rest of my life
I want to touch her long hair as if it were my hair
I want to convince her I believe in everything she believes
but I demand too much of faith
like apples in the market I inspect the curves & creases
put them back at the slightest sign of bruising

FRANCISCO ARAGÓN

Nicaragua in a Voice

More than the poems
—the fruits that sang
their juices; dolls, feverish,
dreaming of nights,

city streets—for me it was
the idle chat *between* the poems:
cordial, intimate almost . . .
like a river's murmur

as if a place—León,
Granada—could speak,
whistle, inhabit
a timbre . . . as if, closing

my eyes, I had it again,
once more within reach:
his voice—my father
unwell, won't speak.

WILLIAM ARCHILA

Duke Ellington, Santa Ana, El Salvador, 1974

He paces the cool, dusty classroom,
hands in his pockets, rows of chairs,
sixth-grade children looking straight
at him, watching his big-band walk.

At the blackboard, he turns
and breaks the silence.
"Instead of crossing an Oriental garden,
picture a desert under a devil sun."

He snaps his fingers two plus one
as if to say one more time.
We shout back a demented version of *Caravan*,
crashing cymbals, drums, bent horns—
muffled rhythms from a line of saxophones.

Edwin Martínez gets on his feet, leans over
the music stand and tortures the trumpet,
pouring all his memories of Egypt from history class.
Douglas Díaz slaps the bongos
exactly the same way he beats on
cans of coffee and milk at home.

Señor Ellington claps his hands along,
dancing a two-step blues, stomping
in the center of everyone like a traffic cop
conducting a busy city street.
Before break he will tell us
stories of a smoky blue spot
called the Cotton Club.
We will learn all the Harlem rhapsodies
from the Latin Quarter up to 125th Street.
He will swing the piano keys, a syncopated phrase
and we will listen: no need to study war no more.

He could be my grandfather,
black boy from Chalatenango—
indigo-blue family
from the Caribbean through Honduras.
He could be the one to write
a tone parallel to Sonsonate,
a trombone to roll to the wheels
of a cart, the wrinkled man,
toothless, pulling his corn.

More than a Congo drum in a cabaret,
more than a top hat and tails before a piano,
I want him to come back,
his orchestra to pound the doors
of a ballroom by the side of a lake.
I want the cracked paint to peel off the walls,
lights to go dim, floors to disappear,
a trumpet to growl,
my country to listen.

RICHARD BLANCO

COMO TÚ / *LIKE YOU* / *LIKE ME*

{for the D.A.C.A. DREAMers and all our nation's immigrants}

> *. . . my veins don't end in me*
> *but in the unanimous blood*
> *of those who struggle for life . . .*

> *. . . mis venas no terminan en mí*
> *sino en la sange unánime*
> *de los que luchan por la vida . . .*
> —*ROQUE DALTON*, Como tú

Como tú, I question history's blur in my eyes
each time I face a mirror. Like a mirror, I gaze
into my palm a wrinkled map I still can't read,
my lifeline an unnamed road I can't find, can't
trace back to the fork in my parents' trek
that cradled me here. *Como tú*, I woke up to
this dream of a country I didn't choose, that
didn't choose me—trapped in the nightmare
of its hateful glares. *Como tú*, I'm also from
the lakes and farms, waterfalls and prairies
of another country I can't fully claim either.
Como tú, I am either a mirage living among
these faces and streets that raised me here,
or I'm nothing, a memory forgotten by all
I was taken from and can't return to again.

Like memory, at times I wish I could erase
the music of my name in Spanish, at times
I cherish it, and despise my other syllables
clashing in English. *Como tú*, I want to speak
of myself in two languages at once. Despite
my tongues, no word defines me. Like words,
I read my footprints like my past, erased by

waves of circumstance, my future uncertain
as wind. Like the wind, *como tú*, I carry songs,
howls, whispers, thunder's growl. Like thunder,
I'm a foreign-borne cloud that's drifted here,
I'm lightning, and the balm of rain. *Como tú*,
our blood rains for the dirty thirst of this land.
Like thirst, like hunger, we ache with the need
to save ourselves, and our country from itself.

DANIEL BORZUTZKY

Let Light Shine Out of Darkness

I live in a body that does not have enough light in it

For years, I did not know that I needed to have more light

Once, I walked around my city on a dying morning and a
decomposing body approached me and asked me why I had
no light

I knew this decomposing body

All that remained of it were teeth, bits of bone, a hand

It came to me and said: There is no light that comes out of
your body

I did not know at the time that there should have been light
in my body

It's not that I am dead

It's not that I am translucent

It's that you cannot know you need something if you do not
know it is missing

Which is not to say that for years I did not ask for this light

Once, I even said to the body I live with: I think I need more
light in my body, but I really did not take this seriously as a
need, as something I deserved to have

I said: I think I need for something blue or green to shine
from my rib cage

Other times when I am talking about lightness I am talking about breath and space and movement

For it is hard to move in a body so congested with images of mutilation

Did you hear the one about the illegal immigrant who electrocuted his employee's genitals? Did you hear the one about the boy in Chicago whose ear was bitten off when he crossed a border he did not know existed?

I want to give you more room to move so I am trying to carve a space, with light, for you to walk a bit more freely

This goes against my instincts, which are to tie you down, to tie you to me, to bind us by the wrist the belly the neck and to look directly into your mouth, to make you open your mouth and speak the vocabulary of obliteration right into your tongue your veins your blood

I stop on a bridge over the train tracks and consider the history of the chemical-melting of my skin

Once, when I poured a certain type of acid on my arm I swore I saw a bright yellow gas seep out of my body

Once, my teeth glowed sick from the diseased snow they had shoved into my mouth when they wanted me to taste for myself, to bring into my body the sorrows of the rotten carcass economy

Once, I dreamwrote that I found my own remains in a desert that was partially in Chile and partially in Arizona

Was I a disappeared body, tossed out of an airplane by a bureaucrat-soldier-compatriot or was I a migrant body who died from dehydration while crossing the invisible line between one civilization and another

I was part of a team of explorers   we were searching for our
own bodies

In the desert I found my feet and I put them in a plastic
bag and photographed them, cataloged them, weighed
and measured them and when I was finished with the
bureaucratization of my remains I lay down in the sand and
asked one of my colleagues to jam a knife into my belly

She obliged

But when the blade entered my skin it was as if my belly were
a water balloon

Water shot into the air

My skin ripped into hundreds of pieces and I watched as the
water covered the feet of my colleagues who were here to
document their disappearances and decomposition

It was at this moment that I saw light in my body   not sun
over the sand but a drip of soft blue on a piece of skin that
had fallen off my body and dissolved into its own resistance

RAFAEL CAMPO

My Voice

To cure myself of wanting Cuban songs,
I wrote a Cuban song about the need
For people to suppress their fantasies,
Especially unhealthy ones. The song
Began by making reference to the sea,
Because the sea is like a need so great
And deep it never can be swallowed. Then
The song explores some common myths
About the Cuban people and their folklore:
The story of a little Carib boy
Mistakenly abandoned to the sea;
The legend of a bird who wanted song
So desperately he gave up flight; a queen
Whose strength was greater than a rival king's.
The song goes on about morality,
And then there is a line about the sea,
How deep it is, how many creatures need
Its nourishment, how beautiful it is
To need. The song is ending now, because
I cannot bear to hear it any longer.
I call this song of needful love my voice.

BRENDA CÁRDENAS

Report from the Temple of Confessions in Old Chicano English

*(after an installation by Guillermo Gómez-Peña
and Roberto Sifuentes)*

Se cruzan canyons   en el templo de confessions.
Language lies   across the barbed lines,
piles of its limbs   pierced y pinchados.
Risky recordings   reveal what we think
of the Other   offering his objectified body
to the river rats   who ride his wet back,
the coro de coyotes   who crave his flesh,
the wheyfaced who   whisper their sin in his ear,
the translators who trap   and trade his tongue,
la raza who receive him,   la raza who repel him.

In this chamber the chill   of chicken flesh—
pollito mojado   picoso y picado,
the black body   bag of the repatriated.
Here the distorted words   of debutantes y do-gooders,
of know-no-betters   y neo-Nazis,
of Beowulfs and other   born-again beasts,
of sandaled sombreros   sleeping under cacti,
of Machiavellian   mentes y mouths
of anthropological   autoethnography,
of pretend pachucas   peeling their layers,
of preachers and poets   with puckered lips
of the misused multi-   cultural machinery,
of the Hispanic hodgepodge   hiding their indio,
of the Quetzalcoatls   concealing their conqueror
de la migra meando   marking its turf.

Here, the hemistiched   hemispheres blend,
a vacuum of voices   absorbed in the velvet

paintings of slick
of the Aztec icon
tripping and turning
of the cyber-cholo
The vato loco's liquid
over borders, their blurred
calling us to come
jaula de joda
the table turned
lit with votives
breakfast bowl
squirming to free

y sexy santos,
at the altar of Aztlán
transvestite warrior,
stripping down—¡Simón!
eye lures us
tumbling barriers,
stare into the cage—
aquí juntándonos—
and tacked to the wall,
licking our luscious
of cucarachas on their backs
their feet and fly.

SANDRA M. CASTILLO

La Fiesta del Globo

Surrounded by the red and blue balloons
that will name our homemade video
when it arrives in Havana,
we drink to primo Alfonso,
the archer, who has just arrived
in time to drink to the new year,
to those on the island we imagine
will see us dancing away the distance
with him, el exiliado, the Pan Am Games deserter,
the stranger who has joined us here,
our exile, our unexpected Miami lives,
to the video camera watching us,
an audience of Donates lining up
to touch the past we drape
with the thick plastic of nostalgia,
the artifice of a reconstructed life
with our Cuba, the Cuba of convenient memory,
those we were twenty-five years ago
when we left him,
a falling afternoon in Artemisa,
a cellophane sky en la Calle Céspedes,
the front porch of Madrina's house
with its connecting doors that opened
to rooms, to other lives,
to whispers of winning back time,
our lives from the Revolution,
of leaving the island
because soon,
he, too, will forget
who he was there.

ADRIAN CASTRO

When Hearing Bàtá Drums . . .

Atandá they say
had the secret
(wrapped in red cloth)
to speak in goatskin
beat a message spiraling into sound
straight to the ears which woke destiny
red rooster's first flutter of wings
first cackle
not wake yet
—the rise of early freedom
  when he woke at four a.m.
    kneeled once on knee
   leather strip in hand
    reciting history
      praise names to remind that we came
        from somewhere

    When we entered our hollowed tunnel
Atandá was standing at the end
hands callused
when we heard the guttural sounds
  the ki-gún call
(there was also Ño José, Obakole, Akinlakpa)
when we waking the Caribbean sun

These bàtá carved like hourglass
speak because of tension on skin
squeezing the bandages of injured history
Once you fell a trunk
you must give it voice—
bitter as cedar or
sweet like almendra
wrap it in red cloth
bury it deep within the trunk

376

voice will echo from tunnel
out the bass end the
other crisp slapping end keeping time

myriad of words
        impregnating rhythm in them
        the flavor of who we are
        our history rhythmic
        bitter & sweet
        hard but
        ours

LISA D. CHÁVEZ

Manley Hot Springs, Alaska: 1975

Independence Day, and I am twelve,
dark hair falling straight, held back
by a blue bandana. My mother rents a room—
above the lodge's bar—and all night, voices rise
in slurred shouts, while outside,
gunfire rends the air in lieu of fireworks.
From the car, our dog's furious barking.
Darkness never comes; the sun doesn't set.

At five, a gunshot in the bar
then shuddering silence.
My mother shifts in her bed. "The dog,"
she says, and I dutifully go to tend her.
Quiet echoes as I edge down narrow stairs.

On the landing, a bearded man and a rifle
aimed angrily at my face.
"I thought I told all you fucking Indians
to get out of my bar."
My legs shake, wanting to run,
all I can think of is the dog
already maybe peeing on the car's seat;
when I open my mouth, words
rush out with tears—my mom and vacation
and the dog. He doesn't lower the gun,
but opens the door, shoves me out
onto the morning's cool grass.

And I am only twelve. I have never seen
a gun before. I have come from California
where night follows day in orderly fashion,
where on the Fourth of July I whirl dizzily
with sparklers in both hands, and place black pellets
on the sidewalk to see them transform

into charcoal snakes. I squeeze my eyes shut,
wish hard for some magic to take me home,
but when I open them, I see only
the unfamiliar spruce, and revelers
swaying unsteadily by. I take the dog
for a walk—I don't know what else to do.

Two young men, Indian, black hair held back
with bandanas like mine, say hello;
I gaze at my feet, whisper a reply.
In the lodge window, I see the gun's
slim shadow, so I crouch by the car
arms tight around the dog's neck, until
she pulls away, shakes herself and stretches.
There is nowhere to go but back.

I try to make myself small,
inoffensive, invisible, but that man
grabs my shoulder hard then lets me go,
rifle still dangling from one hand, an evil
appendage. Cringing like a beat dog, I leap
for the stairs, imagining the rifle raising,
the furious noise, and a sudden sharp
crack in my back.

Hours later, my mother
sends me to breakfast while she searches out
the lodge owner. Her voice rises
from another room like bursts of gunfire.
I mop syrup around my plate
with a scrap of blueberry pancake,
stomach tight. The bearded man comes in,
stares hard at me. "She looks like a goddamn Native."
The other diners nod, and I hang
my head, face burning.

CYNTHIA CRUZ

Self Portrait

I did not want my body
Spackled in the world's
Black beads and broke
Diamonds. What the world

Wanted, I did not. Of the things
It wanted. The body of Sunday
Morning, the warm wine and
The blood. The dripping fox

Furs dragged through the black New
York snow—the parked car, the pearls,
To the first pew—the funders,
The trustees, the bloat, the red weight of

The world. Their faces. I wanted not
That. I wanted Saint Francis, the love of
His animals. The wolf, broken and bleeding—
That was me.

DAVID DOMINGUEZ

Mi Historia

My red pickup choked on burnt oil
as I drove down Highway 99.
In wind-tattered garbage bags
I had packed my whole life:
two pairs of jeans, a few T-shirts,
and a pair of work boots.
My truck needed work, and through
the blue smoke rising from under the hood,
I saw almond orchards, plums,
the raisins spread out on paper trays,
and acres of Mendota cotton my mother picked as a child.

My mother crawled through the furrows
and plucked cotton balls that filled
the burlap sack she dragged,
shoulder-slung, through dried-up bolls,
husks, weevils, dirt clods,
and dust that filled the air with thirst.
But when she grew tired,
she slept on her mother's burlap,
stuffed thick as a mattress,
and Grandma dragged her over the land
where time was told by the setting sun. . . .

History cried out to me from the earth,
in the scream of starling flight,
and pounded at the hulls of seeds to be set free.
History licked the asphalt with rubber,
sighed in the windows of abandoned barns,
slumped in the wind-blasted palms,
groaned in the heat, and whispered its soft curses.
I wanted my own history—not the earth's,
nor the history of blood, nor of memory,

and not the job found for me at Galdini Sausage.
I sought my own—a new bruise to throb hard
as the asphalt that pounded the chassis of my truck.

BLAS FALCONER

The Given Account

Puerto Rico, 1510

They said they were gods, and we believed—
they crossed uncrossable seas, after all,

in ships with sails like wings—but Salcedo
is dead. Pacing river shallows, turning rocks,

sifting sand for flecks of gold, he cut his foot
on stone or shell, sending braids of blood

downstream. Overhead, wind shook trees
so leaves and light spilled in, catching a school

of fish, a silver shimmer. I was there.
Kneeling on the bank, I dressed his wound,

pressing strips of cloth to stop the flood,
but red spots seeped through the weave,

my fingers wet with blood, his blood,
no different from mine. He winced, his face

paled by pain, but nothing, nothing changed,
no dove, no cloud, no beam of light, and he

a god or son of god? I, who came to drink,
struck dumb by one thought—they bleed, they die—

led him back into the pool and pushed
his head below. His arms thrashed, legs kicked,

lungs inhaled mouths of water. He stopped.
Three days I stayed to see him stir, but he,

not strongest, weakest, or cruelest of them,
did not move. I pulled him out. He hung

wet and limp and heavy in my arms—
this man, this man, almost too much to bear.

GINA FRANCO

The Line

a serious surplus population that needs eliminating

So now we are equals, verdad? All along eyeing the same
    banks,
as though we might surface on the same shore, bare backs
to the sun, wet shirts in hand, boots aside, those too.
You keep saying, *El otro lado.* See you there,
face to face, no worries.
                              The last good lynching
was long ago. Ropes, belts, canteens sway in the tree. The
    tree
sings with lightness. In time, the fruit shrank in the heat,
    grinned
wide from the bone, dropped to the dirt.
                                        Rot. The earthworm's
heart, this now. A knot, a fishing spot.
The sweet-blood smell of the hook right through, the
    impaled
form, right through, either soft end writhing on the line.
Beneath the surface, neither vertebral nor articulate, it sways
under water—guts in skin—it sways from the other side,
    verdad,
not a lure but a rumor, a mirror, of a parallel end;

        we'd fished the shallows with stripped willows,
        with a hellgrammite drifting in the current,
        and that's where we trapped our leviathan,
        iridescent scales that slid away from our hands,
        where we crossed the swinging bridge and found
        effigy and sign, *Death to scabs crossing the line,*
        a volleyball head and a pair of shovels for limbs,
        the hanging white sheet, the slashed body of many:

the hanging white sheet, the slashed body of many:
a volleyball head and a pair of shovels for limbs,
effigy and sign, *Death to scabs crossing the line*,
where we crossed the swinging bridge and found
iridescent scales that slid away from our hands,
and that's where we trapped our leviathan,
with a hellgrammite drifting in the current,
we'd fished the shallows with stripped willows

y verdad, the cities on either side of the river watch
one another from the eyes of their televisions.
Their headlines race beneath glass

—they have taken my father's body
and I do not know where they have laid him—

and light. Love as the sinker, the line sinking deep. The last
    time
I saw my father was in a dream, seated on every side of the
    table
of ancestors, and belonging so fully, he ceased
            to exist. They arrived
on the other side, at the tree at the end of this world, and the
    tree
drank deeply. Love as a secret, unbearable map. Tell
    me—*verdad*—
where you have laid the body (and

            I will bear
            him away. I
            will bear him a-
            way. I will bear
            him a way).

SUZANNE FRISCHKORN

Pool

         Desire your name is Miami,
stirred with a snip of sugarcane,
crushed mint, Bacardi, and sunning
yourself by the Biltmore pool. No, Miami,
        I sip mojitos, while I am stroked by the eyes
of the cabana boy—he is heady
with a cocktail of bikini and tropical oil. "You know
how when you go to Little Italy it's all Chinese now?
That's how Little Havana is, but with South Americans."
        We decided to skip it and drink
mojitos by the pool. "Cubans?
They're everywhere," says the concierge
with a Cuban wave of his hand.
     "Maybe, you'll see some signs with Spanish writing . . ."
We drank mojitos by the side of the pool,
while I was desired, and realized
        I don't desire you, Miami.
Miami, you are not what I recalled
yet, only within you do I feel desired.

CARMEN GIMÉNEZ

[Llorona Soliloquy]

The river's dried up once made of my hair
I've left behind rubble but it's thinking
of all of us that I make a tiny baby funeral
of my tears and they make me a reason
for beatings so I had better find the thing
I left behind since it was precious
like the plaza where I used to throw coins
and wish for someplace else to be like the shimmer
of coins in water that newness not the borne-down
appendage like the body is haven as passageway
to life I make to death because it's easier
in the long term shadow of this body and its vacuum

(after Pedro Pietri's "Puerto Rican Obituary")

they work their fingers
to the soul their bones
to their marrow
they toil in blankness
inside the dead yellow
rectangle of warehouse
windows work fingers
to knots of fire
the young the ancients
the boneless the broken
the warehouse does too
to the bone of the good
bones of the building
every splinter spoken for
she works to the centrifuge
of time the calendar a thorn
into the sole dollar of working

without pause work their mortal
coils into frayed threads until
just tatter they worked their bones
to the soul until there was no
soul left to send worked until
they were dead gone
to heaven or back home
for the dream to have USA
without USA to export
USA to the parts under
the leather sole of the boss
they work in dreams of working
under less than ideal conditions
instead of just not ideal
conditions work for the
shrinking pension and never
dental for the illusion
of the doctor medicating them
for work-related disease
until they die leaving no empire
only more dreams that their babies
should work less who instead
work more for less
so they continue to work
for them and their kin
they work balloon payment
in the form of a heart attack
if only that'll be me someday
the hopeless worker said on
the thirteenth of never
hollering into the canyon
of perpetual time
four bankruptcies later
three-fifths into a life
that she had planned
on expecting happiness
in any form it took
excluding the knockoff
cubed life she lived in debt
working to the millionth

of the cent her body cost
the machine's owner
Yolanda Berta Zoila
Chavela Lucia Esperanza
Naya Carmela Celia Rocío
once worked here
their work disappearing
into dream-emptied pockets
into the landfill of work
the work to make their bodies
into love for our own

ARACELIS GIRMAY

Ode to the Watermelon

It is June.
At El TaContento near 17th,
the cook slices clean
through the belly of a watermelon,
  Sandía, día santo!
& honey bees
grown in glistening temples
dance away from their sugary hives,
ants, in lines,
beetles, toward your red,
(if you are east, they are going east)
over & over,
toward your worldly luscious,
blushed fruit freckled with seeds.

Roadside, my obtuse pleasure,
under strings of lights,
a printed skirt, in grocery barrels,
above park grasses on Sunday afternoon
to the moan & dolorous moan
of swings.

Ripe conjugationer of water & sun,
your opening calls
even the birds to land.
& in Palestine,
where it is a crime to wave
the flag of Palestine in Palestine,
watermelon halves are raised
against Israeli troops
for the red, black, white, green
of Palestine. Forever,
I love you your color hemmed
by rind. The blaring juke & wet of it.

Black seeds star red immense
as poppy fields,
white to outsing jasmine.
Again, all that green.

Sandía, día santo,
summer's holy earthly,
bandera of the ground,
language of fields,
even under a blade you swing
your quiet scent
in the pendulum of any gale.
Men bow their heads, open-mouthed,
to coax the sugar
from beneath your workdress.
Women lift you
to their teeth.
Sandía, día santo,
yours is a sweetness
to outlast slaughter:
Tongues will lose themselves inside you,
scattering seeds. All over,
the land will hum
with your wild,
raucous blooming.

The Black Maria

black the raven, black the dapples on the moon & horses,
    black sleep of night & the night's idea,
black the piano, white its teeth but black its gums & mind
    with which we serenade the black maria.

    & the night, wearing its special silver, serenades us, too,
    with metaphors for how the body makes: semen stars,
        egg moon.

1600s: European ships heave fatly with the weight of black
   grief, black flesh, black people, across the sea; the
astronomers think the moon's dark marks are also seas & call
   them "the black maria."

> Meanwhile, the Italian Riccioli, naming the seas
>   according to his language & sensibilities.
> Riccioli naming the dark fur of the moon:

Mare Cognitum, Mare Crisium, Mare Fecunditatis; Sea that
   Has Become Known, Sea of Crises, Sea of Fertility.
If it is up to Riccioli, then these are the names of three of the
   black maria.

> I call the sea "mar." I call the sea "bahri."
> I call the moon "luna." But "far" is my word for both
>   you & the moon.

I heard a story once of a woman in the Sahara who, for years,
   carried a single page of *Anna Karenina*
that she read over & over, the long combers of print
   repeating like the waves of the black maria.

> Language is something like this. A hard studying of
>   cells under a microscope,
> cells on their way to becoming other things: a person,
>   a book, a moon.

Above the bowl, I crack the egg of this idea. Yolk from clear.
   Which is It? Which is Not It?
Does "moon" name the whole thing, or just the side we
   know, the side made dark with the black maria?

> How language is an asha tree, a fool that grows
>   everywhere, a snake shedding its skin.
> A bowl of teeth. A kitchen plate of shadow & ruins,
>   like the moon.

Moon says, "Please, god, crowd my loneliness with stars."
   But the star's life is short compared to Moon's.

There is always a funeral. Moon is always wearing the veil of
   the black maria.

      However pretty the sound, it was a misidentification,
      to name the basalt basins & craters the black maria of
         the moon.

If this is a poem about misseeing—Renisha McBride,
   Trayvon Martin, Rekia Boyd,
then these are also three of the names of the black maria.

      Naming, however kind, is always an act of estrangement.
         (To put into language that which can't be
      put.) & someone who does not love you cannot name
         you right, & even "moon" can't carry the moon.

If this is a poem about estrangement & waters made dark
   with millions of names & bodies—the Atlantic
Ocean, the Mediterranean & Caribbean Seas, the Mississippi,
   then these are also the names of the black maria.

      For days, the beautiful child Emmett swells into
         Tallahatchie. Even now, the moon paints its face
      with Emmett's in petition. Open casket of the night,
         somebody's child, our much more than the moon.

KEVIN A. GONZÁLEZ

How To Survive the Last American Colony

Stop at a *kiosko* in Luquillo, Puerto Rico.
Brush past the table of tourists, cameras hung like medals
from their necks. The bartender
will move to the salsa pouring from a small red
radio, rust on the lone speaker like static. Behind him, a sign
will warn patrons: PROHIBIDO HABLAR DE POLITICA

& in front, everyone at the bar will be silent, as if politics
were the only thing anyone knows in Puerto Rico.
Outside, on the country road, stray dogs will not resign
themselves to hunger as the tourists fork lobster medallions.
Above them, the branches of a Flamboyán will sag, red
as the blood of patriots you can't mention in this bar.

When a man proclaims *Cuba Libre,* notice the bartender
mixing Don Q & Coke: how he ignores the politics,
how he squeezes a lemon & stares at you, eyes redolent
of the O's in PROHIBIDO. You will want to order a *Puerto
   Rico
Libre,* though that is not a drink. Settle for a Medalla,
the national brew, its golden logo's design
suggestive of treasure. The tourists, who can't read the sign,
will begin to praise their expansionist president. The
   bartender
will say nothing as he flicks your Medalla

to make sure it's not frozen. To him, POLITICA

means only one language. You are a tri-colored bead, Puerto
    Rico,

in an island-necklace: ocean-blue annexation, Flamboyán-red

status quo, & mountain-green independence. You are a
    redundant

stalemate machine fueled by misperception. Know that no
    sign

will ever prohibit these thoughts. Every day in Puerto Rico,

we perch our arms like surrendered weapons atop the same
    bar;

every day we come home to the same stuffed politics

steaming on the table. When a tourist looks up from his
    medallion

& tosses an ice cube, the dogs will fight for it, that hollow
    medal

of charity, & bark for more. Here, you will want to speak of
    redemption.

Here, you will want to drop your own politics

like an eggcrate. Don't. Instead, glance once more at the sign,

clutch your beer & drop two bills on the bar,

that mecca of sedatives: Bacardi, Barrelito, Palo Viejo, Ron
    Rico.

Drive off into rural Puerto Rico, sip your Medalla

& remember belief can never be barred. Plunge into the red

speech of the sun. Forget all the signs. Let cool be your
    politics.

ROBERTO HARRISON

a grotesque side of panamá with cooling shadow

i am from a stitch sewn angel's death
his innocent mouth ripped apart by knives

and a sand blast, a blood soaked mass of the meat of the door.

my cover is the brutal silence
of the jungle Lord of disappearances

as i do not stand well
against the patterns of a pure night's grief without trigger.

one day the visions of pain outside the body
lose the sun's directions. the executions

of my intimate outline to extinguish the real
stand for you to be seen, as a knotted time

collects our dripping sweat from the clouds
and our water serves for the death

of a vocable daylight. midnight slices my body
in two as i am so happy to see the human alternative

and my face drops off with a crash
to the other side of each of the earth's symbols.

where can i hunt the threat
to unite with you?

bullshit allowance
for the blank persons of the world, encounter

the amputations of visibility
and the loss of a wandering origin, to be gone

the canal is gone   as the Mississippi pearls to my neck

TIM Z. HERNANDEZ

I've Worn That Feminine Skin

but you refused it—
called me a queer
said my affection with men bothered you,
said I held too long
that I cried too hard
that my hair should smell appropriately male,
said a man who smells of lavender & sage is no man
at all

Wondered aloud about
why I must talk before sex
why I must talk during sex
why I must talk after sex
and still you wonder why men are such liars
ignorant & soulless
empty carcasses of
scar & bone

Truth is—we're born from lies
been nurtured on gun smoke and horse muscle
told grown men can hang
faked the courage of hunters & heroes
of righteous soldiers
erect & stoic in their stance

Our whole lives
we've aimed to reach you,
to keep still that image of us
to chop the logs that fuel the fire
so that we can tender our touch
—and it's been this way for a long time

But secretly, amongst the boys,
amongst the shadow-faced truckers and

slick hot-rodders of gurgling grease
We revel in this lust
We shit-talk 'round bonfires
of our once thriving pasts,
but we speak highly of you
—build you up

This is why we refuse to bathe
To erase the scent
Why we leave the salt
To preserve the sex
Why we scratch our balls
To sniff our fingers
reminding us
of when we entered heaven
through a hole in the thrust
of a woman's wings.

JAVIER O. HUERTA

Toward a Portrait of the Undocumented

The economy is a puppeteer
manipulating my feet.

(Who's in control when you dance?)

Pregnant with illegals, the Camaro
labors up the road; soon, I will be born.

I am the heat
captured by infrared eyes.

(Had you no life before this?)
(Are you not the source of that warmth?)

I am a night shadow; when la migra
shines spotlights, I disperse.

A body snatcher, I steal faces
and walk among the people, unnoticed.

I wear anonymity like an oversized
trench coat; now and then, I flash.

(Is your name perverse?)
(Is your skin not your own?)
(Are you not flesh?)

Read me: I am a document
without an official seal.

(Who authored you?)

MAURICE KILWEIN GUEVARA

Clearing Customs

Returning took thirty years: I fly into Bogotá at night.
Landing in the Andes is like a moth dipping into the side
of a starry bowl.

Of all my luggage, the uniformed woman at Customs is
most suspicious of my electric typewriter. I open it up for
her. "What's it for?" I write poems. "What kind of poems?"
Poems that shine a little flashlight into the guts of my
typewriter. Poems of small children who sleep under bridges.
Poems through which rivers move. Translations hawk-
perched on the shoulder of a statue. Poems like lime juice
falling into soup and the smell of fresh bread down every
alleyway. She almost smiles; I can see only the top half of her
gold tooth in the fluorescent light. Motioning me forward,
"*Siga, siga,*" she says, and I pass.

RAINA J. LEÓN

Southwest Philadelphia, 1988

Our eyes focused on swirled vats:
vanilla ice cream, then cherry water ice,
more vanilla,
cherry for a tower of red
and white stripes that melted
into pink after heat stroll.

We had to wait for tall, plastic cups,
like all the brown
kids, while Papi grumbled. ─────────────
Counter girls sucked their teeth,
gloved their hands,
but we never noticed that then.

⋮
"Miss, why we always
gotta wait?
We were here
first. My
children
were first!"

Children with stain history—
my brother, fair-skinned and universal
prize, and me, Black and not—
walked the block with the evidence there,
cherry crystal-flecked jackets,
happy. Papi held our hands,
brooding the cost.

⋮
only for us

Blackness was catching
the neighborhood

pecking ravens in flight
us   them

403

ADA LIMÓN

Notes on the Below

For Mammoth Cave National Park

Tell me—humongous cavern, tell me, wet limestone,
    sandstone
caprock, bat-wing, sightless translucent cave shrimp,

this endless plummet into more of the unknown,
                tell me how one keeps secrets for so long.

All my life, I've lived above the ground,
            car wheels over paved roads, roots breaking through
                concrete,
and still I've not understood the reel of this life's purpose.

Not so much living, but a hovering without sense.

What's it like to be always night? No moon, but a few lit-up
        circles at your many openings. Endless dark, still time
must enter you. Like a train, like a green river?

Tell me what it is to be the thing rooted in shadow.
        To be the thing not touched by light (no, that's not it)—
to not even need the light? I envy; I envy that.

Desire is a tricky thing, the boiling of the body's wants,
            more praise, more hands holding the knives away.

I've been the one who has craved and craved until I could
    not see
        beyond my own greed. There's a whole nation of us.

To forgive myself, I point to the earth as witness.

To you, your Frozen Niagara, your Fat Man's Misery,
          you with your 400 miles of interlocking caves that
               lead
only to more of you, tell me

what it is to be quiet, and yet still breathing.

          Ruler of the Underlying, let me
speak to both the dead and the living as you do. Speak
to the ruined earth, the stalactites, the eastern small-footed
     bat,

to honor this: the length of days. To speak to the core
     that creates and swallows, to speak not always to what's
shouting, but to what's underneath asking for nothing.

I am at the mouth of the cave. I am willing to crawl.

Cargo

I wish I could write to you from underwater,
          the warm bath covering my ears—
one of which has three marks in the exact
shape of a triangle, my own atmosphere's asterism.

Last night, the fire engine sirens were so loud
they drowned out even the constant bluster
          of the inbound freight trains. Did I tell you,
the R. J. Corman Railroad runs 500 feet from us?

Before everything shifted and I aged into this body,
     my grandparents lived above San Timoteo Canyon
where the Southern Pacific Railroad roared each scorching
California summer day. I'd watch for the trains,
howling as they came.

Manuel is in Chicago today, and we've both admitted
     that we're traveling with our passports now.

Reports of ICE raids and both of our bloods
are requiring new medication.

I wish we could go back to the windy dock,
drinking pink wine and talking smack.
Now, it's gray and pitchfork.

The supermarket here is full of grass seed like spring
                might actually come, but I don't know. And you?
I heard from a friend that you're still working on saving
        words. All I've been working on is napping, and maybe
being kinder to others, to myself.

Just this morning, I saw seven cardinals brash and bold
                as sin in a leafless tree. I let them be for a long while
                        before
I shook the air and screwed it all up just by being alive too.

Am I braver than those birds?

Do you ever wonder what the trains carry? Aluminum ingots,
                plastic, brick, corn syrup, limestone, fury,
                        alcohol, joy.

All the world is moving, even sand from one shore to another
is being shuttled. I live my life half afraid, and half shouting
at the trains when they thunder by. This letter to you is both.

The End of Poetry

Enough of osseous and chickadee and sunflower
and snowshoes, maple and seeds, samara and shoot,
enough chiaroscuro, enough of thus and prophecy
and the stoic farmer and faith and our father and tis
of thee, enough of bosom and bud, skin and god
not forgetting and star bodies and frozen birds,
enough of the will to go on and not go on or how
a certain light does a certain thing, enough
of the kneeling and the rising and the looking
inward and the looking up, enough of the gun,
the drama, and the acquaintance's suicide, the long-lost
letter on the dresser, enough of the longing and
the ego and the obliteration of ego, enough
of the mother and the child and the father and the child
and enough of the pointing to the world, weary
and desperate, enough of the brutal and the border,
enough of can you see me, can you hear me, enough
I am human, enough I am alone and I am desperate,
enough of the animal saving me, enough of the high
water, enough sorrow, enough of the air and its ease,
I am asking you to touch me.

SHERYL LUNA

Bones

Once, as a girl, she saw a woman shrink
inside herself, gray-headed and dwarf-sized,
as if her small spine collapsed. Age
and collapse were something unreal, like war
and loss. That image of an old woman sitting
in a café booth, folding in on herself, was forgotten
until her own bones thinned and hollowed,
music-less, un-fluted, empty.

She says she takes shark cartilage before she sleeps,
a tablet or two to secure flexibility and forget
that pain is living and living is pain.

And time moves like a slow rusty train
through the desert of weeds, and the low-riders
bounce like teenagers young and forgiving
in her night's dream. She was sleek in a red dress

with red pumps, the boys with slick hair, tight jeans.
She tells me about 100-pound canisters of lard
and beans, how she could dance despite her fifth
child, despite being beaten and left
in the desert for days, how she saw an angel
or saint glimmer blonde above her, how she rose
and walked into the red horizon despite
her husband's sin.

I'm thinking how the women
in my family move with a sway, with a hip
ache, and how they each have a disk
slip. The sky seems sullen, gray, and few birds
whisk. It's how the muse is lost
in an endless stream of commercials, how people
forget to speak to one another as our ending skulks

arthritically into our bones, and the dust
of a thousand years blows across the plain,
and the last few hares sprint across a bloodied
highway. Here in the desert southwest, loss
is living and it comes with chapped lips,
long bumpy bus rides and the smog of some man's
factory trap. And there are women everywhere
who have half-lost their souls
in sewing needles and vacuum-cleaner parts.
In maquiladoras there grows a slow poem,
a poem that may only live a moment sharply
in an old woman's soul, like a sudden broken hip.

And yet, each October, this old woman rises
like the blue sky, rises like the fat turkey vultures
that make death something beautiful, something
towards flight, something that circles in a group
and knows it is best not to approach death alone.

Each October she dances, the mariachis yelp
and holler her back to that strange, flexible youth,
back to smoky rancheras and cumbias, songs
rolling in the shadows along the bare Mexican hills.
She tells me, "It's in the music, where I'll always
live." And somehow, I see her jaw relax,
her eyes squint to a slow blindness
as if she can see something I can't.

And I remember that it is good to be born of dust,
born amid cardboard shanties of sweet gloom.
I remember that the bare cemetery stones
in El Paso and Juárez hold the music, and each spring
when the winds carry the dust of loss there is a howl,
a surge of something unbelievable, like death,
like the collapse of language, like the frail bones
of Mexican grandmothers singing.

MARIPOSA

Ode to the Diasporican

(pa' mi gente)

Mira a mi cara Puertorriqueña
A mi pelo vivo
A mis manos morenas
Mira a mi corazón que se llena de orgullo
Y dime que no soy Boricua

Some people say that I'm not the real thing
Boricua, that is
because I wasn't
born on the enchanted island
because I was born in the mainland north of Spanish Harlem
because I was born in the Bronx

Some people think I'm not bonafide
because my playground was a concrete jungle
because my Rio Grande de Loiza was the Bronx River
because my Fajardo was City Island
my Luquillo, Orchard Beach
and summer nights were filled with city noises
instead of coquis
and Puerto Rico was
just some paradise
that we only saw in pictures

What does it mean to live in between
What does it take to realize that being
Boricua is
a state of mind
a state of heart
a state of soul

Mira a mi cara Puertorriqueña
A mi pelo vivo
A mis manos morenas
Mira a mi corazón que se llena de orgullo
Y dime que no soy Boricua

¡No naci en Puerto Rico.
Puerto Rico nació en mí

DEMETRIA MARTINEZ

Discovering America

for P., 1992

Santo Ninõ on a
bedroom desk,
holy water in a
mouthwash bottle
Grandma had the
priest bless,
this house,
a medieval city
you visited,
what you sought
was not here.

Not in wrists
oiled with sage,
Chimayo earth
sprinkled on sheets,
nor San Felipe bells
that pecked away
the dark,
Cordova blanket
we hatched
awake in.

To prove love
I shed still
more centuries,
rung by rung
into a pueblo
kiva where
you touched
the *sipapu*,
canal the universe

emerged from,
brown baby glazed
in birth muds.

You thought
America
was on a map,
couldn't see it
in a woman,
olive skin,
silver loops
in lobes,
one for each
millennium
endured on this
husk of red earth,
this *nuevo méjico.*

Last night
I dreamed
a map of the
continent,
the train
that took you
from me whipped
across tracks
like a needle
on a seam
somewhere
near Canada.

It took me
four years
to heal.
Have you?
Have you
discovered
America
or at least
admitted

a woman grew
maíz here
long before
you named it
corn?

VALERIE MARTÍNEZ

from Count

At the Biscayne National Park welcome center
I arrive too late for a snorkeling trip, refuse the self-

guided tour, exit the building chiding myself. I watch
the boat crowded with snorkelers, little black dots

receding quickly into the distance. When we were little
the blue bathtub was big as a lagoon, and we'd take turns

being *bridge* and *diver*, holding our noses, swimming
end to end, pretending we were Jacques Cousteau,

saying, *I saw a whale, an eel, a sea horse, a starfish*,
plunging again and again until forced to get out,

make room for two more. I'd delay and linger, dive
once more to hold on: dreamy waterlog. At Xel-Há,

Quintana Roo, 1996, numb to my severely sunburned
back, I swam with the magnificents: *Pterophyllum,*

Paracanthurus hepatus, Sphyraena, tried to stay submerged
all the way back to the airport—saltwater blurring eyes

and earshot. I'd become something else. Like the infants
in that swimming pool footage, deep under the surface,

chubby thighs and forearms, pupils half-focused, belonging
to some other world of echo and gills. Relenting, I reenter

the building, wander to the back where dioramas display
creatures so fantastical—fingerprint cyphoma, rainbow

wrasse—I feel an opening, wide, imagine Spider Woman
and the clans actually listen to Sotuknang, abandon

the assault on ice and mountain, walk away
from the back door to the Fourth World.

FARID MATUK

Talk

I am Sicilian today when the skies
are gray with field smoke I share a cigarette
with my friends, nothing is new to me
I've ridden over three hills to get here
and here are my friends at the Irish
again, I love this city and I can walk its length and breadth
when it's cooler, its lights, the road back
from Lido Neptuno. All we talk about is leaving but I know
they love like I love threading our parents' cars
between a salt or phosphor truck
and the oncoming car, I know the tolerances of our Fiat
and I love the stupid, unnecessary hugs my boyfriend gives
and how we smell each other, I think everything
happens beneath the cover
of something else, something prettier
now there are Arab African boys everywhere.
Where have the gypsies gone?
Can gypsies love anything like I love Caltanissetta
the vests on their own backs?
I don't need the kids' Kleenex, my nose is dry in these fires
but I give one a Euro and he stays at our table
plays at taking our cell phones and helmets, Who
would you call? What would you ride? He plays with our fear
of his thievery, I think it's sad, and beneath that? Our sort
of friendship. And beneath that? His thievery.

Talk

I am Moroccan today, I carry
my backpack full of Kleenex
fifty packs across Sicily
I memorize their thirteen
variations of the latest haircut, the shoes
I will buy will raise me, incline me
as the whole of Europe is inclined
this summer. I learn everything about women
from Fendi handbags, from Puma pants
everything about men, I am a boy of eleven
why not a skinny thirteen? and I ask the waiter
"Are you Ireesh?" since this is the Irish Caffetteria
in Caltanissetta, Sicily.
Here are my young Italians
who won't buy the Kleenex
though one woman takes me
for a beggar and I get a half Euro—"not bad," I'd
have said in Tangiers on my way out
of Africa (aren't we all moving out of Africa?)
and nothing, not the dry grass of Sicily, reminds me of it.
I learned about little leather tags on jeans in Africa
there goes the cow hide I'd say, there goes the cow
and I smelled the people's evaporating hotel soaps. It's June
in Sicily, and the skies are gray with field smoke.

RACHEL McKIBBENS

drought (California)

Once they've rid their bodies

of an impossible country,

become flatbed livestock

in migration,

you coin them not of this earth.

Beings of neither flesh

nor light

*

When I was small

I saw men & women—brown terrestrial bodies—

bent in the field

a mile

from the strawberry stand

in ninety-five-degree heat

one hundred

one hundred & three.

I'd ask my father

to stop the car

to gobble each sunlit jewel,

adorn my mouth

in bleeding seeds

NO

he'd answer   sharply

as if their sweat

         contagious
            *

When the woman at the taqueria

      attempted

to speak to me (in audible hieroglyphics)

    I knew it was

      something mine   but not mine.

        No habla español   my father said

my closed mouth

     a thorn

         shoved hard into her lip
          *

When my great-great-grandparents

     arrived from Guanajuato,

they wore no disguises—Mercedes

     vibrant

         in a handmade dress,

   Pedro (my father's namesake)

   in a silent

       gentleman's hat.

Did they, too, imagine

      becoming ghosts

   like I have,

     like I do?

Boneless satellites in lace

     swaying above

their children's heads?

If no child of mine

becomes a poet

will the absence of my tongue   shimmer

like betrayal

in their mouths?

MARIA MELENDEZ

El Villain

"I fled the West Coast to escape them, but I still see illegals
  Everywhere," whines a letter-writer in our rural Utah paper,
  Applauding a local ICE raid. "How does it feel to be a
    problem?"

Everyone (no one) wanted to ask Du Bois, circulating his
    elegant
Diction and mixed-race face among Atlanta glitterati, turn
Of the century, when the White Sixth Sense was "I can smell

Negroes and Jews." The question ices my hair and eyelashes,
All Raza one family of suspects in this age of round-ups; am I
To breathe in prejudice, breathe out light? How does it feel

To be a problem? Some well-meaning White ones want a
    Christ of
Me, sacred heart on display. "Where are your documents
Naming this pain?" They hope for a nibble of rage. I see
    Lourdes,

Seven years old and *sin documentos*, embrace my daughter
    hello,
Good-bye, every day on their school's front steps, the two of
    them
Giddy with girl pacts. When Lourdes solves subtraction
    problems,

Safe at her dim kitchen table, how does her mother, Elva,
    feel,
As her daughter works a language that will never add up to
    home?
Down the street, I see Rodolfo from El Salvador, legal
    refugee, dance

422

The glee of a Jazz victory in front of his big screen. Ask him
    how
Pupusas feel in his mouth, corn-dough communion with
    patria. His wife,
Inez, is fourth-generation Mexican American from Salt Lake
    City.
                        Fuck these pedigrees. How does it feel

For Rodolfo, Inez, Elva, Lourdes, me, to be seen as
    not-quite-right,
Not quite US, not from around here, are ya?
I will not say. I will not display our stigmata.

We shouldn't need papers to cross from familia to politics.
Ask the seer-of-illegals, the maid of ethnic cleansing,
How it feels to hold a broken feather duster.

ANDRÉS MONTOYA

fresno night

a jazz trumpet finds the lips of someone unsuspecting and
    the stars find huge caves

        of light to hide in. i am left with the quiet power
of the heat and a horn echoing off the cages of concrete
        and cars and the cold metal madness of this city.

        off in the distance, perhaps on tulare ave,
a cop's corrupt hand is finding its way around
        the neck of a boy suspected of being illegal

        and in the park, radio park, lovers laugh
at the imagined future of their unnamed children,
        at the stories they'll tell as grandparents

        still savoring the breath of each other's skin.
in this city i sit waiting for the end of the world.
        the neighbors of noah are everywhere

        and a strange sky has come staggering in.
i am not holy or noble or righteous, but i still,
        from my crippled mouth call, "Christ, Christ!

        let your blood bathe me and not night's nasty
glare, let love's power bind peace around the neck
        of my soul, and i will stand confident, clinging

        to the Cross when the storm's scream comes
stinging at the heels of your saints. oh, Lord have mercy!"
        i am not unusual, you see. i am in love, in love

        with a girl from the sea who sleeps with her head
in the valley. i cry and laugh and live in the dust of the earth.
        i am born, bought with blood into the Spirit, but

still this flesh is of clay, of dust, of death.
but hope holds my heart: the word made flesh, laid down
    and picked up again to the right hand of glory.

    here in this city i sit, the trumpet's trembling song
fading away like an adulterous man, and i am left with car horns
    and gunshots and shouts and smells of grapes

    just about to rot on the vine, surrounded by wasps
whispering lies and mothers weeping for children brainwashed
    with insanity, and i am determined to know nothing

    but Christ and him crucified.

JOHN MURILLO

Santayana, the Muralist

Outside Chong's liquor store, you'll meet a man
Spraying corridos along a façade. He carries the soul
Of la raza in his cans, he claims. Hopes to change
The world one wall at a time. His bold blues,
Greens, and golds bring to mind the photos you pour
Over in *National Geographic.* Paint caps

Dot the sidewalk like spilled Skittles. His Dodgers cap
Tilts to one side, more pachuco than painter. This man
Aerosols Aztlán across barrio brick for all the poor
To see: Aztec warriors, old Mexican washwomen, dios del sol.
See his lowriders and zoot suiters battle badges and blue
Uniforms. "¿Sabes qué, hombre? Things don't change

Much around here. Haven't really changed
Since Roosevelt and his American concentration camps."
He fingers the pump on a can of crimson. "Blew
Me away when I read about that shit. The white man
Points at Hitler and calls *him* evil? Please! *His* soul
Should burn the way he locked up them Japanese." A poorly

Dressed elderly man walks over. Santayana pours
A fistful of nickels into his dingy fedora. Fingers more change
In his other pocket. Gives that away too. The sole
Heir to the Rivera legacy—let him tell it—keeps
A buck knife close as skin, but still believes that man's
True nature, "beneath the grime," is gold. His blue

Sputters. Coughs. Falls from his hand. "This blue
Is the hardest of all to match. With aerosol, you can't pour
And blend like the ancients did with plants and clays.
    Nowadays a man
Gotta mix while he sprays. But that could change

426

The whole piece. ¿Tú sabes? And the cap
Don't really tell what's inside the can. Kinda like the soul,
¿Qué no? You can look beautiful on the outside and your soul

Be all fucked up on the inside. How blood drips red, but is
    blue
In your veins? Can't tell shit from the outside, man." His cap
Tilted back, a faded gang tattoo wipes a sweaty brow. He
    pours
A forty down his throat, stares down the sun. "Yep, change
Gonna have to come. Or we all gonna be like that old man.

Not only in his pocket, but in his soul, he's poor.
Singing the blues, in fact. But check it: Begging change,
You think the man just means the coins in his cap?"

MIGUEL MURPHY

Love Like Auto-Sodomy

I was not in love, and I loved to be in love,
I sought what I might love, in love with loving.
—St. Augustine

I am through with smoke and the fire,
through with the intestine of a beautiful city. A man
who is lonely may travel only so far
along its street at night until nearness
is the hand opening so wide

there is nothing it can hold. Even runaways
in their plastics, arms wrapped around
one another in the rain. Why is it

the women in my life unfasten
their faces like my mother when she's sad,
men's voices bruise
the air like my father when he's drunk,
hot, in love? Their memory fingerprints

my life. The drug addict
with her hair and smeared eyeliner, girl
with a red message that marks
the back of her hand—CALL HOME. She runs

around in me. The dark lyric of her
still aching below sleep and the invisible
small something quiet
hovering in city lights: the terrific need
of that seam blackening between things.

It is your name, Michael. *Miguel* it is the dead
still breathing in the dark

428

in the river below your footsteps. Grief
is being so close you can't stand it
anymore. It is saying,

And if you think your lovers in this city
will love you without touching the holy
cross's wound over the length of your body,
then fuck the little boy crying

because pelvicly is the only way I know
to heal. You have to hate

until you hurt no more. You have to be somewhere else.
You have to close your eyes to even bear me at all.

URAYOÁN NOEL

No Longer Ode
Oda Indebida

for my grandmother in Puerto Rico
para mi abuela en Puerto Rico

A hurricane destroyed your sense of home
       El huracán arrasa lo que amas.
and all you wanted was to pack your bags
       Quieres viajar de noche, sin manera,
in dead of night, still waving mental flags,
       sin maletas, izar mental bandera.
forgetting the nation is a syndrome.
       Del mar llevas la espuma, panoramas
All that's left of the sea in you is foam,
       de una patria inasible y sus dolamas,
the coastline's broken voice and all its crags.
       voz ronca de disturbios mar afuera
You hear the governor admit some snags
       inundando ciudades de salmuera.
were hit, nada, mere blips in the biome,
       El gobernador vende melodramas
nothing that private equity can't fix
       para saciar al buitre inversionista;
once speculators pour into San Juan
       le ora a San Ciprián y Santa Clara
to harvest bad seeds of an idea.
       sabiendo que la isla se vacía.
She tells you Santa Clara in '56
       Dice tu abuela, y a primera vista,
had nothing on the brutal San Ciprián,
       que el viento de la muerte no compara.
and yes, your abuela's named María.
       Ella que también se llama María.

Thoughts of Katrina and the Superdome,
   Oh, sol de Nueva Orleans, ¡cómo derramas
el Caribe mapped with blood and sandbags,
   sangre colonial en cualquier acera!
displaced, diasporic, Spanglish hashtags,
   Hay diques y turistas dondequiera,
a phantom tab you keep on Google Chrome,
   fantasmas de un Caribe en hologramas,
days of hunger and dreams of honeycomb.
   hemisféretros. Ya sin más proclamas,
Are souls reborn or worn thin like old rags?
   escupamos al dios de cabecera
The locust tree still stands although it sags,
   (hashtag: #queelverdugoseaelquemuera).
austere sharks sequence the island's genome,
   Cotorras, ¡revoloteen las ramas
and parrots squawk survival politics
   para que el bosque de voces resista!
whose only power grid is the damp dawn.
   Tiburones austeros, ¡pongan cara
There's no other way, no panacea.
   de que al crucero le llego el día!
Throw stuff at empire's walls and see what sticks
   Se acabaron los memes de conquista,
or tear down the walls you were standing on?
   Vivimos para que otro sol brillara,
Why not run that question by María?
   revolución que nadie domaría.

Beyond the indigenous chromosome,
   Pese a los ancestros que reclamas
your gut genealogy's in chains and gags,
   tu genealogía es prisionera:
paraded though the colonies' main drags
   cadenas, mordazas, lucha obrera,
and left to die. So when you write your tome,
   cenizas de carbón sobre las camas.
please note: each word must be a catacomb,
   El ácido vital que desparramas

must be a sepulcher and must be a
　　　　en una extraña especie de aporía
cradle in some sort of *aporía*
　　　　quema las joyas de tu fantasía.
where bodies draw on song as guns are drawn,
　　　　Cual h silenciosa de *huracán,*
resurgent, silent h in *huracán.*
　　　　tus muertos insurrectos gritarán
Your ache song booms ashore. Ashé, María.
　　　　quebranto y contracanto. Ashé, María.

DEBORAH PAREDEZ

Year of the Dog: Walls and Mirrors

Fall 1982
The wall dematerializes as a form and allows the name to become
the object . . .
  —*Maya Lin, designer of the Vietnam Veterans Memorial*

The English translation of my surname is *walls*
misspelled, the original *s* turned to its mirrored
twin, the *z* the beginning of the sound for sleep.

I'm nearly twelve and the mirror is a disaster I
learn to turn away from, the girl looking back
always looking to extract her pound of flesh.

I had a simple impulse to cut into the earth,
Maya Lin is writing as the mirrored wall
of names she's made is arranged and laid

against the riven hillside. *I never looked*
at the memorial as a wall, she writes, *but*
as an edge to the earth, an opened side.

For a wall to become a mirror it must not
absorb or scatter too much light; for a girl
to become the protagonist she must sleep

with the guy or until he kisses her awake.
Sometimes we know she's the fairest one
of all because of the mirror on the wall.

Sometimes she must scale the city's walls
to bury the guy. Antigone cuts into the earth
to give him his proper memorial. She ends

up the heroine and buried alive, an *in-be-
tween thing*, like someone who's eleven or
nearly twelve. When I look at the number

11 I see two walls, my name and its mirrored
twin. Sometimes 11 resembles the mirrored
L's at the end of *wall* or the beginning of *llanto*,

the Spanish word for weeping. Sometimes 11
looks like a pair of railway sleepers arranged
and laid along a track that's always leading me

back to my war-worn father. Sometimes the guy
comes back from battle and has seizures
in his sleep and the girl must shake him awake.

Sometimes the wall and the name are one
and the same. Sometimes the wall is where
we end up to begin letting go our llanto.

WILLIE PERDOMO

Arroz con Son y Clave

My father used to leave sharp sounds
By the door, steady conga heads were
Rare. When you party with grown-ups,
You learn not to suffer dancers a weak
Hand; otherwise a safe return to silence
Becomes less of a road—no yesterday.
The great readers, he would say, quote
From the kitchen. Yes, chops—cook,
Steam like jabs, stories, walls that sob
I'm sorry. In the middle of a sacrifice,
Death always has a shape to introduce:
Breath deflates & balloons a club like
An amateur soul drowning in whisper.

We Used to Call It Puerto Rico Rain

The rain had just finished saying, *This block is mine.*

The kind of rain where you could sleep through two
    breakthroughs, and still have enough left to belly-sing the
    ambrosial hour.

Blood pellets in the dusk & dashes of hail were perfect for
    finding new stashes; that is to say, visitations were never
    announced.

A broken umbrella handle posed a question by the day care
    center.

A good time to crush a love on a stoop, to narrate through
    a window, to find the heartbeat of solitude, and collect
    gallons for the Bruja's next *baño.*

435

Good conditions to be in the dialectic of O Wow Ooo Baby
  O Shit Ooo Damn.

The perfect weather to master the art of standing under a
  bodega awning, shifting crisis to profit.

There's always a dreamer who thinks they can race the rain to
  the building, who loves the smell of wet concrete, and uses
  a good downpour to be discreet.

There's always one toddler who quietly crawls off the top
  step, dodges a thunderbolt, and quickly becomes fluent in
  all things stormy weather.

Story goes that Don Julio was swept up, ripped around the
  corner, stumbled & cartwheeled to the light post, but he
  never let go of his porkpie hat.

An improvised ballet near an improvised rivulet.

Shopping bags, pulverized by branches, contort into a new
  nation of black flags. Our block was our island.

The manhole on the corner perked with popsicle sticks,
  empty beer cans, and the brown sole of a fake karate
  slipper as we started to sink & boil.

The forecast, you said, *was type perfect.*

MAYRA SANTOS-FEBRES

Tinta

tinta para este poema sobre   dejar una isla
de antiguos tontonmacoutes   cielo mediocre
de nuevos tontonmacoutes
que ni para comer
ni para un solo sol de árbol ni maleza en combite.
no hay perros que ahuyenten el derroche
de avisar la llegada de tu muerte.
negra tinta que
sólo un carrefour hecho de agua esta vez
hecho del ojoloco y salitre y ola
aguante los mil pedazos de tu pecho de cartón
          cuatro llantas
                    lo que flote   negresa
lo que vuelva invisible esta locura.
los guardianes del cementerio tienen chalecos contra balas
y tú nada
ni una garza que suba al cielo
para hacer llover sobre la yola.
naufragar
sería un beso de las algas
una camita como el callo entre tus piernas
que ofreces
cuando no queda ni una lágrima qué beberse.
               no existe
               ni tinta hay
               para describir
               tu viaje.

MAYRA SANTOS-FEBRES

Ink

ink for this poem about   leaving an island
old Tonton Macoutes fools   mediocre sky
new Tonton Macoutes
nothing to eat
not even a single sun tree or mangrove in combite.
no dogs to chase away the excess
heralding your death's arrival.
black ink at
crossroads made only of water this time
of wild-eyes and saltpeter and waves
bearing the thousand pieces of your cardboard breast
     four tires
                  whatever floats   negress
whatever makes this madness invisible.
the cemetery guardians have bulletproof vests
and you   nothing
not even a heron rises to the sky to
make it rain on the yawl.
shipwrecked
it would be a seaweed kiss
a little bed like the moss between your thighs
your offering
when there is not even a tear left to drink.
        there's nothing
        not even ink
        to describe
        your journey.

Translated by Vanessa Pèrez-Rosario

IRE'NE LARA SILVA

dieta indigena

what would we be if we were still
what our ancestors ate
there were no cows no pigs no chickens here
there were no domesticated animals
animals fattened beyond their ability
to survive in the wild
bred to feeble-mindedness

there were javelinas serpents turtles fish pheasants
and further north buffalo moose deer
none of them raised in captivity misery
none of them pumped with hormones
no Oestradiol Progesterone Testosterone
no Zeranol Trenbolone Melengestrol
no meat injected with ammonia dioxin
no cloned meat no poisoned meat

500 years and our bodies
cannot adjust to this foreign diet
and not just we but all humans
cannot thrive on a diet of chemicals
and preservatives
sulfur dioxide sodium benzoate sodium nitrate
propyl gallate BHA BHT
food prepared food poisoned with
partially hydrogenated oils trans fats saturated fats

and what have they done to maíz
our first food
the corporations have created maíz
which bears no viable seed
they would have us eating maíz
born infertile born artificial born dead
what is a food that is not fertile

we are the eaters of fruit and seed
the eaters of that which has eaten fruit and seed
sustenance of fertility of blooming of gestating
our lives fed by what is alive

but if we listen to the ancestors
there is still food we can eat
food which can renew our health
food we can grow with our own hands
food which has grown in fields close to us
chiles frijoles tomates aguacate calabaza
nopales chayote cacao amaranth quinoa
food we should eat
food we must eat
sustenance our bodies have craved
all these centuries
let us eat what our ancestors ate
decolonize your diet *mi raza*
it is time to regain our strength

VIRGIL SUÁREZ

El Exilio

White birds over the gray river.
Scarlet flowers on the green hills.
I watch the Spring go by and wonder
if I shall ever return home.

Tu Fu

After his accident in Hialeah where he worked
     as a coffee packer, my father returned home
from the hospital and sat by the window
     of the room where my mother sewed,
and he watched the world through the two-inch
     window bars, *mi prisión*, he called it,
this catatonia of spirit, he sighed,
     breathing with difficulty in the air-
conditioned apartment he shared with my mother,
     and we'd talk on the phone once during
the week, and then on Sundays, he spoke little
     of how he felt, often repeating yesterday's
news or how gray the weather hovered in Miami,
     these cumulus clouds of surrender, a bad
omen for those crossing the Florida Straits on make-
     shift rafts, all trying to get to freedom,
and my father would chuckle his ironic laugh over
     the telephone line as if to say few made it,
and indeed when they made it, *pa' que*, he'd say,
     to lose life in the United States, too much
work, not enough money, too little to show for it,
     but he believed in freedom, in how he came
and went out of his house and not a soul
     asked him for papers or where he was going,
like his old life in Cuba, and the language,
     El Inglés, he never learned, only chewed
on a few necessary words like "mortgage,"
     "paycheck," "punch clock," "bills," . . .

the rest all sounded like the barks of mad
        dogs in an alleyway, the rest sounded
like the poetry he lacked in spirit; *El Exilio*
        he sighed, did this to him, his life,
and my mother would sew a dress's hem,
        and she'd stop long enough to tell him
he was wrong, their (our?) lives here
        had been a blessing, even if hard,
even if they were now alone in this apartment
        in Hialeah where my father watched
the children arrive in the yellow buses
        at the school across the street;
he was there when they came and there when
        they left, his visions of a daily routine,
like clockwork, beyond the barred window,
        his sedentary life without the use
of his hands, and often, he looked at his thin
        fingers and thought of the crows he ran
over by the roadside in Cuba, when younger,
        when he knew bad luck when he saw it,
the way these scavengers of the earth
        flocked over a rotting carcass of a killed
animal, the way he wanted to scream out
        his bad luck in English now, say "Fuck You!"
to his life, to this life of sitting and watching.
        The steeling of his heart.

RODRIGO TOSCANO

Latinx Poet

Sometimes X leans Tang Dynasty
and is glad to tell these Romans
who've stuck around for the last call
chumming it with Delta Blues Folk
razzing Elizabethan bards

Says X, "Ahoy Futurist brutes
on seven stages vogueing to
Post-LangPo cell group epsilon
in harmonic consonance with
3rd wave Xicano *presente*"

And what do they say these Romans
to X wobbling on a bar stool
pensive about collapsing towards
Infrarealists moshing with
Canadian Kootenay Kool Dub?

"3rd wave Harlem Renaissancing
bouncing to Symbolist techno
with acoustic Marxist *lehrstuck*
at Baroque toccata tempi
is true NOLA line strutting *yo*"

And X, supine retorts skyward
just as the Beat Front rounds the curb
sighting the tail end of ConPo
clearing the path for gen-u-wine
Ruskie Constructivism "*yeah*"

To which these Romans saucily
counterpoint to drop precisely
"do all-night donk to donk with *Gronk*
skanking it up to cop a feel
Castilian Lit pre-1610"

EMANUEL XAVIER

Madre America

If I were to give myself to you completely,
would it matter that I didn't come from your womb?
I have been thrown out of homes and abandoned by fathers
looking for a place to settle and offer what little is left
of this spirit.
I speak your tongue and share the beds of your sons.
I would fight in your battles if considered man enough
for you
The dead eyes of innocent faces would not haunt
this empty soul
Would you be my motherland?
Would I be allowed to bathe in your oceans?
Without drowning in your oil spills?
Would you hold me when I die and grant me
a final resting place?
Madre, put down that newspaper and look at me closely,
I much resemble your first kin before you were raped
I have tasted your tears and washed myself in your sorrow
Madre, would you grant me sanctuary for my sin of living?
Of loving?
Your children do not want me to be part of your history.
Your daughters do not care to heal these wounds.
Madre, remind them that I have kept you strong
I have cleansed you, fed you, kept you warm.
You made me who I am today but still, unworthy
of their affection.
You were always full of love for all of us.
You raised us the same even when we took your splendor
for granted.
We may not have the same blood, but we are all connected.
I don't want to lose this family.

This heart belongs to you.
America, you have been my mother and my father.

The autumn leaves are falling, and it is only summer.
Do not let them keep me from coming into your arms.
Do not let them imprison me with lies.
Do not let them kill me
for wanting to share in your devotion.
Remind them that our differences
is what makes this home more beautiful than any other.
I am nourished and wise because of you.
I look out the window and am not afraid of the wilderness
outside.
I only fear not finding my way back.
Madre, I want to stay here with the others to protect you.
I want to read your musings and hear your stories.
I want to stare out at your skies at night
and lay on your lands.
Madre, I know it is not you but they that are jealous of our
bond.
Madre, educate us all to understand more than one
language.
I want to write poetry to someday teach in your schools
Peace belongs to all of us because of you, *madre*
America, I will always be your child.

VI.
MY BODY SANG ITS UNDEATH

ELIZABETH ACEVEDO

La Ciguapa

For the Antilles

They say La Ciguapa was born on the peak of El Pico
    Duarte.
Balled up for centuries beneath the rocks
she sprang out red, covered in boils, dried off black
and the first thing she smelled was her burning hair.

* * *

They say Atabeyra carried La Ciguapa while in frog form—
held her low in the belly until squatting she laid her
into soft dirt: an egg made of ocean. Millenniums later, La
    Ciguapa
poked through and the blue water burst, grafted onto her
    skin.

* * *

They say La Ciguapa pried apart her jaw
and spit herself out, soft and malleable
but at the last second her legs scraped against fangs
and inverted her footing.

* * *

Her backwards-facing feet were no mistake, they say,
she was never meant to be found, followed—
an unseeable creature of crane legs, saltwater crocodile scales,
long beak of a parrot no music sings forth from.

* * *

La Ciguapa, they say, was made on one of those ships;
    stitched
and bewitched from moans and crashing waves. She emerged
entirely formed. Dark and howling, stepped onto the auction
block but none would buy her. They wouldn't even look her
    in the eye.

* * *

They say she came beneath the Spanish saddle of the first
     mare.
Rubbed together from leather and dark mane. Hungry.
That she has a hoof between her thighs and loves men
like the pestle loves the mortar;

                              she hums them into the cotton thick fog
of the mountains. They follow her none word sing-song
and try to climb her, tall and dark and rough as sugarcane
and don't know until they're whittled down how they've
     scraped

themselves dead. They say the men were the first to undo her
     name;
thinking that burying it would rot her magic, that long cry
they were compelled to answer. They hung all five-toed dogs
because they alone knew her scent—

they say there was a time her silhouette shadowed the full
     moon.

                         * * *

They say. They say. They say. Tuh, I'm lying. No one says.
     Who tells
her story anymore? She has no mother, La Ciguapa, and no
     children,
certainly not her people's tongues. We who have forgotten all
     our sacred monsters.

ANTHONY AGUERO

Undetectable Explained to a Primo

What does it mean, you know, to you?

I massage a rose petal onto each temple
And breathe in its perfume.

So, you're like taking care of yourself, right?

My body discovering song.

But I mean can you, like, give it to
Anyone else?

A bird ate from my hand and fluttered away.

Can you be in love with anyone else?

In this lifetime and next and next and—

I guess what I'm trying to ask is
Does it bother you that I'm asking?

My hands using a rosary as expression;
As the blood I'm trying to help you see.

So, you like, take medication every day?

A rose petal floating down my esophagus.

I mean, like, what does it mean to you?

My body sung its undeath.

ALDO AMPARÁN

What I say to my mother after her father dies is soft

as an organ

liquified beneath a swollen chest—a grenade exploding
in a field. Unbearable. & meaningless. What I mean to say:

there's a mountain at the edge of El Paso bathed in the light
of Ciudad Juárez. I dreamed my grandfather standing there

this morning, wearing only his gold
skin. What I mean to say: let's drive

up the bright road to meet him. But what I say
unloads a carcass on the white bathroom tile. I'm sorry
for my words. I'm sorry, Mother, for only now understanding

how cruel
the sudden leaving, the lack

of a flicker monitoring your father's pulse: your father's pulse
still beeping in the blue. The monitor. Slim morsel of night—

the lack. The beat. The lack. The beat.

DIANNELY ANTIGUA

Golden Shovel with Solstice

after Gwendolyn Brooks and Terrance Hayes

When we found her sex positions book, we
didn't think it was real.

My mother wasn't cool
enough for sex. We

flipped through the pages, turning left,
studying where each body fit in this school,

the detailed figures of the man and woman, the parts we
hid under cotton, kept from the lurk-

ing skin, a hand, a finger, the late-
night moon with its borrowed light. We

lay our bodies on the bed, to strike
the pose, mimic the face down, the ass out straight.

We laughed and snorted, we
looked like pigs, sing-

ing oinks, our faces in the trough, this sin.
I don't want to say what we did next, that we

touched our own bodies, thin
arms reaching to what bits of hair we'd grown, the begin-

ing of a secret thing, or that we
reached for each other, a fumbled jazz

of grips, on this solstice in June.
If today, I could replay our hands' song, we

would deny its music, when we each die-
d a little on that bed, notes ending too soon.

GUSTAVO ADOLFO AYBAR

Wallflower Mambo

You ain't Dominican she says
—envious eyes admiring the shorter

gradually balding man a car's length away,
whose arms move like a tropical storm,

twirling his partner at sixty miles per hour.
Pulsing with wild abandon, fingers touching slightly,

spirits dancing swiftly; exchanging alluring glances
and inviting smiles.

Los Dominicanos they're born dancing,
and oye nene, you've already stepped on me twice.

Gaze drifting back to the balding man
wishing to charm him with her enchantress eyes—

believing that executing a fancy dip or an elegant twist
is indicative of a people's essence or a nation's pride.

I stepped on her twice. Like twice the American government
intervened and occupied the country with its military might

during the 20th century. Like twice, the number of times
we fought to gain our independence against French Haiti,

and 2/27 is the day we celebrate our liberation.
Like too many cultures are entwined in our genealogy

to ever simply say
—*I am Dominican.*

Because our sultry Spanish accents stem
from conquistadors, explorers and religious zealots

with an unquenchable thirst for gold and land used to destroy
a jungle of souls which sprung from indigenous fruit.

Because our Taíno culture dates back to around 800 A.D.
and one interpretation of the island's name, Quisqueya,

means mother of the earth. Because our descendants endured
the Middle Passage, sugar cane and rice plantations,

plus the percussive beating of our hearts resembles African
    drumbeats
like Tito's congas and timbales and their steps live in the clave.

So this is my Yoruba song chanted to a Catholic saint,
meant for the thunder god, Changó.

This is my flamenco scream, plucked from inebriated guitars
—clinging to a lover's memory in brokenhearted bachata
    laments.

This is my flamenco stomp echoed in ballet folclórico footfalls.

This is my Dominican hue. This is my Dominican kink.
This is my Dominican twang. This is my Salsa twirl.

This is my Merengue swing. This is my Dominican dance.
This is my Dominican dance. This is my Dominican dance.

DIEGO BÁEZ

Yaguareté White

No jaguars wander my father's village, no panthers
patrol the cane fields caged in bamboo fences,

nestled among the Ybyturuzú, what passes for a mountain
range in Paraguay, the Cordillera Caaguazú. You see,

Spanish adjectives arrive after the noun they describe,
clarifying notes that add color and context.

There is history and then there is history, but there are no
    jaguars
here, only a pool of blood petrified into stone, a place I call
    home,

tierra de arcilla, clay so bright it stains orange. This color we
    call rust in English,
after a chemical reaction used to describe the old, unused,
    out of practice.

And it's true, no mountain lions roam my mother's home-
town of Erie, Pennsylvania, wasted city of industry, named
    for the native

people who once combed its shores, called "Nation du Chat"
by the colonizing French, after the region's Eastern Panther.

By now, every oxidizing firearm and spearhead and family
charm has moved west or died out, like the Lynch clan,

my ancestors, or the only indigenous word to survive
the Erie people: "Chautauqua," co-opted by enterprising
    whites,

literally taken to mean a cross-country, faith-based movement,
a cultural accumulation, which does sound awfully familiar.

Don't worry, because I don't know how to pronounce it
     either,
the Guaraní. I only know Jopara is like Paraguayan Spanglish,

a mixture of Spanish and Guaraní spoken in the hillside
     villages,
los campos, the countryside. But I speak none of the above
     myself.

Even English makes little sense whatsoever, hybrid monster
of predominant whites, but this book is not about albinos.

It's not about willow bark or sugar cane or bartered soil.
It's not about the basilica at Caacupé or the spring of the
     Virgin Mary,

busy with elbows this morning. It's not about anything
real or true. It's not about binaries, ancient or new.

It's not about a tía teaching her sobrino to speak,
spelling out the sound of each color and pointing:

charcoaled remains of last night's fire, *hũ*.
Ash blown and scattered, *morotĩ*.

It's not about mythology, evil Tau
chasing the child Kerana,

fast silhouette of an immigrant couple
racing across the border, seven offspring in tow,

cursed to haunt the forests outside my father's village.
It's not about a story I only learn online:

the death of Arasy, mother to Rupave and Sypave,
the sun and moon, murdered by celestial jaguars.

The siblings avenged their mother, killing all
but one pregnant jaguar, their end and their beginning.

They are now entangled, twinned. Jaguars come to represent
the souls of all the dead. Inseparable from each other,

this people and their origin. So it is, and so am I,
here now in the temple.

OLIVER BAEZ BENDORF

My Body the Haunted House

This house is haunted you know. Someone died in here.
Where is the basement of the body I don't know. Where is
the attic I don't know. I carry her around with me. Stillborn
in my boy-womb. There was a girl died young no funeral.
A haunted house is always alone. People come to be scared
because they like it they like to be scared knowing they can
leave anytime and they do they always do they always leave.
Back to their safe and warm without me, I mean the house.
A haunted house is always alone. I carry your body (in my
body). I live for both of us now. Cannot pinpoint what I
miss. Looking for the chicken exit. Desire wrapped in a
sheet. Where is the body I said I don't know. No body no
case everyone knows that. Am I free to go now. I want to go
home. I said I want to go.

ROSEBUD BEN-ONI

All Palaces Are Temporary Palaces

My niece calls with questions of asteroid mining.
At six she's worried & can't tell me why.
So we talk it out. I hear there is gold, silver, platinum
On spent comets. Who would say *I do* on a stony
Asteroid? People are already getting married underwater,
The very rich driving cars on coral reefs.
& if the newest frontiers require technology
Smaller than an atom, well, now there's the pentaquark
Which is almost all quark save for one
Antiquark, & if not for the anti-
Quark, would anything, any-
Thing at all, be? What's next is never
Enough. All left to chance shrinking. My dear, dear girl
Calling on this overcast day in the spring, where sky is one
    long cover
Of impassivity. *Why are we here?* She's asking for the first time,
& I hear the anxiety of one who's stumbled upon a burning
Temple in the fields. We listen to each other
Breathe. I miss my train, linger on a winding staircase
In Woodside, Queens. I remember the day I discovered
This small stretch of exposed track subverting the sky &
    knew
I'd come home. One more day, & I will tell her this.
One more day for life on asteroids without fences or fracking,
& dreams know no deep inelastic scattering. Let it be
Where silence is never summoned, where rays
Collide in charm & strange.

DAVID CAMPOS

Lizard Blood

My grandfather asks me to drink lizard blood.
"It's good," he says, "gives you ganas."

I gag, but I swallow
the warm and slimy liquid down

and don't protest. The bitter taste
lingers in my mouth like the words

of my poli-sci teacher at Clovis Community
who said I should drop his class,

that I wasn't going to pass, and that I would need
near-perfect scores on all my exams.

In that office, I didn't put up a fight;
I studied while I slapped out pizzas.

"I don't feel anything," I tell him.
My face contorts in disgust while

I rinse out the taste.
My spit stained purple-red.

The headless reptile lies across a rock.
I passed that class without this blood.

No other tongue will determine
which myths I accept.

"Now you have ganas," he says. A smile across his face
as he throws the bloodless body into the bushes.

NATASHA CARRIZOSA

Mejiafricana

born with two tongues
i speak of—hablo de
i write of—escribo de
mi vida cultura colorada
pintada—painted a picture
para que puedan ver
that i am
mejiafricana

that's half and half
but whole—as in
an entire empire of aztec warriors
breathed orange red fire into my lungs
that's half and half
but whole—as in
an entire tribe from the congo
rained blue black blood into my soul

i am that red brown black sista
thinking and breathing them poetic thoughts
that prolific prophetic poet
with them red brown twisted locks
i see and record the world in black ink
like the skin of my people
i am fierce like panthers
militant with pen as they be
hot water cornbread oxtails and collard greens
chanting down babylon with
jah! rastafari beats
i am ghetto soliloquies of haitian refugees
spoken underneath harlem's balconies
i represent the black freedom
of which the negro spiritual speaks

i am all things black
and all black things I be

yo soy la morena
la poema
que despierta su mente
que enciende su alma
con papel y pluma
i can make the sun and moon rise
at the same time
i am el viento que viene de méxico

el este y el oeste
esta es la verdad
i am the song on pancho's lips
as he sits and eats un burrito de chorizo con huevo
praying for a job to feed his niños
salsa picosa
como willie colón frankie ruiz y celia
una mariposa en may
and may i say that brown and proud
is what i will remain
staining this life with my mark
because you see
my sico is just as bad as my bark
because porque
i am una niña del yucatán
chichén itzá
quetzacoatl kissed my mother
and here i am
landed on this land with pen in hand
to tell the tales of mi gente
mayans aztecs and incans
roofers day laborers carpenters
lo que sea
es la misma cosa
sangre
i am una niña de mi país
una de una raza tan fuerte
una niña de méxico y así me quedo

born with two tongues
i speak of—hablo de
i write of—escribo de
mi vida
cultura colorada
pintada
painted a picture para que puedan ver
that i am
mejiafricana

MARCELO HERNANDEZ CASTILLO

Wetback

After the first boy called me a wetback,
I opened his mouth and fed him a spoonful of honey.

     I like the way you say "honey," he said.

I made him a necklace out of the bees that have died in my yard.

       How good it must have felt before the small
         village
       echoed its grief in his throat; before the sirens
         began ringing.

How fallow their scripture.

Perhaps we were on stage which meant it was a show,
which meant our only definition of a flower was also a flower.

I waved to the crowd
like they taught me,
like a mini-miss something.

       Thank you.
       Thank you.

Yes, I could have ripped open his throat.
I could have blown him a kiss from the curtain.

I wanted to dance by myself in a dark room
filled with the wingless bodies of bees—

to make of this our own Old Testament
with all the same beheaded kings
pointing at all the same beheaded prophets.

The same Christ running through every door
like a man who forgot his child in the car.

But the lights were too bright.
I couldn't hear him because I wasn't on stage.

I could have been anyone's
idea of pity.

How quiet our prophets.
Let my bare back remind him of every river he's
swam in.

Miel and *miel.*

I pulled the bees off the string
and cupped them in my palm.

I told him my Spanish name.

There was nothing dry on my body—
The lamps falling over in the dark of me.

ANDRÉS CERPA

The Distance between Love & My Language

She, no one, can hold my blood like a trembling mirror in
   which the stars can weep,

& therefore, I walk the city unknown. I'd like to vow my
   silence & be done.
I can't. I keep a belief in salvation,

in a hand reaching gently out. The click of dice in lamplight,
   a chewed cigar,
   & my friends raising guns to the air on a rooftop,

painting the sky with their anger. The wolves' communion,
   my death,

my box of ashes in a pause of wind. I don't wanna be holy,
I want my breath to flock & spiral like birds,

but like a girl, so far from the ocean, whistling a hollow-
   point into the wheat fields

at twilight, as she watches her song carry, I think, *Where does
   it end?*

Powerless in love, I dreamt the deep shade of Berlin; that
   distance was my savior,
yet I still wanted to hold the birdcage & dwindling song: my
   father's chest,

& hold my mother's strength, to be there when she weeps.
   I wanted another life,

one in which my love could save them. Years after our love
   had ended, in its first form,

an old lover asked if I could speak, if I could finally let a
   woman in,

& then I remembered how she began to shatter plates as her
   hands trembled,
when I had no words but a bottle's silence or shatter. We broke

everything that night, & cared deeply at the end. We thought
   about their beauty,
about the waste, the money we'd have to spend.

The language of our anger was frail.

It was the cheap nourishment of forgetting, not the hand,
   the thumb moving in a slight circular
motion to ease & say, *I'm ready.*

There is a language I can't take back, a rib cage cleaned by
   the wolves & scattered,
a tint of red in a snow which lays my love distant. I remember
   taking my father's throat

in my left hand, while my right hesitated, made snow of the
   Sheetrock beside him.

MAYA CHINCHILLA

Central American-American

Centralamerican   American
does that come with a hyphen?
a space?
Central   America
America
América
Las   Américas

Español chapín
black beans and white rice
tortillas de maíz almost an inch thick
refugees and exiles
as playmates
movies with trembling
mountains, bombs and
gunfire raging in my heart.
black lists and secrets.
Hüipiles and mysterious people
passing through my home.

Where is the center of America, anyway?
Are there flowers on a volcano?

You can find the center in my heart
where I imagine the flowers never die

But today the volcano explodes in the way
it has every day for 30 years.
No it is not a sacrifice it desires,
for we already have sacrificed too much,

They want us out of this country
they say we don't belong here

vamos pa' el norte
they tell us the American dream is the truth
but that our stories of escape from horror are not.
When can we rest from running?
When will the explosions in my heart stop
and show me where my home is?

Are there flowers on a volcano?
am I a CENTRAL
          American?
Where is the center of America?

ANTHONY CODY

How to Lynch a Mexican (1848–Present)[*]

ose a Mexican.
isappear a Mexican.
nd drag a Mexican off.
nd a Mexican with a gun shot in a Mexican head
hoot a Mexican in front of a Mexican wife.
ury a Mexican.
ake a Mexican from jail, beat a Mexican, and secretly
xecute a Mexican.
ake a Mexican from a Mexican village to the hillside and
apture a Mexican, transport a Mexican, and shoot a Mexican.
hoot a Mexican
ie wire around a Mexican neck, drag a Mexican, and
mishap happens to a Mexican on the way to jail.
hoot a Mexican and leave a Mexican.
ake a Mexican from a hospital and hang a Mexican.
ce log, and throw a Mexican into the river.
hoot a Mexican, decapitate a Mexican, tie a Mexican to a
hoot a Mexican and let a Mexican rot.
eat a Mexican with a mob of 200 men.
ear a Mexican and drag a Mexican by buggy.
ang a Mexican during interrogation.
ll a Mexican to their door and shoot a Mexican.
ash a Mexican 300 times, then hang a Mexican.

Torture a Mexican and hang a Mexican.
Decapitate a Mexican and pickle a Mexican head in a jar.
Hang a Mexican until a Mexican is freed and a
Mexican goes back to jail and go back to the jail
and take a Mexican to the nearest tree, and hang a
Mexican.
Drag a Mexican down main street.
Hang a Mexican from a bridge.
Execute a Mexican with a posse.
Hang a Mexican after a mock trial.
Hang a Mexican from a telephone poll.
Hang a Mexican in front of a crowd.
Hang a Mexican under the cover of night.
Hang a Mexican in broad daylight.
Shoot a Mexican and cut off each ear of a Mexican.
From a vigilance committee and hang a Mexican
from a windmill.
Burn a Mexican.
Mutilate a Mexican, shoot a Mexican, and drag a Mexican.
Pound a Mexican head in and hang a Mexican
inside a courtroom.

Whip a Mexican.

Shoot a Mexican with a gun.

Shoot a Mexican with a rifle.

Lash a Mexican 75 times, then hang a Mexican.

Beat a Mexican, then hang a Mexican,

Hang a Mexican from a Live Oak.

Construct a platform over a river, apply the noose on a Mexican on the platform, and tell a Mexican to leap.

Overpower the deputy to seize a Mexican from the courthouse, drag a Mexican by horse to a tree, hang a Mexican.

Abduct a Mexican from a Mexican home and hang a Mexican.

Abduct a Mexican from a Mexican home while they are sleeping and hang a Mexican.

Hang a Mexican with a log-chain.

Tie a Mexican to a mesquite tree, pour kerosene on a Mexican, and light a Mexican on fire, do not shoot a Mexican.

Bind a Mexican, then decapitate a Mexican.

Drag a Mexican down main street and hang a Mexican.

Take a Mexican from a steamboat and hang a Mexican from the yard-arm of the dock.

Hang a Mexican, then burn the corpse of a Mexican.

Burn a Mexican alive.

Hang a Mexican indiscriminately.

Put on masks to take a Mexican from authorities and hang a Mexican.

Hang a Mexican, then shoot a Mexican.

Hang a Mexican, then shoot a Mexican in a Mexican face.

Round up a Mexican, round up a Mexican, round up a Mexican, hang a Mexican, hang a Mexican, and hang a Mexican.

Beat a Mexican with a club.

Shoot a Mexican in the back of a Mexican head.

Find a Mexican at a dance and shoot a Mexican.

Take a Mexican on the road and shoot a Mexican.

Capture a Mexican and cut a Mexican throat with an axe.

Trample a Mexican with a horse.

Slice a Mexican throat.

Seize a Mexican, take a Mexican to a river, shoot a Mexican, and throw a Mexican into the river.

Kill a Mexican and feed a Mexican to hogs.

Shoot a Mexican with a mob of 20 men.

Shoot a Mexican in jail.

* When possible, the poem should be read simultaneously by 4 readers, or in groups of 4, with each reader or group picking a different direction to read.

EDUARDO C. CORRAL

In Colorado My Father Scoured and Stacked Dishes

in a Tex-Mex restaurant. His co-workers,
unable to utter his name, renamed him Jalapeño.

If I ask for a goldfish, he spits a glob of phlegm
into a jar of water. The silver letters

on his black belt spell *Sangrón*. Once, borracho,
at dinner, he said: Jesus wasn't a snowman.

Arriba Durango. Arriba Orizaba. Packed
into a car trunk, he was smuggled into the States.

Frijolero. Greaser. In Tucson he branded
cattle. He slept in a stable. The horse blankets

oddly fragrant: wood smoke, lilac. He's an illegal.
I'm an Illegal-American. Once, in a grove

of saguaro, at dusk, I slept next to him. I woke
with his thumb in my mouth. ¿No qué no

tronabas pistolita? He learned English
by listening to the radio. The first four words

he memorized: In God We Trust. The fifth:
Percolate. Again and again I borrow his clothes.

He calls me Scarecrow. In Oregon he picked apples.
Braeburn. Jonagold. Cameo. Nightly,

to entertain his cuates, around a campfire,
he strummed a guitarra, sang corridos. Arriba

Durango. Arriba Orizaba. Packed into
a car trunk, he was smuggled into the States.

Greaser. Beaner. Once, borracho, at breakfast,
he said: The heart can only be broken

once, like a window. ¡No mames! His favorite
belt buckle: an águila perched on a nopal.

If he laughs out loud, his hands tremble.
Bugs Bunny wants to deport him. César Chávez

wants to deport him. When I walk through
the desert, I wear his shirt. The gaze of the moon

stitches the buttons of his shirt to my skin.
The snake hisses. The snake is torn.

Want

abandoned by his coyote, my
father, sand seething beneath
his sneakers,   trekked
through   southern Arizona:
maze of acacia   & cholla
cold sweat cut   his face like
a razor   in his pocket: a fine-
tooth comb, dice, & a photo
of a girl playing a violin   on
the third day,   he picked up
a rock,   killed a blue lizard
with a single strike he tore it
apart,   shoved guts & bones
into his mouth   the first
time I knelt for a man,   my
lips   pressed to his zipper,
I suffered   such hunger

RIO CORTEZ

Ars Poetica with Mother and Dogs

I turn and don't expect my mother's face
                    I ask *how did you enter this poem*
she says it wasn't easy

she is dressed in my favorite horse-print silk sheath
                    and dripping lake water
says she wore it to trick my lover

I want to ask *How could you* but instead
                    I reach behind her and break a vase
she used to love but we are surrounded

by dogs some of them used to sleep
                    at our bedsides but don't
anymore she grabs my hand and who am I anyway

to keep asking
                    her to leave why not take her face
and explain the damned line

JOSEPH DELGADO

dirty sheets

he shifted his skin
in the cold dark

        his veins numbed
                collapsed
                the wet green
                bruises
      extended to a moonless
      night

he licked the stretched skin
of my belly   the
        hairs on his chin
        catching the faint
        light of
        cigarettes   burning

or was it a car?
a flash in the thick
        cold of winter

our   wind blistered lips
        cracking breaking loose

        split open to the cool
            spittle of two men.

he pressed his thumb
        deep inside
        warm
the wild grasses
        howling at our ankles
        pulling   calling

the wind scratching, gnawing
at my body
          flesh sliding in and out of flesh

BLAS MANUEL DE LUNA

To Hear the Leaves Sing

Going down Highway 99, to Modesto,
I see an orange glow in the sky.
At first I think it is a fire, but, as I get closer,
it is the lights of a packinghouse,
where women work through the night,
giving up the fire of their lives,
to get the peaches to market.

Ten minutes later I pass
the Avenue 20 off-ramp, the ramp
that, in summers, would take me
to the peach fields of Madera,
where, as the sun rose to its peak
in the brilliant sky,
and the bitter dust
settled in my throat,
I would stand on a ladder,
my heavy sack pulling me down,
and throw peaches, as fast
as I could, into the trees,
to hear the leaves sing,
the tiny branches break.

NATALIE DIAZ

Tortilla Smoke: A Genesis

In the beginning, light was shaved from its cob,
white kernels divided from dark ones, put to the pestle
until each sparked like a star. By nightfall, tortillas sprang up
from the dust, billowed like a fleet of prairie schooners
sailing a flat black sky, moons hot white
on the blue-flamed stove of the earth, and they were good.

Some tortillas wandered the dry ground
like bright tribes, others settled through the floury ceiling
el cielo de mis sueños, hovering above our tents,
over our beds—floppy white Frisbees, spinning, whirling
like project merry-go-rounds—they were fruitful and
    multiplied,
subduing all the beasts, eyeteeth, and bellies of the world.

How we prayed to the tortilla god: to roll us up
like burritos—tight and fat *como porros*—to hold us
in His lips, to be ignited, lit up luminous with Holy Spirit
dancing on the edge of a table, grooving all up and down
the gold piping of the green robe of San Peregrino—
the saint who keeps the black spots away,

to toke and be token, carried up up
away in tortilla smoke, up to the steeple
where the angels and our grandpas live—
    porque nuestras madres nos dijeron que viven allí—
high to the top that is the bottom, the side, the side,
the space between, back to the end that is the beginning—

a giant ball of *masa* rolling, rolling, rolling down,
riding hard the arc of earth—gathering rocks, size, lemon
trees, Joshua trees, creosotes, size, spray-painted
blue bicycles rusting in gardens, hunched bow-legged
    grandpas in white

undershirts that cover cancers whittling their organs like
   thorns
and thistles, like dark eyes wide open, like sin—leaving behind
bits and pieces of finger-sticky dough grandmas mistake
for Communion *y toman la hostia*—it clings to their ribs
like gum they swallowed in first grade.

The grandmas return from *misa*, with full to the brim
estómagos and overflowing souls, to empty homes.
They tie on their aprons. Between their palms they sculpt
   and caress,
stroke and press, dozens and dozens of tortillas—stack them
from basement to attic, from wall to wall, crowding closets,
jamming drawers, filling cupboards and *el vacío*.

At night they kiss ceramic statues of Virgin Marys,
roll rosary beads between their index fingers and thumbs,
weep tears prettier than holy water—
    sana sana colita de rana si no sanas ahora sanarás
      mañana—
When they wake they realize frogs haven't had tails in ages,
they hope gravity doesn't last long, and they wait—
y esperan y esperan y esperamos—to be carried up
   up—anywhere—
on round white magic carpets and tortilla smoke.

If Eve Side-Stealer & Mary Busted-Chest
Ruled the World

          What if Eve was an Indian
          & Adam was never kneaded
          from the earth, Eve *was* Earth
          & ribs were her idea all along?

          What if Mary was an Indian
          & when Gabriel visited her wigwam
          she was away at a monthly WIC clinic

receiving eggs, boxed cheese
& peanut butter instead of Jesus?

What if God was an Indian
with turquoise wings & coral breasts
who invented a game called White Man Chess
played on silver boards with all white pieces
pawns & kings & only one side, the white side
& the more they won the more they were beaten?

What if the world was an Indian
whose head & back were flat from being strapped
to a cradleboard as a baby & when she slept
she had nightmares lit up by yellow-haired men & ships
scraping anchors in her throat? What if she wailed
all night while great waves rose up carrying the fleets
across her flat back, over the edge of the flat world?

Postcolonial Love Poem

I've been taught bloodstones can cure a snakebite,
can stop the bleeding—most people forgot this
when the war ended. The war ended
depending on which war you mean: those we started,
before those, millennia ago and onward,
those which started me, which I lost and won—
these ever-blooming wounds.
I was built by wage. So I wage love and worse—
always another campaign to march across
a desert night for the cannon flash of your pale skin
settling in a silver lagoon of smoke at your breast.
I dismount my dark horse, bend to you there, deliver you
the hard pull of all my thirsts—
I learned *Drink* in a country of drought.
We pleasure to hurt, leave marks
the size of stones—each a cabochon polished
by our mouths. I, your lapidary, your lapidary wheel
turning—green mottled red—

the jaspers of our desires.
There are wildflowers in my desert
which take up to twenty years to bloom.
The seeds sleep like geodes beneath hot feldspar sand
until a flash flood bolts the arroyo, lifting them
in its copper current, opens them with memory—
they remember what their god whispered
into their ribs: *Wake up and ache for your life.*
Where your hands have been are diamonds
on my shoulders, down my back, thighs—
I am your culebra.
I am in the dirt for you.
Your hips are quartz-light and dangerous,
two rose-horned rams ascending a soft desert wash
before the November sky untethers a hundred-year flood—
the desert returned suddenly to its ancient sea.
Arise the wild heliotrope, scorpion weed,
blue phacelia which hold purple the way a throat can hold
the shape of any great hand—
Great hands is what she called mine.
The rain will eventually come, or not.
Until then, we touch our bodies like wounds—
the war never ended and somehow begins again.

ANGEL DOMINGUEZ

Dear Diego,

I write to you in a distant tongue. When I speak Spanish, I feel like I'm trying on shorts I know won't fit. They might button up, but I muffin top, and I'm painfully aware. I slip on English like a nighty; I'm comfortable when it's loose, it breathes with my body. It doesn't hurt me, at least not always. Diego, the present continues and I imagine the fabric of English upon my body—what would be its print? I guess I'd say the fabric would be blood-drenched cotton, the cut would be short, mid-thigh, I see a flower print, but I want the color to be blood before it dries. A shy sheen. It's intimate but I wear it often. I never take it off really. Crumpling up the smallest bits of myself into its pockets; rewriting those bits until I'm convinced I'm over-writing and trying so desperately to disappear. I guess I'll write again if the writing happens.

Love,
A

CAROLINA EBEID

Punctum / Image of an Intifada

And then you were standing under a red arcade of flyers.
The military said it dispersed leaflets over Gaza warning
residents to keep away—leaflets, I wanted to say, fell like
autumn, an artificial autumn in a school play, & we know it's
a tragicomedy because the dead lovers get up again—

Abid for the adorer, worshipper, he gets up again, the
anonymous one, *Munhit* whose voice is in his chest, the man
throwing a rock, my husband, *Samer* who talks smoothly at
night, I am a perfect wife to a revolution, he is a chain-link
fence collecting snow, *Sildin* who doesn't care what happens,
he is a black-figure athlete on a water jug in a museum,
Hamza who won't let go, *father,* I call out to him, *Khalil* is
the beautiful friend, he is a squeaky pink balloon twisted &
twisted into an elephant—what will you name him?

ROBERT FERNANDEZ

flags

Choose a flag,
one that itches, raw
glass, and draw it close

—

Comfort is for those
whose eyes can shut but
all wallets close at once, all eyes

—

All hands all hearts, blood
chambers—no-
thing speaks,
in the vast hall nothing speaks,
the air conditioner blows and the glass
tomb's color is perfect

—

I would bend you toward speed of day you
are not yet aligned you
are too slow slow slow or or or
you're not quite yes yes yes and must
align perfectly with break of day,
unwrapping inch by inch of stubborn canvas
to winds that would clean their teeth on you

—

So the day is murder;
still there's a bit, here and there, to say to day—
say ears are enfolded listening, colored flags, yes
again say nothing and no one
is ever enough there is no time yes yes never sorrow
never enough

ARIEL FRANCISCO

Along the East River and in the
Bronx Young Men Were Singing

I heard them and I still hear them
above the threatening shrieks of police sirens
above the honking horns of morning traffic,
above the home-crowd cheers of Yankee Stadium
above the school bells and laughter
lighting up the afternoon
above the clamoring trudge of the 1 train
and the 2 and 4, 5, 6, the B and the D
above the ice-cream trucks' warm jingle
above the stampede of children
playing in the street,
above the rush of a popped fire hydrant
above the racket of eviction notices
above the whisper of moss and mold moving in
above the High Bridge and the 145th Street Bridge
above mothers calling those children
to come in for dinner, to come in
before it gets dark, to get your ass inside
above them calling a child who may never come home
above the creaking plunge of nightfall
and darkness settling in the deepest corners
above the Goodyear blimp circling the Stadium
above the seagulls circling the coastal trash
along the East River and in the Bronx
young men are singing and I hear them,
eastbound into eternity even
as morning destars the sky.

VANESSA JIMENEZ GABB

Xunantunich

You are in my mouth sweet when I hear Belize
Oh, my sweet Belize

On TV they are eating panadas
We ate panadas just this week
I fried them barefoot like a mother
Even though I am no mother
I was one once for eight weeks
Then we were in Belize

Remember the ruins
Xunantunich, the stone woman
We took a boat to land
To a bus that delivered us rum-drunk

Post-colonial
I didn't recall what fell from my uterus
We saw the sun and fried for days and tasted better

Photos of us exist somewhere
We were so there
The mosquitos took our blood

JENNIFER GIVHAN

Coatlicue Defends, Amongst Others, the Tunguska Event

after Gloria Anzaldúa

First I stole just two of Jupiter's moons, sliced
midline, let flow their bowels until
my sluicing mouth bared jawbone, chewed white
meat, its death-cud & onions.
For my hair, their jagged rinds
like two little tusks knifing my forehead.
On my back I carried contempt—
a cradle sweet as cake.

Next came Venus, whose half-eaten peach
I peeled, his sulfur-stained teeth
crushed like old tin cans
then I left him to tend the planetarium
like a sad vegetable garden in his abuela's backyard—
the one place in the solar system most like Hell.
His transit, a red bellybutton
brutalizing the sun, but it's my
embryonic eye. My bruja's caldron
aftermath.

Did I do them wrong? My men
& their babies? Bruises of womb
breeching stone gods, pit vipers spitting
cotton-mouth black. There's no unwashing these deserts
I create. I couldn't admit
accident.

This is a story of
catastrophe, honey. You're the result of ancient
impacts. So too your bright new moon, horns

tilted toward the East,
split in two—I set
it wobbling, swinging like a bell
or flying mountain. Those Siberian trees?
Birthday candles
        I blew
then made a wish.

RODNEY GOMEZ

Coatlicue

Rattles delivered me. I was covered in mud. A nun.

I had my first meal in a diner on Closner Road:
chilaquiles, barbacoa, y chorizo con huevo.

Me tragué toda la basura. Me tragué la cocina y los carros.
Con gente o sin. My breath was holocaust.

I rumbled through laundromats. Sleeves of discarded uniforms
crawled to me. Soiled briefs, tattered bras, I accepted them.

Wilted sunflowers suckled at my breasts to become new again.

At night I slunk through black bars listening to the flim
of border patrol agents. They were bombardiers with no eyes.

I slept in a patchwork warehouse, drawing to me all neglected
     things.

The river changed its course, flowered through me.

Abandoned children were born in the entryway steps.
Children with crooked teeth, crinkled hair.
Children fueled by black holes. Drowned children & escapees.

I gave them my blood to drink.

I gave them my hands. They used them to pray.

CYNTHIA GUARDADO

Parallel Universe

after a five-hour flight from El Salvador to Los Angeles

In the dark of my mother's room
a portal opens into my abuela's house in Buena Vista:

tall ceilings, revealed beams, bats hanging in the shadows,
& another sleepless me afraid of night. I lie

next to my mother, my nails digging into the back of her
night gown (afraid she will disappear like abuela

into the portal's open mouth). After weeks en el cantón
we have travelled back in time to los Estados

(where no one we love exists). I'm nine years old
& the world has split in two. In the portal's eye I can still see

abuela's body shrinking in the distance on an endless road.
I hear the wind howling against the veranda of her house,

electricity trembling in the storm. The portal
in my mother's room flickers a message—Morse code between

spaces, across the wreckage of time—telling us to teleport
back to the only place we call home. The day we left

the dog chased our lingering scent for miles,
Tio's truck kicked up dirt & still the dog chased us

through the clouds. He ran faster & faster like he knew
we weren't coming back. I believed he would leap onto

the back of the truck-bed his teeth clinging to my clothes
like a plea for us to listen, to stay a little while longer.

LAURIE ANN GUERRERO

Put Attention

Put attention, grandma would say, as if attention
    were a packet of salt to be sprinkled, or a mound
        we could scoop out of a carton like ice cream.

Put attention, put attention. Put it where? In her hands?
    In the percolator? On top of the television set
        that seeps fat red lips and Mexican moustaches?

Next to the jade Buddha? Between La Virgen and Cousin
    Pablo's sixth-grade class photo—marshmallowy teeth
        jumping out of his mouth? We never corrected her.

Like the breast, Spanish lulled grandma's tongue, as we threw
    down shards of English, laughing, for her to leap in and
    around.
        Put attention, put attention. Put it where?

Shall I put attention in my glass and drink it soft like
    Montepulciano
        d'Abruzzo? Like Shiner Bock? Horchata? *Put attention*.
        Ponga atención, she tried to say in our language.

Put attention somewhere large. Back into her eyes.
    In the part of her brain that doesn't remember her own
        daughters, how to make rice, translate instructions.

LETICIA HERNÁNDEZ-LINARES

Translating the Wash

The lady who washes what
the neighborhood wears
doesn't pretend to like you,
so when she asks where
my clean clothes will travel,
she really wants to know.

El Salvador, my parents' country,
registers no recognition.
Offering a pen and interest,
she urges a drawing
on the back of an already
opened envelope.

Her expression doesn't follow
the tiny dots and hasty marks
I ink on the paper. Central America
below Mexico, the longitude
graphs itself around us.

Vietnamese sputters
from the twenty-something-year-old
radio without an antenna saving us
from an awkward silence.

Maybe if I say the country
is not too different
from her Vietnam—a thought
that makes a hole
in the counter, filling with sand,
the comparison muddled before translation.

Fifteen years and only a terminally
vacant apartment, a church

she can't pray in but that she worships
outside her window,
she has sewn my ripped fabric
together, erased stains, polished delicates.
Always open, except Sundays and holidays.

The cut and color of my clothing change
over fifteen years, and she wraps
safe travel wishes in plastic,
congratulating me on my births, describing
her father's death—first trip back home.

A long stretch between visits,
I bring her my post-maternity
pants to hem and a newborn.
His bouncy bare feet
unearth laughter, tender confession,
jagged-edged warnings from her.

No children, because she didn't have
enough money. This business—her child.
Wondering about me just this morning,
inquires after my first born. Sends me away
with a promise of shorter pants and relief
that the older one is not just crazy.

In her hometown, a little girl was so mad
at the baby her mother brought home,
she yelled her dissatisfaction
out the window—jumped out after it.
Just crazy. Probably better with boys.

I pack her story in my bag, wait and wish
for shock, dismay, but they don't come.
Some things are not lost in translation.

I try to send her customers,
but her refusal to feign
contentment with the folding of days

between other people's creases
scares them away.

Tired of giving directions at the coordinates
that mark an immigrant woman's arrival
and where she finds bread and breath,
I don't bother to translate.

DARREL ALEJANDRO HOLNES

Cristo Negro de Portobelo

It's when they see me naked that they finally believe
I'm from Panamá. The crucifix
hanging on my Black chest, underneath
the little hair I inherited from my father,
sweats as I perform what priests
and their laws call *unnatural acts.*
Only men grow body hair.
Only men are this dark and when
my hands finally darkened enough
to color even the blackest swans
I was sad to see them suddenly turn into wings,
plumed palms, hollow finger bones,
limp wrists. But then again, the struggle
of first flight against the moon's night
can be a freedom beyond heaven and
its wanting eternity. So now
rebellion is my new religion
or something else romantic and American
like a crownless king, perhaps an immigrant one
atop a throne, in native disguise.

JOE JIMÉNEZ

Some nights, I just want to hold a man in my arms because this would make everything better in my life—.

a comfort I frame—biceps and all
of my Mexican tattoos, my bulldog chest, and stuttering
    lung,
whispers that come only from another man's scalp
when the whole world inside him is a fingernail
or quiet like a small bucket of snails.
Even when I'm a remolino,
more so, then, especially, I wish my kiss tenderness,
enough to make a man's heart burst
into a thousand desert owls—wingbeat,
featherness, beak prod, and screech.
Last week, I was a pendulum in a fantasy—versatile,
swinging back, forth, into, deeply.
Being entered is when I know I am human.
Being entered is when I know I'm a part of something bigger.
Again. Equilibrium.
Evenness. And here it is: I've come here to love
breath in my bones when skin falls off the world.
and who doesn't carry some sort of trap on his knuckles?
The moment inside the body
when joy is not born as much as it is made out of anything
the rest of the world doesn't want.

ANTONIO DE JESÚS LÓPEZ

Convert Glossary

Tabula Rasa: Latin for I first prayed
       on a used bath towel.

Salaam: to shake after months filled
       with fitna, the cloro'd hands
of a Honduran convert,
       cuarenta cuaresmas old.

Shukr: when I lent him my tasbih
       for a lifetime, in honor of wiping
hospital floors; of staying
       after every jumu'ah

       to put away chairs.

Tajweed: the way he pronounced
       Fa-yet-vil,
the Carolina city
       donde tomó su testigo.

Sujud: when an egret bends its mouth
       inside a sea,

       the cheap incense
of sin that singes his MEChAs,
       as he learns to drink

from the Qur'an's ink.

Tawbah: to claw towards repentance,
       like los peregrinos en la Basílica
de Guadalupe;

       like the legless man
inside this masjid
       who bends over his wheelchair.

Istighfar: to clothe my loneliness
       with a pair of lace panties, join
the drowned hornets who floated
       atop red cups, guzzled

all the pineapple chunks
       of this dunya; to betray
You, skip salah tantas veces;

these dedos that groped for moans,
       now count Your names;

       my beads of sweat that thread
this negligee neglect.

DAVID TOMAS MARTINEZ

The Only Mexican

The only Mexican that ever was Mexican, fought in the
    revolution
and drank nightly, and like all machos, crawled into work
    crudo,

letting his breath twirl, then clap and sing before sandpaper
juiced the metal. The only Mexican to never sit in a Catholic
    pew

was born on Halloween, and ate his lunch wrapped in foil
    against
the fence with the other Mexicans. They fixed old Fords
    where my

grandfather worked for years, him and the welder Juan
    wagered
each year on who would return first to the Yucatán. Neither
    did.

When my aunts leave, my dad paces the living room and then
    rests,
like a jaguar who once drank rain off the leaves of Cecropia
    trees,

but now caged, bends his paw on a speaker to watch crowds
    pass.
He asks me to watch grandpa, which means, for the day; in
    town

for two weeks, I have tried my best to avoid this. Many times
    he will swear,
and many times grandpa will ask to get in and out of bed,
    want a sweater,

he will ask the time, he will use the toilet, frequently ask for
    beer,
about dinner, when the Padres play, por que no novelas,
    about bed.

He will ask about his house, grandma, to sit outside, he will
    question
while answering, he will smirk, he will invent languages
    while tucked in bed.

He will bump the table, tap the couch, he will lose his
    slipper, wedging it in
the wheel of his chair, like a small child trapped in a well,
    everyone will care.

He will cry without tears—a broken carburetor of sobs.
    When I speak
Spanish, he shakes his head, and reminds me, he is the only
    Mexican.

J. MICHAEL MARTINEZ

Lord, Spanglish Me

I.
Lord, Spanglish mi abuela para mi

      boil the orange rind
      beneath the syntax
      peeled of her name

      translate *naranja*   into *familia*
      the grove   into tea,
      the tea   into the talisman

      of her hand's soft work,
      the color of fold,

      unfolded,
           & sung.

II.
Lord, Spanglish mi abuela para mi

      her kingdom creation come,
      her gray hair grown down the fears,

      her pale hand plucking
      my tears as plums
      as love ransoms

      the noun within,
      her childhood unseeded

        beneath the ravage,
      the creek drowning

her colony home,
the aphids   & the oak.

her velvet Christ flood-spent,
        & Godless.

                    III.
Lord, Spanglish mi madre para ti

        carve shipless the light
        my world is etched by
        the wreck-salt
        so she may move
        among the beryl water,
        tide red with the silt
        beneath baptism, her eyes cast
        in the shadow of the soft
        of lavender grown there.

                    IV.
Lord, Spanglish mi lengua para ti

        that I may break open
        the promise-space of my fear,
        & become ladder, &

I may finally skin my ravage,

        that I may bear the estranged seasons,
        for I know we are creatures of metal
        without answer,

        a lost Spring
        whose lips rest
        where intimacy resigned
                the shapes of want,

        our honey succored from dust.

JASMINNE MENDEZ

Machete

call me what you want

gift / weapon / thief

from the inside out a CT scan
slices you a photograph
you cannot forget a memory
you cannot hold

Dominican - American / Haitian -
American / American - American

I hyphenate you into the you
that you are tissue rot stem
cells bundle of knuckles
harvest of fingertips

hold still / just breathe / count to ten

I swing

after the fog a rusty tongue
sticks and clicks your heavy metal
breath a metronome marks
my song a ballad that begins
and ends in blood

a cacophony of green hands and blue
mouths migrate towards your borders
draw a line where they will pull
apart your ligaments to collect
scars cut from the altar
of your almost fist

steel cut / sharp needle / silk scalpel

your stemmed finger a rot root
eviction notice where blood trembles
and I belong bent like stripped winds

soft / silent / serene

sink under then sleep between
saltgrass and palmas

I swing

call me by my name

Kukiri / Hawkbill / Cane

YESENIA MONTILLA

Maps

for Marcelo

Some maps have blue borders
like the blue of your name
or the tributary lacing of
veins running through your
father's hands. & how the last
time I saw you, you held
me for so long I saw whole
lifetimes flooding by me
small tentacles reaching
for both our faces. I wish
maps would be without
borders & that we belonged
to no one & to everyone
at once, what a world that
would be. Or not a world
maybe we would call it
something more intrinsic
like forgiving or something
simplistic like river or dirt.
& if I were to see you
tomorrow & everyone you
came from had disappeared
I would weep with you & drown
out any black lines that this
earth allowed us to give it—
because what is a map but
a useless prison? We are all
so lost & no naming of blank
spaces can save us. & what
is a map but the delusion of
safety? The line drawn is always
in the sand & folds on itself

before we're done making it.
& that line, there, south of
el rio, how it dares to cover
up the bodies, as though we
would forget who died there
& for what? As if we could
forget that if you spin a globe
& stop it with your finger
you'll land it on top of someone
living, someone who was not
expecting to be crushed by thirst—

JUAN J. MORALES

Discovering Pain

I was sixteen and skateboarding on a failed double-kick flip,
ankle's loud pop. I went on with my day in the swell of pain,
small ankle bone floating with snapped cartilage, one of
the first moments of learning my fragility. I used to always
sacrifice body and told myself, "It'll heal, no worries." Now,
I sometimes bang a finger or suffer a magnificent garden
scratch and claim them for the attention. But in instances
with more at stake, moments of failing family or mourning
love's purest hurt, I am paralyzed to speak. Perhaps this
paradox, hiding in the open, helps me study my obsessions,
like conquests centuries earlier, the Incan reign coming
undone as an ache I did not witness but read in the Andes
and in pages. I am guided toward historical pain, a shrine
built on the journey to museums, the pondering of a PBS
documentary on Friday night, a National Geographic in a
waiting room eerily similar to Bishop's childhood memory,
the untouched structures still buried around Machu Picchu,
but what happens when the hurt I reference involves a
skateboard, an ankle, or a childhood's bloodied kneecap,
minor images hundreds of years later and still a continent
removed, coming too late, coming too late?

ADELA NAJARRO

And His Name Is Nixon

Not Richard Nixon. His name is just a name,
this Nixon, this one Nica from Nicaragua
who walks into a kitschy little hot spot
and begins lilting his Spanish,
dropping the "s" *y vocificando.*
I know I've heard that Spanish
before and of course, *son de Nicaragua,*
Nixon y su compañero wittier than wit
and fast with one-liners, in Spanish
of course, Nicaraguan Spanish, that Spanish
interwoven between the vowels of my English.

And his name is Nixon, but how
did one boy out of Bluefields, Nicaragua,
acquire a moniker chiming
infamously through history, an American
history, a history of Empire: the capital,
commerce and dollars. So often
we've sent in the Marines followed by freight
tankers chugging through
playas del sol and waterways south:
México, el Caribe, El Salvador,
Nicaragua, Panamá, Colombia y Chile.

I tell Nixon that my mother was raised
on a farm in Bluefields: the *fincas*, rivers,
my mother's memories turned into stories
about rabbits, crocodiles, and Tía Pinita
spooning out rice and beans.

It was his turn, at age twelve, to traverse
borders, from Nicaragua to the US
con un coyote, alone by himself.
"*No me hicieron nada,*" he says, implying

that his body survived intact, perhaps a bit tired,
near exhaustion, but whole, with his soul
still fluttering inside a prepubescent body.

When *los coyotes* took his passport,
he put on a show, pleading
ignorance, that he didn't know
how to write his name, that he needed
to copy the letters out, and somehow
this worked. They let him keep
the passport. Then one evening,
he jumps out of a bedroom window.

Debajo los llantos de la luna,
through the breathing pulse of night,
his feet landed with a soft thud,
and he joined those who had gone before,
those who crossed borders,
those across centuries,
those who fled
only to continuously flee
rusted wire, chains, locks,
our doors bolted shut.

JOSÉ OLIVAREZ

Mexican American Disambiguation

after Idris Goodwin

my parents are Mexican who are not
to be confused with Mexican Americans
or Chicanos. i am a Chicano from Chicago
which means i am a Mexican American
with a fancy college degree & a few tattoos.
my parents are Mexican who are not
to be confused with Mexicans still living
in México. those Mexicans call themselves
mexicanos. white folks at parties call them
pobrecitos. American colleges call them
international students & diverse. my mom
was white in México & my dad was mestizo
& after they crossed the border they became
diverse. & minorities. & ethnic. & exotic.
but my parents call themselves mexicanos,
who, again, should not be confused for mexicanos
living in México, those mexicanos might call
my family gringos, which is the word my family calls
white folks & white folks call my parents interracial.
colleges say put them on a brochure.
my parents say que significa esa palabra,
i point out that all the men in my family
marry lighter-skinned women. that's the Chicano
in me. which means it's the fancy college degrees
in me, which is also diverse of me. everything in me
is diverse even when i eat American foods
like hamburgers, which, to clarify, are American
when a white person eats them & diverse
when my family eats them. so much of America
can be understood like this. my parents were
undocumented when they came to this country
& by undocumented, i mean sin papeles, &

by sin papeles, i mean royally fucked, which
should not be confused with the American Dream
though the two are cousins. colleges are not
looking for undocumented diversity. my dad
became a citizen which should not be confused
with keys to the house. we were safe from
deportation, which should not be confused
with walking the plank, though they're cousins.
i call that sociology, but that's just the Chicano
in me, who should not be confused with the diversity
in me or the mexicano in me who is constantly fighting
with the upwardly mobile in me who is good friends
with the Mexican American in me, who the colleges love,
but only on brochures, who the government calls
NON-WHITE, HISPANIC or WHITE, HISPANIC, who
my parents call mijo even when i don't come home so much.

ALAN PELAEZ LOPEZ

"Sick" in America

before the crossing[1] our family could understand the
whispers of the water[2]. we bathed our cuerpos morenos as
if we were holy: as if our humanity was valuable, as if we
were worth life. it is hard to remember anything before the
crossing[3]. how do i tell myself i had a childhood if at the
age of five i am a fugitive[4] of the law? it would be easier
to remember life before the crossing[5] if we didn't become
paralyzed for the rest of our lives: the doctor tells me i have
post traumatic stress disorder. he says it is because i am an
immigrant[6], but that in a few years, i will be american[7].

[1] during the crossing // we were faced with // the reality // of what it
means // to be black and indian // in an empire // that constantly measures
us // on production // production // and production. // our blood // a
sustenance // for those // who deem us "illegal."

[2] the water here // has been cut through // by wooden logs // that demand
// we show them // papers that say // we are not poor // nor indian or black.

[3] i only crossed once // (location: // san diego/tijuana border // age //
five // how // by foot and car.) // but every story heard // becomes another
crossing // my body remembers every crossing // every crossing becomes
mine // my body has experienced every crossing // in dreams.

[4] fugitive: runaway slave // fugitive: runaway NDN // fugitive: runaway
soon-to-be-lynched negro // fugitive: assata shakur // fugitive: mike brown
// fugitive: sandra bland // fugitive: alan carlos pelaez lopez.

[5] crossing: the precise location in a five-year-old's life where they lose their
humanity, health, and livelihood. // the site where the child realizes their
guiding spirit is weakening // the body, changing // the mind, confused //
the flesh, shivering // eyes, watering // digits, dancing. // the site where
"americans" will blame the child for "infecting" the "american dream." //
the site where a child is just a child visiting occupied NDN land.

[6] "the black body does not migrate . . . it is shipped"— tavia nyong'o

[7] american: i guess i'll be forever "sick."

EMMY PÉREZ

Laredo Riviera

I could love you all day
in a Laredo swimming
pool, ears under water,
eyes to the sky. Clouds

can't hear German
shepherds barking post-
shift before they're detained
near the river, our view

from the hotel room window,
in that dusky, almost stadium
light. Two cities facing each
other. What is it to love

within viewing distance of night
vision goggles and guns, mud
and the Republic of the Rio Grande
Museum? We're tourists skipping

churches, living off of credit
and elotes, trying to forget
our maquiladora conveniences.
We toast compañeros-compañeras

who slide along live conjunto
and sticky floors. We imagine who lives
with each other, who only for the night.
Euphoria more ancient than any vow.

Earth is earth. And kryptonite,
kryptonite. You and me, me and you.

ANA PORTNOY BRIMMER

A hurricane has come and gone.
What do we tell our children now?

Tell them about the waters. The ones they wade
     in, taste on their lips. Tell them not to fear the waves

that baptized them. That heat grows
     like a fetus, and come June, another swell will miscarry

into the wind. Tell them of Guabancex.
     A goddess whose fury destroys everything.

Juracán, the storm she swirls,
     the word *hurricane*, a bastardized translation—

drifts from one mouth to another.
     Tell them *hurricane* lies arid and unmoving

on the tongue—in bite-sized headlines,
     quick conscientious exchanges on the way to work.

Hurricane sounds like "hurry, cane"
     and sugar boils in the bile and rises

in the throat. Tell them not to speak
     this word. Say, *Juracán*. Let it thrash your mouth

open, shriek it like a prayer,
     sing it like a *son*. Our bodies are potholed

roads of chaos. Sweat tendrils
     down our spine. The way we dance, the whirl

in our walk. The way our desire
      spirals, how we coil and curl—thrust

forward, when touching,
      how we breathe up storms.

GABRIEL RAMIREZ

On Realizing I Am Black

I.

What the   oh nah,   forreal?
Wowwww!   Blessings!   This makes sense!
    Y'all!   It's wild nobody told me   right?!

II.

Born american. Raised Dominican.
Was called   spanish. (ALLTHETIME!)
Found Black. Found God. Found home.

III.

You're kidding me right?
I mean, don't you eat
rice and beans every night?
When the last time
you had some mac-n-cheese,
collard greens, and some
neck bones? You know
speaking spanish means
you're spanish?! Which means,
you're european. Which means,
you're white. Which means,
you're greedy. Would you like
some neck bones? Along with
the vertebrae of America's
hung foundation fathers?

Ain't that what you wanted?
To call African ancestors
yours too? Afro-Latino?
Taino-Indian? Drinks
you spanish people get
during happy hour?! Ha!

Ain't no happy hour when
the hands of your clock are shackled,
dragged, baton beaten, bullethole
bleed out. Countless moments
drowning in alcoholism
trying to forget you were born
cause when you are murdered every
28 hours it'll just be another bump
from a stranger on the sidewalk.

IV.

I hold elevator doors
for every racist
I look better than.
I reach into my pockets.
They grab their bags tighter.

V.

My hair curls into an Afro.
My grandfather would tell me
stop looking like a nigga! I'd tell him:
I'm celebrating the way God made me.
His teeth: the 13th, 14th, and 15th amendments
shredded into 32 pieces of bigotry.

VI.

My   grandfather   died
the moon.   I am   not him.
I am   Black   and full
of stars.   I am   not the absence of light.
I am   who allows light
to exist.   Don't confuse   me for only   Hip-Hop and Rap.
Those are my   fraternal twin
grandchildren   who   won't stop
asking for money.
You remember   Biggie?   Pac?   Pun?
Stars died and   have come home
to me.   I am
not ugly.   I am   who allows you
to be beautiful.   Now isn't that
the blackest thing   you've ever heard God say?

JULIAN RANDALL

Biracial Ghazal: Why Everything Ends in Blood

And what language exists with no word for blood?
What gets across the legend as quickly as blood?

Where I am from there are no words for my shade
Only nicknames   approximations for the blood

Blacktino   Lanegro   Halfbreed   Mutt   Progress
confused   a turmoil of skin   bouquet of hunted blood

I am a burden in every mouth   my name a minefield
people forget what I am exactly   but I end in blood

Two tone sacrament   Where the soil meets the sky
but never the horizon   child with the invisible blood

Like a sunset I am considered most beautiful when
I am disappearing   stitching a gown of my blood

Child with too many tongues   gone twice over
aftermath   a failed experiment of the blood

People ask *what are you*   and I have no house
I bite my tongue into copper   search my blood

For a key   for a name that is not a translation for
Once there was a war   here is what we did with the blood

ALEXANDRA LYTTON REGALADO

La Mesa

After Carolyn Forché

Yes, what you've written is true. A Salvadoran colonel might
have collected a sack full of human ears in the late 70s. I
know a retired colonel and I've heard his talk to consider
it possible. The death squads of the 80s—certainly not a
subject for dinner conversation, which according to my
grandmother, should glide over pleasant topics and promote
easy digestion. I've sat with threaded lips listening to stories
of the ex-guerrilla-leader now our current president, of the
former president's shopping binges and a totaled Ferrari, of
a winning mayor's campaign: go-go dancers grinding on a
table in their political-party-colored thongs, of gang leaders
watching their flat screens alongside lovers in their hotel-
prisons, of 6pm city buses overturned and lit on fire. The
men pound their hands on the polished wood and the wine
goblets jump, the red liquid sloshes in the crystal wells. I've
watched the waiters dressed in white tuxedo jackets, the
black moth of death clinging to their throats as they listen,
offering a second helping of roast lamb. We've left behind the
sandbagged street corners and now it's only the bodyguards
driving us around in bulletproof SUVs that keep us from
the gun-toting assailant at the stoplight. The thick glass that
separates us from the children begging at their mother's
side—and my own child asking, *What does she want mom?*
Where is her car? Where is her house? And the driver staring
ahead at the road through the tinted glass, his ears listening
and listening for my reply. What to answer: this is something
for my poetry, no? Would my hand move toward the knife as
those on the left and right argue for their piece, the country
carved up like a pie? In the morning I'll hold my grand-
mother's porcelain cup and pour sugar into the bitter black
while I read the newspaper, guaranteed a ladle of casualties,

dead bodies splayed across page two, all this news sounding like the maid saying, *A dish broke*—the action disembodied of any blame or fault—an object finished or disappeared of its own volition. My husband across the table says with his eyes, say nothing. And I think of this life: of pears stewed in wine, the instant gratification of artichoke hearts, the chalice always refilled, music in stereo and the velvet wind through the pines, a pair of loyal dogs sleeping at our feet. The moon shines its white beam across the lawn's smooth plane.

YOSIMAR REYES

TRE (My Revolutionary)

You tell me you don't like the city
That these buildings, this concrete
Numbs the senses
Cages the spirit and baby
Your spirit was meant to be free
You my love
Were born to be revolutionary

Like the winds we felt sitting on top of the world
Free like the tobacco you offered me to blow blessings
Free like palabras sagradas que salen de tu boca
Y las rimas femeninas y masculinas that you bust on
stage
You are my revolutionary
Not a guerrero but a healer
Because in times of conflict
Mi rey you heal
And more than body I must agree with you that you are
    spirit
Because more than your flesh I am in love con el Corazón
    que tienes

You are the reason why I love men with noble hearts
The reason why I don't mind sharing a bed with someone
For men like you I would ride a million BARTs
Get lost in Oakland
And find your house beneath the brightest star

Mi Vida
You come from tierra
Where the spirits of those who failed to cross over roam
You come from el desierto
But baby we all know you are not deserted
You got me and together we are 4 spirits

Like the 4 directions
You got the creator behind you
you are his creation
His masterpiece

And in this journey you are traveling you have managed to
    leave
Your footprints in my heart
I carry your breath in my hair
Your teachings in my two spirits
You are fluid
Como los Ríos que nuestra gente ha cruzado

You remind me that the only possessions we have in this
    world
Are our bodies and our voice
And the combination of the two must be used
To honor the spirits of los antepasados
This life is a ritual
And in its sacredness
I am so glad that I am able to hug you

You are my revolutionary . . .
And as you make your transition back home
Into the arms of your mother
Into the lips of your father
I ask that you take this poem with you
Take a memory of me with you
Plant these
En la tierra que te vio nacer
En esa tierra que ha sido bautizada
Con la sangre sagrada de nuestra gente
And I will assure you
that where ever you be
This love will sprout anew
Como el sol por las mañanas this poem will shine on you

Now go
to where ever home is
Knowing that in San Jose

You leave a brown boy
That has nothing but love and respect for you.

In the mean time,
I will stay here
in this cage, in this shitty city

Singing and singing
Till this system crumbles
Till borders break
Till the earth shakes
And our people become awake

I will be here
Singing and singing till the day
We are all free to return

HOME.

ILIANA ROCHA

Elegy Composed of a Thousand Voices in a Bottle

¿Girl, why you trying to be white? Güera. Sinvergüenza.
The fortune cookie's jaw cracks, on its tongue: Remember
this day, three months from now. Mija, querida linda. Lazy
daisy. You were my first Mexican girl. ¡Mexicana, habla en
español! I thought you were twenty-six. No me gusta hablar
en español porque mi español es muy mal. No. Me. Siento.
Bien. Hablo. Hablas. Habla. Let's talk a while. Cautionary
tales about machismo, your father con la puta. Never marry
a Mexican. They dismantled the gun that killed Selena &
threw it off the Corpus Christi Harbor Bridge. Como la flor.
"Put the Blame on Mame" by acoustic guitar. Pizza & yeast
infections. Fireworks. Virginity. A machine makes ice. Your
father disappears again into the Gulf. You're no Mexicana.
Another man suicides middle age like your father. Your ass
is like Selena's. My mother's humming while she picked
cotton, my mother speaking en inglés. Me hicieron ojo.
Code switching, faces somewhat reflected in glass, passing.
¿Where you from? Your Spanish is like a confetti cannon. ¡Ya
tu sabes! Is that guy your sancho? Dismantled. The gun. You
are the saddest girl I've ever seen. A rooster's crow, kikirikí:
You are selfish & lonely.

JOSÉ ANTONIO RODRÍGUEZ

La Migra

The grownups sat on their long chair called couch
And talked of the weather, the dew of the blossoms'
 morning,
And what might happen to us, the children.
Mom said don't leave the house, not without
Papers. Do I dare speak of the papers hoarded
In corners? How many more poems can you write
About a face spackled with fear before
It holds you? The reader aiming, too.
Let us find a darkened corner, you and I,
Where we will lay these words. Leave children
To sleep in windowless rooms. The mother
Biting a prayer. The country weaving a tomb.

Shelter

Don't misunderstand me, I love a good poem
Like half my Facebook friends, one that transports you
To a corner of the soul you didn't know was there
Because you couldn't find the precise metaphor,
Even if you felt it, like that time my parents saw
A local news story of an older woman asking for help
With an ailing husband, and I volunteered to drive them
To the address onscreen, a neighborhood
I'd never driven through, though it looked familiar
With its usual poverty: a few leaning boards called a house
And inside the woman from the news in half-light
Thanking us for the comforters in our hands and pointing
To a foldout chair where we could place them
Before introducing us to her husband, a scraggly beard
Beneath a crinkled blanket on a cot right there

In what would have been the living room, groaning
In the muted manner of those who know this is
As good as it'll get, the woman's non-stop small talk
About "So it is, life's a struggle" and "Please stay awhile"
And "Take a seat," as if we were long-missed relatives,

All this in Spanish, though I translate it here
Because I want to reach the widest audience
And not burden the monolingual English reader
When they've already gifted me their time by reading this,
Which I'll call a poem, one that my parents can't read,
As they only speak Spanish with that poor Mexican lilt of
    apology
Which kept them from interrupting the woman, a Spanish
I've kept but rarely use, though I did that moment
When I kept telling my mother "We have to go"
With an almost impolite urgency, because I couldn't bear
One more minute in that near-replica of the room of my
    childhood,
Even as the woman said "He seems to be in such a hurry"
And my mother smiled, making excuses as we turned to
    leave,
While I bemoaned my parents' passive politeness
So common in the Mexican in America, though by then
I was already a grad student in upstate New York
And down in South Texas for the winter break
Between semesters of reading Adichie and Alexie
And risking words together to find something
Like the point of this, some search for the reason
For the speaker's love of poems, that pull
Of the written word as artifact, as a kind of tool
Against the sometimes overwhelming sadness about all of
    it—
Including the fact that some of us it seems will never be
    allowed
The time and energy to sit with a poem, like them
In that illusion of shelter, though perhaps
They were closer to poetry's pursuit, that edge of oblivion
Where words begin becoming insufficient—the woman

With her frantic speech beseeching us and the man
Extending his bony hand out, as if from the cot itself,
The tremor of it trying to say something that sounded
Like a greeting, that sounded like a plea.

ROQUE RAQUEL SALAS RIVERA

they

what do we eat when a name dies?
yesterday your mother stopped by, but she didn't
recognize me as your friend's friend, the previous one.
what is that about, having a dead friend
in the wallet with a picture of a kidnapped kid?
have you seen my son?
he is short and collects photos of swings.

my short hair isn't professional;
your long hair doesn't prepare you.
between the two of us, we figure out how
to fake we are marionettes, not people.
it's difficult to count the days
since the last time we went out.

what is that about, going out
and not having to explain
you aren't that her
or that thing?

in this, our language,[1]
there exists no plural that doesn't deny me.

if time is queer/and memory is trans/and my hands hurt in the cold/then

there are ways to hold pain like night follows day
not knowing how tomorrow went down.

[1] our language is spanish. ours, but never quite mine.

it hurts like never when the always is now,
the now that time won't allow.

there is no manner of tomorrow, nor shape of today
only like always having to leave
from and toward the future's could-be,
in order to never more see
the sí;

and if forever proves me wrong,
it'll hurt with the hurt of before the before.
it'll have to take me along:
all the never-enough of why and therefore.

life has given me much to believe,
but more is the doubt that undid what i know,

for, like night follows day, the pleasure is sure,
of forever beginning once more.

C. T. SALAZAR

All the Bones at the Bottom of the Rio Grande

stick up like a cradle growing out of the mud. All the bones
    at the bottom
of the Rio Grande know the same song but cannot

sing. They raise the river, but only a little, as when
    Archimedes lowered
the gold crown into the bath to study displacement.
    Displacement: *noun.*

The moving of something from its place. All the bones at the
    bottom of
the Rio Grande know this definition. To replace with oneself
    what would

otherwise be occupied with fluid. To be as much the river as
the river—all the bones at the bottom of the Rio Grande
    have changed

        their name to Rio Grande. The Rio Grande has so
        many names.
                Río Bravo del Norte: Great River of the
                North, or Hanapakwa
            in the Towa, or boundary or border to the
            desperate, or my love
                I swear I'll come back for you. In
                between two halves of me
            a river is running. I've named that river
            Rio Grande.

That river named me survivor, named me *lucky*. Is there
    a word
for the opposite of a miracle? There must be a sound.
    Punctured whistle

of air leaving the raft. All the bones at the bottom of the Rio
    Grande
needed a home more than they needed a lifeboat. All the
    bones at the

bottom of the Rio Grande I've inherited the way my mother
    inherited
my grandmother's teapots. I've seen two shatter. They fell
    with no river

> to catch them. Is ruin by land a sweeter
>   heirloom?
> Imagine to be gone. Record   destroyed.
>   Archimedes's book
>   of handwritten mathematics a thirteenth-
>   century monk erased
>   page after page and filled with prayers to the
>   Lord. All the bones
>   at the bottom of the Rio Grande rattle at the
>   word *erased*.

All the bones at the bottom of the Rio Grande have
    finally found
    a place willing to make room for them, and all the bones

at the bottom of the Rio Grande will reverse this river when
    their children call.

RUTH IRUPÉ SANABRIA

Distance

My grandfather asked me: could I remember
him, the park, the birds, the bread?
I'll be dying soon, he said.

His voice would stretch the ocean and end there,
inside the olive phone in our tiny kitchen.
My mother would stretch the green shell to my ear,
speak, say something, speak. My fingers tugged the cord
across our red wooden table. Listening to the dark adios,
I carved half moons into the wood with my fingernails.
In case I am dead by your next birthday, hija, *remember . . .*

We ate without him, without any elders
and the world was fine.

We have yet to bury our bones in this foreign land.
When we do, where will we come from then?
Already, *home* is a carnation pinned to our cold breasts.

ERIKA L. SÁNCHEZ

Narco

Highway of Death—the indifference
of snakes. Sky is ripe and everywhere
the colors are breaking. *¿Quién es el jefe
más jefe?* In the filmy stillness, Possum-face
carries a bucket of heads and spills them
like marbles. *La yerba, el polvo, las piedras—
Que traguen fierro los cabrones,
¡yo soy el más chingón de Pisaflores!*
Rompe-madres, gazing at mountains
the color of elephant skin, pulls a woman
from a bus and onto the thorns and dirt:
White hiss of heat. Hummingbirds. Milkweed.
A pack of spotted horses turn to the foaming
moon. *May God bless you all and lead you
toward righteousness.* Under the final gash
of light, Rompe-madres wipes the sweat
from his eyes, and ties her panties to a creosote bush—
a colony of vultures waiting for its tribute.

JACOB SHORES-ARGÜELLO

Paraíso

We escape with Guatemalan rum
through the city's petroleum night,

through rain-washed asphalt
and taxi smog, up the volcanic hills

of San José, through neighborhoods
roofed by zinc, and fincas where

shade trees stand watch over coffee,
up the mountain's lava-made trail,

into the theater of the sky
where we can see the naked body

of the city, and higher to where
we point to our far pueblo,

and to the ocean eating up the coast,
and higher into the cold

until we can hold all of Costa Rica
in our eye, and then higher

until Mexico bulges into the ocean—
up and up until we stare out at the mingling

Americas, Florida kissing Cuba
in the blue distance, and we open our rum

and drink so long that we forget ourselves,
and remember ourselves again.

BRANDON SOM

Chino

The olla knocked with steam. The masa cooked.
    She said her eyes are china. The vowel
    switched
on an aura, a shine that sheens the threshold.
      The vowel was spell: an *i* that
      might we,
an *i* that echoes how we're seen and see.
     *Eye*dentity. Ay Dios, she exclaimed
surrounded by photos—niños and nietos—
      where I'm the only chino. How
      might I
see through my family's eyes—an owl's eyes
     in ojos and one in its lid turned sideways
     目—
I wondered with her at the table where we
      placed one olive—ojo negro—in
      each hoja,
that worn folio for field corn's field notes.
     What does that dark eye in the ear's husk
     see?

CHRISTOPHER SOTO

The Joshua Tree // Submits Her Name Change

She stepped across our chest
   Dragging her shadow & fraying // All the edges
     Our nipples bloomed // Into cacti // Fruit & flower
      She ate // Then we did // A needle pricked her

We've seldom seen this woman cry // Squeezed like a raincloud
   She cried because // Two men // Two men
     Built a detention center // From bone & clay

The first bone // Our clavicle The second // Her spine
   She howled // As the fence // Surrounded her
     She coughed & combed the floor // Our chest shiv
     Shivering

Inside the detention center // She was renamed Ill // Egal
   She forgot 15 pounds & mental health & her feet were
     Cracked tiles // Dirty dishes

This border // Isn't a stitch // Where nations meet
   This border's a wound // Where nations part

VINCENT TORO

Sonata of the Luminous Lagoon

after Pedro Pietri

Crickets, coquis corrobórate. Mezzo.
Alto. Tenor. Chemical coladas are pumped

like stale petroleum from fracked rocks.
The joy of combustion at five dollars a pop.

Surf shops collide with Desecheo Island.
Silicon Valley Spanish stings like chlorine,

an ill refuge from portfolios and defaulted
mortgages seared on grills that serve no native

dish. The esclavos fed-exed to Co-op City,
Humboldt Park, Kensington, where nature

is a cable program shot from a satellite dish
in twenty minute cycles and sunsets come

with membership fees. Coconuts, cangrejos
are gathered and stacked. For tonight there

will be a fiesta in the hacienda overlooking
Culebra, but the residents did not receive

an invitation, Coral contorts into ads for cell
phones. Panorama in flux. Coffee plantation

permutated into port. Cracked conch serves
as chrysalis for research station. A naval base

etched into islet. Yucca fields tailored into
spa resort. The new natives will boast of job

creation and toast to how the quality of life
has improved for the mosquitos who now

feast on sweet meat of plump and primped
immigrants blown in from el norte.

DAN VERA

Small Shame Blues

I live with the small shame
of not knowing the multiple names for blue
to describe the nightsky over New Mexico
to describe the light in my lover's eyes.

It is a small shame that grows.

I live with the small shame
which resides in the absences of my speech
as I pause to search for the word in Spanish
to translate a poem to my Father
who sits there waiting
who scans my eyes to see
what I cannot fully describe
who waits for the word from me
the word that escapes me in the moment
the word I fear has never resided within me.

It is a small shame that grows
when indigo and cerulean are merely azul
and not *añil* and *cerúleo.*

LAURA VILLAREAL

Home Is Where the Closet Is

Home is where I put my whole self away
    in the garage or the attic or inside
        a part of me I won't visit soon.

My identity knots around everyone else's finger in Texas.
    I forgot I was brown
        until Texas pointed to the border.

I forgot my orientation was straight
    to hell if I love another woman.
        I'm having trouble adjusting

the light so I look straight enough not to get fired.
    I whisper the word queer
        over & over like a spell—

to remind myself I'll come back for it again later
    in a new city, with a new job,
        when there's enough money to be alive.

Most days I want to grieve
       & I want all the stars to grieve with me
        because in Texas even the moon hides

herself behind the clouds—
    away from every woman she loves.

VANESSA ANGÉLICA VILLARREAL

A Field of Onions: Brown Study

*dedicated to the immigrants buried in mass graves
in and near Falfurrias, Texas*

1. I walk through a bald field blooming violet onions. I will know I am absolved when there is no more dirt underfoot, when I have flipped the earth and the river runs above us, a glassed belldark sound.

2. To find: liver, lung, womb. A lens cut from vulture eye. This is what it is to miss a thing.

3. At the McDonald's, a man in a parked car will talk himself awake. This is another kind of hunger.

4. A prayer for the king: forty pears, all bloomed from young throats. Long life, a sea of rice, a thicket of braids.

5. Problem: Four boats arranged in a cross drift away from each other in opposing directions. What theory states that, all conditions remaining equal, they can reach each other again on the other side of a perfect globe?

6. To understand a map is to shrink the world; to plan; to color.

7. Can you smell the vinegar blood in the babes, stardappled. The survivors ride the beast train toward the North, over those rolled off onto the tracks. See their legs, scattered.

8. Olga in Minnesota: to be with her mother amidst rags of spring snow. For now, she is curled in the glovebox of a Chevrolet Cavalier.

9. Bless you, all that meat and milk, threaded. Pass, you fairer animal. Not you. I have seen the door in the water.

10. Solution: Magical thinking.

11. To panic is to feel all your wildness at once.

12. A flock of geese felled to the open plain, the lush grass confounds even the birds for passable angles.

13. We the holy, are never really still. Agitation pulls even at hanging planets.

14. Four sirens twist their voices—four dead in the desert borderlands.

15. In this dream, I am on a plane. I wake up to the pilot smiling down on me. No one flies the plane. Or, I am flying the plane.

16. The threads fly loose on each body, some sown to others, some not. But let's not take this metaphor too far; we are better than the obvious.

17. A hero is a plane of being.

18. I think of a girl at space camp, perched above a better telescope than she has in her room. Tonight, she figures space as a map of horses. Blur, focus. Blur and focus. Tonight, the clouds will pull apart for her. Tonight, we will all dream of horses.

19. My ancestor says: *Later, when I arrive at your house, I will hang a crown of flowers at your door. And yours. And yours.*

20. And: *Sometimes I choose to come through your television. In sleep, you will mistake me for dripping water. You will think you heard your father. We visit each other in these ways.*

21. Plan B. From the moon, the earth is a crown of dark marble.

22. There are varying kinds of tragedy that produce the same outcome: paperwork.

23. And even if we did save the trees, or the whales, the hunger would still be so great the people who need saving would still need saving.

24. The heads of violet onions, rooted child fingers, blue-leafed lips. An orchard, a mass grave.

25. I give you my coat and scarf in offering. I have no choice, I was born to saints in pilgrimage.

26. Paper-purple skin. Grounded bodies. The border. A field of onions.

27. Thesis: I swallow a bee for each ill deed done. I am a hive walking. I strain to hear you over the regret.

JAVIER ZAMORA

El Salvador

Salvador, if I return on a summer day, so humid my thumb
　　will clean your beard of salt, and if I touch your volcanic face,

kiss your pumice breath, please don't let cops say: *he's gangster.*
　　Don't let gangsters say: *he's wrong barrio.* Your barrios

stain you with pollen. Every day cops and gangsters pick at you
　　with their metallic beaks, and presidents, guilty.

Dad swears he'll never return, Mom wants to see her mom,
　　and in the news: black bags, more and more of us leave.

Parents say: *don't go; you have tattoos. It's the law; you don't know
　　what law means there.* ¿But what do they know? We don't

have greencards. Grandparents say: *nothing happens here.*
　　Cousin says: *here, it's worse. Don't come, you could be . . .*

Stupid Salvador, you see our black bags, our empty homes,
　　our fear to say: *the war has never stopped,* and still you lie

and say: *I'm fine, I'm fine,* but if I don't brush Abuelita's hair,
　　wash her pots and pans, I cry. Tonight, how I wish

you made it easier to love you, Salvador. Make it easier
　　to never have to risk our lives.

BIOGRAPHICAL NOTES

NOTE ON THE TEXTS
AND ACKNOWLEDGMENTS

NOTES

INDEX OF TITLES
AND FIRST LINES

INDEX OF POETS

BIOGRAPHICAL NOTES

Alexander Abreu (b. 1976) b. Cienfuegos, Cuba. Graduated from Cuba's Escuelas Nacionales de Arte in Havana. Trumpet player, composer, arranger, and singer who leads the band Havana D'Primera, which he founded in 2007.

Elizabeth Acevedo (b. 1988) b. New York, NY, to Dominican immigrant parents. Raised in New York City. Earned BA in Performing Arts from George Washington University and MFA in Creative Writing from the University of Maryland. Taught eighth-grade English in Prince George's County, Maryland. Named National Poetry Slam Champion in 2014. Chapbook *Beastgirl & Other Origin Myths* was published in 2016; *Inheritance* appeared in 2022. Has won several awards for her young adult novels, including the National Book Award for *The Poet X* (2018).

Marjorie Agosín (b. 1955) b. Bethesda, MD, and raised in Chile in Santiago and Quisco; returned to U.S. at age sixteen. Earned BA from University of Georgia and MA and PhD from Indiana University. First published poetry collection, *Gemidos y cantares* (Groans and Chants), was brought out in Chile in 1977. Returned to South America on a 1984 Fulbright fellowship. Other publications include the memoir *A Cross and a Star: Memoirs of a Jewish Girl in Chile* (1995); the poetry collections *Toward the Splendid City* (1994), winner of the 1995 Latino Literature Prize, and *At the Threshold of Memory: New and Selected Poems* (2003); and the young adult novel *I Lived on Butterfly Hill* (2015), winner of an International Latino Book Award. Edited anthology *These Are Not Sweet Girls: Poetry by Latin American Women* (1994). A human rights activist, she is recipient of a United Nations Leadership Award for Human Rights; other honors include a Gabriela Mistral Award for Life Achievement and a Letras de Oro prize. Is Andrew W. Mellon Professor in the Humanities and professor of Spanish at Wellesley College.

Anthony Aguero (b. 1992) b. Los Angeles, CA. Received BA from Antioch University. First poetry collection, *Burnt Spoon Burnt Honey*, was published in 2022.

Jack Agüeros (1934–2014) b. New York, NY, to parents recently arrived from Puerto Rico. Served in U.S. Air Force for four years. Earned BA at Brooklyn College and MA in Urban Studies from Occidental College in 1990. Worked as community organizer; after dismissal from post as deputy commissioner for New York City's main antipoverty agency (due to his not having filed tax returns for prior years), staged five-day hunger strike demanding greater Puerto Rican representation in the city's government. Served as director of El Museo del Barrio. Author of books in several genres, including the poetry collections *Correspondence Between the Stone Haulers* (1991), *Sonnets from the Puerto Rican* (1996), and *Lord, Is This a Psalm?* (2002). Short stories collected in *Dominoes and Other Stories from the Puerto Rican* (1993). Wrote plays. Translations of Julia de Burgos's and José Martí's work published, respectively, as *Songs of the Simple Truth* (1997) and *Come, Come, My Boiling Blood* (2007; with Lidia Torres).

Francisco X. Alarcón (1954–2016) b. Wilmington, CA, and grew up in Guadalajara, Mexico. Returned to Southern California at age seventeen. Earned BA from California State University, Long Beach, and MA from Stanford. Served as director of the Spanish for Native Speakers Program at the University of California, Davis, and taught for the California Poets in the Schools program. Publications include the poetry collections *De amor oscuro/Of Dark Love* (1991), the American Book Award–winning *Snake Poems: An Aztec Invocation* (1992), and *From the Other Side of Night/Del otro lado de la noche* (2002); among his books for children are the bilingual poetry collection *From the Bellybutton of the Moon and Other Summer Poems/Del ombligo de la luna: y otros poemas de verano* (1998). Winner of a Chicano Literary Prize and the Fred Cody Lifetime Achievement Award, and other honors.

Claribel Alegría (1924–2018) b. Estelí, Nicaragua, to Nicaraguan and Salvadoran parents. Father's criticism of the U.S.-backed government forced family's move to Santa Ana in El Salvador when she was a small child. Came to the United States and earned BA in Philosophy and Letters at George Washington University, studying with Juan Ramón Jiménez, who chose the poems gathered in her début collection, *Anilo de silencio* (Ring of Silence, 1948). Traveled widely, living in Mexico, Chile, Uruguay, the United States, France, and Mallorca. Novel written with her husband, Darwin J. Flakoll, *Cenizas de izalco* (Ashes of Izalco), set during the civil war in El Salvador in the 1930s, was published in 1966 (English translation by Flakoll, 1989). Unable to return to El Salvador during its civil war (1979–92), she settled in Nicaragua in the 1980s. Books in several genres include the poetry collections *Sobrevivo* (I Survive, 1978), which won a Casa de Las Américas prize; *Flores del volcán* (Flowers from the Volcano, 1982); and *La Mujer del río* (Woman of the River, 1989). In 2006, awarded the Neustadt International Prize for Literature.

Miguel Algarín (1941–2020) b. San Juan, Puerto Rico; moved to New York City at age nine. Received BA from University of Wisconsin and

MA in English Literature from Pennsylvania State University. Returned to New York City, where he was at the center of a group of artists and writers who would regularly meet at his apartment, the genesis of the Nuyorican Café, founded in 1973. Taught U.S. ethnic literature, Shakespeare, and creative writing at Rutgers University. Books include *Mongo Affair: Poems* (1978), *Time's Now/Ya es tiempo* (1985), *Love Is Hard Work: Memorias de Loisaida* (1997), *Survival Superviviencia* (2009), and the translation *Song of Protest: Poems by Pablo Neruda* (1985). Co-edited, with Miguel Piñero, *Nuyorican Poetry: An Anthology of Puerto Rican Words and Feelings* (1975). Recipient of four American Book Awards, including a Lifetime Achievement Award.

Alurista (b. 1943) b. Alberto Baltazar Urista Heredia in Mexico City; family relocated to San Diego, CA, when he was thirteen. Earned BA in Psychology from San Diego State; received MA in Literature from San Diego State and PhD in Literature from University of California, San Diego. Adopted pen name Alurista in 1965. In 1967, while at San Diego State, cofounded Movimiento Estudiantil Chicano de Aztlán (MECHA, Chicano Student Movement of Aztlan); involved in activism his entire career. Books include *Timespace Huracan: Poems 1972–1975* (1976), *Et Tú . . . Raza?* (1996), and *Tunaluna* (2010). Has taught at California Polytechnic State University, 1986–90, as well as Denver's Escuela Tlatelolco and the University of Texas at Austin.

Julia Alvarez (b. 1950) b. New York, NY. Lived until age ten in the Dominican Republic; family then returned to the United States after her father was involved in a plot to overthrow dictator Rafael Trujillo. Earned BA from Middlebury College and MFA from Syracuse University. *Homecoming* was published in 1984, followed by other poetry collections, including *Homecoming: New and Collected Poems* (1996) and *The Woman I Kept to Myself* (2004). Her novels include *How the García Girls Lost Their Accents* (1991), *In the Time of the Butterflies* (1994), and *The Cemetery of Untold Stories* (2024). With her husband, started an organic coffee farm in the Dominican Republic. Has written essays and children's books. Awarded in 2013 the National Medal of Arts, among other honors. Writer-in-residence at Middlebury College, where she has taught since 1988.

Steven Alvarez (b. 1979) b. Safford, AZ. Received BA in English Literature and in Creative Writing from University of Arizona; earned his MA and PhD at the Graduate Center of the City University of New York. Publications include the novels-in-verse *The Pocho Codex* (2011), *The Xicano Genome* (2013), and *The Codex Mojaodicus* (2017). Was associate professor at University of Kentucky; is currently professor of English at St. John's University in Queens, NY.

Eloisa Amezcua (b. 1989) b. Arizona. Received BA in English from the University of San Diego, followed by an MFA from Emerson College. Publications include *From the Inside Quietly* (2018) and *Fighting Is Like a Wife* (2022). Founder of Costura Creative, an agency for poets and writers, and the poetry journal *The Shallow Ends*. Currently a professor in Randolph College's MFA program.

Aldo Amparán (b. 1988) Raised in El Paso, TX, and Ciudad Juárez, Mexico. Received BA and MFA at University of Texas at El Paso, where he has also taught. Inaugural poetry collection *Brother Sleep* was published in 2020. Currently Visiting Assistant Professor in Poetry at New Mexico State University.

Diannely Antigua (b. 1989) b. Haverhill, MA. Received BA in English from the University of Massachusetts, Lowell, and MFA from New York University. Début collection *Ugly Music* (2019) was followed by *Good Monster* (2024). Founder of the *Bread & Poetry* podcast. Named Poet Laureate of Portsmouth, NH.

Gloria Anzaldúa (1942–2004) b. Raymondville, TX. Earned BA from Pan American College (now University of Texas Rio Grande Valley) and MA in English from the University of Texas at Austin; was nearly finished with doctoral degree at University of California, Santa Cruz, when she died of complications from diabetes (was awarded posthumously). Taught in public schools in the 1960s and early 1970s. Moved to Bay Area, 1977–1981. With Cherríe Moraga, co-edited the influential anthology *This Bridge Called My Back: Writings by Radical Women of Color* (1981). Lived in Cambridge, New Haven, and Brooklyn before moving back to Bay Area in 1985. Publications include the book of poetry and prose *Borderlands/La Frontera: The New Mestiza* (1987) and *Making Face, Making Soul/Haciendo Caras: Creative and Critical Perspectives by Feminists of Color* (1990); also wrote bilingual children's books. Among her honors is a Lambda Lesbian Small Press Book Award.

Francisco Aragón (b. 1965) b. San Francisco, CA, the son of Nicaraguan immigrants. Awarded degrees in Spanish from the University of California, Berkeley, and New York University as well as graduate degrees in Creative Writing from University of California, Davis, and the University of Notre Dame. Lived in Spain for several years before returning to the U.S. in 1998. First collection, *Puerta del Sol*, was published in 2005, followed by the anthology *The Wind Shifts: New Latino Poetry* (2007) and the books *Glow of Our Sweat* (2010) and *After Rubén* (2020). Has translated several Spanish-language poets, including Francisco X. Alarcón, Federico García Lorca, and

Rubén Darío. On the faculty, since 2003, of the University of Notre Dame's Institute for Latino Studies, home of the literary organization Letras Latinas, which he founded and directs.

William Archila (b. 1968) b. Santa Ana, El Salvador; immigrated with his family to the U.S. in 1980 following the outbreak of civil war the year before, living in Los Angeles. Worked as English teacher. Earned MFA from the University of Oregon. Books include *The Art of Exile* (2009), winner of the International Latino Book Award, and *The Gravedigger's Archaeology* (2015), winner of the Letras Latinas/ Red Hen Poetry Prize.

Rane Arroyo (1954–2010) b. Chicago, IL, to parents from Puerto Rico. Earned BA from Elmhurst College, MA from University of Illinois Springfield, and PhD in English and Cultural Studies from the University of Pittsburgh. Was a performance artist in Chicago during the 1980s. Taught creative writing at the University of Toledo. Publications include ten poetry collections as well as chapbooks, along with books of short stories and plays.

Gustavo Adolfo Aybar (b. 1976) b. Dominican Republic; moved to the United States when he was four. Earned BA and MA from University of Missouri–Kansas City. First book of poems, *Between Line Breaks* (2016), was followed by *We Seek Asylum* (2017).

Jimmy Santiago Baca (b. 1952) b. Santa Fe County, New Mexico, of Chicano and Apache heritage. Abandoned by his parents at a young age and then placed in an orphanage at thirteen by his grandmother. Incarcerated for five years on drug-related charges in a maximum-security prison at twenty-one, during which time he taught himself to read and then began to write poetry. Publications include the collection *Immigrants in Our Own Land* (1979), the autobiography-in-verse *Martín and Meditations on the South Valley* (1987), winner of an American Book Award, the collection of essays *Working in the Dark* (1991), the memoir *A Place to Stand* (2001), and the screenplay for the film *Bound by Honor* (1993), directed by Taylor Hackford. Founder of Cedar Tree, an organization that offers literary workshops and support for inmates and at-risk youth.

Diego Báez (b. 1984) b. Bloomington, IL, where he also grew up. Received BA in English from Illinois Wesleyan University and MFA in Poetry from Rutgers University–Newark. He is the author of *Yaguareté White* (2024). Has served on the boards of the National Book Critics Circle and the International David Foster Wallace Society. Currently an assistant professor in poetry and composition at the Harry S Truman City College of Chicago.

Oliver Baez Bendorf (b. 1987) b. Iowa City, IA. Received BA from University of Iowa and MFA from University of Wisconsin–Madison. Publications include *Consider the Rooster* (2024), *Advantages of Being Evergreen* (2019), and *The Spectral Wilderness* (2015). Currently works as the teen services librarian at Boulder Public Library

Rosebud Ben-Oni (b. 1978) b. Harlingen, TX, to a Mexican mother and a Jewish father. Earned a BA at New York University and an MFA at the University of Michigan. Publications include the collection *turn around, BRXGHT XYXS* (2019), the chapbook *20 Atomic Sonnets* (2020), and *If This Is the Age We End Discovery* (2021). Created the video essay *My Judaism is a Wild Unplace* for a Jewish Heritage Month campaign commissioned by Paramount. Previously a weekly contributor to the *Kenyon Review* blog. Participated in the QUEENSBOUND project.

Richard Blanco (b. 1968) b. Madrid, Spain, and raised in Miami, the son of Cuban exiles. Earned a BS in Civil Engineering and an MFA in Creative Writing from Florida International University. Publications include the poetry collections *City of a Hundred Fires* (1998), *Directions to the Beach of the Dead* (2005), *Looking for the Gulf Motel* (2012), *How to Love a Country* (2019), *Homeland of My Body: New and Selected Poems* (2023), as well as a memoir, *The Prince of Los Cocuyos: A Miami Childhood* (2014). He read his poem "One Today" at the inauguration for President Barack Obama's second term in 2013. On August 14, 2015, he read his poem "Matters of the Sea/Cosas del mar" at the reopening ceremony for the United States Embassy in Havana. Appointed the first Poet Laureate of Miami-Dade County in 2022. Currently associate professor at Florida International University and education ambassador for the Academy of American Poets.

Daniel Borzutzky (b. 1974) b. Pittsburgh, PA, to Chilean parents. Received a BA in Philosophy from the University of Pittsburgh in 1997 and an MFA from the School of the Art Institute of Chicago. Short stories collected in *Arbitrary Tales* (2007). Poetry volumes include *The Book of Interfering Bodies* (2011), the National Book Award–winning *The Performance of Becoming Human* (2016), and *Written after a Massacre in the Year 2018* (2021); has translated works by Jaime Luis Huenún, Galo Ghigliotto, and Raúl Zurita. Currently teaches in the department of Latin American and Latino studies at the University of Illinois Chicago.

Giannina Braschi (b. 1953) b. San Juan, Puerto Rico, and in her late teens traveled to Madrid, Rome, London, and Paris before settling in New York City. Received her PhD in Hispanic Literatures from the State University of New York, Stony Brook. Publications include the cross-genre poetic epic *El imperio de los sueños* (1988; translated as *Empire of Dreams* in 1994), the Spanglish novel *Yo-Yo Boing!* (1998), and the novel *United States of Banana* (2011). The subject of *Poets, Philosophers, Lovers: On the Writings of Giannina Braschi* (2020). Has taught at Rutgers University, Colgate University, and City University of New York.

Rafael Campo (b. 1964) b. Dover, NJ, son of a Cuban father and an Italian mother. Received BA and MA from Amherst College (which later awarded him an honorary doctorate in Literature) and MD from Harvard Medical School. Began practicing internal medicine in the 1990s. First poetry collection, *The Other Man Was Me* (1994), followed by *What the Body Told* (1996) and other collections, including *Comfort Measures Only: New and Selected Poems 1994–2016* (2018). Other books include *The Poetry of Healing* (1997) and *The Healing Art: A Doctor's Black Bag of Poetry* (2003). Is poetry editor of the *Journal of the American Medical Association*. Teaches and practices medicine at Harvard Medical School, where he has served as director of literature and writing programs of the arts, and at Beth Israel Deaconess Medical Center in Boston.

David Campos (b. 1984) b. Ventura, CA, to Mexican immigrant parents. Earned BA from California State University, Fresno, and MFA from University of California, Riverside. Was member of the Parking Lot Prophets, a spoken-word troupe. Hosted *Pákatelas*, a literary radio program in Fresno. His books are *Furious Dusk* (2015) and *American Quasar* (2021), with art by Maceo Montoya. Currently teaches English at Fresno City College.

Ernesto Cardenal (1925–2020) b. Granada, Nicaragua. Studied at Autonomous University of Mexico in Mexico City, 1943–47. First poetry book, *La Ciudad deshabitada* (The Uninhabited City), was published in 1946, as well as his anthology of Nicaraguan poetry, published in Spain. Studied at Columbia University for two years before returning to Nicaragua in 1950. Jailed briefly for opposition to Somoza government in 1952; took part in failed attempt to oust Somoza in 1954. Had intensive religious experience in 1956. The following year he became a novice at Gethsemani Abbey in Kentucky, where he was a disciple of Trappist monk Thomas Merton, who subsequently translated his poetry. After two years moved to Colombia, living in a Benedictine monastery. Ordained a priest in 1962. Returned to Nicaragua. Embraced liberation theology and supported the Sandinista National Liberation Front. In 1966, founded religious community on Mancarrón in the Solentiname Islands, which became known for its art and its poetry and literacy workshops. Site was destroyed by Nicaraguan government forces in 1977 and Cardenal went into exile in Costa Rica until Sandinista revolution in Nicaragua in 1979; appointed minister of culture. Requests from Rome that he and other priests in the Sandinista government resign were resisted; in 1983, on papal visit to Nicaragua, greeted pope, who wagged his finger disdainfully at him. Suspended from the priesthood in 1984 (suspension was lifted by Pope Francis in 2019). Resigned as minister of culture in 1987. Publications in translation include *With Walker in Nicaragua and Other Early Poems 1949–1954* (1984) and *Pluriverse: New and Selected Poems* (2009).

Brenda Cárdenas (b. 1961) b. Milwaukee, WI. Received BA from the University of Wisconsin–Milwaukee and MFA from the University of Michigan. Author, in addition to chapbooks, of the poetry collection *Boomerang* (2009). Co-edited the anthologies *Between the Heart and the Land: Latina Poets in the Midwest* (2001) and *Resist Much/Obey Little: Inaugural Poems to the Resistance* (2017). Milwaukee's Poet Laureate, 2010–12. Teaches at University of Wisconsin–Milwaukee.

Natasha Carrizosa (b. 1975) b. Fort Worth, TX, to African American mother and Mexican immigrant father. Publications include *Of Fire and Rain* (with Joaquin Zihuatanejo, 2011) and *Crown* (2018). Is facilitator and speaker for Coolspeak, a youth engagement program.

Lourdes Casal (1938–1981) b. Havana, Cuba, of African, Chinese, and European descent. Attended the Universidad Católica de Santo Tomás de Villanueva in Havana, first studying chemical engineering, then psychology. At first allying herself with Fidel Castro's revolution against the Batista regime, she soon went into the anti-Castro opposition and left Cuba, becoming an American citizen in 1962. Traveled to Africa on a trip underwritten by the CIA. Earned MA and PhD in Psychology from The New School for Social Research. *El caso Padilla: Literatura y revolución en Cuba*, her book on the treatment of Cuban poet Heberto Padilla, who was placed under house arrest for his antigovernment sentiments, was published in 1971. Taught at several universities, including the City University of New York and Rutgers University, where she cofounded the Institute for Cuban Studies. Cofounded journal *Revista Areito*. Accepted invitation from Cuban government to visit the island; became sympathetic to Castro regime. Cowrote, with Rafael Prohias, the sociological study *The Cuban Minority in the United States* (1974). Founded the Antonio Maceo Brigade, composed of exiles seeking to establish good relations with the Cuban government, and took part in negotiations between exiles and Cuban officials about matters such as family visits and political prisoners. Kidney ailment necessitated dialysis; hospitalized during a trip to Cuba in December 1979, she decided to live the remainder of her life there. Collection *Palabras juntan revolución* (Words Join Revolution), published shortly after her death in 1981, was awarded a Casa de las Américas prize.

Ana Castillo (b. 1953) b. Chicago, IL. Earned BA from Northwestern Illinois University, MA from the University of Chicago, and PhD from the University of Bremen, Germany. Publications include the novels *The Mixquiahuala Letters* (1986), which won an American Book Award from the Before Columbus Foundation, and the Lambda Award–winning *Give It to Me* (2014); the poetry collections *My Father Was a Toltec: and Selected Poems* (1995) and *My Book of the Dead: New Poems 2012–2020* (2021); and the memoir *BLACK DOVE: Mamá, Mi'jo, and Me* (2016), winner of an International Latino Book Award and a Lambda Award. *Massacre of the Dreamers: Essays on Xicanisma* was published in 1994. Given the Sor Juana Achievement Award by the National Museum of Mexican Art in Chicago, among other honors. Inducted into the Chicago Literary Hall of Fame. Held the first Sor Juana Inés de la Cruz Endowed Chair at DePaul University, 2001–6, among several other appointments. Edits journal *La Tolteca*.

Marcelo Hernandez Castillo (b. 1988) b. Zacatecas, Mexico; moved to California at age five. Earned a BA from Sacramento State University and an MFA from the University of Michigan. Books include the poetry collection *Cenzontle* (2018) and the memoir *Children of the Land* (2020). Cofounder of Undocupoets, initiative founded to change citizenship requirements for poetry awards. Named Yuba and Sutter County Poet Laureate. Teaches poetry workshops for incarcerated youth. Teaches in the MFA program in creative writing at Ashland University.

Sandra M. Castillo (b. 1962) b. Havana, Cuba; moved to Florida in 1970. Received MA in Creative Writing from Florida State University. Publications include the chapbook *Red Letters* (1991) and the poetry collections *My Father Sings to My Embarrassment* (2002) and *Eating Moors and Christians* (2016). Currently teaches at Miami-Dade College.

Adrian Castro (b. 1967) b. Miami, FL. Of Afro-Caribbean, Cuban-Dominican heritage. Début poetry collection *Cantos to Blood & Honey* (1997) was followed by *Wise Fish: Tales in 6/8 Time* (2005) and *Handling Destiny* (2009). Has taught at University of Miami, Miami Dade College, and Florida International University.

Andrés Cerpa (b. 1990) b. New York, NY, and raised on Staten Island, the child of Puerto Rican parents. Earned BA from the University of Delaware and MFA from Rutgers University–Newark. Author of the poetry books *Bicycle in a Ransacked City: An Elegy* (2019) and *The Vault* (2021). Currently teaches high school English at Rye Country Day School in Rye, NY.

Lorna Dee Cervantes (b. 1954) b. San Francisco, CA, and raised in San José; of Mexican, Chumash, and Tarascan heritage. As a teenager took part in poetry workshops at San José State with Robert Hass. In 1974 an unscheduled reading of her poem "Refugee Ship" at a festival in Mexico City was publicized in newspapers and journals. Founded the small press Mango Publications in 1976. First poetry collection, *Emplumada* (1981), won an American Book Award. Stopped writing for several years in the wake of her mother's murder in 1982; earned BA from San José State University in 1985, followed by PhD in the History of Consciousness from the University of California, Santa Cruz. *From the Cables of Genocide: Poems of Love and Hunger* (1991) won a Latino Literature Prize. Later books of poetry include *Drive: The First Quartet: New Poems, 1980–2005* (2006), *Ciento: 100 100-Word Love Poems* (2011), and *Sueño: New Poems* (2013). Co-editor of the poetry journal *Red Dirt*. Has taught at the University of Houston, the University of Colorado Boulder, where she directed the creative writing program, and the University of California, Berkeley.

Lisa D. Chávez (b. 1961) b. Los Angeles, CA, and raised in Alaska. Earned BA at University of Alaska Fairbanks, MFA at Arizona State University, and MA with additional doctoral study at University of Rochester. Author of the poetry collections *Deconstruction Bay* (1998) and *In an Angry Season* (2001). Teaches creative writing at University of New Mexico.

Maya Chinchilla (b. 1976) b. Long Beach, CA, of Guatemalan heritage. Earned BA from University of California, Santa Cruz, and MFA from Mills College. Author of *The Cha Cha Files: A Chapina Poética* (2014). Founder of the performance group Las Manas and director of several documentaries. Formerly a lecturer in Chicano/a Studies at University of California, Davis. Hosts podcast *Live and Queer*.

Sandra Cisneros (b. 1954) b. Chicago, IL. Earned BA at Loyola University Chicago and MFA from the University of Iowa Writers' Workshop. Published chapbook *Bad Boys* in 1980. Traveled to Italy on a writer's residency; spent summer in Sarajevo. Novel *The House on Mango Street* (1984) won American Book Award; other books include *Woman Hollering Creek and Other Stories* (1991) and the poetry collections *Loose Woman* (1994) and *Woman Without Shame* (2022). Founder of the Alfredo Cisneros Del Moral Foundation and the Macondo Foundation. Has taught at the University of California, Berkeley, and the University of Michigan, among other universities. Among her many honors are a MacArthur Foundation fellowship, the Premio Napoli prize, and, in 2016, the National Medal of Arts.

Anthony Cody (b. 1981) b. Fresno, CA. Earned BA and MFA from California State University, Fresno. Co-edited *How Do I Begin?: A Hmong American Literary Anthology* (2011). His *Borderland Apocrypha* (2020), which won an American Book Award, was followed by *The Rendering* (2023). Also an artist. Has collaborated with and translated Juan Felipe Herrera. Currently copublisher for Noemi Press and a professor of poetry in Randolph College's low-residency MFA program.

Lucha Corpi (b. 1945) b. Jáltipan, Mexico. Moved to Berkeley, CA, with her former husband, a Berkeley student, in 1964. Earned BA at University of California, Berkeley, and MA from San Francisco State University. Taught English as a Second Language in the Oakland public school system. Poetry collection *Variaciones sobre una tempestad/Variations on a Storm* was published in 1990, followed by *Palabras de mediodía/Noon Words* (2001). Began writing mystery novels with *Eulogy for a Brown Angel* (1992); *Cactus Blood* (1995) featured detective Gloria Damasco, who would appear in three other novels. Honors include an International Latino Book Award.

Eduardo C. Corral (b. 1973) b. Casa Grande, AZ. Earned BA at Arizona State University and MFA at the University of Iowa's Writers' Workshop. With *Slow Lightning* (2012), became the first Latino poet to win the Yale Series of Younger Poets award. *Guillotine* was published in 2020. Currently an associate professor in the MFA program at North Carolina State University.

Rio Cortez (b. 1985) b. Salt Lake City, UT. Earned MFA from New York University. Publications include the chapbook *I Have Learned to Define a Field as a Space Between Mountains* (2016), the poetry collection *Golden Ax* (2022), as well as the picture book *The ABCs of Black History* (2020).

Cynthia Cruz (b. 1968) b. Wiesbaden, Germany, and raised in Northern California. Earned a BA in English at Mills College, an MFA in Poetry at Sarah Lawrence College, an MFA in Art Writing from the School of Visual Arts, and an MA in German Language and Literature from Rutgers University. *Hotel Oblivion* (2022), one of

Cruz's eight poetry collections, won the National Book Critics' Circle Award; other works include *Disquieting: Essays on Silence* (2019), *The Melancholia of Class: A Manifesto for the Working Class* (2021), and the novella *Steady Diet of Nothing* (2023). Co-edits *Schlag* magazine. Is pursuing a PhD at the European Graduate School and teaches creative writing in the MFA program at Sarah Lawrence College.

Silvia Curbelo (b. 1955) b. Matanzas, Cuba; family immigrated to the U.S. when she was eleven, living first in Florida, then Iowa, before returning to Florida. Earned BA from University of South Florida. Published first poetry book, *The Geography of Leaving*, in 1991, followed by *The Secret History of Water* (1997), *Ambush* (2004), and *Falling Landscape* (2015). Served as editor of *Organica Quarterly*.

José Dávila Semprit (1902–1958) b. Tona Baja, Puerto Rico. Moved in his twenties to New York City, where he worked as a postman. Poetry collection *Brazos Bronce* was published in 1933. Active in workers' groups and was an advocate for Puerto Rican independence; was a prominent member of Committee to Aid Puerto Rico, which was under surveillance by the FBI (one memo referring to Semprit and his colleagues as "known communists"). Worked on anthology of Puerto Rican poets in New York City, "Florilegio lirico," in the 1950s. Returned to Puerto Rico in 1956, where he died of peritonitis two years later. Also edited an anthology of poems about mothers, *Poemario de la madre* (1958).

Julia de Burgos (1914–1953) b. Julia Constanza Burgos García in Carolina, Puerto Rico. Earned degree at the University of Puerto Rico and became an elementary school teacher. A political activist, she became an official in the Nationalist Party advocating for Puerto Rican independence. First poetry collection, *Poema en veinte surcos* (Poem in Twenty Furrows), was published in 1938. Moved to New York City in 1940, where apart from two years in Cuba she lived for the rest of her life. Wrote column in the Spanish-language New York periodical *Pueblos Hispanos*. Suffered from alcoholism, cirrhosis of the liver, and respiratory problems. Collapsed on the street and died at Harlem Hospital at age thirty-nine.

Angela de Hoyos (1940–2009) b. Coahuila, Mexico. At age three suffered severe burns from a gas heater and underwent a long convalescence, to which she traces her origins as a writer. As a child moved to San Antonio, TX. Took art and writing courses at University of Texas at San Antonio, San Antonio College, the Witte Museum, and the San Antonio Art Institute. Publications include the poetry collections *Arise, Chicano! and Other Poems* (1975), *Chicano Poems* *for the Barrio* (1975), *Selecciones* (1979), and *Woman, Woman* (1995). Cofounded and served as an editor for M&A/Manda Publications and as the director of *Huehuetitlan* magazine.

Joseph Delgado (b. 1979) b. Albuquerque, NM. Attended the College of Santa Fe. Author of the poetry collections *Buzzard Songs* (2010), *Ditch Water* (2013), and *Broken Mesas* (2021). Featured in the anthology *Collective Brightness: LGBTIQ Poets on Faith, Religion & Spirituality* (2011) and elsewhere. Currently lives on the Fort Mojave Indian Reservation in Mojave Valley, AZ.

Abelardo "Lalo" Delgado (1931–2004) b. Chihuahua, Mexico, and moved to El Paso, TX, at twelve. Earned BA in Spanish Studies at University of Texas at El Paso, then taught at Metropolitan State College and University of Colorado. Participated in the farm labor movement with Cesar Chavez, and remained committed to civil rights causes throughout his life. Served as executive director of the Colorado Migrant Council and later as client-services specialist at the Justice Information Center in Denver. Considered himself a people's poet, who wrote poems for special occasions. Author of fourteen books, many of which were self-published, including *Chicano: 25 Pieces of a Chicano Mind* (1969), *It's Cold: 52 Cold-Thoughts Poems of Abelardo* (1974), and *Letters to Louise* (1982). Much of his work was republished posthumously in *Here Lies Lalo: The Collected Poems of Abelardo Delgado* (2011). Posthumously named Denver's first Poet Laureate.

Blas Manuel de Luna (b. 1969) b. Tijuana, Mexico; raised in Madera, CA. Received BA and MA from California State University, Fresno, and MFA from the University of Washington. Author of the poetry collection *Bent to the Earth* (2005).

Natalie Diaz (b. 1978) b. Fort Mojave Indian Village in Needles, CA. She is Mojave and an enrolled member of the Gila River Indian Tribe. Earned BA and MFA from Old Dominion University. Publications include *When My Brother Was an Aztec* (2012), winner of an American Book Award, and *Postcolonial Love Poem* (2020), winner of the Pulitzer Prize. Awarded fellowships from the MacArthur Foundation, among other honors. Elected a chancellor of the Academy of American Poets in 2021. Currently the Maxine and Jonathan Marshall Chair in Modern and Contemporary Poetry, a director at the Center for Imagination in the Borderlands, and a professor of English in the MFA program at Arizona State University.

Angel Dominguez (b. 1989) b. Los Angeles, CA, and raised in Van Nuys; of Yucatec Maya descent. Earned BA at University of California,

Santa Cruz, and MFA at Naropa University. Publications include the hybrid work *Black Lavender Milk* (2015) and the poetry books *RoseSunWater* (2020) and *Desgraciado (the collected letters)* (2022). Was writer-in-residence at San Francisco State University. Currently works as graduate services counselor at University of California, Santa Cruz.

David Dominguez (b. 1971) b. Fresno, CA. Earned BA in Comparative Literature from the University of California, Irvine, and an MFA in Creative Writing from the University of Arizona. Publications include the chapbook *Marcoli Sausage* (2000) and the collections *Work Done Right* (2003) and *The Ghost of César Chávez* (2010). Cofounder and editor of *The Packinghouse Review*. Teaches English at Reedley College.

Carolina Ebeid (b. 1976) Raised in West New York, NJ; of Palestinian and Cuban descent. Earned MFA from the Michener Center for Writers at the University of Texas at Austin. Debut poetry collection, *You Ask Me to Talk About the Interior*, was published in 2016. Currently an editor at *The Rumpus* and *Visible Binary*. Teaches at Brown University, Regis College, and University of Texas at El Paso.

Fray Alonso Gregorio de Escobedo (mid-sixteenth century–early seventeenth century) b. southern Spain. A Franciscan friar about whom little is known. Arrived in Florida in October 1587. Author of *La Florida* (1587), long poem most likely written in the 1590s after his return to Spain.

Martín Espada (b. 1957) b. Brooklyn, NY. Puerto Rican father was a community organizer and photojournalist; mother was Jewish. Family moved to Long Island when he was sixteen. Earned BA from the University of Wisconsin–Madison and a JD from Northeastern University. Worked wide range of jobs, including as a groundskeeper in a minor-league baseball park, a radio journalist in Nicaragua, and an attorney representing low-income tenants in housing cases in the greater Boston area. First poetry collection, *The Immigrant Iceboy's Bolero* (1982), was published while he was a law student. Numerous subsequent collections include *Imagine the Angels of Bread* (1996), which won an American Book Award; *The Trouble Ball* (2011), winner of an International Latino Book Award; and the National Book Award–winning *Floaters* (2021). Edited anthology *Poetry Like Bread: Poets of the Political Imagination* (1994) and was cotranslator of *The Blood That Keeps Singing: Selected Poems of Clemente Soto Vélez* (1991). Also edited *What Saves Us: Poems of Empathy and Outrage in the Age of Trump* (2019). Among his many honors is the 2018 Ruth Lilly Prize for lifetime achievement. Has long been a professor of English at the University of Massachusetts Amherst.

Rhina P. Espaillat (b. 1932) b. Santo Domingo, Dominican Republic. Family spent part of 1937 in Washington, D.C., where father was a diplomatic attaché; due to her family's criticism of the Trujillo regime, parents remained in U.S. After returning to Dominican Republic for two years, joined her parents in New York City. As a teenager published poetry in *Ladies' Home Journal* and at sixteen was the youngest member to be inducted into the Poetry Society of America. Earned BA from Hunter College and MA in Education from Queens College. Taught at Jamaica High School in Queens for fifteen years. Moved to Newburyport, MA, in 1990. *Lapsing to Grace* was published in 1998, followed by *Where Horizons Go* (1998) and several other books and chapbooks. Has translated Richard Wilbur and Robert Frost into Spanish and Sor Juana Inés de la Cruz, Vicente Huidobro, and others into English. Cofounded and directed the Powow River Poets, group of poets based in Newburyport.

Sandra María Esteves (b. 1948) b. Bronx, NY, of Dominican and Puerto Rican descent. Also a visual artist, playwright, and performer. Was prominent in the first generation of Nuyorican poets. Served as the executive director of the African Caribbean Poetry Theater. First book of poetry, *Yerba Buena*, was published in 1980; other publications include *Bluestown Mockingbird Mambo* (1990) and the spoken-word recordings *DivaNations* (2010) and *Wildflowers* (2009).

Noel Estrada (1918–1979) b. Isabela, Puerto Rico, and grew up in San Juan. Composer best known for "En mi Viejo San Juan," written during World War II when his brother, stationed in Panama, requested he write a song to lift morale among Puerto Rican soldiers serving in the U.S. military. First recorded in 1943 by the Puerto Rican singing group Trio Vegabajeño, it was later covered by many artists and translated into German, English, French, and other languages.

Blas Falconer (b. 1971) b. Virginia. Earned MFA from the University of Maryland and PhD in Creative Writing and Literature from the University of Houston. Poetry collections include *A Question of Gravity and Light* (2007) and *Rara Avis* (2024). Co-edited *The Other Latin@: Writing Against a Singular Identity* (2011) and *Mentor & Muse: Essays from Poets to Poets* (2010). Teaches in the MFA program at San Diego State University.

Robert Fernandez (b. 1980) b. Hartford, CT, and grew up in Hollywood, FL. Earned MFA at the University of Iowa Writers'

Workshop. Publications include the poetry collections *We Are Pharoah* (2011), *Pink Reef* (2013), and *Scarecrow* (2016). Cotranslated Stéphane Mallarmé's *Azure* (2015); portions of his translation of Haitian writer Félix Morisseau-Leroy's *Antigòn* have appeared in print. Creates visual art, music, and artists' books. Lives in Lincoln, NE.

Eugenio Florit (1903–1999) b. Spain (sources give different birthplaces, such as Madrid and Salamanca), of Spanish and Cuban parentage. Spent much of his childhood in the coastal city of Port-Bou. At age fifteen he moved to Cuba, where he graduated from the University of Havana and with a degree in law. Worked at the state secretariat and as actor for radio and theater. First poetry collections include *32 poemas breves* (1927), *Trópico* (1930), and *Doble acento* (1937), with a preface by his lifelong friend the Spanish poet Juan Ramón Jiménez. In 1940 Florit moved to New York City, working as an attaché at the Cuban consulate until accepting, in 1945, a teaching appointment at Barnard College. Served as editor for the *Revista Hispánica Moderna*. Retired from Barnard in 1969; left New York for Miami in 1982. Author of numerous volumes of poetry, as well as translations, works of criticism such as *Hispanic-American Poetry Since Modernism* (1968), and anthologies, including *Antología de la poesía norteamericana contemporánea*.

Ariel Francisco (b. 1990) b. Bronx, NY, to Dominican and Guatemalan parents; raised in Miami. Earned a BA and MFA in Poetry from Florida International University and an MFA in Literary Translation at Queens College CUNY. Served as editor of *Gulf Stream Literary Magazine*. Author of five books of poetry, most recently *All the Places We Love Have Been Left in Ruins* (2024). Translator of Carolina Sanchez's *Viaje/Voyage* (2020), Hael Lopez's *Routines/Goodbyes* (2022), and Jacques Viau Renaud's *Poet of One Island* (2023). Currently assistant professor in poetry at Louisiana State University.

Enrique Franco (1938–2013) b. Enrique Franco Aguilar in Mazatlán, Mexico. Family moved to Tijuana when he was six. As bandleader of Los Cometas de Enrique Franco, recorded and toured Mexico and the United States over a period of fifteen years. Served as artistic director at Fama Records; in the 1980s moved to San José, CA, where he continued to write songs and worked as a producer, collaborating most notably with the popular Mexican *corrido* group Los Tigres del Norte. Acted in films. Received a Lifetime Achievement Award in 2010 from Mexico's Society of Authors and Composers.

Gina Franco (b. 1968) b. Clifton-Morenci, AZ. Earned BA from Smith College and MFA and PhD from Cornell University. Author of the two poetry collections *The Keepsake Storm* (2004) and *The Accidental* (2019). Is also an oblate with the monastic order of the Community of St John. Teaches at Knox College.

Suzanne Frischkorn (b. 1970) Cuban American. Earned BA at Fairfield University. Author of *Girl on a Bridge* (2010), *Lit Windowpane* (2008), *Fixed Star* (2022), and five chapbooks. Is an editor for the journal *$—Poetry Is Currency;* serves on the editorial board of terrain.org.

Vanessa Jimenez Gabb (b. 1983) b. Brooklyn, NY, of Colombian and Belizean descent. Received MA in English from St. John's University and MFA from Brooklyn College. First collection, *Images for Radical Politics* (2016), was followed by *Basic Needs* (2021). Cofounded *Five Quarterly*. Currently teaches at Newark Academy in Livingston, NJ.

Diana García (b. 1950) b. San Joaquin Valley, CA, in a migrant farm labor camp. Earned BA and MFA in Creative Writing from San Diego State University. Her book *When Living Was a Labor Camp* (2000) won an American Book Award for poetry. Co-edited *Fire and Ink: An Anthology of Social Action Writing* (2009). Has long taught at California State University, Monterey Bay.

Richard Garcia (b. 1941) b. San Francisco, CA. First published poems were included in Beat collection *Beatitude Anthology* (1960). Attended San Francisco State University. After publication of chapbook *Selected Poems* (1972), stopped writing poetry for several years; admiring letter from Mexican poet Octavio Paz in 1978 spurred him to resume. Bilingual children's book *My Aunt Otilia's Spirits/ Los Espíritus de mi tía Otilia* published in 1978. First full-length collection, *The Flying Garcias*, published in 1993; earned MFA in Creative Writing from Warren Wilson College Writers' Program the following year. Has served as poet-in-residence at Children's Hospital Los Angeles and has taught in Antioch University Los Angeles's MFA program.

Carmen Giménez (b. 1971) b. New York, NY, to a Peruvian mother and an Argentine father. Grew up in New York City and San José. Earned BA in English from San Jose State University and MFA in Creative Writing from the University of Iowa. First full-length poetry collection was *Odalisque in Pieces* (2009), followed by *Goodbye, Flicker* (2012), *Milk & Filth* (2013), and *Be Recorder* (2019), as well as the memoir *Bring Down the Little Birds: On Mothering, Art, Work, and Everything Else* (2010), winner of an American Book Award. Co-edited *Angels of the Americlypse: New Latin@ Writing* (2015).

Founded and for twenty years was publisher of Noemi Press. In 2017, began teaching in the creative writing MFA program at Virginia Tech University and was named a poetry editor at *The Nation*. Awarded Academy of American Poets Fellowship Prize in 2020. In 2022 left academia and began serving as publisher and executive director of Graywolf Press.

Aracelis Girmay (b. 1977) b. Santa Ana, CA. Earned BA from Connecticut College and MFA from New York University. Her poetry collections are *Teeth* (2007), *Kingdom Animalia* (2011), and *The Black Maria* (2016). Editor of *How to Carry Water: Selected Poems of Lucille Clifton* (2020) and *So We Can Know: Writers of Color on Pregnancy* (2023). Taught at Hampshire College and is currently a professor of English at Stanford University.

Jennifer Givhan (b. 1984) b. Imperial Valley, CA; of Mexican American and Indigenous heritage. Earned MFA from Warren Wilson College and MA in English Literature from California State University, Fullerton. Author of five poetry volumes, most recently *Belly to the Brutal* (2022), as well as the novels *Trinity Sight* (2019), *Jubilee* (2020), and *River Woman, River Demon* (2022). Has taught creative writing at the University of Washington Bothell, Western New Mexico University, and the University of New Mexico.

Rodney Gomez (b. 1975) b. Brownsville, TX, the son of migrant farmworkers. Earned BA in Philosophy from Yale University, MA in Philosophy from Arizona State University, and MFA and MPA from the University of Texas Rio Grande Valley. Chapbook *Mouth Filled with Night* was published in 2014; full-length collection *Citizens of the Mausoleum* appeared in 2018, followed by *Baedeker from the Persistent Refuge* (2019) and other books. Named 2020–21 Poet Laureate of McAllen, TX. Serves as advisory editor for FlowerSong Press.

Rodolfo "Corky" Gonzales (1928–2005) b. Denver, CO. Worked as laborer and farmhand as a child and youth. Attended University of Denver for one quarter. Was professional boxer in the late 1940s and early 1950s. Owned bar and a bail-bonds business. Worked for Democratic Party through the mid-1960s, including as district captain and for John F. Kennedy's campaign in Colorado, as well as heading a regional antipoverty program. Made several unsuccessful attempts to win elective office. Founded in 1963 the Chicano civil rights organization Los Voluntarios (The Volunteers), followed by the Crusade for Justice; was leader of a Chicano contingent in the Poor People's Campaign's March on Washington in 1968. Long poem *I Am Joaquín* first published in 1967, followed by a best-selling trade paperback in 1972. Established school in Denver, the Escuela Tlatelolco, and organized first Chicano Youth Liberation Conference, out of which came the "Plan Espiritual de Aztlán" ("Spiritual Plan of Aztlán"), manifesto advocating Chicano self-determination. Was injured in an automobile accident in 1978, and later suffered heart attack; health problems limited his later activity. His poems, plays, and other writings are collected in *Message to Aztlán: Selected Writings* (2001).

Kevin A. González (b. 1981) b. San Juan, Puerto Rico. Earned BA at Carnegie Mellon University and MFAs from University of Wisconsin–Madison and the Iowa Writers' Workshop. Chapbook *The Night Tito Trinidad KO'ed Ricardo Mayorga* was published in 2007, followed by the full-length collection *Cultural Studies* (2009). Co-edited *The New Census: An Anthology of Contemporary American Poetry* (2013). Currently professor of English at Carnegie Mellon University.

Ray Gonzalez (b. 1952) b. El Paso, TX. Earned BA from University of Texas at El Paso and MFA in Creative Writing from Texas State University. Author of books including the poetry collections *The Heat of Arrivals* (1997) and *Tierra Grande* (2003); the story collection *The Ghost of John Wayne* (2001), winner of a Latino Heritage Award; and *The Underground Heart: A Return to a Hidden Landscape* (2002), a book of essays. Edited *Touching the Fire: Fifteen Poets of Today's Latino Renaissance* (1998) and *No Boundaries: Prose Poems by 24 American Poets* (2002); co-edited *Sudden Fiction Latino* (2010). Was poetry editor of *The Bloomsbury Review*. Founded poetry magazine *LUNA*. Received Lifetime Achievement Award in Literature from the Border Regional Library Association, among other honors. Currently professor in the MFA in creative writing program at University of Minnesota.

Cynthia Guardado (b. 1985) b. Los Angeles, CA, to Salvadoran immigrant parents. Earned BA from University of California, Santa Cruz, and MFA from California State University, Fresno. Transcribed and translated interviews with exile Cuban journalist Normando Hernandez Gonzalez in *The Madrid Conversations* (2013). Author of the poetry collections *ENDEAVOR* (2017) and *Cenizas* (2022). Currently associate professor in the English department at Fullerton College.

Juan Luis Guerra (b. 1957) b. Santo Domingo, Dominican Republic. Singer-songwriter of bachata and merengue music as well as other genres. Studied at the National Conservatory of the Dominican Republic, the Autonomous University of Santo Domingo, and

Berklee College of Music in Boston, which later awarded him an honorary doctorate. His many recordings include *Bachata Rosa* (Romantic Bachata, 1990) and *La Llave de mi Corazón* (The Key to My Heart, 2007). Winner of numerous Latin Grammy Awards, among other accolades.

Laurie Ann Guerrero (b. 1978) b. San Antonio, TX. Earned BA in English Language and Literature from Smith College and MFA in Poetry from Drew University, Madison, NJ. Poetry collections include *A Tongue in the Mouth of the Dying* (2013), recipient of an International Latino Book Award and the Andrés Montoya Poetry Prize; *A Crown for Gumecindo* (2015), a collaboration with the artist Maceo Montoya; and *I Have Eaten the Rattlesnake: New & Selected Poems* (2021). Served as Poet Laureate of San Antonio, 2014–16, and of Texas, 2016–17. Currently associate professor and writer-in-residence at Texas A&M University, San Antonio.

Roberto Harrison (b. 1962) b. Corvallis, OR, to Panamanian parents; sent to Panama to live soon after he was born, first with his grandmother and then with his parents; moved in 1969 to Wilmington, DE, where he was raised mostly by his mother. Pursued graduate studies in mathematics at Indiana University in Bloomington and earned MA in Library and Information Science at University of Wisconsin–Milwaukee. Publications include the poetry collections *Os* (2006), *bicycle* (2015), *Yaviza* (2017), and the compilations of poetry and drawings *Tropical Lung exi(s)t(s)* (2021) and *Isthmus to Abya Yala* (2024). Co-editor of the anthology *Resist Much/Obey Little: Inaugural Poems to the Resistance* (2017). Milwaukee's Poet Laureate, 2017–19.

José María Heredia y Heredia (1803–1839) b. Santiago de Cuba, Cuba, to parents who had fled colonial Santo Domingo in the wake of the Haitian Revolution; lived in Cuba and Venezuela as a child and spent a year in Mexico as a teenager. Entered college at age fourteen; received law degree from the University of Havana in 1823. Became involved with Cuban independence efforts; Spanish colonial authorities issued warrant for his arrest. Lived in the U.S. from late 1823 through mid-1825, residing in Boston, New York City, Philadelphia, New Haven, and elsewhere. His first poetry collection, *Poesías* (1825), was published in New York. Upon the invitation of the Mexican president he moved to Mexico, where he held positions in governmental and educational institutions, returning only once to Cuba.

Tim Z. Hernandez (b. 1974) b. Dinuba, CA, and raised in the San Joaquin Valley. Earned BA from Naropa University and MFA from

Bennington College. Publications include the poetry collections *Skin Tax* (2004), winner of an American Book Award, *Natural Takeover of Small Things* (2013), and *Some of the Light: New and Selected Poems* (2023), as well as the novel *Mañana Means Heaven* (2013), winner of an International Latino Book Award, and the hybrid nonfiction work *All They Will Call You* (2017). Currently an associate professor at the University of Texas in El Paso's bilingual MFA program.

Victor Hernández Cruz (b. 1949) b. Aguas Buenas, Puerto Rico; moved to New York City at age five. As a teenager, cofounded Calle Once Publications, which published a small run of his first collection, *Papo Got His Gun! And Other Poems* (1966); several of its poems were then published in *Evergreen Review*. Became an editor of *Umbra* magazine and cofounded the East Harlem Gut Theater. Moved to Northern California in 1968. *Snaps* published by Random House in 1969. Later collections include *Red Beans* (1991), *Maraca: New and Selected Poems 1965–2000* (2001), and *Beneath the Spanish* (2017). Co-editor of *Paper Dance: 55 Latino Poets* (1995). Cofounded, with Ishmael Reed, the Before Columbus Foundation. Served as chancellor of the Academy of American Poets. Lives in Morocco and Puerto Rico.

Leticia Hernández-Linares (b. 1971) b. Los Angeles, CA, to Salvadoran parents. Earned BA from Scripps College, MA from University of Pennsylvania, and MFA from San Francisco State University in 2020. Publications include the poetry collections *Razor Edges of My Tongue* (2002) and *Mucha Muchacha, Too Much Girl* (2015), as well as the picture book *Alejandria Fights Back!/¡La Lucha de Alejandria!* (2021). Co-editor of *The Wandering Song: Central American Writing in the United States* (2017). Also a multidisciplinary artist who has performed and exhibited work at the Smithsonian Museum and SOMArts Gallery. Currently assistant professor in the College of Ethnic Studies at San Francisco State University.

Juan Felipe Herrera (b. 1948) b. Fowler, CA, to migrant farmers. Spent his years growing up moving throughout the San Joaquin and Salinas Valleys. Received BA in Anthropology at the University of California, Los Angeles, through the Educational Opportunity Program, an MA from Stanford University, and an MFA from the University of Iowa Writers' Workshop. Led a trip through Mexico with fellow Chicano artists, which greatly influenced his poetry. Publications include the novel-in-verse *Crashboomlove* (1999), which received the Americas Award; the poetry collections *187 Reasons Mexicans Can't Cross the Border: Undocuments 1971–2007* (2007), *Half of the World in Light: New and Selected Poems* (2008), and *Every Day*

We Get More Illegal (2020); and the children's book *Jabberwalking* (2018), which won an International Latino Book Award. Has taught Chicano and Latin American studies and creative writing at California State University, Fresno, and University of California, Riverside. Holds honorary doctorate from California State University. His visual art has been featured in the Monterey Museum of Art. Recipient of a Latino Hall of Fame Award, he was also California's Poet Laureate, 2012–15, and U.S. Poet Laureate, 2015–17.

Darrel Alejandro Holnes (b 1987) b. Panama City, Panama. Received BA at the University of Houston and MFA at the University of Michigan. Publications include the chapbook *Migrant Psalms* (2021) and the poetry collection *Stepmotherland* (2022), winner of the Andrés Montoya Poetry Prize. His plays have been produced at the Kennedy Center for the Arts American College Theater Festival, Kitchen Theater Company, Primary Stages, and elsewhere. Currently assistant professor of English at Medgar Evers College and part-time professor at New York University's Gallatin School of Individualized Study.

Javier O. Huerta (b. 1973) b. Nuevo Laredo, Mexico; immigrated to the U.S. in 1981, living in Houston. Attended the bilingual MFA program at the University of Texas at El Paso, then earned PhD from the University of California, Berkeley. Publications include the poetry collection *Some Clarifications y otros poemas* (2007) and the multi-genre book *American Copia: An Immigrant Epic* (2012). Currently professor of English at Mission College, Santa Clara, CA.

Joe Jiménez (b. 1976), b. San Antonio, TX. Earned MFA at Antioch University. Author of the poetry collections *The Possibilities of Mud* (2014) and *Rattlesnake Allegory* (2019), as well as the young adult novels *Bloodline* (2016) and *Hot Boy Summer* (2024).

Maurice Kilwein Guevara (b. 1961) b. Belencito, Colombia; family moved to Pittsburgh when he was two. Earned BA and BS from the University of Pittsburgh, MFA from Bowling Green State University, and PhD in English and Comparative Literature from the University of Wisconsin–Milwaukee. Traveled on Fulbright fellowship to Colombia in 1993. Is also a playwright and actor. Publications include the poetry collections *Postmortem* (1994), *Autobiography of So-and-So: Poems in Prose* (2001), *POEMA* (2009), winner of an International Latino Book Award, and the play *The Last Bridge/El Ultimo Puente* (1999). Currently a professor at the University of Wisconsin, Milwaukee.

Tato Laviera (1950–2013) b. Jesús Abraham Laviera in San Juan, Puerto Rico; moved to New York City when he was nine. "Tato" is family nickname. Studied at Cornell University and Brooklyn College. Worked as community organizer before devoting himself to writing full-time; was central figure among Nuyorican poets and playwrights. Taught at Rutgers University, 1979–81. First collection *La Carreta Made a U-Turn* (1979) was followed by the American Book Award–winning *Enclave* (1981) and other collections. Attended White House gathering of poets in 1980. Complications from diabetes led to him being legally blind in later years. Wrote more than a dozen plays, including *King of Cans,* which premiered in 2012 at New York's Red Carpet Theatre, renamed Tato Laviera Theatre shortly after his death. *Bendición: The Complete Poetry of Tato Laviera* (2014) published posthumously.

Raina J. León (b. 1981) b. Philadelphia, PA. Earned BA from Pennsylvania State University, MA in Teaching of English from Teachers College, Columbia University, MA in Educational Leadership from Framingham State University, MFA in Poetry from Saint Mary's College of California, and PhD in Education from University of North Carolina in Chapel Hill. An Afro-Boricua poet, she is the author of *Canticle of Idols* (2008), *Boogeyman Dawn* (2013), *black god mother this body* (2022), and other books. Also a visual artist. Founding editor of *The Acentos Review.* Was professor in the School of Education at Saint Mary's College of California; currently teaches in the Stonecoast MFA program at the University of Southern Maine.

Aurora Levins Morales (b. 1954) b. Maricao, Puerto Rico. Family moved to Chicago in 1967. Attended Franconia College. Relocated to the Bay Area in the 1970s. Involved in the Chicago Women's Liberation Union, anti–Vietnam War movements, Jewish Voice for Peace, and the disability justice movement. Went back to school in the late 1980s, attending Mills College. Holds a PhD from Union Institute & University. Hosts eco-justice podcast *Letters from Earth* and is the creator of the Rimonim Liturgy Project. Publications include *Getting Home Alive* (1986), *Kindling: Writings on the Body* (2013), *Medicine Stories: Essays for Radicals* (2019), and *Silt: Prose Poems* (2019).

Frank Lima (1939–2013) b. New York, NY, of Mexican and Puerto Rican descent. Childhood marked by violence and sexual abuse at home; dropped out of school at fourteen, and as a teenager was involved with gangs and addicted to heroin, necessitating stays at a juvenile drug rehabilitation center. Met painter Sherman Drexler, who sent Lima's early poems to poets, including Kenneth Koch and Robert Lowell. Worked as a professional chef. First published poems appeared in *Evergreen Review* in 1962. Became close with painters and New York School poets, especially Frank O'Hara, with whom he collaborated on a play for an unrealized Andy Warhol film project. Worked as drug counselor and nonprofit administrator. Earned MFA from Columbia University in 1975. Resumed work as chef, then taught for many years at the New York Restaurant School. Rejected label of "Latino" applied to his poetry. Publications include the poetry collections *Inventory* (1964), *Underground with the Oriole* (1971), *Inventory: New & Selected Poems* (1997), and the posthumous *Incidents of Travel in Poetry: Selected Poems* (2016).

Ada Limón (b. 1976) b. Sonoma, CA. Earned MFA from New York University. Author of six poetry collections, including *The Carrying* (2018), which won a National Book Critics Circle Award. Hosted poetry podcast *The Slowdown*, September 2021–October 2022. Her many awards include a MacArthur fellowship. Appointed Poet Laureate of the United States in 2022. One of her poems will be engraved on NASA's Europa Clipper Spacecraft, scheduled to be launched in October 2024.

Antonio de Jesús López (b. 1994) b. Palo Alto, CA, to Mexican immigrant parents. Earned BA from Duke University, MFA from Rutgers University–Newark, and MPhil from the University of Oxford, which he attended as a Marshall Scholar. Elected to city council of East Palo Alto in 2020. Author of poetry collection *Gentefication* (2021); currently pursuing a PhD in Modern Thought and Literature at Stanford University.

Sheryl Luna (b. 1965) b. El Paso, TX. Earned BA at Texas Tech University, MFA from the University of Texas at El Paso, and PhD in Contemporary Literature from the University of North Texas. Author of the poetry collections *Pity the Drowned Horses* (2004), *Seven* (2013), and *Magnificent Errors* (2022). Has taught at the University of Colorado and the Metropolitan State College of Denver.

Jaime Manrique (b. 1949) b. Baranquilla, Colombia; moved to Lakeland, FL, at the age of seventeen with his mother. Received BA in English Literature from the University of South Florida. Publications include the poetry collections *Los adoradores de la luna* (1976), which won Colombia's Eduardo Cote Lamus National Poetry Award; *My Night with Federico García Lorca* (1997), translated by Edith Grossman; the essay collection *Eminent Maricones: Arenas, Lorca, Puig, and Me* (1999); as well as the novels *Our Lives Are the Rivers* (2006), which won an International Latino Book Award, and *Cervantes Street* (2012). Co-editor of *Bésame Mucho: An Anthology of Gay Latino Fiction* (1999). With Joan Larkin, translated Sor Juana

Inés de la Cruz's *Love Poems/Poemas de amor* (2003) into English. Taught in the MFA writing program at Columbia University and was a Distinguished Lecturer at The City College of New York. Received a Bill Whitehead Award for Lifetime Achievement.

Mariposa (b. 1971) b. Mariposa María Teresa Fernández in the Bronx, NY, a third-generation Puerto Rican. Earned both a BA in Women's Studies with a concentration in English Literature and an MA in Education from New York University. Poetry collection *Born Broxeña: Poems on Identity, Love, and Survival* was published in 2001.

José Martí (1853–1895) b. Havana, Cuba. At sixteen, founded the newspaper *La Patria Libre*, where he published patriotic verse epic *Abdala*. Shortly afterwards, letter dissuading a classmate from joining Spanish army led him to be sentenced to six years in prison; fell ill after six months of hard labor. Deported to Spain. Published *El presidio político en Cuba* (1871) on his experience as a political prisoner. Attended the Central University of Madrid and later the University of Zaragoza, earning degrees in Law and Philosophy and Letters. In 1875, traveled to Mexico City and wrote for Mexican newspapers such as *El Socialista*, *Revista Universal*, and *El Federalista*; was pressured to leave the country due to his criticism of the dictatorial presidency of Porfirio Díaz. Moved to Guatemala City before returning to Cuba in 1878, was again exiled to Spain the following year, but soon moved first to Caracas, Venezuela, and then in 1881, to New York City. Became a leader of Cuban exiles and wrote prolifically for newspapers in New York and throughout Latin America, including a regular column for *La Nación* in Buenos Aires. First book of poems, *Ismaelillo* (Little Ishmael), was published in 1882. Prolifically recorded his observations of American social and political life and admiration for cultural figures such as Walt Whitman. In 1890 became consul of Argentina and Paraguay and cofounded La Liga, a school for Black Cubans and Puerto Ricans in New York. In 1891 his poetry collection *Versos sencillos* (Simple Verses) was published. Began to dedicate ever more time to Cuban independence, traveling to Florida and the Caribbean to arouse revolutionary fervor among exiles. In 1892 cofounded and became a delegate of the Cuban Revolutionary Party and founded the newspaper *La Patria*. In 1895, arrived in Santo Domingo and was subsequently promoted to major general of the Liberation Army. With General Máximo Gómez, drafted *El Manifiesto de Montecristi*. On May 18, 1895, died at the hands of the Spanish at the Battle of Dos Ríos, seven years before Cuba gained its independence.

David Tomas Martinez (b. 1976) b. San Diego, CA. Earned BA and MFA at San Diego State University. Publications include the poetry collections *Hustle* (2014) and *Post Traumatic Hood Disorder* (2018). Formerly the reviews and interviews editor for *Gulf Coast Journal*.

Demetria Martinez (b. 1960) b. Albuquerque, NM. Earned BA at Princeton University. Publications include the poetry collection *Breaking Between the Lines* (1997), the novella *The Block Captain's Daughter* (2012), which won an American Book Award, the essay collection *Confessions of a Berlitz-Tape Chicana* (2005), which won the International Latino Book Award, and the novel *Mother Tongue* (1994). Deeply involved in the sanctuary movement. *Mother Tongue* is partially based on her experience being tried and acquitted for allegedly helping two undocumented Salvadoran women to enter the U.S.

Dionisio D. Martínez (b. 1956) b. Havana, Cuba; raised in Spain and the U.S. Publications include the poetry collections *Climbing Back* (2001), selected for the National Poetry Series, *Bad Alchemy* (1995), and *History As a Second Language* (1992).

J. Michael Martinez (b. 1978) b. Greeley, CO. Earned BA from the University of Northern Colorado and MFA from George Mason University. Publications include the poetry collections *Heredities* (2010), which won a Walt Whitman Award, selected by Juan Felipe Herrera, *In the Garden of the Bridehouse* (2014), and *Museum of the Americas* (2018). Former poetry editor at Noemi Press.

Valerie Martínez (b. 1961) b. Santa Fe, NM, of Pueblo, Diné, and Latino heritage. Earned BA from Vassar College and MFA from the University of Arizona. Her poetry collections include *Absence, Luminescent* (1999), *Each and Her (Camino del Sol)* (2010), and *Count* (2021). Translated the Uruguayan poet Delmira Agustini in *A Flock of Scarlet Doves* (2005). Santa Fe's Poet Laureate, 2008–10.

Farid Matuk (b. 1974) b. Lima, Peru, to a mother of Syrian heritage and a Peruvian father. Immigrated to Anaheim, CA, at age six. Earned BA in Comparative Literature from University of California, Irvine, and MFA at University of Texas at Austin. Lived in Santiago, Chile, on a Fulbright fellowship, awarded in 1998, and began writing poetry and translating there. Publications include the poetry collections *This Isa Nice Neighborhood* (2010), *My Daughter La Chola* (2013), *The Real Horse* (2018), and, with visual artist Nancy Friedemann-Sánchez, *Redolent* (2022). Served as poetry editor for *FENCE* magazine. Currently a professor of English at the University of Arizona.

Rachel McKibbens (b. 1975) b. Santa Ana, CA. Publications include the poetry collections *Pink Elephant* (2009), *Into the Dark and*

Emptying Field (2013), and *blud* (2017). A Women of the World Poetry Slam champion, among other honors. Has led poetry workshops in the Healing Arts Program at Bellevue Hospital in Manhattan.

Pablo Medina (b. 1948) b. Havana, Cuba; moved to New York City with his family at age twelve. Received BA and MA from Georgetown University. Publications include the poetry collections *The Floating Island* (1999), *Points of Balance/Puntos de apoyo* (2005), and *The Man Who Wrote on Water* (2011); the memoir *Exiled Memories: A Cuban Childhood* (1990); and the novel *Cubop City Blues* (2012). Cotranslated Federico García Lorca's *Poet in New York* (2008) with Mark Statman. Professor Emeritus at Emerson College and former director of its creative writing MFA program.

Maria Melendez (b. 1974) b. Tucson, AZ, and grew up in the Bay Area. Received BA from Colorado State University and MFA from the University of California, Davis. Her poetry collections include *How Long She'll Last in This World* (2006) and *Flexible Bones* (2010). Writes short stories and crime fiction, including her début *The White Redwood* (2024). Since 2019 a professor of English at Dodge City Community College.

Jasminne Mendez (b. 1984) b. Alabama. Earned BA and MEd from the University of Houston and MFA from the Rainier Writing Workshop at Pacific Lutheran University. Publications include the picture book *Josefina's Habichuelas* (2021), the poetry book *City Without Altar* (2022), the young adult memoir *Islands Apart: Becoming Dominican American* (2022), and the youth novel *Aniana del Mar Jumps In* (2023). Translator of youth and children's literature by Amanda Gorman, Nikole Hannah-Jones, Reneé Watson, and Claribel Ortega.

Orlando Ricardo Menes (b. 1958) b. Lima, Perú, to Cuban parents; moved to Miami at age ten. Studied at the University of Florida and obtained his PhD at the University of Illinois Chicago. Author of several poetry collections, including *Rumba Atop the Stones* (2001), *Fetish* (2013), *Heresies* (2015), and *The Gospel of Wildflowers & Weeds* (2022). Translator of work by Alfonsina Storni and José Kozer, and editor of *Renaming Ecstasy: Latino Writings on the Sacred* (2003). Teaches in the creative writing program at the University of Notre Dame and edits the *Notre Dame Review*.

Chucho Monge (1910–1964) b. Jesús Monge Ramírez in Morelia, Mexico. Composer whose notable works include "La feria de las flores," "Sacrificio," and "México lindo y querido." He worked extensively in film, with composing credits including *Los bohemios*

(1935) and *Cuando los hijos se van* (1941). A cofounder of the Sociedad de Autores y Compositores de Música de México (Society of Authors and Composers of Music of Mexico).

Yesenia Montilla (b. 1974) b. New York, NY, an Afro-Latina of Cuban and Dominican descent. Received MFA from Drew University. Publications include the poetry collections *The Pink Box* (2015) and *Muse Found in a Colonized Body* (2022).

Andrés Montoya (1968–1999) b. Central Valley, CA. Earned BA from California State University, Fresno, and MFA from the University of Oregon. Author of *the iceworker sings and other poems* (1999), which won a Chicano/Latino Literary Prize and an American Book Award, and of the posthumously published poetry collection *a jury of trees* (2017). Cofounder of the Chicano Writers and Artists Association. Died of leukemia at age thirty-one, with the Andrés Montoya Poetry Prize created in his honor.

José Montoya (1932–2013) b. Albuquerque, NM, to migrant farm-worker parents; grew up in California's Central Valley. Served in the U.S. Navy during the Korean War. Earned BA at the California College of Arts and Crafts and MFA at California State University, Sacramento, where he later taught art, education, and Chicana/o studies. Founder of the art collective Rebel Chicano Art Front (later known as the Royal Chicano Air Force), a group of artist-activists protesting the Vietnam War and advocating for farmworkers and laborers, and the Barrio Art Program, which offers community art classes throughout Sacramento. A visual artist who created sketches and political posters. Publications include *El sol y los de abajo (The Sun and Below) and Other R.C.A.F. Poems* (1972) and the book of poetry and sketches *In Formation: 20 Years of Joda* (1992). Named Poet Laureate of Sacramento in 2002.

Pat Mora (b. 1942) b. El Paso, TX. Studied at University of Texas at El Paso, where she later taught. Publications include the poetry collections *Aunt Carmen's Book of Practical Saints* (1997) and *Agua Santa/Holy Water* (1995), the memoir *House of Houses* (1997), and other books of prose and poetry for adults, teens, and children. Honored with a lifetime achievement award from the Texas Institute of Letters, among other honors. Founder of Children's Day, Book Day.

Juan J. Morales (b. 1980) b. Iowa City, IA, and raised in Colorado Springs, CO, son of an Ecuadorian mother and Puerto Rican father. Earned BA at Colorado State University–Pueblo and MFA at University of New Mexico. Publications include the poetry collections *Friday and the Year That Followed* (2006), *The Siren*

World (2015), and *The Handyman's Guide to End Times* (2018), which won an International Latino Book Award. Currently associate dean of the College of Humanities, Arts & Social Sciences and professor of English at Colorado State University–Pueblo.

John Murillo (b. 1971) b. Upland, CA. Earned BA from Howard University and MFA from New York University. Has published the two collections *Up Jump the Boogie* (2010, 2020) and *Kontemporary Amerikan Poetry* (2020). Cofounded poets' collective The Symphony. Currently a professor at Wesleyan University.

Miguel Murphy (b. 1974) b. Los Angeles, CA. Earned BA and MFA from Arizona State University. Publications include the poetry collection *A Book Called Rats* (2003), *Detainee* (2016), and *Shoreditch* (2021). Currently a professor of English at Santa Monica College, instructor of creative writing for UCLA Extension, and lecturer at UC Riverside's MFA program.

Adela Najarro (b. 1962) b. San Francisco, CA, of Nicaraguan descent. Received MFA from Vermont College and PhD in Literature and Creative Writing from Western Michigan University. Her poetry collections include *Split Geography* (2015), *Twice Told Over* (2015), and *Volcanic Interruptions* (2023), featuring art by Janet Trenchard. Currently a creative writing and poetry instructor at Cabrillo College.

Urayoán Noel (b. 1976) b. San Juan, Puerto Rico, and raised in Río Piedras. Earned BA in English from Universidad de Puerto Rico, Río Piedras, and MA and PhD in Spanish from Stanford University and New York University, respectively. Publications include the poetry collections *Kool Logic/La Lógica Kool* (2005), *Hi-Density Politics* (2010), and *Transversal* (2021); the critical study *In Visible Movement: Nuyorican Poetry from the Sixties to Slam* (2014), winner of the LASA Latino Studies Book Award; and translations of the Chilean poet Pablo de Rokha, *Architecture of Dispersed Life: Selected Poetry* (2018). Currently associate professor of English and Spanish at New York University.

José Olivarez (b. 1988) b. Chicago, IL, son of Mexican immigrants. Earned BA from Harvard University. Début collection, *Citizen Illegal* (2018), was followed by *Promises of Gold* (2023). Cohosted poetry podcast *The Poetry Gods*, 2016–17. Co-editor of the poetry anthology *The BreakBeat Poets, Vol. 4: LatiNEXT* (2020).

Judith Ortiz Cofer (1952–2016) b. Hormigueros, Puerto Rico; when she was young her family relocated to Paterson, NJ, but she made frequent lengthy trips back to Puerto Rico during her youth. Moved to Augusta, GA, at age fifteen. Earned BA from Augusta College and MA from Florida Atlantic University; studied at Oxford University on a fellowship. Was Franklin Professor of English and Creative Writing at the University of Georgia, where she taught from 1984 to 2013. Books include the poetry collections *Reaching for the Mainland* (1995) and *Love Story Beginning in Spanish* (2005) as well as the novel *The Line of the Sun* (1989) and *The Latin Deli: Prose & Poetry* (1993). Inducted in 2010 into the Georgia Writers Hall of Fame.

Américo Paredes (1915–1999) b. Brownsville, TX. Grew up along U.S.–Mexico border, spending time on both sides. Published poems as a teenager in newspapers. Earned degree at Brownsville Junior College. Worked as journalist, including on the staff of *Brownsville Herald*. First poetry collection, *Cantos de adolescencia* (Songs of Adolescence), was published in 1937. Performed regularly on local radio station as singer and guitarist. Joined U.S. Army in 1944, working as a reporter and becoming political editor of *Pacific Stars and Stripes* during the occupation of Japan. Traveled in Asia during his military service through 1950. Earned BA from the University of Texas at Brownsville and PhD from the University of Texas, Austin, in 1956; two years later his dissertation about the folk hero Gregorio Cortez, *With His Pistol in His Hand: A Border Ballad and Its Hero,* was published as a book. Was for decades a professor at the University of Texas at Austin, teaching and publishing extensively on folklore and related topics. His *A Texas-Mexican Cancionero: Folksongs of the Lower Border* was published in 1976; novel *George Washington Gómez,* parts of which date from the 1930s, was brought out in 1990. Other books include the poetry collection *Between Two Worlds* (1991). Among his honors and awards is La Orden del Águila Azteca from the government of Mexico.

Deborah Paredez (b. 1970) b. San Antonio, TX. Father, a Mexican immigrant, served in the U.S. military during the Vietnam War, which informs her 2020 collection *Year of the Dog.* Earned a BA in English from Trinity University and a PhD in Interdisciplinary Theatre and Performance from Northwestern University. In addition to *This Side of Skin* (2002), a book of poems, she is author of the critical study *Selenidad: Selena, Latinos, and the Performance of Memory* (2009). Cofounder and director, 2009–19, of CantoMundo. Currently associate professor of creative writing and ethnic studies at Columbia University.

Alan Pelaez Lopez (b. 1993) b. Oaxaca, Mexico, of Afro-Indigenous descent. Migrated to the United States at age five. Earned his PhD in Ethnic Studies from University of California, Berkeley. Publications include the visual poetry collection *Intergalactic Travels: poems from a fugitive alien* (2020). Edited *When Language Broke Open: An Anthology of Queer and Trans Black Writers of Latin American Descent* (2023). Currently assistant professor in Chicana/o Studies at University of California, Davis.

Willie Perdomo (b. 1967) b. New York, NY, of Puerto Rican descent. Earned MFA at Long Island University. Has published five poetry volumes, including *The Essential Hits of Shorty Bon Bon* (2014) and *Smoking Lovely: The Remix* (2021), as well as children's books. State Poet of New York, 2021–23. Teaches at Phillips Exeter Academy.

Emmy Pérez (b. 1971) b. Santa Ana, CA. Earned BA from the University of Southern California and MFA from Columbia University. Moved to Texas, living first in El Paso and then McAllen. Publications include *Solstice* (2003) and *With the River on Our Face* (2016). A former Texas Poet Laureate. Currently chairs the creative writing program at the University of Texas Rio Grande Valley.

Gaspar Pérez de Villagrá (1555–1620) b. Puebla de Los Ángeles (now Puebla de Zaragoza, Mexico). Studied at University of Salamanca. Served in several capacities in the army of Juan de Oñate, whose expedition established the first European settlements in New Mexico and engaged in brutal violence against the Indigenous population. Was regional magistrate, 1601–3, in the mines of Guanacevi and Nuestra Señora de Alancón in Nueva Vizcaya (now Durango, Mexico). His epic poem *Historia de la Nueva México* (1610), written upon his return to Spain c. 1605, is an account of Oñate's expedition, a work intended to persuade Philip III to assign him a new post in New Spain. Tried and convicted in absentia in 1614 for the executions of two deserters from Oñate's expedition, among other charges. In 1620, granted mayorship of Zapotitlán in Guatemala, but he died at sea en route.

Gustavo Pérez Firmat (b. 1949) b. Havana, Cuba. Fleeing the Cuban Revolution, family came to the U.S. when he was eleven, settling in Miami. Earned BA from the University of Miami and PhD from the University of Michigan. Publications include the poetry collections *Bilingual Blues* (1995) and *Scar Tissue* (2005), the novel *Anything but Love* (2000), the memoir *Next Year in Cuba: A Cubano's Coming-of-Age in America* (1995), and *Life on the Hyphen* (1994), a book about Cuban American culture. Taught at Duke University, 1979–99, then Columbia University, where he is currently Professor Emeritus.

Pedro Pietri (1943–2004) b. Ponce, Puerto Rico. Moved to Spanish Harlem in early childhood. Served in the U.S. Army in the Vietnam

War. Joined the Young Lords, a Puerto Rican civil rights organization; cofounded the Nuyorican Poets Café in the early 1970s. Became known for eccentric performances; nicknamed himself "Reverend" and carried leaflets of his poems in a suitcase labeled "Coffin for Rent." Recorded two LPs in 1979, *One Is a Crowd* and *Loose Joints: Poetry by Pedro Pietri*. Books include the poetry collection *Puerto Rican Obituary* (1973) and the satirical play *The Masses are Asses* (1984). Was an AIDS activist. Died of stomach cancer.

Miguel Piñero (1946–1988) b. Gurabo, Puerto Rico, and raised on the Lower East Side of Manhattan. Spent time in juvenile prison; struggled with addiction. Convicted on charges of armed robbery in 1971; while incarcerated at Sing Sing prison he took part in theater workshops and wrote the play *Short Eyes* (1974), which was staged off-Broadway and won a New York Drama Critics' Circle Award and an Obie. Cofounded the Nuyorican Poets Café and was co-editor of the anthology *Nuyorican Poetry: An Anthology of Puerto Rican Words and Feelings* (1975). Wrote screenplay for and appeared in film adaptation (1977) of *Short Eyes*. Début poetry collection, *La Bodega Sold Dreams*, was published in 1980. Career as an actor included several films and the television show *Miami Vice*. Collaborated with the artist Martin Wong, who was also his partner. *Piñero*, biographical film starring Benjamin Bratt, was released in 2001.

Ana Portnoy Brimmer (b. 1995) b. New York, NY, and raised in Puerto Rico. The daughter of Mexican Jewish immigrants. Earned BA and MA in English Literature from the University of Puerto Rico and MFA in Creative Writing from Rutgers University–Newark. Holds a certification in Communal, Indigenous, and Popular Feminisms in Abya Yala from the Rodolfo Kusch Institute at the National University of Jujuy. Publications include *To Love an Island* (2021) and *Que Tiemble* (2023).

Leroy V. Quintana (b. 1944) b. Albuquerque, NM. Served in U.S. Army's 101st Airborne Division during the Vietnam War. Studied at University of New Mexico and New Mexico State University. Taught at San Diego Mesa College. Author of several poetry collections, including *Sangre* (1981) and *The History of Home* (1993), both winners of American Book Awards, and the short story collection *La Promesa and Other Stories* (2002). Co-editor of the anthology *Paper Dance: 55 Latino Poets* (1995).

Miguel de Quintana (1677–1748) b. Mexico City. Came to New Mexico in the 1690s, settling first in Santa Fe and then Santa Cruz. Along with writing poetry, he was a playwright, town scribe, farmer, and assistant and notary to local civil and ecclesiastical authorities. Denounced as a "hypocrite and heretic" by two friars who wanted him to cease writing, he was investigated by the Inquisition, and in his defense claimed that inner voices were dictating his poems and plays; he was exonerated in 1735.

Gabriel Ramirez (b. 1994) b. New York, NY. Poems featured in *The Breakbeat Poets Vol. 4: LatiNEXT* (2020) and other anthologies.

Ramito (Florencio Morales Ramos) (1915–1990) b. Caguas, Puerto Rico. A prolific artist who made important contributions to *jíbaro* music. Toured widely in the U.S. and across Latin America; popular songs include "Que Bonita Bandera" ("What a Beautiful Flag"), which became an unofficial independentist anthem. Lived and performed in New York City, 1960–72. Committed suicide in 1990 in the wake of a cancer diagnosis.

Julian Randall (b. 1993) b. Chicago, IL. Earned MFA from the University of Mississippi. Author of poetry collection *Refuse* (2018), as well as the middle-grade novel *Pilar Ramirez and the Escape from Zafa* (2022) and *The Dead Don't Need Reminding: In Search of Fugitives, Mississippi, and Black TV Nerd Shit* (2024).

Alexandra Lytton Regalado (b. 1972) b. El Salvador; grew up in Miami. Received MFA in Poetry from Florida International University and MFA in Fiction from Pacific University. Publications include *Matria* (2017) and *Relinquenda* (2022). Editor of *Vanishing Points: Contemporary Salvadoran Prose* (2017). Has published translations of several Latin American poets. Is an editor at *SWWIM* (Supporting Women Writers in Miami). Returned to live in El Salvador in the late 1990s. Currently creating ongoing photo-essay about El Salvador, *through_the_bulletproof_glass*. Cofounder, Kalina Publishing. Lives in San Salvador.

Yosimar Reyes (b. 1988) b. Guerrero, Mexico; raised in San Jose, CA. Earned BA in Creative Writing from San Francisco State University. Author of the chapbook *For Colored Boys Who Speak Softly* . . . (2008).

Alberto Ríos (b. 1952) b. Nogales, AZ. Received BA and MFA from the University of Arizona. Began teaching at Arizona State University in 1982. His books include the poetry collections *Whispering to Fool the Wind* (1982), *The Smallest Muscle in the Human Body* (2002), and *Not Go Away Is My Name* (2020). *Capirotada: A Nogales Memoir* (1999) was given a Latino Literary Hall of Fame Award. Named Arizona's Poet Laureate in 2013, the state's first. Among his many honors are the Western Literature Association Distinguished Achievement award and election as chancellor of the Academy of American Poets. Currently Regents' Professor at Arizona State.

Iliana Rocha (b. 1981) b. Victoria, TX, and grew up in the surrounding area. Earned BA at the University of Houston, MFA at Arizona State University, and PhD in English Literature and Creative Writing from Western Michigan University. Début poetry collection, *Karankawa* (2015), was followed by *The Many Deaths of Inocencio Rodriguez* (2022). Is a poetry editor at *Waxwing Literary Journal*. Currently assistant professor at the University of Tennessee, Knoxville.

José Antonio Rodríguez (b. 1974) b. La Sierrita, Mexico, a small farming community in the state of Tamaulipas; immigrated to U.S. with his family at age five, settling in McAllen, TX. Earned BS in Biology, BA in Theatre Arts, and MA in English from the University of Texas–Pan American, and a PhD in English and Creative Writing from Binghamton University. Books include the poetry collections *Backlit Hour* (2013), *This American Autopsy* (2019), and *The Day's Hard Edge* (2024), as well as the memoir *House Built on Ashes* (2017). Currently associate professor in MFA program at the University of Texas–Rio Grande Valley.

Luis J. Rodriguez (b. 1954) b. El Paso, TX; grew up in Los Angeles. Early involvement in gangs recounted in his 1993 memoir *Always Running: La Vida Loca—Gang Days in L.A.* Deeply involved in Chicano activism and community organizing; founded the Guild Literary Complex in Chicago and Tia Chucha Press, among other initiatives. Ran as vice-presidential candidate for the Justice Party in the 2012 U.S. presidential election; ran for governor of California in 2014 and 2022 endorsed by the Green Party. Author of books in several genres, including fiction and the poetry collection *My Nature Is Hunger: New and Selected Poems, 1989–2004* (2005). Memoir *It Calls You Back: An Odyssey Through Love, Addiction, Revolutions, and Healing* (2012) won a National Book Critics Circle Award. Poet Laureate of Los Angeles, 2014–16. Honors include the Hispanic Heritage Award for Literature and the *Los Angeles Times*'s Robert Kirsch Lifetime Achievement Award.

Lola Rodríguez de Tió (1834–1924) b. San Germán, Puerto Rico. Participated in the 1868 Lares uprising against Spanish rule and wrote independentist lyrics to a song set to a dance tune, later the basis (with words changed) for the Puerto Rican national anthem "La Borinqueña." With her husband, deported to Venezuela. First book of poetry, *Mis cantares* (My Songs), published in 1876. Returned to Puerto Rico in 1885 for four years before being deported again, this time to Cuba, where she supported Cuban independence. Forced to flee the island in 1892, lived in New York City, where she met poet José Martí and other Cuban revolutionaries. In 1899 returned to Cuba, where she lived the rest of her life. Named to the newly established Cuban Academy of Arts and Letters in 1910. Served in several positions for the Cuban Ministry of Education.

Leo Romero (b. 1950) b. Chacón, NM, and raised in West Las Vegas, NM. Earned BA from University of New Mexico and MA from New Mexico State University. Worked as technical writer for Los Alamos National Laboratory before opening a bookstore with his wife in Santa Fe. Books include the poetry collections *During the Growing Season* (1978), *Celso* (1980), and *Agua Negra* (1981), as well as plays and short stories. Currently runs and operates Books of Interest in Santa Fe.

Benjamin Alire Sáenz (b. 1954) b. Old Picacho, NM. Earned BA in Humanities and Philosophy from St. Thomas Seminary in Denver and MA in Creative Writing from the University of Texas at El Paso. Pursued graduate study at Stanford University. Taught in the bilingual MFA program at the University of Texas El Paso. Publications include the poetry collection *Calendar of Dust* (1991), winner of an American Book Award, the short story collection *Everything Begins and Ends at the Kentucky Club* (2012), for which he became the first Latino author to win the PEN/Faulkner Award for fiction, and the young adult novel *Aristotle and Dante Discover the Secrets of the Universe* (2012).

Roque Raquel Salas Rivera (b. 1985) b Mayagüez, Puerto Rico, and grew up between Puerto Rico and the U.S. Received BA from the Universidad de Puerto Rico and PhD from the University of Pennsylvania. Publications include the poetry collections *lo terciario/the tertiary* (2019), winner of the Lambda Literary Award for Transgender Poetry, *while they sleep (under the bed is another country)* (2019), *x/ex/exis (poemas para la nación) (poems for the nation)* (2020), and *antes que isla es volcán/before island is volcano* (2022), which won the Juan Felipe Herrera Best Poetry Book Award. Translated *The Book of Conjurations* by Irizelma Robles and *The Rust of History* (2022) by grandfather Sotero Rivera Avilés. Editor of *Puerto Rico en mi corazón* (2019) and *La piel del arrecife: Antología de poesía trans puertorriqueña* (2023). Cofounder and translation supervisor for El proyecto de la literatura puertorriqueña/The Puerto Rican Literature Project. A Poet Laureate of Philadelphia, among other honors.

C. T. Salazar (b. 1992) b. Columbus, MS. Received MFA from creative writing program at Mississippi University for Women.

Publications include the chapbook *American Cavewall Sonnets* (2021) and the poetry collection *Headless John the Baptist Hitchhiking* (2022). Currently an assistant professor and librarian at Delta State University.

Excilia Saldaña (1946–1999) b. Havana, Cuba. Graduated from the Pedagogical Institute of Havana, then worked as a high school teacher and later as an editor for Editorial Casa de las Américas, *El Caimán Barbudo,* and Editorial Gente Nueva. Taught as a visiting professor at the Felix Varela Teaching Institute. Publications include the children's stories *Soñando y viajando* (1980), *La Noche* (1989), and the posthumous bilingual poetry collection *In the Vortex of the Cyclone: Selected Poems* (2002). Recipient of the Nicolás Guillén Award and an International José Martí Prize for children's literature, among other honors.

Luis Omar Salinas (1937–2008) b. Robstown, TX. Spent early years in Texas and Monterrey, Mexico. Mother died of tuberculosis in 1941 and he was sent by his father to live with his aunt, an event that figures in his poetry. The racism faced by his adoptive family in Nueces County, TX, pushed them to move to California in 1946. Earned an AA in Art History at Bakersfield City College, then studied poetry under Philip Levine at Fresno State College (now California State University, Fresno), where he later taught. Co-editor of the poetry anthology *From the Barrio: A Chicano Anthology* (1973). Poetry collections include *Crazy Gypsy* (1970), *The Sadness of Days: Collected and New Poems* (1987), and *Elegy for Desire* (2005).

Raúl R. Salinas (1934–2008) b. San Antonio, TX. Incarcerated on drug-related charges, 1959–72, and in prison developed his poetic practice, first publishing what became *Un Trip Through the Mind Jail* (1999) in the prisoner newspaper *Aztlán de Leavenworth*, which he coproduced. Studied and taught at the University of Washington in Seattle and later at Saint Edwards University, Austin. In 1981 he opened Resistencia Bookstore in East Austin. Active in Chicano, American Indian, and prisoners' rights movements; member of the Leonard Peltier Defense Committee and taught writing in juvenile detention facilities through his nonprofit organization Red Salmon Arts. Other publications include *Indio Trails: A Xicano Odyssey through Indian Country* (2006), spoken-word CD *Red Arc: A Call for Liberación con Salsa y Cool* (2005), and the essay collection *raúlsalinas and the Jail Machine: My Weapon is My Pen* (2006), edited by Louis G. Mendoza. Awarded the Louis Reyes Rivera Lifetime Achievement Award and the 2004 National Association for Latino Arts and Cultures Lifetime Achievement Award, among other honors.

Ruth Irupé Sanabria (b. 1975) b. Bahia Blanca, Argentina, and grew up between Seattle and Washington, D.C., after going into exile with her mother during Jorge Rafael Videla's dictatorship. Received BA from Rutgers University–Newark and MFA from New York University. Publications include *The Strange House Testifies* (2009) and *Beasts Behave in Foreign Land* (2017). Currently teaches high school English in Perth Amboy, NJ.

Erika L. Sánchez (b. 1984) b. Cicero, IL, to Mexican immigrant parents. Attended the University of Illinois Chicago. Earned a Fulbright scholarship to teach English in Madrid, during which time she began writing poetry. Received MFA in Creative Writing from the University of New Mexico. Publications include the poetry collection *Lessons on Expulsion* (2017), the young adult novel *I Am Not Your Perfect Mexican Daughter* (2017), adapted for the stage by Steppenwolf Theatre Company and for a forthcoming film directed by America Ferrera, and the memoir *Crying in the Bathroom* (2022).

Ricardo Sánchez (1941–1995) b. El Paso, TX. Served in the U.S. Army and earned his GED. Imprisoned in California and Texas for nine years for armed robbery. Following his release, received a Frederick Douglass journalism fellowship. *Canto y Grito Mi Liberacion/The Liberation of a Chicano Mind* was published in 1971. Earned PhD in American Studies from Union Institute & University; later taught writing and Chicano studies at Washington State University. Other publications include the poetry collections *Hechizospells* (1976) and *Eagle-Visioned/Feathered Adobes* (1990). Author of columns in the San Antonio *Express News* and the El Paso *Herald-Post*.

Mayra Santos-Febres (b. 1966) b. Carolina, Puerto Rico. Received BA from the University of Puerto Rico and MA and PhD from Cornell University. The author of numerous books of poetry and prose, including *Anamú y manigua* (1991), *El orden escapada* (1991), *Sirena Selena vestida de pena* (2000), *Nuestra Señora de la noche* (2006), winner of Puerto Rico's Premio Nacional de Literatura, and *Boat People* (2005), republished with translations by Vanessa Pérez-Rosario in 2021. A professor of creative writing at the University of Puerto Rico, Río Piedras, where she specializes in African, Caribbean, and feminist literature.

Salomón de la Selva (1893–1959) b. León, Nicaragua. First left Nicaragua at thirteen for New Jersey. Briefly attended Cornell University and Williams College. In 1915, with Thomas Walsh, translated a small published collection of Nicaraguan poet Rubén

Darío's work. In 1916 appointed as faculty member at Williams College; taught Spanish and French. In 1918 *Tropical Town and Other Poems* was published. Frequented New York literary circles and became associated with figures such as Edna St. Vincent Millay; hosted Latin American poets such as Rubén Darío. In 1918, founded short-lived *Pan-American Poetry* magazine featuring translations in English and Spanish of well-known modernist poets. Also that year, enlisted in the British army and was placed in a reserve unit at Felixstowe. Did not see combat but drew from this experience to write his book-length poem *El soldado desconocido* (The Unknown Soldier), published in 1922 in Mexico City with a cover illustration by Diego Rivera. Active in the American labor movement and was secretary to labor leader Samuel Gompers. In 1925 returned to Nicaragua and remained involved in labor struggle; served as director of newspaper *Nicaragua Libre*. Began publishing articles in support of anti-American Nicaraguan revolutionary Augusto César Sandino in journals such as *Diario de Costa Rica*. Spent time in exile in Costa Rica, Panama, and Mexico, where he served as advisor to President Miguel Alemán Valdés. Became honorary member of the Mexican Academy of Language. Returned to Nicaragua in 1955 and served as European ambassador for Nicaraguan president Luis Anastasio Somoza Debayle, whose father, Anastasio Somoza García, had called for Sandino's assassination.

Jacob Shores-Argüello (b. 1978) b. Miami, FL; grew up between Tres Ríos, Costa Rica, and Oklahoma City, OK. Received BA from the University of Central Oklahoma, MFA from the University of Arkansas, and PhD from Texas Tech University. Author of poetry and fiction, including the collections *In the Absence of Clocks* (2012) and *Paraíso* (2017). Currently an assistant professor in the department of English at Baylor University.

ire'ne lara silva (b. 1975) b. Edinburg, TX, to migrant parents; moved frequently throughout Texas, New Mexico, and Oklahoma while growing up. Attended Cornell University. Author of poetry collections *furia* (2010), *Blood Sugar Canto* (2015), *CUICACALLI/ House of Song* (2019), and *the eaters of flowers* (2024), as well as the short story collection *flesh to bone* (2013). Co-editor of the anthology *Imaniman: Poets Writing in the Anzaldúan Borderlands*. Named Texas Poet Laureate in 2023.

Brandon Som (b. 1975) born in Phoenix, AZ, of Mexican and Chinese descent. Earned BA from Arizona State University, MFA in Poetry from the University of Pittsburgh, and PhD in Literature and Creative Writing from the University of Southern California.

Publications include the chapbook *Babel's Moon* (2011) and *The Tribute Horse* (2014). Currently associate professor of literature and creative writing at the University of California, San Diego.

Christopher Soto (b. 1991) b. Los Angeles, CA, to Salvadoran parents. Received MFA in Poetry at New York University. Publications include *Diaries of a Terrorist* (2022) and the chapbook *Sad Girl Poems* (2016). Editor of *Nepantla: An Anthology Dedicated to Queer Poets of Color* (2018). Alongside Javier Zamora, cofounder of the Undocupoets Campaign, which began as an effort to remove proof-of-citizenship barriers from book contests and now offers fellowships to undocumented writers. Also cofounded Writers for Migrant Justice in response to family separation at the U.S.–Mexico border.

Gary Soto (b. 1952) b. Fresno, CA. Spent his early life working in the fields in the San Joaquin Valley. Attended Fresno City College and California State University, Fresno, where he studied under Philip Levine, and earned MFA from the University of California, Irvine. Publications include the poetry collections *The Elements of San Joaquin* (1977), *The Tale of Sunlight* (1978), *Neighborhood Odes* (1992), *New and Selected Poems* (1995), *Canto Familiar/Familiar Song* (1996), *A Fire in My Hands* (2006), the memoir *Living Up the Street* (1985), and the young adult short story collections *Baseball in April and Other Stories* (1990) and *Petty Crimes* (1998). Produced the film *The Pool Party* and the libretto for the opera *Nerdlandia* (1999).

Clemente Soto Vélez (1905–1993) b. Lares, Puerto Rico. Orphaned at seven and raised by his godfather. In 1918 moved to San Juan. Studied electrical engineering at Ramírez Commercial School. Worked for newspaper *El Tiempo* until he was fired for writing an article condemning the sugar industry. In 1929, founded the movement El Atalaya de los dioses (The Watchtower of the Gods), which sought to unite literary and political aspirations to free Puerto Rico from U.S. colonialism. In 1932, joined the Puerto Rican Nationalist Party, and in 1934 was arrested for instigating a sugar strike. Following the assassination by two Nationalists of the police chief E. Francis Riggs in 1936 as reprisal for the murder of four Nationalists by police (known as the Río Piedras Massacre), Vélez was convicted of sedition and imprisoned. Barred from Puerto Rico, he settled in New York City after his release in 1942. Joined Communist Party and became involved with American Labor Party. Founded the magazine *La Voz de Puerto Rico en Estados Unidos* (The Voice of Puerto Rico in the United States), as well as the Club Cultural del Bronx (Bronx Cultural Club) and Casa Borinquen. Served as the president of the Círculo de Escritores y Poetas Iberoamericanos. Returned to Puerto

Rico in the 1980s. Publications include *La tierra prometida: Poema* (1979), *Obra poética* (1989), and *The Blood That Keeps Singing/La Sangre que Sigue Canta* (1995).

Virgil Suárez (b. 1962) b. Havana, Cuba, and moved to the United States in 1974. Earned BA from California State University, Long Beach, and MFA from Louisiana State University. Publications include the collections *Banyan* (2001), *90 Miles (Selected and New Poems)* (2005), *The Painted Bunting's Last Molt* (2020), the short story collection *The Soviet Comes to Havana & Other Stories* (2014), and the memoir *Spared Angola* (1997). Is professor of creative writing and Latino/a literature at Florida State University.

José Juan Tablada (1871–1945) b. Mexico City, Mexico. First poetry collection, *El florilegio*, was published in 1899. Traveled to Japan in 1900–1901. Expanded version of *El florilegio* published in 1904. Introduced haiku to Spanish-language poetry and created calligrammes. Lived in Paris, 1911–12. His study of Japanese artist Hiroshige was published in 1914. Supported Victoriano Huerta during the Mexican Revolution; after Huerta's defeat in 1914, Tablada fled to New York City, where he lived through 1935, interspersed with diplomatic postings in Colombia and Venezuela, 1918–20. Returned to Mexico in 1935. Wrote prolifically and in many genres, including under various pseudonyms. Died in New York City.

Carmen Tafolla (b. 1951) b. San Antonio, TX. Earned BA from Austin College and PhD in Bilingual Education from the University of Texas, Austin. Served as director of the Mexican-American Studies Center at Texas Lutheran College. *Get Your Tortillas Together*, joint collection with Reyes Cardenas and Cecilio Garcia-Camarillo, was published in 1976. Wrote for bilingual children's television show *Sonrisas*. Début full-length poetry collection, *Curandera,* was published in 1983, followed by the study *To Split a Human: Mitos, Machos, y la Mujer Chicana* (1984) and numerous books across several genres. One-woman show *My Heart Speaks a Different Language* performed internationally. Poet Laureate of San Antonio, 2012–14, and of the state of Texas, 2015–16. Named president of the Texas Institute of Letters. Among her honors are the Americas Award from the Library of Congress, six International Latino Book Awards, and other honors. Taught at California State University, Fresno, and is Professor Emerita at the University of Texas, San Antonio.

Vincent Toro (b. 1975) b. New York, NY; raised in northern New Jersey. Earned MFA at Rutgers University. Author of the poetry collections *Stereo.Island.Mosaic* (2016) and *Tertulia* (2020). Also a playwright.

Director of performing arts and literature at the Guadalupe Cultural Arts Center, San Antonio, 2016–11. Is poetry editor at *Kweli Journal* and assistant professor in the English department at Rider University.

Edwin Torres (b. 1958) b. Bronx, NY. Earned degree in graphic design from Pratt Institute. Also a performer and artist. In 1988 began performing readings under the aegis of the fictitious art movement I.E. Interactive Eclecticism. Read frequently at Nuyorican Poets Café. His recording *Holy Kid* (1998) was included in part two of the Whitney Museum's exhibition *The American Century: Art & Culture 1900–2000*. Publications include the poetry books *Yes Thing No Thing* (2011) and *quanundrum [i will be your many angled thing]* (2021).

Rodrigo Toscano (b. 1964) b. San Diego, CA. Moved in the 1990s to San Francisco, where he helped found the Labor Party. First of his many books, *Arbiter*, was published in 1995; other works include *Collapsible Poetics Theatrics* (2008). Lived in Brooklyn, then in 2015 moved to New Orleans. Works for the Labor Institute.

Luis Alberto Urrea (b. 1955) b. Tijuana, Mexico, to a Mexican father and American mother; moved to San Diego at age three. Earned BA at the University of California, San Diego, and MFA from the University of Colorado Boulder. First book, *Across the Wire: Life and Hard Times on the Mexican Border*, was published in 1993. Writings in several genres include *Nobody's Son: Notes from an American Life* (1998), recipient of an American Book Award, and the poetry collection *A Fever of Being* (1994). Inducted into the Latino Literature Hall of Fame, among other honors. Currently Distinguished Professor of Creative Writing at the University of Illinois Chicago.

Robert Vasquez (b. 1955) b. Central Valley, California. Earned BA from California State University, Fresno, and MFA from the University of California, Irvine. Author of the poetry book *At the Rainbow* (1995) and *Braille for the Heart* (2007). Teaches at College of the Sequoias.

Dan Vera (b. 1967) b. Kingsville, TX, to Cuban parents; spent childhood in Raymondville and Corpus Christi. Earned BA in History and Sociology at Southwestern University and attended the Iliff School of Theology in Denver. Author of *The Space Between Our Danger and Delight* (2008) and *Speaking Wiri Wiri* (2013). Co-edited the anthology *Imaniman: Poets Writing in the Anzaldúan Borderlands* (2016). Served as chair of the social-justice poetry organization Split This Rock. Also a watercolorist.

Cecilia Vicuña (b. 1948) b. Santiago, Chile. Her poetry is interwoven with her work as a visual artist, performer, and filmmaker. Developed "Arte Precario" (precarious art; her coinage) in the 1960s, incorporating debris and ephemeral materials; what she has called her *basuritas* use plastic and other forms of industrial waste. Over her career she has created numerous textile assemblages called *quipus* (Quechua for "knot"). Was in London when Augusto Pinochet mounted a coup against the government of Salvador Allende in 1973; refusing to return to Chile, stayed in London until 1975, then moved to Bogotá and, in 1980, New York City. Major solo exhibitions of her works have been mounted internationally in museums, including London's Tate Modern and New York's Guggenheim Museum; more than thirty books of her art and poetry have been published. Elected honorary member of American Academy of Arts and Letters. Awarded the Gold Lion for Lifetime Achievement in 2022 at the fifty-ninth Venice Biennale (2022). In 2023, received Chile's 2023 Premio Nacional de Artes Plásticas.

Alma Luz Villanueva (b. 1944) b. Lompoc, CA, and raised in San Francisco; of Yaqui and Mexican descent. Earned BA from City College of San Francisco and MFA from Vermont College of Norwich University. Taught at University of California, Santa Cruz, Cabrillo College, and in the MFA program at Antioch University of Los Angeles. Publications include the American Book Award–winning novel *The Ultraviolet Sky* (1988). Lives in San Miguel de Allende, Mexico.

Tino Villanueva (b. 1941) b. San Marcos, TX; parents were migrant workers. Drafted into the U.S. Army in 1963 and sent to Panama Canal zone. Earned BA at Southwest Texas State University, MA from State University of New York at Buffalo, and PhD from Boston University. First collection of poems, *Hay Otra Voz*, was published in 1972. In the 1970s Villanueva cofounded Imagine Publishers and edited *Imagine: International Chicano Poetry Journal*; also edited the anthology *Chicanos: Antología Histórica y Literaria* (1980). Book-length poem series *Scenes from the Movie GIANT* (1993) won an American Book Award. Taught at Boston University and elsewhere.

Laura Villareal (b. 1992) b. San Antonio, TX. Earned BA from Texas State University in San Marcos and MFA from Rutgers University–Newark. Author of poetry collection *Girl's Guide to Leaving* (2022). Currently works for Letras Latinas at the University of Notre Dame's Institute for Latino Studies.

Vanessa Angélica Villarreal (b. 1982) b. McAllen, TX, to formerly undocumented Mexican immigrants; moved to Houston at age five.

Received BA in English and Creative Writing at the University of Houston and MFA at the University of Colorado Boulder. Author of the poetry collection *Beast Meridian* (2017) and *Magical/Realism: Essays on Music, Memory, Fantasy, and Borders* (2024). Currently pursuing PhD in English Literature and Creative Writing at the University of Southern California in Los Angeles.

William Carlos Williams (1883–1963) b. Rutherford, NJ, to an English father and a Puerto Rican mother. Spanish was dominant language at home. Entered University of Pennsylvania school of dentistry in 1902, transferred to medical school a year later; interned at two New York City hospitals, 1906–9. Published first book, *Poems* (1909), at his own expense. Studied pediatrics at University of Leipzig before returning to Rutherford in 1910 and establishing medical practice. Friends and acquaintances included many modernist poets and visual artists, including Ezra Pound (whom he had met at Penn) and Mina Loy. Was contributor to Pound's imagist anthology *Des Imagistes* (1914). Wrote prolifically while working full-time as a doctor, including as an essayist and fiction writer; worked for many years on long poem *Paterson*, published 1946–58. Was corecipient of 1953 Bollingen Prize. Suffered stroke shortly after appointment as consultant to the Library of Congress in 1952; claims that he was a Communist sympathizer prompted an FBI investigation, suspended when the Library of Congress rescinded Williams's appointment on grounds of his health problems. Posthumously awarded Pulitzer Prize for poetry collection *Pictures from Breughel* (1962).

Emanuel Xavier (b. 1970) b. Brooklyn, NY; father was Puerto Rican, and he was raised by his Ecuadorian mother. Kicked out of his home after he came out as gay; became involved in New York City's ballroom subculture in the 1980s. Self-published first poetry collection, *Pier Queen* (1997); other books include *Love(ly) Child* (2023) and the novel *Christ Like* (1999). Founded annual Glam Slam poetry competition in 1998. Edited anthologies *Bullets & Butterflies: queer spoken word poetry* (2005), *Mariposas: A Modern Anthology of Queer Latino Poetry* (2008), and *Me No Habla with Acento: Contemporary Latino Poetry* (2011). Founded, in 2011, the Penguin Random House LGBTQ Network.

Daisy Zamora (b. 1950) b. Managua, Nicaragua. Father imprisoned for taking part in failed coup against the Samoza government in 1954. Earned degree in Psychology from Nicaragua's Universidad Centroamericana. Taught at a school at a sugar mill. Joined the Sandinista National Liberation Front, organizing workers and engaging in revolutionary activity; was involved in attacks on National

Palace and police stations in 1978. Fled to Honduras, Panama, and Costa Rica, where she made broadcasts from the clandestine revolutionary radio station Radio Sandino. After Sandinista victory she returned to Managua and served as vice minister of culture in the new government. First of several poetry collections, *La violenta espuma* (The Violent Foam), was published in 1981. In addition to writing poetry and other literary works she founded and edited a journal devoted to economics and the social sciences. Currently teaches at San Francisco State University. Lives in Managua and San Francisco.

Javier Zamora (b. 1990) b. San Luis Herradura, El Salvador. Parents fled El Salvador in the 1990s; raised by grandparents after mother's departure in 1995. At age nine migrated to the U.S. unaccompanied by family, as would later be recounted in his memoir *Solito* (2022). Earned BA at the University of California, Berkeley, and MFA at New York University. Author of the poetry collection *Unaccompanied* (2017). Cofounder of the Undocupoets Campaign, which began as an effort to remove proof-of-citizenship barriers from book contests and now offers fellowships to undocumented writers.

NOTE ON THE TEXTS AND
ACKNOWLEDGMENTS

This volume contains 253 poems by 186 poets, including anonymous poets, published from the early seventeenth century through the present (2023, at the time of this writing). Poems written in Spanish are presented here in the original Spanish accompanied by English translations; otherwise the poems were composed in English (or a hybrid of English and Spanish).

The texts of the poems are, in most cases, taken from their first publications in books by their authors or, in certain instances, later collected or posthumous editions. Only if a poem has not been collected in one of the poet's books will the text be drawn from periodical, anthology, or online publications. Of the translations from the Spanish, ten are published here for the first time. With regard to copyright, great care has been taken to locate and acknowledge all owners of copyrighted material included in this book. If any such owner has inadvertently been omitted, acknowledgment will gladly be made in future printings.

The following list accounts for the sources of the texts for all poems printed in this volume, accompanied by copyright information.

Alexander Abreu, Me dicen Cuba: Spanish text transcribed from *Havana D'Primera—Me dicen Cuba/Official Lyric Video.* Copyright © Alexander Abreu. Reprinted with the permission of Páfata Productions S. L. They Call Me Cuba: English translation for this volume by Mahsa Hojjati.

Elizabeth Acevedo, La Ciguapa: *Beastgirl and Other Origin Myths* (Portland, OR: Yesyes Books, 2016). Copyright © 2016 by Elizabeth Acevedo. Reprinted with the permission of the author.

Marjorie Agosín, Lejos/Far Away: *At the Threshold of Memory* (Buffalo, NY: White Pine Press, 2003). Copyright © 2003 Marjorie Agosín. Reprinted with the permission of the author. La Extranjera/The Foreigner: *At the Threshold of Memory: New and Selected Poems* (Buffalo, NY: White Pine Press, 2003. Copyright © 1997, 2003 Marjorie Agosín. Reprinted with the permission of The Permissions Company, LLC, on behalf of White Pine Press, whitepine.org.

Anthony Aguero, Undetectable Explained to a Primo: *Burnt Spoon Burnt Honey* (McAllen, TX: FlowerSong Press, 2022). Copyright © 2022 by Anthony Aguero. Reprinted with the permission of Flowersong Press.

Jack Agüeros, Sonnet for the #6; Sonnet: The History of Puerto Rico: *Sonnets from the Puerto Rican* (Brooklyn: Hanging Loose Press, 1996). Copyright © 1996 Jack Agüeros. Reprinted with the permission of Hanging Loose Press.

Francisco X. Alarcón, Un Beso Is Not a Kiss; In Xochitl In Cuicatl: *From the Other Side of Night/Del otro lado de la noche* (Tucson: University of Arizona Press, 2002). Both poems copyright © 2002 Francisco X. Alarcón and reprinted with the permission of the University of Arizona Press. De *De amor oscuro*/from *Of Dark Love*: *Of Dark Love*, trans. Francisco Aragón (Santa Cruz: Moving Parts Press, 1991). Copyright © 1991 Francisco X. Alarcón. Reprinted with the permission of Moving Parts Press.

Claribel Alegría. Ars poetica/Ars Poetica; Carta a un desterrado/Letter to an Exile: *Fugues*, trans. D. J. Flakoll (Willimantic, CT: Curbstone Press, 1993). Copyright © 1993 Claribel Alegría. Translation copyright © 1993 D. J. Flakoll. Reprinted with the permission of Northwestern University Press.

Miguel Algarín, Nuyorican Angel Papo; HIV: *Love Is Hard Work* (New York: Scribner, 1997). Copyright © 1997 Miguel Algarín. Reprinted with the permission of Scribner, a division of Simon & Schuster, Inc. All rights reserved.

Alurista, sliver; with: *Return: Poems Collected and New* (Ypsilanti, MI: Bilingual Press, 1982). Copyright © 1982 Bilingual Press. Reprinted with the permission of Bilingual Press/Arizona State University, Tempe, AZ.

Julia Alvarez, All-American Girl; Museo del Hombre: *The Woman I Kept to Myself* (Chapel Hill, NC: Algonquin Books, 2004). Both poems previously published in *Beauty's Nothing* (Santa Fe, NM: Arena Editions, 2001). Copyright © 2001, 2004 Julia Alvarez. Reprinted with the permission of Susan Bergholz Literary Services, Lamy, NM.

Steven Alvarez, 1992/5th sun/our present: *The Codex Mojaodicus* (Albany, NY: Fence Books, 2017). Copyright © 2017 Steven Alvarez. Reprinted with the permission of Fence Books.

Eloisa Amezcua, The Witch Reads Me My Birthchart: *Fighting Is Like a Wife* (Minneapolis: Coffee House Press, 2022). Copyright © 2022 Eloisa Amezcua. Reprinted with the permission of The Permissions Company, LLC, on behalf of Coffee House Press, coffeehousepress.org.

Aldo Amparán, What I say to my mother after her father dies is soft: *Brother Sleep* (Farmington, ME: Alice James Books, 2022). Copyright © 2022 Aldo Amparán. Reprinted with the permission of The Permissions Company, LLC, on behalf of Alice James Books, alicejamesbooks.org.

Anonymous, El Corrido de Gregorio Cortez: María Herrera-Sobek, *Chicano Folklore: A Handbook* (Westport, CT: Greenwood Press, 2006). The Ballad of Gregorio Cortez: English translation for this volume by Susana Plotts-Pineda.

Anonymous, La Indita de Plácida Romero: *Herencia: The Anthology of Hispanic Literature of the United States*, ed. Nicolás Kanellos et al. (Oxford: Oxford University Press, 2002). Copyright © 2002 Oxford University Press.

Reprinted with the permission of Arte Público Press–University of Houston. Little Indian Ballad of Plácida Romero: English translation for this volume by Mahsa Hojjati.

Anonymous, de *Los Comanches*/from *The Comanches*: *Los Comanches: A Spanish Heroic Play of the Year Seventeen Hundred and Eighty*, ed. Aurelio M. Espinosa (Albuquerque: University of New Mexico, 1907). English translation for this volume by Lawrence Schimel.

Diannely Antigua, Golden Shovel with Solstice: *Ugly Music* (Portland, OR: Yesyes Books, 2019). Copyright © 2019 Diannely Antigua. Reprinted with the permission of Yesyes Books.

Gloria Anzaldúa, To live in the Borderlands means you: *Borderlands: The New Mestiza = La Frontera* (San Francisco: Aunt Lute Books, 1999). Copyright © 1999. Reprinted with permission of Aunt Lute Books.

Francisco Aragón, Nicaragua in a Voice: *After Ruben* (Pasadena, CA: Red Hen Press, 2020). Copyright © 2020 Francisco Aragón. Reprinted with the permission of Red Hen Press.

William Archila, Duke Ellington, Santa Ana, El Salvador, 1974: *The Art of Exile* (Tempe, AZ: Bilingual Press, 2009). Copyright © 2009 Bilingual Press/Editorial Bilingüe. Reprinted with the permission of Bilingual Press/Editorial Bilingüe/Arizona State University, Tempe, AZ.

Rane Arroyo, A Chapter from *The Book of Lamentations*; That Flag: *The Buried Sea: New and Selected Poems* (Tucson: University of Arizona Press, 2008). Copyright © 2008 Rane Arroyo. Reprinted with the permission of the University of Arizona Press.

Gustavo Adolfo Aybar, Wallflower Mambo: *Manteca! An Anthology of Afro-Latin@ Poets*, ed. Melissa Castillo-Garsow, (Houston: Arte Público Press, 2018). Copyright © 2010 Gustavo Adolfo Aybar. Reprinted with the permission of Arte Público Press–University of Houston.

Jimmy Santiago Baca, "I love the wind . . .": *Martín and Meditations on the South Valley* (New York: New Directions, 1987). Copyright © 1987 Jimmy Santiago Baca. Reprinted with the permission of New Directions Publishing Corp. Knowing the Snow Another Way: *Black Mesa Poems* (New York: New Directions, 1989). Copyright © 1986, 1987, 1988, 1989 Jimmy Santiago Baca. Reprinted with the permission of New Directions Publishing Corp.

Diego Báez, Yaguareté White: *Freeman's: The Best New Writing on Animals* (New York: Grove Atlantic, 2022). Copyright © 2022 Diego Báez. Reprinted with the permission of Grove Atlantic, Inc.

Oliver Baez Bendorf, My Body the Haunted House: *Advantages of Being Evergreen* (Cleveland: Cleveland State University Poetry Center, 2019).

© 2017 Natasha Carrizosa. Reprinted with the permission of Arte Público Press–University of Houston.

Lourdes Casal, Para Ana Veldford: *Palabras juntan revolución* (Havana: Casa de las Américas, 1981). For Ana Veldford, trans. David Frye in *Bridges to Cuba/Puentes a Cuba*, ed. Ruth Behar (Ann Arbor: University of Michigan Press, 1995). Copyright © 1995 Lourdes Casal. Reprinted with the permission of University of Michigan Press.

Ana Castillo, A Christmas Carol: c. 1976: *My Father Was a Toltec and Selected Poems 1973–1988* (New York: Norton, 1995). Copyright © 1995 Ana Castillo. Reprinted with the permission of Writers House LLC, acting as agent for the author.

Marcelo Hernandez Castillo, Wetback: *Cenzontle* (Rochester, NY: BOA Editions, 2018). Copyright © 2018 Marcelo Hernandez Castillo. Reprinted with the permission of The Permissions Company, LLC, on behalf of BOA Editions Ltd., boaeditions.org.

Sandra M. Castillo, La Fiesta del Globo: *My Father Sings to My Embarrassment* (Buffalo, NY: White Pine Press, 2002). Copyright © 2002 Sandra M. Castillo. Reprinted with the permission of The Permissions Company, LLC, on behalf of White Pine Press, whitepine.org.

Adrian Castro, When Hearing Bàtá Drums: *Handling Destiny* (Minneapolis: Coffee House Press, 2009). Copyright © 2009 Adrian Castro. Reprinted with the permission of The Permissions Company, LLC, on behalf of Coffee House Press, coffeehousepress.org.

Andrés Cerpa, The Distance between Love & My Language: *Bicycle in a Ransacked City: An Elegy* (Farmington, ME: Alice James Books, 2019). Copyright © 2019 Andrés Cerpa. Reprinted with the permission of The Permissions Company, LLC, on behalf of Alice James Books, alicejamesbooks.org.

Lorna Dee Cervantes, Poem for the Young White Man Who Asked Me How I, an Intelligent, Well-Read Person Could Believe in the War Between Races; Visions of México While at a Writing Symposium in Port Townsend, Washington: *Emplumada* (Pittsburgh: University of Pittsburgh Press, 1981). Both copyright © 1981 Lorna Dee Cervantes. Reprinted with the permission of the University of Pittsburgh Press. Flatirons: *From the Cables of Genocide* (Houston: Arte Público, 1991). Copyright © 1991 Lorna Dee Cervantes. Reprinted with the permission of Arte Público Press–University of Houston. Bananas: *Drive: The First Quartet* (San Antonio, TX: Wings Press, 2005). Copyright © 2005 Lorna Dee Cervantes. Reprinted with the permission of the author.

Lisa D. Chávez, Manley Hot Springs, Alaska: 1975: *Deconstruction Bay* (Albuquerque, NM: West End Press, 1999). Copyright © 1999 Lisa D. Chávez. Reprinted with the permission of the author.

Maya Chinchilla, Central American-American: *The Cha Cha Files: A Chapina Poética* (San Francisco: Kórima Press, 2014). Copyright © 2014 Maya Chinchilla. Reprinted with the permission of the author.

Sandra Cisneros, You Bring Out the Mexican in Me; Loose Woman: *Loose Woman* (New York: Knopf, 1994). Both copyright © 1994 Sandra Cisneros. Reprinted with the permission of Susan Bergholz Literary Services, Lamy, NM. Instructions for My Funeral: *Woman Without Shame* (New York: Knopf, 2022). Copyright © 2017, 2022 Sandra Cisneros. Reprinted with the permission of Stuart Bernstein Representation for Artists, New York, NY, and protected by the Copyright Laws of the United States. All rights reserved. The printing, copying, redistribution, or retransmission of this Content without express permission is prohibited.

Anthony Cody, How to Lynch a Mexican (1848–Present): *Borderland Apocrypha* (Oakland, CA: Omnidawn, 2010). Copyright © 2001 Anthony Cody. Reprinted with the permission of Omnidawn Publishing.

Lucha Corpi, México/Mexico: *Palabra de mediodía/Noon Words* (Houston: Arte Público, 1995). Originally published in *Fireflight: Three Latin American Poets.* Copyright © 1976, 1980, 1995 by Catherine Rodríguez-Nieto. Reprinted with the permission of Catherine Rodríguez-Nieto and Arte Público Press–University of Houston. Emily Dickinson/Emily Dickinson: *Palabra de mediodía/Noon Words* (Houston: Arte Público, 1995). Originally published by El Fuego de Aztlán Publications. Copyright © 1980, 1995 Lucha Corpi. Reprinted with the permission of Arte Público Press–University of Houston.

Eduardo C. Corral, In Colorado My Father Scoured and Stacked Dishes; Want: *Slow Lightning* (New Haven, CT: Yale University Press, 2012). Copyright © 2012 Eduardo C. Corral. Reprinted with the permission of Yale University Press.

Rio Cortez, Ars Poetica with Mother and Dogs: *Golden Ax* (New York: Penguin, 2022). Copyright © 2022 Rio Cortez. Reprinted with the permission of Penguin Books, an imprint of Penguin Publishing Group, a division of Penguin Random House LLC.

Cynthia Cruz, Self Portrait: *The Glimmering Room* (Village Station, NY: Four Way Books, 2009). Copyright © 2012 Cynthia Cruz. Reprinted with the permission of The Permissions Company, LLC, on behalf of Four Way Books, fourwaybooks.com.

Silvia Curbelo, Between Language and Desire: *Falling Landscape* (Tallahassee, FL: Anhinga Press, 2015). Copyright © 2015 Silvia Curbelo. Reprinted with the permission of Anhinga Press.

José Dávila Semprit, Los Estados Unidos: *Papiros de Babel: Antología de la poesía puertorriqueña en Nueva York*, ed. Pedro Lopez (San Juan: University of Puerto Rico, 1991). The United States: trans. Edna Acosta-Belén and Susan Liberis-Hill in *The Norton Anthology of Latino Literature*, ed. Ilan Stavans et al. (New York: Norton, 2010). Copyright © 2010 W. W. Norton & Company. Reprinted with the permission of the translators.

Julia de Burgos, To Julia de Burgos/A Julia de Burgos; Puerto Rico Is in You/ Puerto Rico está en tí: *Song of the Simple Truth: The Complete Poems of Julia de Burgos*, trans. Jack Agüeros (Willimantic, CT: Curbstone Press, 1997). Copyright © 1997, 2001, 2008 Julia de Burgos. Translation copyright © 1996 Jack Agüeros. Reprinted with the permission of Northwestern University Press.

Angela de Hoyos, La gran ciudad: *Selected Poems* (Houston: Arte Público Press, 2014). Copyright © 2014 Angela de Hoyos. Reprinted with the permission of Arte Público Press–University of Houston.

Joseph Delgado, dirty sheets: *Ditch Water* (Oakland, CA: Kórima Press, 2013). Copyright © 2013.

Lalo Delgado, Stupid America; De Corpus a San Antonio: *Here Lies Lalo: The Collected Poems* (Houston: Arte Público, 2011). Copyright © 2011 Lalo Delgado. Reprinted with the permission of Arte Público Press–University of Houston.

Blas Manuel de Luna, To Hear the Leaves Sing: *Bent to the Earth* (Pittsburgh: Carnegie Mellon University Press, 2005). Copyright © 2005 by Blas Manuel de Luna. Reprinted with the permission of the author.

Natalie Diaz, Tortilla Smoke: A Genesis; If Eve Side-Stealer & Mary Busted-Chest Ruled the World: *When My Brother Was an Aztec* (Port Townsend, WA: Copper Canyon Press, 2012). Copyright © 2012 Natalie Diaz. Reprinted with the permission of The Permissions Company, LLC, on behalf of Copper Canyon Press, coppercanyonpress.org, and Faber and Faber Ltd. Postcolonial Love Poem: *Postcolonial Love Poem* (Minneapolis: Graywolf Press, 2020). Reprinted with the permission of The Permissions Company, LLC, on behalf of Graywolf Press, graywolfpress.org, and Faber and Faber Ltd.

Angel Dominguez, Dear Diego,: *Desgraciado: The Collected Letters* (New York: Nightboat Books, 2022). Copyright © 2022 Angel Dominguez. Reprinted with the permission of Nightboat Books.

David Dominguez, Mi Historia: *Work Done Right* (Tucson: University of Arizona Press, 2003). Copyright © 2003 David Dominguez. Reprinted with the permission of the University of Arizona Press.

Carolina Ebeid, Punctum/Image of an *Intifada*: *You Asked Me to Talk About the Interior* (Las Cruces, NM: Noemi Press, 2016). Copyright © 2016 Carolina Ebeid. Reprinted with the permission of Noemi Press.

Fray Alonso Gregorio de Escobedo, de *La Florida*: Fray Alonso Gregorio de Escobedo, *La Florida* (New York: Colección Plural Espejo, Academia Norteamericana de la Lengua Española, 2015). From *La Florida*: English translation for this volume by Lawrence Schimel.

Gonzales. Reprinted with the permission of Arte Público Press–University of Houston.

Kevin A. González, How To Survive the Last American Colony: *Cultural Studies* (Pittsburgh: Carnegie Mellon University Press, 2009). Copyright © 2009 Kevin A. González. Reprinted with the permission of The Permissions Company, LLC, on behalf of Carnegie Mellon University Press, cmu.edu /universitypress.

Ray Gonzalez, At the Rio Grande at the End of the Century: *Cabato Sentora* (Rochester, NY: BOA Editions, 1999). Copyright © 1999 Ray Gonzalez. Reprinted with the permission of The Permissions Company, LLC, on behalf of BOA Editions, Ltd., boaeditions.org. The Head of Pancho Villa: *Consideration of the Guitar: New and Selected Poems* (Rochester, NY: BOA Editions, 2005). Copyright © 2005 Ray Gonzalez. Reprinted with the permission of The Permissions Company, LLC, on behalf of BOA Editions, Ltd., boaeditions.org.

Cynthia Guardado, Parallel Universe: *Cenizas* (Tucson: University of Arizona Press, 2022). Copyright © 2022 Cynthia Guardado. Reprinted with the permission of the University of Arizona Press.

Juan Luis Guerra, Ojalá que llueva café: Spanish text transcription based on *Juan Luis Guerra—Ojalá Que Llueva Café (Lyric Video)*, https://www .youtube.com/watch?v=w3vWGZgV-N4. Copyright © 1989 Universal Musica Unica Publishing. All Rights Reserved. Reprinted by Permission of Hal Leonard LLC. Let Us Hope It Rains Coffee: English translation for this volume by Mahsa Hojjati.

Laurie Ann Guerrero, Put Attention: *A Tongue in the Mouth of the Dying* (South Bend, IN: Notre Dame University Press, 2013). Copyright © 2013 by the University of Notre Dame. Reprinted with the permission of the publisher.

Roberto Harrison, a grotesque side of panamá with cooling shadow: *Tropical Lung exi(s)t(s)* (Oakland, CA: Omnidawn, 2001). Copyright © 2001 Roberto Harrison. Reprinted with the permission of Omnidawn Publishing.

José María Heredia y Heredia, Niágara: *Poesias de Don José María Heredia* (Boston: Roe Lockwood & Son, 1858). Niagara: *United States Review and Literary Gazette* 2 (January 1827), translated by Thatcher Taylor Payne.

Tim Z. Hernandez, I've Worn That Feminine Skin: *Skin Tax* (Berkeley, CA: Heyday Press, 2004). Copyright © 2004 Tim Z. Hernandez. Reprinted with the permission of the author.

Victor Hernández Cruz, Latin & Soul: *Maraca: New and Selected Poems 1965–2000* (Minneapolis: Coffee House Press, 2001). Copyright © 2001 Victor Hernández Cruz. Reprinted with the permission of The Permissions Company, LLC, on behalf of Coffee House Press, coffeehousepress.org. Trio Los

Dionisio D. Martínez, History as a Second Language: *History as a Second Language* (Columbus: Ohio State University Press, 1993). Copyright © 1993 by Dionisio D. Martínez. Reprinted with the permission of Dionisio D. Martínez.

J. Michael Martinez, Lord, Spanglish Me: *Museum of the Americas* (New York: Penguin, 2018). Copyright © 2018 J. Michael Martinez. Reprinted with the permission of Penguin Books, an imprint of Penguin Publishing Group, a division of Penguin Random House LLC.

Valerie Martínez, from *Count*: *Count* (Tucson: University of Arizona Press, 2021). Copyright © 2021 Valerie Martínez. Reprinted with the permission of the University of Arizona Press.

Farid Matuk, Talk; Talk: *This Isa Nice Neighborhood* (Chicago: Letter Machine Editions, 2010). Copyright © 2010 Farid Matuk. Reprinted with the permission of the author.

Rachel McKibbens, drought (California): *blud* (Port Townsend, WA: Copper Canyon Press, 2017). Copyright © 2017 Rachel McKibbens. Reprinted with the permission of The Permissions Company, LLC, on behalf of Copper Canyon Press, coppercanyonpress.org.

Pablo Medina, The Exile: *Arching into the Afterlife* (Tempe, AZ: Bilingual Press, 1991). Copyright © 1991 Bilingual Press/Editorial Bilingüe. Reprinted with the permission of Bilingual Press/Editorial Bilingüe/Arizona State University, Tempe, AZ. The Floating Island: *The Floating Island* (Buffalo, NY: White Pine Press, 1999). Copyright © 1999 Pablo Medina. Reprinted with the permission of The Permissions Company, LLC, on behalf of White Pine Press, whitepine.org.

Maria Melendez, El Villain: *Flexible Bones* (Tucson: University of Arizona Press, 2010). Copyright © 2010 Maria Melendez. Reprinted with the permission of the University of Arizona Press.

Jasminne Mendez, Machete: *City Without Altar* (Las Cruces, NM: Noemi Press, 2022). Copyright © 2022 Jasminne Mendez. Reprinted with the permission of Noemi Press.

Orlando Ricardo Menes, Doña Flora's Hothouse: *Rumba Atop the Stones* (Leeds, UK: Peepal Tree Press, 2001). Copyright © 2001 Orlando Ricardo Menes. Reprinted with the permission of Peepal Tree Press, Leeds, UK.

Chucho Monge, México, lindo y querido: for Spanish text, transcription based on *México Lindo y Querido (Remasterizado)—Jorge Negrete Full HD*, https://www.youtube.com/watch?v=gq8WILYkhAY. Mexico Sweet and Beloved: English translation for this volume by Mahsa Hojjati.

Yesenia Montilla, Maps: *Muse Found in a Colonized Body* (Village Station, NY: Four Way Books, 2022). Copyright © 2017, 2022 Yesenia Montilla. Reprinted with the permission of The Permissions Company, LLC, on behalf of Four Way Books, fourwaybooks.com.

Ana Portnoy Brimmer, A hurricane has come and gone./What do we tell our children now?: *To Love an Island* (Portland, OR: YesYes Books, 2021). Copyright © 2021 Ana Portnoy Brimmer. Reprinted with the permission of Yesyes Books.

Leroy V. Quintana, Etymologies: *My Hair Turning Gray Among Strangers* (Tempe, AZ: Bilingual Press, 1996). Copyright © 1996 Bilingual Press/ Editorial Bilingüe. Reprinted with the permission of Bilingual Press/ Editorial Bilingüe/Arizona State University, Tempe, AZ.

Miguel de Quintana, Jesús, María y José: Clark A. Colahan and Francisco Lomelí, "Miguel de Quintana, Poeta Nuevomexicano ante la Inquisicion, con Muestras de Su Obra" (1983). https://digitalrepository.unm.edu/shri _publications/22. Jesus, Mary and Joseph: *Defying the Inquisition in Colonial New Mexico: Miguel de Quintana's Life and Writings*, ed. and trans. Francisco Lomelí and Clark A. Colahan (Albuquerque: University of New Mexico Press, 2006). Copyright © 2006 University of New Mexico Press. Reprinted with the permission of the University of New Mexico Press.

Gabriel Ramirez, On Realizing I Am Black: https://buttonpoetry.com /gabriel-ramirez-on-realizing-i-am-black-100k-views/. Copyright © 2016 Gabriel Ramirez. Reprinted with the permission of the author.

Ramito (Florencio Morales Ramos), Que bonita bandera: Spanish text transcription based on Ramito, "Que Bonita Bandera," track 1 on *El Cantor De La Montaña, Vol. 2*, Ansonia, digital album adding 1971 recording of the song to the original 1960 vinyl LP. Copyright © 1971. What a Beautiful Flag: English translation in this volume by Mahsa Hojjati.

Julian Randall, Biracial Ghazal: Why Everything Ends in Blood: *Refuse* (Pittsburgh: University of Pittsburgh Press, 2018). Copyright © 2018 Julian Randall. Reprinted with the permission of the University of Pittsburgh Press.

Alexandra Lytton Regalado, La Mesa: *Matria* (Pittsburgh: Black Lawrence Press, 2017). Copyright © 2017 by Alexandra Lytton Regalado. Reprinted with the permission of Black Lawrence Press.

Yosimar Reyes, TRE (My Revolutionary): http://yosimarreyes.com/poetry. Copyright © Yosimar Reyes. Reprinted with the permission of the author.

Alberto Ríos, Carlos; Nani: *Whispering to Fool the Wind* (New York: Sheep Meadow Press, 1982). Both poems copyright © 1982 Alberto Ríos. Reprinted with the permission of Alberto Ríos. The Vietnam Wall: *The Lime Orchard Woman* (New York: Sheep Meadow Press, 1988). Copyright © 1988 Alberto Ríos. Reprinted with the permission of Alberto Ríos. Rabbits and Fire: *The Smallest Human Muscle in the Body* (Port Townsend, WA: Copper Canyon Press, 2002). Copyright © 2002 Alberto Ríos. Reprinted with the permission of The Permissions Company, LLC, on behalf of Copper Canyon Press, coppercanyonpress.org.

Iliana Rocha, Elegy Composed of a Thousand Voices in a Bottle: *Karankawa* (Pittsburgh: University of Pittsburgh Press, 2015). Copyright © 2015 Iliana Rocha. Reprinted with the permission of the University of Pittsburgh Press.

José Antonio Rodríguez, La Migra: *This American Autopsy* (Norman: University of Oklahoma Press, 2019). Copyright © 2019 José Antonio Rodríguez. Reprinted with the permission of the University of Oklahoma Press. Shelter: *The New Yorker*, March 30, 2020. Copyright © 2020 José Antonio Rodríguez. Reprinted with the permission of the author.

Luis J. Rodriguez, The Monster; *Jarocho* Blues; The Rabbi and the Cholo: *My Nature Is Hunger: New and Selected Poems* (Willimantic, CT: Curbstone Press, 2005). Copyright © 2005, 2016 Luis J. Rodriguez. 2016 edition published by Curbstone/Northwestern University Press by arrangement with the author. Reprinted with the permission of Northwestern University Press.

Lola Rodríguez de Tió, La Borinqueña: *Poesias patrioticas/Poesias religiosas* (Barcelona: Ediciones Rumbos, 1968). The Song of Borinquen: trans. José Nieto in *Borinquen: An Anthology of Puerto Rican Literature*, ed. María Teresa Babín and Sam Steiner (New York: Knopf, 1974). Copyright © 1974.

Leo Romero, The Goat's Cry: *Agua Negra* (Boise, ID: Ahsahta Press, 1981). Copyright © 1981 Leo Romero. Reprinted with the permission of the author.

Benjamin Alire Sáenz, The Fifth Dream: Bullets and Deserts and Borders: *Dreaming the End of War* (Port Townsend, WA: Copper Canyon Press, 2006). Copyright © 2006 Benjamin Alire Sáenz. Reprinted with the permission of The Permissions Company, LLC, on behalf of Copper Canyon Press, coppercanyonpress.org.

Roque Raquel Salas Rivera, they; if time is queer/and memory is trans/and my hands hurt in the cold/then: *x/ex/exis: poemas para la nación* (Tempe, AZ: Bilingual Press, 2020). Both poems copyright © 2000 by Raquel Salas Rivera. Reprinted with the permission of the University of Arizona Press.

C. T. Salazar, All the Bones at the Bottom of the Rio Grande: *Headless John the Baptist Hitchhiking* (Cincinnati: Acre Books, 2022). Copyright © 2022 C. T. Salazar. Reprinted with the permission of Acre Books.

Excilia Saldaña, Danzón inconcluso para Noche e Isla/Unfinished Danzón for Night and Island: *In the Vortex of the Cyclone: Selected Poems*, trans. Flora María González Mandri and Rosamond Rosenmeier (Gainesville: University Press of Florida, 2002). Copyright © 2002 Excilia Saldaña. Reprinted with the permission of University Press of Florida.

Luis Omar Salinas, Ode to the Mexican Experience; That My Name Is Omar: *The Sadness of Days* (Houston: Arte Público, 1987). Copyright © 1987 Luis Omar Salinas. Reprinted with the permission of Arte Público Press–University of Houston.

Raúl R. Salinas, Unity Vision: *Up Through the Mind Jail* (Houston: Arte Público, 1999). Copyright © Raúl R. Salinas. Reprinted with the permission of Arte Público Press–University of Houston.

Ruth Irupé Sanabria, Distance: *Beasts Behave in Foreign Land* (Pasadena, CA: Red Hen Press, 2017). Copyright © 2017 Ruth Irupé Sanabria. Reprinted with the permission of Red Hen Press.

Erika L. Sánchez, Narco: *Lessons on Expulsion* (Minneapolis: Graywolf Press, 2017). Copyright © 2017 Erika L. Sánchez. Reprinted with the permission of The Permissions Company, LLC, on behalf of Graywolf Press, graywolfpress.org.

Ricardo Sánchez, canto: *Canto y Grito Mi Liberación* (New York: Anchor, 1973). Copyright © 1971, 1973 Ricardo Sánchez. Reprinted with the permission of the Ricardo Sánchez Eagle Feather Research Institute.

Mayra Santos-Febres, Tinta/Ink: *Boat People*, trans. Vanessa Pérez-Rosario (Phoenix: Cardboard House Press, 2021). Copyright © 2021 Mayra Santos-Febres. Reprinted with the permission of Cardboard House Press. Poem title provided by the author.

Salomón de la Selva, A Song for Wall Street; My Nicaragua: *Tropical Town and Other Poems* (New York: John Lane, 1918).

Jacob Shores-Argüello, Paraíso: *Paraíso* (Fayetteville: University of Arkansas Press, 2017). Copyright © 2017 Jacob Shores-Argüello. Reprinted with the permission of The Permissions Company, LLC, on behalf of The University of Arkansas Press, uapress.com.

ire'ne lara silva, *dieta indigena: Blood Sugar Canto* (Hilo, HI: Saddle Road Press, 2015). Copyright © 2015 ire'ne lara silva. Reprinted with the permission of Saddle Road Press.

Brandon Som, Chino: *Tripas* (Athens: University of Georgia Press, 2023). Copyright © 2017 Brandon Som. Reprinted with the permission of The University of Georgia Press and the author.

Christopher Soto, The Joshua Tree // Submits Her Name Change: *Diaries of a Terrorist* (Port Townsend, WA: Copper Canyon Press, 2022). Copyright © 2022 Christopher Soto. Reprinted with the permission of The Permissions Company, LLC, on behalf of Copper Canyon Press, coppercanyonpress.org.

Gary Soto, Salt: *The Elements of San Joaquín*, rev. and exp. ed. (San Francisco: Chronicle Books, 2018). Copyright © 2018 Gary Soto. Reprinted with the permission of Chronicle Books LLC, San Francisco, chroniclebooks.com. Mexicans Begin Jogging; Bulosan, 1935: *New and Selected Poems* (San Francisco: Chronicle Books, 1995). Copyright © 1995 Gary Soto. Reprinted with the permission of Chronicle Books LLC, San Francisco, chroniclebooks .com. Fresno's Westside Blues: *The Elements of San Joaquin*, rev. and exp.

ed. (San Francisco: Chronicle Books, 2018). Copyright © 2018 Gary Soto. Reprinted with the permission of Chronicle Books LLC, San Francisco, chroniclebooks.com.

Clemente Soto Vélez, from *The Wooden Horse*: #3, #29: *The Blood That Keeps Singing*, trans. Martín Espada and Camilo Perez-Bustillo (Willimantic, CT: Curbstone Press, 1991). Copyright © 1991 Clemente Soto Vélez. Reprinted with the permission of Northwestern University Press.

Virgil Suárez, El Exilio: *90 Miles: Selected and New Poems* (Pittsburgh: University of Pittsburgh Press, 2005). Copyright © 2005 Virgil Suárez. Reprinted with the permission of the University of Pittsburgh Press.

José Juan Tablada, Haiku seleccionados/Selected Haiku; Luna Galante/ Gallant Moon: *The Experimental Poetry of José Juan Tablada*, trans. A. Scott Britton (Jefferson City, NC: McFarland & Co., 2016). Copyright © 2016 José Juan Tablada. Reprinted with the permission of McFarland & Co., Box 611, Jefferson, NC 28640, mcfarlandbooks.com.

Carmen Tafolla, Mujeres del Rebozo Rojo: *New and Selected Poems* (Fort Worth, TX: Texas Christian University Press, 2018). Copyright © 2018 Carmen Tafolla. Reprinted with the permission of Texas Christian University Press.

Vincent Toro, Sonata of the Luminous Lagoon: *Stereo.Island.Mosaic.* (Boise, ID: Ahsahta Press, 2016). Copyright © 2016 Vincent Toro. Reprinted with the permission of the author.

Edwin Torres, [no yoyo]: *quanundrum [I will be your many angled thing]* (New York: Roof Books, 2021). Copyright © 2021 Edwin Torres. Reprinted with the permission of Edwin Torres.

Rodrigo Toscano, Latinx Poet: *The Charm & the Dread* (Hudson, NY: Fence Books, 2021). Copyright © 2021 Rodrigo Toscano. Reprinted with the permission of Fence Books.

Luis Alberto Urrea, The First Lowrider in Heaven: *Ghost Sickness* (Louisville, KY: Cinco Puntos Press, 1997). Copyright © 1997 Luis Alberto Urrea. Reprinted with the permission of Cinco Puntos Press, an imprint of Lee & Low Books, leeandlow.com.

Robert Vasquez, At the Rainbow: *At the Rainbow* (Albuquerque: University of New Mexico Press, 1995). Copyright © 1995 Robert Vasquez. Reprinted with the permission of the author.

Dan Vera, Small Shame Blues: *Speaking Wiri Wiri* (Pasadena, CA: Red Hen Press, 2013). Copyright © 2013 Dan Vera. Reprinted with the permission of Red Hen Press.

Cecilia Vicuña, Luxumei/Luxumei; Eclipse en Nueva York/Eclipse in New York: *New and Selected Poems*, trans. Rosa Alcalá (Berkeley, CA: Kelsey Street

Press, 2018). Copyright © 2018 Cecilia Vicuña. Reprinted with the permission of Kelsey Street Press.

Alma Luz Villanueva, Child's Laughter: *Soft Chaos* (Tempe, AZ: Bilingual Press, 2009). Copyright © 2009 Bilingual Press/Editorial Bilingüe. Reprinted with the permission of Bilingual Press/Editorial Bilingüe/Arizona State University, Tempe, AZ.

Tino Villanueva, Scene from the Movie *GIANT: Scene from the Movie* GIANT (Willimantic, CT: Curbstone Press, 1993). Copyright © 1993 Tino Villanueva. Reprinted with the permission of Northwestern University Press.

Laura Villareal, Home Is Where the Closet Is: *Girl's Guide to Leaving* (Madison: University of Wisconsin Press, 2022). Copyright © 2022 Board of Regents of the University of Wisconsin System. Reprinted with the permission of the University of Wisconsin Press.

Vanessa Angélica Villarreal, A Field of Onions: Brown Study: *Beast Meridian* (Las Cruces, NM: Noemi Press, 2017). Copyright © 2017 Vanessa Angélica Villarreal. Reprinted with the permission of Noemi Press.

William Carlos Williams, All the Fancy Things: *The Dial* 82 (June 1927). The Poet and His Poems: *The Collected Poems: Volume II, 1939–1962*, ed. Christopher MacGowan (New York: New Directions, 1988). Copyright © 1939 William Carlos Williams. Reprinted with the permission of New Directions Publishing Corp. and Carcanet Press Limited.

Emanuel Xavier, Madre America: *The Selected Poems of Emanuel Xavier* (New Orleans: Rebel Satori Press, 2021). *The Selected Poems of Emanuel Xavier*. Copyright © 2021 Emanuel Xavier. Reprinted with the permission of Rebel Satori Press.

Daisy Zamora, Carta a una hermana que vive en un país lejano/Letter to My Sister Who Lives in a Foreign Land; 50 versos de amor y una confesión no realizada a Ernesto Cardenal/50 Love Poems and an Unfulfilled Confession to Ernesto Cardenal: *Clean Slate: New and Selected Poems*, trans. Margaret Randall and Elinor Randall (Willimantic, CT: Curbstone Press, 1993). Copyright © 1993 Daisy Zamora. Translation copyright © 1993 Margaret Randall and Elinor Randall. Reprinted with the permission of Northwestern University Press.

Javier Zamora, El Salvador: *Unaccompanied* (Port Townsend, WA: Copper Canyon Press, 2017). Copyright © 2017 Javier Zamora. Reprinted with the permission of The Permissions Company, LLC, on behalf of Copper Canyon Press, coppercanyonpress.org.

This volume presents the texts of the original printings chosen for inclusion here, but it does not attempt to reproduce nontextual features of their typographic design. The texts are presented without change, except for the correction of typographical errors. Spelling, punctuation, and capitalization are often expressive features and are not altered, even when inconsistent or irregular. The following is a list of typographical errors corrected, cited by page and line number: 86.5, Soltraron; 86.31, ararrar; 88.10, la; 92.10, son; 94.8, lo; 100.9, talismans; 104.19, Jose; 104.19, Munoz; 125.27, black; 126.18, Tamany; 152.8, medioeval,; 152.23, financia"; 157.1, seem; 170.4, O; 170.7, Con; 182.12, Nezahualcóyotl,; 186.38, Alfego; 188.19, stripped; 196.17 (and *passim*), Bogard; 203.20, Hunts; 216.24, *Xochitl*; 217.3, *xochitl*; 229.12, dening; 229.26, elixir; 248.33, Ixtaccíhuatl; 249.14, *mi*,; 249.27, Tlazoltéotl; 252.18, Otomí; 267.25, Sony; 267.26, Rhasaan; 271.8, though; 331.7, cancion; 331.31, Pendelton; 340.17, entrañas; 343.13, want you; 426.7, pore; 438.23, caillo; 455.22, genealogy; 456.9, resemble; 464.20, I will; 464.26, chichenizta; 464.27, quezacoatl; 494.9, parent's; 501.16, Yucatan; 518.2, I am; 518.30, *Taino-Indian*?; 523.13, rímas; 523.19 and 21, then; 524.11, Rios; 524.11, a cruzado; 524.16, oflos; 524.28, hacido; 524.32, a new; 524.33, mananas; 539.8, surf; 539.12, city.

NOTES

In the notes below, the reference numbers denote page and line of this volume (line counts include headings but not section breaks). No note is made for material included in standard desk-reference books or comparable internet resources such as Merriam-Webster's online dictionary. Translated words and phrases are from Spanish unless otherwise indicated. In general, translations are not provided when words have close English cognates, are clear from context, or appear in Merriam Webster's online English dictionary. Biblical quotations are keyed to the King James Version. Quotations from Shakespeare are keyed to *The Riverside Shakespeare*, edited by G. Blakemore Evans (Boston: Houghton Mifflin, 1974).

3.5　One shipwrecked Spaniard] At age thirteen, the Spanish explorer, writer, and translator Hernando de Escalante Fontaneda (c. 1535) survived a shipwreck off the Florida Keys and was captured by the Calusa people. In 1566, he was freed through the efforts of Spanish governor Pedro Menéndez de Avilés (1519–1574).

3.24　King Philip] Philip II (1527–1598), king of Spain, 1556–98.

5.4　cross of Saint James] A red cross against a white background, the emblem of the Knights of the Order of Santiago, to which Menéndez belonged.

5.13–14　Quiñones . . . fortification of Havana] Diego Fernández de Quiñones, chief administrator of the fortifications in Havana, 1582–86.

9.3　*Acoma*] Acoma Pueblo, established in the twelfth century or earlier in present-day New Mexico and built entirely upon a mesa. The first recorded European contact was in 1539, followed by mainly peaceful encounters throughout the next decade, until the expedition led by Juan de Oñate y Salazar (1550–1626), colonial governor of the province of Santa Fe de Nuevo Mexico in New Spain, and its accompanying violence.

9.3　Zutacapán] Acoma warrior who questioned Perez de Villagrá and received news of Oñate's encroaching attack. After a skirmish in which Oñate's nephew Juan de Zaldívar was killed, presumably as planned by Zutacapán, some eight hundred Acoma villagers, approximately 20 percent of the population, were massacred.

9.6　Tempal and Cotumbo] Members of Zutacapán's party.

11.18　Chumpo] Acoma elder who dissuaded Zutacapán from war with the Spaniards due to the fear of violence and, allegedly, a belief that the Spaniards might be immortal.

13.35 Numantia] Town in Spain that resisted several attacks by the Roman Republic, until survivors eventually capitulated following an eight-month siege in 133 BCE.

19.29 Zaldívar] See note 9.4.

33.2 *Los Comanches*] Anonymous play written c. 1780 (though possibly later), a time when the Comanches were overpowered by Spanish and Hispanic settlers after nearly a century of dominance in the region; the play celebrates their defeat. A text of the drama was first published in 1822, succeeded in 1907 by an edition annotated by the folklorist Aurelio Espinosa. Likely the first secular play written in the colonial Southwest, *Los Comanches* was popular throughout the nineteenth century, staged like other folk dramas in the region as an outdoor pageant.

33.3 CUERNO VERDE] Name given by the Spanish to the eighteenth-century Comanche leader Tavibo Naritgant ("Dangerous Man") for the green horned headdress he wore into battle. His attacks on colonial New Mexico settlements made him a target of the colonial government. He was killed by Juan Batista de Anza's forces on September 3, 1779.

33.35 Caslana nation] Refers to Eastern Apache tribe of southern Colorado driven out by the Comanches in the first half of the eighteenth century.

39.3 *Niagara*] The translation printed here, first published anonymously in 1827, is a somewhat free adaptation of Heredia's poem that had long been believed to have been written by American poet William Cullen Bryant (1794–1878), who edited the translation for publication, suggesting numerous changes. The authorship of the translation has since been attributed to Thatcher Taylor Payne (1796–1863). Payne's version has been included here to show how Heredia's poetry was presented in English to nineteenth-century American readers.

43.34 I am an exile] See Biographical Note for Heredia y Heredia.

47.2 *Song of Borinquen*] In 1868 De Tió wrote "La Borinqueña," a call to arms against Spanish rule, to be sung to a dance tune. The tune still accompanies "La Borinqueña" when sung as the official anthem of the Commonwealth of Puerto Rico, but in the later version Rodriguez de Tió's lyrics were replaced by words written in the early twentieth century by Manuel Fernández Juncos (1846–1928). "Borinquen" is Puerto Rico in Taíno, an Indigenous language once widely spoken on the island and elsewhere in the Caribbean; "Boricua" is used to designate people of Puerto Rican heritage.

47.11 The Cuban will soon be free] The song was written at the outset of the Ten Years' War, 1868–78, the first of Cuba's three wars of independence against Spanish rule.

75.26 let us be!] Refers to the U.S. occupation of Nicaragua, 1912–33.

77.7–8 Nelson Lost his left eye] British naval hero Vice-Admiral Horatio, Lord Nelson (1758–1805), as a twenty-two-year-old captain, was one of the leaders of a British expedition that invaded coastal Nicaragua in 1780; he later suffered an injury to his right (not his left) eye at the siege of Calvi in Corsica in 1794.

79.1 CORRIDOS] Narrative ballads from Mexico and from along the U.S.–Mexico border region whose subject matter has often been historical episodes, folk histories, or the exploits of vaqueros and bandits. Its narrative structure frequently consists of a prologue, the primary story, and a moral and farewell from the singer. Though related to other folk traditions, the corrido has responded to specific social conditions and events and bears unique thematic characteristics, among them a sense of Mexican pride and a spirit of masculine bravado.

81.1 *Plácida Romero*] On August 8, 1881, a raiding party of Apaches and their Navajo allies abducted Plácida Romero Gallegos, killing her husband and separating her from her nine-month-old daughter. During her forty-nine days of captivity Romero was detained at a camp in Chihuahua in Mexico. After she escaped, a group of Mexican civilians encountered her and brought her to the Mexican consulate in Isleta, TX.

84.2 *Gregorio Cortez*] Mexican-born Cortez (1875–1916) was living in Karnes County, TX, when, on June 12, 1901, following a dispute over the sale of a mare, Sheriff W. T. Morris shot Romaldo (also known as Román) Cortez, Gregorio's brother; Gregorio returned fire, killing Morris, then fled. In pursuit the Texas Rangers launched a massive manhunt, June 14–22, sometimes with groups numbering up to three hundred men. In a standoff in Belmont, Cortez killed Sheriff Robert Glover and Constable Henry Schnabel. He then traveled along the Texas-Mexico border for hundreds of miles, first on horse, then on foot, before being captured near Laredo after an acquaintance betrayed his whereabouts. (Romaldo was arrested with other members of the Cortez family and died in prison of his gunshot wounds.) Tried and acquitted of charges related to the killings of Morris and Schnabel, he was convicted of murdering Glover. He was pardoned in 1913. During the manhunt and following Cortez's capture, newspaper accounts of a nonexistent Cortez gang led to the Rangers at times indiscriminately shooting Mexican Americans. For many in the Mexican American border community, Cortez became a folk hero and was immediately the subject of a corrido.

97.17 Borinquen] See note 47.2.

105.19 José de Diego, Bentances and Muñoz Rivera] José de Diego (1867–1918), Puerto Rican poet, lawyer, and politician. Ramón Emeterio Betances (1827–1898), Puerto Rican poet, physician, and public-health activist. Luis Muñoz Rivera (1859–1916), poet and politician who advocated for Puerto Rican autonomy.

109.23   Martí] See Biographical Notes.

109.23   Guillén] The Cuban poet and political activist Nicolás Guillén (1902–1989).

109.24   guayabera] Loose-fitting lightweight pleated shirt, worn untucked.

109.24   guano hat] Or yarey hat, worn widely in Cuba particularly by peasants.

111.11   Boncó] Cuban slang: close friend.

117.10   *mapuey*] A species of yam.

117.15   *pitisalé*] Salted, sun-dried bacon.

117.18   Conuco] Small agricultural plot, derived from the Taíno word for garden.

125.19   Sacco, Vanzetti] In 1921 Nicola Sacco (1891–1927) and Bartolomeo Vanzetti (1888–1927) were convicted of murdering two men during a robbery in South Braintree, MA, the previous year. Their case became an international cause célèbre, with their defenders arguing that the two men had been unfairly convicted because of their Italian immigrant backgrounds and anarchist beliefs. Despite appeals and a commission to investigate the case, the two men were executed by electric chair.

125.20   Mooney] The American labor leader Thomas J. Mooney (1882–1942) was tried and convicted for the bombing that killed nine and wounded forty during a parade in San Francisco on July 22, 1916. His death sentence was commuted to life imprisonment in 1918. A worldwide campaign was mounted seeking his release. He was pardoned in 1938.

125.20   the blacks of Scottsboro] On March 25, 1931, nine Black youths, aged thirteen to twenty, were accused of having raped two young white women on a freight train in northern Alabama. They were tried in Scottsboro, AL, beginning on April 6, 1931, and on April 9 eight of the defendants were sentenced to death. In 1932 the U.S. Supreme Court overturned the verdicts; two defendants were retried and again sentenced to death in 1933, despite the recantation by one of the alleged victims of her previous testimony (the remaining defendants' trials were postponed pending the appeal of the new conviction). The U.S. Supreme Court overturned one of the new convictions in 1935. All the defendants were then reindicted by Alabama authorities. Four were retried and convicted from January 1936 to July 1937; one was sentenced to death (commuted in 1938 to life imprisonment), one to ninety-nine years in prison, and two to seventy-five-year terms. A fifth defendant received twenty years for assaulting a deputy while in custody, and charges against the remaining four were dropped in July 1937.

127.19   Tammany Hall] The Tammany Society, 1789–1961, known as Tammany Hall after its headquarters on 14th Street, was the political machine that controlled Democratic Party politics in New York City through the 1930s, when its influence waned.

127.23   Ginart] Roque Guinart, bandit in part II of Cervantes's *Don Quixote* (1605–15).

131.11   Jagua castle] Fortress in Cuba, south of Cienfuegos.

131.12   *vicaria* flower] Periwinkle (*Catharanthus roseus*).

139.24   Rocinante] Don Quixote's steed in Cervantes's *Don Quixote*, a worn-out workhorse.

143.15   Gilberto Concepción de Gracia] Lawyer (1909–1968) and founder of the Puerto Rican Independence Party.

145.25   Ithaca] Island home of Penelope and her absent husband, Odysseus, in Homer's *Odyssey*.

145.29   your son] Telemachus, the son of Odysseus and Penelope.

147.37–38   I know . . . Calypso and Circe.] In Homer's *Odyssey*, the nymph Calypso detains Odysseus for several years on her native island of Ogygia. Circe is a powerful nymph whose magic turns Odysseus's men into swine; he spends a year with her as her lover before he resumes his voyage home.

149.9–11   Menelaus . . . mad war] The Trojan War was triggered when Paris, a son of the Trojan king Priam, absconded with Helen, wife of the Greek king Menelaus.

153.22   Ed Lewis] American film producer and author (1919–2019).

163.3   *I have two homelands. . . . night.*] From José Martí's "Dos patrias" from *Flores del destierro* (Flowers of exile), posthumously published in 1933.

169.8   *Li-Tai-Po*] Chinese poet (701–762) transliterated in Pinyin as Li Bai.

171.17   April Rebellion] Unsuccessful uprising in 1954 against Nicaraguan dictator Anastasio Somoza García (1896–1956), in which Cardenal took part.

173.4   Solentiname church] At the religious community that Cardenal founded on Mancarrón in the Solentiname Islands; Nicaraguan government forces razed the site in 1977 but it was rebuilt in 1979 after the revolution that brought the Sandinistas (the Sandinista National Liberation Front, FSLN) to power. See also Biographical Note for Cardenal.

173.8   after the Insurrection of '78] Takeover of the National Palace in Managua on August 24, 1978, by the Sandinistas in the wake of anti-government demonstrations triggered by the assassination in January of

Pedro Joaquín Chamorro, publisher of the opposition newspaper *La Prensa*. The Sandinista fighters took hundreds of prisoners, exchanging them for the release of political prisoners, ransom money, and other demands. See also Biographical Note for Zamora.

173.10–23 clandestine Radio Sandino . . . organizing the Ministry of Culture] See Biographical Note for Daisy Zamora.

173.26 Mejía-Sánchez] The Nicaraguan poet Ernesto Mejía-Sánchez (1923–1985).

173.31 Saint John of the Cross] The Spanish Catholic priest and mystical poet Juan de la Cruz (Juan de Yepes y Álvarez, 1542–1591).

173.32 Saint Theresita of the Child Jesus] St. Thérèse de Lisieux (1873–1897), a Carmelite nun known as "The Little Flower of Jesus."

180.9 September the Sixteen] Mexico's Independence Day.

182.3 Cuauhtémoc] Final Aztec ruler (1496–1525) who resisted the Spanish and their four-month siege of the Aztec capital Tenochtitlan. After his capture he was executed at the order of Hernán Cortés (1485–1547).

182.12–13 Nezahualcoyotl] Fifteenth-century Aztec ruler of Texcoco, also a poet and philosopher.

182.17–18 the Eagle and Serpent of the Aztec civilization.] According to legend the god Huitzilopochtli led the Aztecs from their homeland of Aztlán and told them to build a settlement at the place where an eagle, perched on a cactus, was swallowing a snake. They encountered an eagle devouring a snake at the site of what became Tenochtitlan. The iconography of the eagle, cactus, and snake is featured on Mexico's national emblem, which also appears on its flag, coins, and documents containing an official government seal.

183.15–19 Hidalgo . . . El Grito de Dolores] In the early morning hours of September 16, 1810, the Catholic priest Miguel Hidalgo y Costilla (1753–1811), in what became known as "El Grito de Dolores" (the Cry of Dolores), rang the church bell to summon his parishioners in Dolores (now Dolores Hidalgo) in Guanajuato and gave a speech calling for an uprising against Spanish rule.

183.21 La Virgen de Guadalupe] The Virgin of Guadalupe, a representation of a dark-skinned Virgin Mary who is believed to have appeared to one of the first Christian converts in North America, Juan Diego, on December 9, 1531, in the Villa de Guadalupe Hidalgo, north of Mexico City.

183.22–27 I sentenced him . . . I killed him.] The insurrection led by Hidalgo was suppressed by the Spanish; he was executed on July 30, 1811.

184.23 Don Benito Juárez] Politician and lawyer (1806–1872), president of Mexico, 1858–72. He led the republican forces that defeated Emperor

Maximilian (the Habsburg archduke Ferdinand Maximilian, 1832–1867), installed by the French in 1864 in the wake of their invasion of Mexico in 1862.

184.37   Little Zapotec] Juárez was Zapotec, an Indigenous group in Oaxaca (where he was born and raised) and elsewhere in Mexico.

185.4   I rode with Pancho Villa] The supporters of Mexican revolutionary Pancho Villa (Doroteo Arango Arámbula, 1878–1923) killed twenty-four Americans during a raid on Columbus, NM, on March 9, 1916. In response a punitive expedition commanded by Brigadier General John J. Pershing (1860–1948) entered Mexico on March 15. Tensions increased after twelve American cavalrymen were killed and twenty-three taken prisoner at Carrizal on June 21 while fighting troops loyal to Mexican president Venustiano Carranza (1859–1920), but the prisoners were released on July 1 and war was averted. The last U.S. troops left Mexico on February 5, 1917, with Villa still at large. Villa was assassinated in 1923.

185.10   Emiliano Zapata] Mexican revolutionary and peasant leader (1879–1919), leader of the Liberation Army of the South, formed in 1910.

185.38   Yaqui] Indigenous peoples in Arizona and what is now the state of Sonora, Mexico.

185.39   Tarahumara] Indigenous people of the current state of Chihuahua, Mexico.

185.40   Chamula] Located in the mountainous area of Chiapas, Chamula was an important center for Tzotzil peoples before the Spanish conquest.

186.9–12   despots Díaz and Huerta . . . Francisco Madero] The long rule of Porfirio Díaz (1830–1915), president of Mexico, 1877–80 and 1884–1911, ended during the Mexican Revolution. According to the terms of the Treaty of Ciudad Juárez (1911), Díaz ceded the presidency to the revolutionary leader Francisco Madero (1873–1913), who was then overthrown in a coup d'état led by General Victoriano Huerta (1850–1916) on February 18, 1913. Under Huerta's orders, Madero was assassinated five days later.

186.24   Tonantzin, Aztec goddess too.] The Virgin of Guadalupe is associated with the Aztec mother goddess Tonantzin, which can also refer more generally to the feminine archetype or the feminine aspect of different deities.

186.30–35   Joaquín Murrieta . . . my Wife] A group of American miners nearly fatally assaulted the Mexican-born Joaquín Murrieta (1829–1853) in northern California, raping his wife, Rosita, and murdering his brother. After the attack Murrieta, along with Rosita and a companion called Three Finger Jack (also known as Bernardino Garcia), became an outlaw and a stagecoach robber. In July 1853, the two men were killed by a group of California Rangers under the leadership of Harry Love (1810–1868). Preserved in a jar of whiskey, the decapitated head of Murrieta and the hand of Three Finger Jack were brought to San Francisco and exhibited for the admission price of one dollar.

186.38   Elfego Baca] Baca (1865–1945), as a nineteen-year-old deputy sheriff, held off a group of about eighty cowboys in a protracted 1884 shoot-out in Frisco (now Reserve), NM. In addition to his career in law enforcement he was a lawyer and politician. His life was mythologized in comic books and the Disney television series *The Nine Lives of Elfego Baca*, 1958–60.

186.40   the Espinosa brothers] The brothers Felipe and Vivian Espinosa and their nephew José Espinosa went on a killing spree in 1863 that claimed thirty-two victims in the Territory of Colorado.

188.16   Moctezuma] Moctezuma II (1466–1520), Aztec emperor who has also been known as Montezuma, under whose reign, 1502–20, the Aztec empire was at its most expansive. He was killed in the early stages of the Spanish conquest led by Hernán Cortés.

188.30   Hacendado] Patron of an estate known as a *hacienda* in prerevolutionary Mexico, part of a landholding system dating back to the Spanish conquest. Laborers were provided protection against conquerors and conquerors were given grants in repayment for the labor of Indigenous people. Work performed under this system continued to be a form of indentured labor that was mostly uprooted during the revolution of 1910.

188.34   tower of Chapultepec] Chapultepec Castle, during the Mexican-American War the site of the Battle of Chapultepec, September 12–13, 1847, an American victory led by General Winfield Scott (1786–1866), after which U.S. troops occupied Mexico City.

188.36–38   My country's flag . . . Los Niños] In Mexico "Los Niños Héroes" are the six teenage military cadets who died in the Battle of Chapultepec rather than be taken prisoner; one of them wrapped himself in the Mexican flag so it would not be captured and leapt to his death. Their story is lauded in Mexico as a heroic episode in the nation's history.

189.38   the Treaty of Hidalgo] Treaty of Guadalupe Hidalgo, February 2, 1848, ending armed conflict between the United States and Mexico, 1846–48, under whose terms Mexico ceded two-fifths of its territory to the United States.

190.36   Diego Rivera] Mexican painter and muralist (1886–1957).

190.37   Siqueiros] The Mexican painter and muralist David Alfaro Siqueiros (1896–1974).

190.38   Orozco] The Mexican painter and muralist José Clemente Orozco (1883–1949).

196.3 Hoy enterraron al Louie] Louie was buried today. Other Spanish in the poem—*San Pedro o san pinche?*: Saint Peter or saint fucker?; *un vato de atolle*: a cool dude; *y la vida dura*: and the hard life; *Carnal del*: close friend; *Buenas garras*: good rags, i.e. nice clothes; *Rucas*: slang for women (lit. "elderly women"); *como*: like; *siempre con Liras bien afinadas*: always with well-tuned lyres; *Cantando La Palma*: Singing La Palma [a Mexican ballad]; *la Que andaba en el florero*: the one in the flower vase [lyrics from "La Palma"]; *porque Fowler no era nada como Los*: because Fowler was nothing like Los Angeles; *los Mambos y cuatro suspiros Del alma y nunca faltaba*: the Mambos and four sighs of the soul and we never lacked . . . [lyrics from "La Palma"]; *Trucha, esos! Va 'ver Pedo! Abusau, ese!*: Dude, watch out! There's going to be a fight! Stay sharp!; *No llores*: Don't cry; *Ese, 'on tal Jimmy?*: Dude, where is Jimmy?; *Horale*: Damn!; *Primo*: Cousin; *Va 'ver catos!*: There's going to be a fight; *jura*: police; *Trais filero*: Do you have your knife?; *Simon!*: Yes!; *Nel!*: No!; *Chale, ese!*: Damn, man!; *Y en Korea fue soldado de Levita con huevos*: And in Korea, he was a brave soldier; *del soldado razo*: of the buck private; *Mire*: Look; *comadre*: title given to the godmother of your child (literally means "co-mother"), but also a term used among very close friends; *ahí va el hijo De Lola!*: there goes Lola's son!; *pisto*: alcoholic drink; *en el Jardin Canales/Y en el Trocadero*: [names of bars]; *Despues/Enpeñaba su velardo de la/Peluca*: Afterwards he would pawn his barber's tools; *pa' jugar pocar serrada*: to play closed poker; *chukes*: derogatory term for Mexican Americans; *Se acuerdan de*: They remember; *la vez Que lo fileriaron en el Casa Dome*: the time that they knifed him at the Casa Dome; *y cuando se catio con La Chiva*: and when he fought with The Goat; *Porque no murio en accion-/ No lo mataron los vatos/ Ni los gooks en Korea*: Because he did not die in action/ The guys did not kill him nor the gooks [derogatory term] in Korea.

196.17–18 Bogart, Cagney . . . Raft.] James Cagney (1899–1986) and George Raft (1895–1980) were American film actors often cast in tough-guy roles in the 1930s and 1940s.

196.24 '48 Fleetline] Either a two- or a four-door sedan manufactured by Chevrolet.

197.5 Los, 'ol E.P.T.] Los Angeles, or El Paso, Texas.

198.19 Bronze Stars] The Bronze Star is a medal awarded by the U.S. Army for acts of bravery, heroism, or merit.

198.27 "Legs Louie Diamond"] Jack "Legs" Diamond (1897–1931) was a well-known Prohibition-era bootlegger and racketeer.

199.3–4 Casa Dome] Ballroom and dance hall in Selma, CA.

201.13 Dallas Chicanito deaths] Refers to the murder of twelve-year-old Santos Rodriguez by Dallas police officer Darrell Cain (1943–2019) on July 24, 1973. Accusing the boy and his thirteen-year-old brother David of stealing from a vending machine, Cain forcibly removed the brothers from their home and fatally shot Santos in the face while questioning him. (Cain claimed he believed the chamber was empty when he pulled the trigger.) Protests and riots in Dallas roiled the city in the days that followed. Cain was convicted on murder charges and served two and a half years of a five-year sentence.

201.18 WOUNDED KNEE] Refers to two events. The U.S. Seventh Cavalry massacred more than 150 Lakota Sioux on December 29, 1890, at Wounded Knee Creek in South Dakota. On February 27, 1973, activists from the American Indian Movement (AIM) began a seventy-one-day armed occupation of Wounded Knee, SD, on the Pine Ridge Indian Reservation.

201.22–24 The Trail . . . of Broken Treaties] Activist caravan traveling through much of the United States in 1972 en route to Washington, D.C., where it arrived in November seeking reforms from the federal government in its relationship to Indigenous tribes.

202.12 Pedro Bissonette lies dead] On October 18, 1973, Bissonette (1944–1973), an Oglala Sioux leader of the 1973 Wounded Knee occupation and at the time fleeing two arrest warrants, was fatally shot by Bureau of Indian Affairs police near Pine Ridge, SD.

203.9 Huracan] The Taíno deity of storms (see also note 460.8), also the Spanish word for hurricane.

203.24 Pelham or Parnassus] Pelham is a town in Westchester County bordering New York City. Mount Parnassus was the home of the Muses in Greek mythology.

208.18 SS] Abbreviation of *Schutzstaffel* (German for "Protection Detachment"). Originally founded in 1929 as Adolf Hitler's Nazi Party bodyguard. By 1939 the SS controlled the German police, the secret state police (Gestapo), and the Nazis' concentration camps, and had formed its own security service (the SD) and its own military force, known after 1940 as the Waffen (Armed) SS.

216.3–12 un beso . . . testigos] a kiss/is a door/that opens/a secret/shared/a mystery/with wings//a kiss/does not admit/witnesses.

217.1 *Xochitl . . . Cuicatl*] Nahuatl: Flower, Song; Flowery Song or Flower and Song.

220.30 Loisaida] Manhattan's Lower East Side.

221.11 "Straight out of Brooklyn,"] Film (1991) directed by Matty Rich (b. 1971).

225.12 sierras] Mountain ranges. Other Spanish in the poem—*lunas*: moons.

227.15–16   *cortesía . . . alegría*] Courteousness . . . joy.

228.3–4   the Taíno queen Anacaona] Ruler (c. 1474–c. 1503) of the Xaraguá kingdom in southwest Hispaniola, executed by the Spanish; she was also a poet and composer.

228.5   Duarte's . . . barred from his beloved patria] Juan Pablo Duarte (1813–1876), Francisco del Rosario Sánchez (1817–1861), and Ramón Matias Mella (1816–1864) were the three leaders of the Dominican resistance to Haitian occupation in the eastern part of Hispaniola that led to the Dominican Republic declaring itself an independent nation in 1844; they are regarded as the country's founding fathers. Duarte was forced into exile by the Dominican Republic's dictatorial first president, Pedro Santana (1801–1864), and spent most of his later life in exile in Caracas.

228.9   Salome's] In the Gospels of Matthew and Mark, the wish of Herod Antipas's stepdaughter (unnamed but traditionally called Salomé) for the head of John the Baptist is fulfilled. The story, including a seductive dance before Herod, was adapted several times in nineteenth-century art, music, and literature.

228.31   *¡Tu tiempo ya llegó!*] Your time has come!

229.4   *gabacha*] A Chicano term for a white woman (Anzaldúa's note). Other translations from Anzaldúa's notes to her poem—*rajetas*: literally, "spilt," that is, having betrayed your word; *burra*: donkey; *buey*: oxen; *sin fronteras*: without borders.

233.6   calles de polvo] Streets of dust.

236.2   *Soy Boricua*] I am Puerto Rican (see also note 47.2).

238.30   ¿Ya ves? Pórtate bien y a ver qué te trae] See? Behave well and we'll see what he brings you.

242.6   Cantinflas] Stage name of popular Mexican actor and comedian Mario Fortino Alfonso Moreno Reyes (1911–1993).

242.7   Pancho Villa] See note 185.4.

243.1   *Flatirons*] A series of rock formations in the mountains near Boulder, CO.

243.18   winter of their genocide still Ghost Dances] "Ghost Dances" refers to a late nineteenth-century pan-Indigenous religious movement originating among the Northern Paiutes of Nevada, which had as its most important ritual a ceremonial round dance repeated on successive nights. Participants in the Ghost Dance movement hoped, through dance, song, and prophecy, to bring about an end to white expansion, reunite the living with the dead, and restore traditional ways of life. In 1890, fearing a revolt because of the practice of Ghost Dance religious rites among the Lakota Sioux, General Nelson A. Miles (1839–1925) ordered the arrest of Lakota chief and holy man Sitting Bull (c. 1831–1890), who was killed while resisting capture on the Standing Rock Reservation in South Dakota. The massacre committed by the U.S. Seventh Cavalry at Wounded Knee Creek (see note 201.18) occurred two weeks later.

244.18   Colombia, 1928, bananas rot in the fields.] A strike against the United Fruit Company (since 1984 called Chiquita) by Colombian plantation workers advocating for better conditions began on November 12, 1928, at that time the largest labor stoppage ever to have occurred in Colombia. United Fruit refused to negotiate with the strikers, and in the following weeks labor unrest spread more widely in the country. On the night of December 5–6, 1928, Colombian army troops opened fire on a crowded square in the town of Ciénaga filled with striking workers and their families. The death toll of the massacre is uncertain, with wide variations in estimates ranging from forty-seven to two thousand.

244.35   Tláloc] Aztec god associated with weather cycles and with rain, thunder, and lightning.

245.3   quetzal] Brightly colored green and red birds native to tropical regions in Guatemala and Mexico.

245.31   y canela] And cinnamon.

245.38   At Big Mountain uranium] Big Mountain, Hopi and Navajo land in northeastern Arizona, is also known as Black Mesa, and is located in a region that contains uranium ore deposits. Uranium mining in Monument Valley, about seventy-five miles away, employed many Navajo individuals as miners, to whom respiratory protection was not provided; they endured high mortality rates from lung cancer, tuberculosis, and other diseases.

246.6   four corners] The unique point at which the borders of Arizona, Colorado, New Mexico, and Utah meet.

247.3   Vandenberg] Now Vandenberg Space Force Base (formerly Vandenberg Air Force Base), a space and missile testing site near Lompoc, CA.

247.4   Kwajalein] An island in the Republic of the Marshall Islands, designated as an American "trust territory" in 1944 and thereafter under the control of the U.S. military.

248.7   *lágrimas*] Tears. Other Spanish in the poem—*navajas*: folding-blade knives or pocketknives; *berrinchuda*: a girl or woman who makes *berrinche*, i.e., makes a fuss; *bien-cabrona*: real bitch; *Me sacas lo mexicana en mi*: You bring out the Mexican in me; *barbacoa*: pit-baked lamb; *Piñón*: Pine nuts used in Mexican gastronomy; *Quiero ser tuya. . . . Quiero amarte. Atarte. Amarrarte*: I want to be yours. . . . I want to love you. Tie you. Tie you up.

248.15   Dolores del Río] Mexican actor (1904–1983) and an international film star, active for more than fifty years in Hollywood and in Mexican cinema.

248.16   Mexican spitfire] The popular film comedy *Mexican Spitfire* (1940), starring Mexican actor Lupe Vélez (1908–1944), was one of a series of eight films produced from 1939 to 1943; the moniker was often applied to Vélez herself in media accounts.

248.20   eagle and serpent] See note 182.17–18.

248.32   Mexico City '85 earthquake] Massive earthquake with a magnitude of 8.1 that struck Mexico City on September 19, 1985.

248.33   Popocatepetl/Iztaccíhuatl] Popocatepetl is an active volcano in Mexico connected to the dormant Iztaccíhuatl volcano. According to one Aztec legend, the princess Iztaccíhuatl, having been erroneously told the warrior Popocatepetl has been killed, dies of a broken heart. Popocatepetl then kneels by her grave and dies of sadness, whereupon the couple are turned into mountains.

249.2   Agustín Lara] Prolific and beloved Mexican composer (1897–1970) and songwriter known for his boleros; his numerous hits include "Granada" (1932) and "Piensa en mí" (Think of me, 1935, written with his sister María Teresa Lara). See also note 265.2–3.

249.27   the filth goddess Tlazolteotl] Aztec deity associated with sexual desire and transgression, especially adultery; "filth goddess" is a translation of her name in Nahuatl.

250.2   *Virgen de Guadalupe*] See note 183.21.

250.2   *diosa Coatlicue*] Goddess Coatlicue, referring to the important Aztec earth goddess; her name means "serpent skirt" in Nahuatl, referring to the garment of snakes she wears.

251.13   Pancho Villa] See note 185.4.

251.22   *Que se vayan a la ching chang chong!*] Variation on "que se vayan a la chingada," i.e., they can go to hell. Other Spanish in the poem—*¡Wáchale!*: Spanish conjugated form of the English word *watch*, i.e., Chicano slang for watch out.

252.7   smoke me with *copal.*] Resin from copal trees was used as incense on altars in Mexico.

252.10   *petate*] Sitting or sleeping mats woven from dried *palma* leaves.

252.11   "Disco Inferno."] Hit song (1976) by The Trammps, an American disco group.

252.16   witch woman] A *curandera* or traditional natural healer.

252.18　Otomí] Indigenous people and a language spoken in central Mexico.

252.23　*maguey*] Agave.

252.25　*Ni Modo*] A phrase to show that nothing else can be done; similar to "Oh well."

252.27　Music, Fellini-esque] Like the music from the films of Federico Fellini (1920–1993), Italian director whose films include *La Dolce Vita* (1960) and *8½* (1963). Many of Fellini's films were scored by the Italian composer Nino Rota (1911–1979).

259.2　*La gran ciudad*] The big city. Other Spanish in the poem—*Una mujer de tantas/sola/divorciada/separada/largada*: A woman like so many others/alone/divorced/separated/left; *llegué a la gran ciudad/con mi niño en los brazos/por sembrar su camino trigueño/con las blancas flores/de la esperanza*: I arrived in the big city/with my son in my arms/to sow his wheaty path/with the white flowers/of hope [*trigueño* also refers to someone who is tan, olive-skinned, and/or sometimes dark-skinned or Black depending on context]; *El barrio, indefenso*: The defenseless neighborhood; *Mi raza: el ay por todas partes*: My people: woe everywhere; *Y la pregunta, que ofende*: And the question, which offends; *Y yo le contesto*: And I answer him; *Pero se cobró*: He was able to get even; *el muy pinche*: although it's not a translation, "the very big son of a bitch" is what would be said in the same situation; *a su modo*: in his way; *algún día nos olvidará por completo*: someday it will completely forget us; *Hijito, ¿nos comemos hoy/esta fiesta de pan/o lo dejamos para mañana?*: Son, shall we eat today/this celebration of bread/or shall we leave it for tomorrow?; *lárgense con su cuento/a otra parte!* get lost with your story/somewhere else!

261.4　Jayuya] A town in Puerto Rico.

262.9　*Alabanza*] Praise.

262.21–22　Roberto Clemente, his plane . . . Nicaragua] Roberto Clemente (1934–1972), star outfielder for the Pittsburgh Pirates, was killed in a plane crash off the coast of Puerto Rico shortly after takeoff on December 31, 1972. He was traveling to Nicaragua to personally deliver relief supplies to earthquake victims there.

264.14　Wise Men lost on their way to Bethlehem.] In Matthew 2 the Magi or "wise men" travel to Bethlehem from the East to visit the infant Jesus, to whom they bring gifts of gold, frankincense, and myrrh.

264.15　José Martí] See Biographical Notes.

266.31　Shangó—Cabio Sile] For adherents of Santería the invocation of Shangó, the Yoruba warrior god of thunder and lightning, is accompanied by the salutation "Cabio Sile" (often translated as "Welcome to the king").

267.10 *"You Do Something To Me"*] Song (1929) by Cole Porter (1891–1964), a jazz standard.

267.11 *Gerry González and The Fort Apache Band*] New York–born musician Jerry González (1949–2018), of Puerto Rican descent, was the bandleader of the Latin jazz ensemble the Fort Apache Band for more than thirty years.

267.18 bembé] Here, Afro-Cuban drumming with its origins in West Africa.

267.19 Mezclando manos] Mingled hands.

267.25–30 Miles 'n Sonny, across John, Rahsaan . . . Dalto's] Jazz greats the trumpeter Miles Davis (1926–1991), the saxophone players Sonny Rollins (b. 1930) and John Coltrane (1926–1967), the saxophone and flute player Rahsaan Roland Kirk (1935–1977), the pianist Thelonious Monk (1917–1982), and the trumpeter Dizzy Gillespie (1917–1993); followed by members of the Fort Apache Band: Jerry González (who played trumpet, flugelhorn, and congas), his brother the double bassist Andy González (1951–2020), the percussionist Nicky Marrero (b. 1950), and the pianist Jorge Dalto (1948–1987).

269.2 *Operation Wetback*] Mass deportations of more than one million Mexicans living on the U.S. side of the border with Mexico, 1954–55, by the Immigration and Naturalization Service.

269.8 *Mijo*] Short for "*mi hijo*," my son or more broadly my dear.

269.22 viejo sinvergüenza] Shameless old man, someone who takes advantage.

270.4 Teddy Roosevelt in Cuba.] During the Spanish-American War the future president Theodore Roosevelt (1858–1919) led the First U.S. Volunteer Cavalry, whose exploits at the Battle of San Juan Hill in Cuba, July 1, 1898, made them national heroes.

270.5 Ozzie Nelson] Actor (1906–1975) who with his wife, Harriet, and their sons, David and Ricky, was the epitome of mid-century American familial domesticity as expressed in the ABC television sitcom *The Adventures of Ozzie and Harriet*, 1952–66.

270.11 Butch Cassidy] Pseudonym of the outlaw Robert Leroy Parker (1866–1906), Utah-born criminal and leader of the Wild Bunch gang whose exploits have been romanticized in books and movies.

270.20–21 Message from Garcia] Cf. "Message to Garcia" (1899), widely circulated inspirational essay by Elbert Hubbard (1856–1915) recounting the heroism of an American lieutenant during the Spanish-American War.

271.9 "Stars and Stripes Forever"] "The Stars and Stripes Forever" (1896), march by John Philip Sousa (1854–1932).

273.4 *Pancho Villa*] See note 185.4.

274.3 *Joe Bataan*] Afro-Filipino American bandleader and composer (b. 1942) known for his groundbreaking innovations in Latin soul music.

276.1 *Trio Los Condes*] Puerto Rican band formed in New York in 1959, popular throughout Latin America and the United States.

276.8 Taíno Areyto] Celebratory ceremonies of Taíno peoples.

277.2–3 "Amor de mis amores" . . . skinny Agustín Lara] "Amor de mis amores" (1935) was one of Lara's better-known songs. Lara (see note 249.2) was also known for his thinness, with one of his nicknames being "El flaco de oro" (the Golden Skinny).

277.4–5 Rubén Darío's poems] Rubén Darío (pseud. Félix Rubén García Sarmiento, 1867–1916) was a Nicaraguan poet, journalist, and diplomat; he is a foundational figure in Latin American poetic *modernismo*.

277.15 Pedro Flores] Well-known Puerto Rican composer (1894–1979) of ballads and boleros.

281.15 Kashmir] Partitioned Himalayan region, with parts administered by India and Pakistan and both countries making claims to the other side's territory. Some Kashmiris want independence.

281.15 Fallujah] City in Iraq, the site of intense fighting and destruction during the U.S. war against Iraq.

284.20 chicano "ese" talk] Talk among buddies (fellow Chicanos).

285.1 vallenato] A genre of Colombian folk music.

285.8 cumbias] Musical genre and dance from Colombia. *Andino*: from the Andes.

285.12–13 tres por cuatro cubanities con los pasos firmes de aztecas] Three times four "Cubanities" with the firm steps of the Aztecs.

285.26 big stick] Cf. "Speak softly, and carry a big stick—you will go far," phrase by Theodore Roosevelt, first publicly used in a speech at the Minnesota State Fair, September 2, 1901.

288.18 Rousseau] The French naïve painter Henri Rousseau (1844–1910), also called "Le Douanier" (the toll collector) because of his job as a customs official.

291.23 *Translated by Edith Grossman*] In her book *Why Translation Matters* (2010), Grossman reflected on her translation of Manrique's poem: "A composition by Manrique in which the translation focused on transferring rhythms and capturing a certain domestic tone is called 'Mambo.' The original re-creates the dance rhythm of the mambo, using it to highlight the whirling images of the past that flash before the reader's eyes like a series of snapshots. In the translation, I tried to duplicate those dance rhythms and that representational, photographic quality with what is essentially a trimeter (although Spanish meter is not based on feet)—that is, an English version of the three-beat line that dominates the original. [   ] This has always seemed to me an affecting piece of writing. It presents the kind of subjective, emotional connection to a theme or feeling or state of mind that one normally does not encounter in the work of Nicanor Parra, for example, another ordinary-language poet from the opposite end of South America."

293.24–25 *brillando contra el sol y contra los poetas . . . —Heberto Padilla*] Shining against the sun and against the poets. From "A veces Me zambullo" (Sometimes I Dive) from *Provocaciones* (1973) by the Cuban poet Heberto Padilla (1932–2000). In what became an international literary cause célèbre, Padilla was placed under house arrest for his antigovernment sentiments and endured a show trial.

295.12 African St. Barbara] In Cuban Santería the Catholic saint Barbara is associated with the Yoruba deity Changó.

295.20 Ilé-Ifé] Ancient Yoruban city in southwestern Nigeria.

295.26 *zunzuncito* hummingbird] Or bee hummingbird, a tiny creature known as the world's smallest bird.

295.29 *sones*] Plural of *son*.

296.9 *jutía* rat] Or tree rat, a large rodent native to Cuba.

297.23 *zempasúchitl*] Or *cempasúchil*, marigold flowers used in Day of the Dead celebrations in Mexico.

298.2 La Llorona] In Mexican folklore, a woman who, deceived by the father of her children, despairs and drowns the children, then weeps over what she has done, wandering near rivers or lakes.

300.25 que a veces me sirva mi cena] May he serve me my dinner sometimes. Other Spanish in the poem—*como él que no haya igual*: may there not be another like him; *que me traiga florecitas*: may he bring me flowers.

303.23 *la lucha*] The struggle.

304.13 Azul] Blue. Other Spanish in the poem—*mi cielo, mi mar*: my sky, my sea.

306.2 *Last-Mambo-in-Miami*] When this poem was first published it was titled "Bilingual Blues."

306.3 Soy un ajiaco de contradicciones.] I am a jumble of contradictions (*ajiaco* is a soup with varying ingredients mixed in). Other Spanish in the poem—*tema*: subject; *cerca*: fence; *cantando voy*: I go singing; *tu madre*: your mother; *en casa*: at home; *un puré de impurezas*: a puree of impurities; *que nadie nunca acoplará*: that nobody will ever make fit in.

306.13–17   You say tomato . . . Let's call the hole] Alluding to "Let's Call the Whole Thing Off" (1937), music by George Gershwin (1898–1937), lyrics by Ira Gershwin (1896–1983), first performed in a dance duet by Fred Astaire and Ginger Rogers in the film *Shall We Dance?*: "You like potato and I like potahto,/You like tomato and I like tomahto,/Potato, potahto, tomato, tomahto!/Let's call the whole thing off!"

306.16   Pototo] Leopoldo Fernández (1904–1985), one half of the Cuban mambo and comedy duo Pototo y Filomeno.

308.6   Mira] Look.

310.27   the irish sweepstakes] International lottery organized in Ireland to aid Irish hospitals, 1930–87.

319.1   lady bird johnson] Claudia Alta Taylor "Lady Bird" Johnson (1912–2007), wife of President Lyndon Johnson (1908–1973), first lady of the United States, 1963–69.

319.8   en mi casa toman bustelo] "In my house we drink Bustelo," marketing slogan for Bustelo Coffee.

321.21   Rockefeller's] American businessman and politician Nelson Rockefeller (1908–1979), governor of New York, 1959–73; later vice president of the United States, 1974–77.

322.8   vecina] Neighbor. (fem.)

323.1   MARIGUILOS] Marigolds.

323.32   *The Twilight Zone*] Science-fiction television show that in its original iteration, 1959–64, on CBS was hosted by Rod Serling (1924–1975). The episode referred to here is "The Mighty Casey" (1960).

324.2   Hobo Concephers] I.e., the fictional Hoboken Zephyrs baseball team.

326.5   sopa de arroz] Lit. "rice soup," a side dish of rice.

326.12   albondigas] Meatballs.

331.1   *Jarocho*] *Son jarocho*, folk genre of music from the Mexican state of Veracruz.

331.7   Una nueva canción] A new song.

331.8   Exitos] Hits. For Lara, see notes 249.2 and 265.2–3.

331.18   *copas de vino*] Glasses of wine.

333.20   *carnitas*] Pork meat, deep-fried in pork lard.

340.3   oye] Listen. Other Spanish in the poem—*bato loco*: Chicano slang meaning "crazy dude"; *cabrón*: slang, asshole; *reflejos de años pasados*: reflections of past years; *en el refuego juareño*: in the Juárez chaos; *avenida juárez calle mariscál*: Juárez Avenue, Mariscal Street; *cuando la gente real/espresaba víscera y entrañas*: when real people/expressed guts, i.e., deeply; *jovencito*: young; *bebiendo sauza con limón*: drinking Sauza tequila with lime; *tristemente sentía/los trastornos*: sadly felt the disturbances; *dentro refuego y desmadre*: in chaos and drunkenness; *angustia*: anxiety; *chingo*: can mean persistence in working or trying very hard, or can mean a lot of something; *y me chingan todavía*: they still screw me.

342.7   *Conejo*] Rabbit.

343.23   *Bulosan*] Born in the Philippines, the writer Carlos Bulosan (1911?–1956) immigrated to the United States in 1930 or 1931; his best-known work, the autobiographical novel *America Is in the Heart*, was published in 1946.

343.32   *carabao*] Water buffalo.

345.16   *Oye, carnal*] Hey, brother. Other Spanish in the poem—*vato*: dude, guy.

346.2   *Mujeres del Rebozo Rojo*] Women of the Red Shawl.

348.5   *Trigueño*] Wheat-colored, referring to skin complexion (can refer to someone who is tan, olive-skinned, or sometimes dark-skinned or Black, depending on context). Other Spanish in the poem—*Puerto*: Port; *el Coco*: the Coconut (can also mean "brain"); *que hablas*: what do you speak; *toro*: bull.

349.3   Vato] Dude, guy. Other Spanish in the poem: *muy chucote*: very gangster; *el buey*: lit. Oxen or bull, but in slang buey or guey used neutrally means "guy" or used angrily can be an insult; *bien jodido*: very much screwed; *porque*: because; *rucas*: literally means "old women," but used here to refer to women in general; *loca*: crazy; *pedo*: in slang que pedo means "what's up?"; *pinche*: in slang can mean "fucking" or "damn"; *menudo*: a soup made with tripe and hominy; *onda*: literally wave, in slang it can mean "feeling."

350.21   a magnum, just like Dirty Harry] The fictional San Francisco police inspector Harry Callahan, played by Clint Eastwood (b. 1930) in *Dirty Harry* (1971) and its sequels, carries a Smith & Wesson .44 Magnum revolver.

355.5   Tiwa] Pre-Columbian Indigenous language spoken in parts of New Mexico.

356.2   *the Movie* GIANT] Film (1956) directed by George Stevens (1904–1975), starring Rock Hudson (1925–1985), Elizabeth Taylor (1932–2011), and James Dean (1931–1955).

356.13–14   their daughter Luz, and daughter-in-law Juana and grandson Jordy] Played, respectively, by Mercedes McCambridge (1916–2004), Elsa Cárdenas (b. 1932), and Dennis Hopper (1936–2010).

361.4   AZtlán] Name for the mythical homeland of the Aztecs thought to be in the Southwestern United States.

361.6   Chaley Chastitellez] Protagonist of Alvarez's verse novel *McTlán*.

361.7   Xingadx] I.e., Chingadx: fucker (gender neutral). Other Spanish in the poem—*Xicanxs*: i.e., Chicanxs; *la migra*: border police; *los vendidos agringadxs*: those Americanized sellouts; *boca*: mouth; *lengua*: tongue; *chavalito*: little kid.

361.14–16   Puebla . . . Sinaloa . . . Chihuahuas] States in Mexico.

361.25   Dedalus] Stephen Dedalus, protagonist of *A Portrait of the Artist as a Young Man* (1916), novel by the Irish writer James Joyce (1882–1941), and a major character in Joyce's *Ulysses* (1922).

361.26   Oneigen] Eugene Onegin, titular hero of the verse novel (1833) by the Russian writer Alexander Pushkin (1799–1837).

365.13   *Caravan*] Jazz composition (1937) written by Juan Tizol (1900–1984) and Duke Ellington (1899–1974), associated with Ellington's orchestra.

365.28   the Cotton Club] New York City nightclub of the 1920s and 1930s in Harlem and, from 1936 to 1940, on Times Square; Duke Ellington's orchestra was its house band from 1927 to 1931.

365.30   Latin Quarter] New York nightclub on Times Square at 48th Street.

365.32   no need to study war no more.] Cf. "Ain't gonna study war no more," repeated phrase in the work song and spiritual "Down by the Riverside," often played in jazz and other arrangements.

366.2   Chalatenango] Department in northern El Salvador, and its capital city; Sonsonate is a department in western El Salvador and the name of its capital city as well.

367.3   *D.A.C.A. DREAMers*] Since 2012, conferral of DACA (Deferred Action for Childhood Arrivals) status by the U.S. Citizenship and Immigration Services has protected undocumented minors from being deported. (DACA was declared illegal by a judge in Texas in September 2023, barring the acceptance of new applications during the appeals process concerning its legality.) "DREAMers" refers to potential beneficiaries of the Development, Relief, and Education for Alien Minors (DREAM) Act, legislation that would provide a path to U.S. citizenship for undocumented immigrants who arrived as minors; various versions have been introduced in Congress since 2001 but none have passed into law.

367.10   *ROQUE DALTON*] Salvadoran poet and writer (1935–1975), a Communist who spent much of his career in exile; he was executed by El Salvador's People's Revolutionary Army (ERP). His "Como tú" (Like you) was included in the posthumous collection *Poemas clandestinos* (Clandestine Poems, 1984).

373.4   *an installation*] *Temple of Confessions* (1996) by the performance artist Guillermo Gómez-Peña (b. 1955) and Roberto Sifuentes (b. 1967).

373.6   Se cruzan] They cross. Other Spanish in the poem—*en el templo de*: in the temple of; *pinchados*: punctured; *coro de*: choros of; *pollito mojado*: wet chicken; *picoso y picado*: spicy hot and chopped up; *mentes*: minds; *pachuca*: feminine form of pachuco, member of youth subculture that emerged in the 1940s; *la migra*: border police; *meando*: peeing; *Simón!*: a way of saying sí, yes; *juala de joda*: fucked/ing cage; *aquí juntándonos*: huddled together here; *cucarachas*: cockroaches.

374.2   Aztlán] See note 361.4.

375.2–11   *La Fiesta del Globo* . . . Pan Am Games deserter] *Fiesta del Globo*: Balloon Party. In November 1993, during the Central American and Caribbean Games in Ponce, Puerto Rico, the nineteen-year-old Cuban archer Alfonso Donate, along with his father, joined a contingent of numerous defectors from Cuba among the athletes.

375.24   Madrina] Godmother.

376.3   Atandá] "Yorubá. Proper name of one of the first drummers brought to Cuba as a slave. Famous for consecrating the first set of bàtá drums in Cuba, Ño José, Obakole, Akinlakpa were other historical drummers" (Castro's note).

383.6   Salcedo] The sixteenth-century Spanish conquistador Felipe de Salcedo.

385.3   *a serious surplus population that needs eliminating*] See the website of the organization Refusing to Forget (https://refusingtoforget.org/the -history/), which seeks to raise awareness about violence against ethnic Mexicans on the U.S.–Mexico border from 1910 to 1920: "the violence was welcomed, celebrated, and even instigated at the highest levels of society and government. As thousands fled to Mexico and decapitated bodies floated down the Rio Grande, one Texas paper spoke of 'a serious surplus population that needs eliminating.'"

385.4   verdad?] Right?

385.8   *El otro lado*] The other side.

388.2   Llorona] See note 298.2.

389.1–2   mortal coils] Hamlet speaks of "shuffl[ing] off this mortal coil" during his "To be, or not to be" soliloquy in *Hamlet*, III.i.55–87.

391.7   *Sandía, día santo!*] Watermelon, holy day!

393.5   the Italian Riccioli, naming the seas] In *Almagestum Novum* (1651), bk. 4, by the Italian astonomer Giovanni Battista Riccioli (1598–1671).

393.12   "bahri."] Arabic: marine, maritime.

394.6   Renisha McBride] A nineteen-year-old Black woman fatally shot by a white man, Theodore Wafer, through the screen door of his home in Dearborn Heights, MI, in the early morning hours of November 2, 2013. Wafer was convicted of second-degree murder for McBride's killing.

394.7   Trayvon Martin] While walking home on the evening of February 26, 2012, Trayvon Martin (b. 1995) was followed by George Zimmerman (b. 1983), a neighborhood watch volunteer for a gated community in Sanford, Florida. Zimmerman called the police and was told to remain in his vehicle; he nonetheless got out and in a scuffle with Martin he fatally shot the unarmed teenager in the chest. Zimmerman was acquitted of second-degree murder and manslaughter charges in a verdict that led to widespread protests.

394.7   Rekia Boyd] Twenty-two-year-old woman fatally shot in the back of the head by the off-duty Chicago police officer Dante Servin, who fired at Boyd and her group of friends in a park on March 21, 2012. Servin was cleared of involuntary manslaughter charges in 2015.

394.17   the beautiful child Emmett] Fourteen-year-old Emmett Till (1941–1955) was murdered on August 28, 1955, while visiting Leflore County, Mississippi, from Chicago; he was beaten and shot to death after he allegedly whistled at a white woman. His murder and the acquittal on September 23 of Roy Bryant and J. W. Milam, the two white men charged with the crime (both of whom later admitted to a journalist that they had killed Till), attracted widespread public attention.

394.19   Open casket of the night] Mamie Till (1921–2003) insisted that her murdered son be viewed by mourners at his funeral in an open casket so that the atrocity of the violence against him was visible. Photographs of Emmett Till in the open casket by David Jackson (1922–1966) appeared in *JET* magazine, September 15, 1955.

395.8   PROHIBIDO HABLAR DE POLITICA] Speaking about politics is forbidden.

395.13   Flamboyán] Tree native to Puerto Rico, also known as flame tree.

402.16   "*Siga, siga,*"] Continue, keep going.

405.1   Frozen Niagara . . . Fat Man's Misery] In Mammoth Cave in Kentucky, a section with a dense collection of stalactites and a narrow one-hundred-foot passageway, respectively.

406.1   ICE] Immigration and Customs Enforcement.

410.3   *pa' mi gente*] For my people. Other Spanish in the poem—*Mira a mi cara Puertorriqueña/A mi pelo vivo/A mis manos morenas/Mira a mi corazón que se llena de orgullo/Y dime que no soy Boricua*: Look at my Puerto Rican face/At my lively hair/At my brown hands/Look at my heart that fills with pride/And tell me I'm not Boricua; *coquis*: a frog native to Puerto Rico; *Mira!*: Look!; ¡*No nací en Puerto Rico/Puerto Rico nació en mi!*: I wasn't born in Puerto Rico/Puerto Rico was born in me!

412.4   *Santa Niño*] The Holy Child.

412.17   Chimayo] Site of El Santuario de Chimayo, a shrine and pilgrimage destination in the Sangre de Cristo Mountains of New Mexico.

412.19   San Felipe] San Felipe de Neri Church in Albuquerque's Old Town, first built in 1706 and rebuilt in 1793.

415.10   Jacques Cousteau] French oceanic explorer (1910–1997).

416.1–4   Spider Woman . . . Fourth World.] Hopi creation mythology posits a succession of seven worlds; the god Taiowa created Sotuknang who, in the First World, created Kokyangwuit, the Spider Woman who helped her create life. Our current worldly universe is the Fourth World.

422.5–7   "How does it feel to be a problem?" . . . Du Bois] See the beginning of the first chapter of *The Souls of Black Folk* (1903) by W.E.B. Du Bois (1868–1963): "Between me and the other world there is ever an unasked question[. . . .] All, nevertheless, flutter round it. They approach me in a half-hesitant sort of way, eye me curiously or compassionately, and then, instead of saying directly, How does it feel to be a problem? they say, I know an excellent colored man in my town; or, I fought at Mechanicsville; or, Do not these Southern outrages make your blood boil? At these I smile, or am interested, or reduce the boiling to a simmer, as the occasion may require. To the real question, How does it feel to be a problem? I answer seldom a word."

426.11   Aztlán] See note 361.4.

426.12   dios del sol] God of the sun. Other Spanish in the poem—¿*Sabes qué, hombre?*: You know what, man?

426.16   Roosevelt and his American concentration camps."] Internment without trial or hearing of more than 120,000 Japanese Americans and Japanese residents living on the West Coast, based on an executive order signed by President Franklin D. Roosevelt on February 19, 1942.

426.24   Rivera] Diego Rivera.

430.30   brutal San Ciprián] Destructive hurricane that made landfall in Puerto Rico on September 27, 1932.

431.1   Katrina and the Superdome] The Superdome in New Orleans became an enormous makeshift shelter for evacuees fleeing Hurricane Katrina in August 2005.

433.26–27   Antigone . . . proper memorial.] Antigone, title character of tragedy (441 BCE) by the Greek dramatist Sophocles, defies an order not to bury the corpse of her treasonous brother Polynices, is arrested, and hangs herself.

435.28   *baño*] A ritual bath for spiritual cleansing.

438.4   Tontonmacoutes] Tonton Macoutes; Haitian secret police.

442.2   *El Exilio*] The exile. Other Spanish in the poem—*mi prisión*: my prison; *pa' que*: for what.

442.3–6   *White birds . . . home.*] The complete text of "Another Spring," version by the American poet Kenneth Rexroth (1905–1982) of a poem by the Chinese poet Tu Fu (713–770) in Rexroth's *One Hundred Poems from the Chinese* (1971).

444.20   *lehrstuck*] *Lehrstück*, German for "teaching play," a didactic theater piece developed by playwright Bertolt Brecht.

449.2   *La Ciguapa*] Supernatural figure in Dominican folklore who roams the mountainsides in the form of a naked woman with ankle-length hair and backward-facing feet. In many versions of her legend she transfixes men with her eyes and kills them.

449.9   Atabeyra] Mother goddess, one of the two supreme Taíno deities.

453.2–3   *Golden Shovel . . . after Gwendolyn Brooks and Terrance Hayes*] The poet Terrance Hayes (b. 1971) invented the "Golden Shovel" poetic form, in which words from a poem, most frequently by Gwendolyn Brooks (1917–2000), are selected to be end words in a new poem. Here the Brooks poem is "We Real Cool."

455.12   *oye nene*] Hey boy.

455.17–18   twice the American government intervened and occupied the country] In 1916–24 and in 1965–66, the latter as part of an inter-American peacekeeping force.

455.19–20   twice, the number of times we fought to gain our independence against French Haiti] In 1805, when Haiti's emperor Jean-Jacques Dessalines (1758–1806) mounted an unsuccessful invasion of Santo Domingo, and in the Dominican War of Independence, 1844–56, which ended Haiti's twenty-two-year occupation of what became the Dominican Republic.

456.11   Tito's] Tito Puente (1923–2000), a Manhattan-born Puerto Rican bandleader and percussionist, founder in 1949 and leader of the Tito Puente Orchestra.

456.12   a Catholic saint] Santa Barbara (see note 299.12).

457.2   *Yaguareté*] Jaguar.

457.13   tierra de arcilla] Clay soil. Other Spanish in the poem—*tía*: aunt; *sobrino*: nephew.

457.25–458.2   "Chautauqua," co-opted by enterprising whites, . . . cultural accumulation which does sound awfully familiar.] The Chautauqua community, founded in 1874 in Jamestown, New York, was designed to promote intellectual and spiritual development. "Chautauqua" came to be used as a generic term for various troupes that traveled throughout the country presenting cultural entertainments.

458.19–20 *hū . . . morotī*] Guarani: black . . . white.

458.21–22 evil Tau chasing the child Kerana] In Guarani mythology, the supreme god Tupã created the good spirit Angatupyry and the evil spirit Tau, who fell in love with the princess Kerana. When Angatupyry defeated Tau after a seven-day battle Tau was banished to the underworld, but Tau returned to abduct Kerana. Their offspring, cursed by the moon goddess Arasy, were seven monsters.

458.27 Rupave and Sypave] In Guarani mythology, the first humans.

462.4 ganas] A sense of drive and desire.

463.2 *Mejiafricana*] Mexican African.

463.5–6 escribo de/mi vida cultura colorada/pintada] I write of/my colorful culture life/painted. Other Spanish in the poem—*para que puedan ver*: so that they can see; *yo soy la morena*: I am the brown woman; *la poema*: poem, usually masculine, made feminine here; *que despierta su mente*: who wakes their mind; *que enciende su alma*: who lights up their soul; *con papel y pluma*: with paper and pen; *el viento que viene de méxico*: the wind that comes from Mexico; *el este y el oeste*: the east and the west; *esta es la verdad*: this is the truth; *un burrito de chorizo con huevo*: a burrito of chorizo and egg; *niños*: children; *salsa picosa*: hot salsa; *una mariposa*: a butterfly; *sico*: mouth [slang]; *una niña del yucatán*: a girl from yucatán; *chichén itzá*: i.e., an ancient Mayan city; *quetzalcoatl*: i.e., Quetzalcoatl, the Mesoamerican feathered serpent deity; *mi gente*: my people; *lo que sea/es la misma cosa*: whatever/it's the same thing; *sangre*: blood; *una niña de mi país*: a girl from my country; *una de una raza tan fuerte*: one from a race so strong; *una niña de méxico y así me quedo*: a girl from Mexico and that's how I will remain.

464.19 willie colon frankie ruiz and celia] Trombonist and salsa musician Willie Colón (b. 1950); salsa singer Frankie Ruiz (1958–1998); Cuban-born singer Celia Cruz (1926–2003).

467.15 *Miel*] Honey.

470.10 chapín] Informal word for fellow Guatemalan.

471.1 vamos pa' el norte] Let's go north.

474.8 *Sangrón*] Arrogant, annoying person. Other Spanish in the poem—*borracho*: drunk; *Arriba*: Let's go; *Frijolero*: Beaner [derogatory term for Mexicans]; ¿*No qué no/tronabas pistolita?*: Literally "Didn't you say you didn't go off, little gun?", commonly used expression meaning "I thought you didn't have it in you"; *cuates*: friends; ¡*No mames*!: lit. "Don't suck," slang for "No way!"

474.10 Arriba Durango. Arriba Orizaba.] Exclamatory pride for two distinct regions in Mexico.

475.6 águila perched on a nopal.] See note 182.17–18.

475.8 César Chávez] American farmworker and labor organizer (1927–1993) who cofounded the National Farm Workers Association (later the United Farm Workers) in 1962.

480.11 *el cielo de mis sueños*] The sky of my dreams. Other Spanish in the poem—*como porros*: like cigarettes (tobacco or marijuana); *porque nuestras madres nos dijeron que viven allí*: because our mothers told us that they live there; *masa*: corn dough; *y toman la hostia*: and take the host [during the rite of communion]; *misa*: mass; *estómagos*: stomachs; *el vacío*: the emptiness; *sana sana colita de rana si no sanaras ahora sanarás mañana*: heal, heal, tail of the frog, if you don't heal now, you'll heal tomorrow [said to children when they get hurt]; *y esperan y esperamos*: and they wait and we wait.

483.11 culebra] Snake.

488.2 *Xunantunich*] Site ("Stone Woman") of Mayan ruins in Belize near the border with Guatemala. It is named for the ghost of the woman who, according to local folklore, haunts the site.

489.2 *Coatlicue*] See note 250.2.

489.3 *Tunguska Event*] On the morning of June 20, 1908, an asteroid exploded over a remote area of Siberia. The impact of the blast flattened an estimated eighty million trees over an area of 830 square miles.

489.21 bruja's] *Bruja*: witch.

491.2 *Coatlicue*] See note 250.2.

491.4 Closner Road] Closner Boulevard in Edinburg, TX.

491.6–7 *Me tragué toda la basura/Me tragué la cocina y los carros/Con gente o sin*] I swallowed all the garbage. I swallowed the kitchen and the cars./With or without people.

493.9 La Virgen] The Virgin of Guadalupe (see note 183.21).

497.2 Cristo Negro de Portobelo] An eight-foot-tall wooden statue in the Iglesia de San Felipe in Portobelo, Panama, known as El Nazareno, a representation of a Black Jesus Christ. Portobelo is the site of an annual Festival of the Black Christ.

498.11 remolino] Whirlwind.

499.6 fitna] Arabic: trial, strife. Other non-English words in the poem—
cuarenta cuaresmas [Sp.].: forty Lents; *Shukr* [Ar.]: Thankfulness, gratitude;
tasbih [Ar.]: prayer beads; *jumu'ah* [Ar.]: Friday; *Tajweed* [Ar.]: Rules for
reciting the Qu'ran; *donde tomó su testigo* [Sp.]: where he took his witness;
Sujud [Ar.]: Prostration; *Tawbah* [Ar.]: Repentance to Allah; *los peregrinos
en la Basílica/de Guadalupe* [Sp.]: the pilgrims in the Basilica of Guadalupe
[cathedral in Mexico City]; *masjid* [Ar.]: mosque; *Ishtighfar* [Ar.]: Seeking
forgiveness; *dunya* [Ar.]: the earthly world; *salah* [Ar.]: referring to obligatory
prayers for Muslims; *tantas veces* [Sp.]: many times; *dedos* [Sp.]: fingers.

499.24 mike brown] Michael Brown (1996–2014) was killed by police
officer Darren Wilson (b. 1986) in Ferguson, MO, on August 9, 2014.
Wilson had driven his SUV in front of Brown and twenty-two-year-old
Dorian Johnson to question them about a reported theft of cigarillos from
a nearby convenience store. According to the report (2015) of a Department
of Justice investigation into Brown's death, Wilson fired his gun twice
during a scuffle between himself and Brown while Wilson was still inside the
vehicle, wounding Brown's right hand. Brown then fled, pursued by Wilson
on foot. When Brown turned around and faced Wilson, the police officer
fired several times, including a fatal gunshot to the head. A crowd soon
formed at the scene; Brown's corpse lay on the ground on Canfield Road
for at least four hours. Brown's death, which according to some accounts
had occurred while he was surrendering to Wilson, led to days of vigils,
protests, and civil unrest, which in turn were met with a curfew and a highly
militarized response by the Ferguson Police Department, the Missouri State
Highway Patrol, and the National Guard. The events in Ferguson received
widespread national and international attention. Further protests and unrest
took place in November after a grand jury declined to indict Wilson for the
killing.

501.6 crudo] Hungover.

502.3 por que no novelas] Why no soap operas.

503.8 *naranja*] Orange.

504.17 mi lengua para ti] My tongue for you.

509.17–18 in a waiting room . . . Bishop's childhood memory] As recalled in
the poem "In the Waiting Room" from *Geography III* (1976) by the American
poet Elizabeth Bishop (1911–1979).

510.7 y vocificando] And shouting. Other Spanish in the poem—*son de
Nicaragua*: they are from Nicaragua; *y su compañero*: and his friend; *playas
del sol*: beaches of sun; *fincas*: farms; *con un coyote*: with a person who illegally
guides people across the border; *no me hicieron nada*: they didn't do anything
to me; *Debajo los llantos de la luna*: Under the cries of the moon.

512.3 *after Idris Goodwin*] The poem is in part inspired by "A Preface" from Idris Goodwin's book *These Are the Breaks* (2011).

512.24 que significa esa palabra] What does this word mean. Other Spanish in the poem—*sin papeles*: without papers; *mijo*: my son.

514.4 cuerpos morenos] Brown bodies.

514.23 NDN] Slang term for Indigenous Americans.

514.24 assata shakur] The radical activist Assata Shakur (b. JoAnne Deborah Byron in 1947), a member of the Black Liberation Army, was convicted of first-degree murder in the death of a New Jersey state policeman during a shoot-out on the New Jersey Turnpike on May 2, 1973. After her escape from prison on November 2, 1979, she went to Cuba, where she has since lived. In 2013 she was placed on the FBI's Most Wanted Terrorists list.

514.25 sandra bland] On July 10, 2015, Bland (1987–2015) was pulled over by Texas state trooper Brian Encinia on a traffic stop and, after a confrontation, was taken into custody in a Waller County jail on assault charges. Three days later, she was found hanging in a fifteen-by-twenty-foot cell in what was ruled a suicide. The actions of Encinia and the jail's employees in their treatment of Bland elicited national criticism and protests. A grand jury declined to indict Encinia in December 2015 on charges related to Bland's death, though he was dismissed from the state police force and was later indicted for perjury; these charges were dropped after he agreed not to seek further employment in law enforcement.

514.32 tavia nyong'o] Critic and professor (b. 1974), author of *The Amalgamation Waltz: Race, Performance, and the Ruses of Memory* (2008).

515.20 elotes] Corn. Other Spanish in the poem—*compañeros-compañeras*: dance partners; *conjunto*: musical ensemble of the region.

516.8 Guabancex] Taíno goddess of the winds and storms (sometimes referred to as Juracán or Huracan).

516.21 a *son*] Piece of Afro-Cuban music, marked by African rhythms and ostinato patterns often played on piano.

519.33 Biggie? Pac? Pun?] The rival rappers Notorious B.I.G. (Christopher George Latore Wallace (1972–1997), also known as Biggie Smalls, and Tupac Shakur (Lesane Parish Crooks, 1971–1996), as well as the rapper Big Pun, short for Big Punisher (Christopher Lee Rios, 1971–2000).

521.3 *Carolyn Forché* . . . what you've written] In the poem "The Colonel" (1981) by the American poet Carolyn Forché (b. 1950).

523.12–13 palabras sagradas . . . masculinas] Sacred words that leave your mouth/and the feminine and masculine rhymes. Other Spanish in the poem—*guerrero*: warrior; *mi rey*: my king; *con el Corazón que tienes*: with the Heart you have; *Mi Vida*: my Life; *tierra*: earth; *el desierto*: the desert; *Como los Ríos que nuestra gente ha cruzado*: like the Rivers that our people have crossed; *los antepasados*: the ancestors; *En la tierra que te vio nacer*: in the land that saw you be born; *En esa tierra que ha sido bautizada*: in this land that has been baptized; *Con la sangre sagrada de nuestra gente*: with the sacred blood of our people; *Como el sol por las mañanas*: like the sun in the mornings.

526.3   Güera] White or light-skinned. Other Spanish in the poem— *Sinvergüenza*: shameless, scoundrel; *Mija*: my daughter; *habla en español*: speak in Spanish; *No me gusta hablar en español porque mi español es muy mal*: I don't like to speak Spanish because my Spanish is much bad; *No. Me. Siento. Bien. Hablo. Hablas. Habla*: I. Don't. Feel. Well. I speak. You speak. Speak; *la puta*: the whore; *Me hicieron ojo*: they put the evil eye on me; *Ya tu sabes!*: you know it!; *sancho*: the lover of a married woman.

526.11–12   killed Selena . . . flor.] The enormously popular Tejano music singer Selena (Selena Quintanilla-Pérez, 1971–1995) was murdered by Yolanda Saldívar, the president of her fan club and the director of her beauty line and boutique, in a hotel in Corpus Christi, TX, on March 31, 1995. "Como la Flor" (Like the Flower) refers to Selena's 1992 recording of a song written for her by her brother A. B. Quintanilla III (b. 1963) and Pedro Astudillo (b. 1963). It was the closing song of her last concert before she was murdered.

526.13   "Put the Blame on Mame"] Song best known for the version in the 1946 film noir *Gilda*, in which Rita Hayworth (b. Margarita Carmen Cansino, 1918–1987), playing a nightclub chanteuse in Buenos Aires, teasingly peels off her full-length black opera gloves while singing.

527.2   *La Migra*] The border police.

528.26   Adichie and Alexie] Nigerian novelist Chimamanda Ngozi Adichie (b. 1977), whose books include *Half of a Yellow Sun* (2006), and the American writer Sherman Alexie (b. 1966), whose books include the novel *The Absolutely True Diary of a Part-Time Indian* (2007).

532.2–9   Archimedes . . . Displacement.] While in a bathtub the Greek mathematician and philosopher Archimedes (c. 287–212 BCE) discovered the principle of displacement, which he applied to test the gold purity of King Hiero's crown.

533.12–16   Archimedes's book . . . filled with prayers to the Lord.] The texts of treatises on mathematics by Archimedes, originally written on papyrus (now lost), were copied onto parchment by a scribe in tenth-century Constantinople. In the thirteenth century the text was erased and the parchment leaves were used, along with parchment from other books, to fashion a Greek Orthodox prayer book. Conservation and the use of imaging technology from 1999 to 2008 succeeded in making the erased text legible.

535.5–6   *¿Quién es el jefe/más jefe?*] Who's the boss of bosses? Other Spanish in the poem—*La yerba, el polvo, las piedras—/Que traguen fierro los cabrones,/¡yo soy el más chingón de Pisaflores!*: The herb, the dust, the stones [referring respectively to marijuana, cocaine, and crack cocaine]—/They can swallow metal the assholes /I am the greatest in Pisaflores [a municipality in Hidalgo]!; *Rompe-madres*: lit. Mother-breaker; someone who beats people up.

537.3   olla] Pot. Other Spanish in the poem—*masa*: dough; *niños*: children; *nietos*: grandchildren; *ojos*: eyes; *ojo negro*: black eye; *hoja*: leaf, sheet.

539.8   Desecheo Island.] Uninhabited .6-square-mile island off the west coast of Puerto Rico, now administered by the U.S. Fish and Wildlife Service as a wildlife preserve. It is closed to the public because of unexploded ordnance dating back to the island's use from the 1940s through the 1970s by the U.S. military.

539.12   esclavos] Slaves. Other Spanish in the poem—*cangrejos*: crabs.

543.3–4   *the immigrants buried in mass graves in and near, Falfurrias, Texas*] Beginning in 2013, a team led by forensic scientists from Baylor University and the University of Indianapolis, working with a laboratory at Texas State University, exhumed a series of mass graves at the Sacred Heart Burial Park in Falfurrias in Brooks County, TX, in an effort to identify the remains of unknown migrants who had died in Brooks County, TX, after crossing the U.S.–Mexico border.

546.11   presidents, guilty.] Antonio Saca (b. 1965), president of El Salvador 2004–9, pled guilty in 2018 to criminal embezzlement and money-laundering charges.

546.13   the news: black bags] News reports of a 2012 trial of a Salvadoran gang accused of homicides in Sonsonate contained accounts detailing how victims' body parts were put in black bags.

INDEX OF TITLES AND FIRST LINES

INDEX OF POETS

This book is set in 10 point ITC Galliard, a face designed
for digital composition by Matthew Carter and based
on the sixteenth-century face Granjon. The paper is acid-free
lightweight opaque that will not turn yellow or brittle with age.
The binding is sewn, which allows the book to open easily and lie flat.
The binding board is covered in Brillianta, a woven rayon cloth
made by Van Heek–Scholco Textielfabrieken, Holland.
Composition by Westchester Publishing Services.
Printing by Sheridan, Grand Rapids, MI.
Binding by Dekker Bookbinding, Wyoming, MI.
Designed by Bruce Campbell.

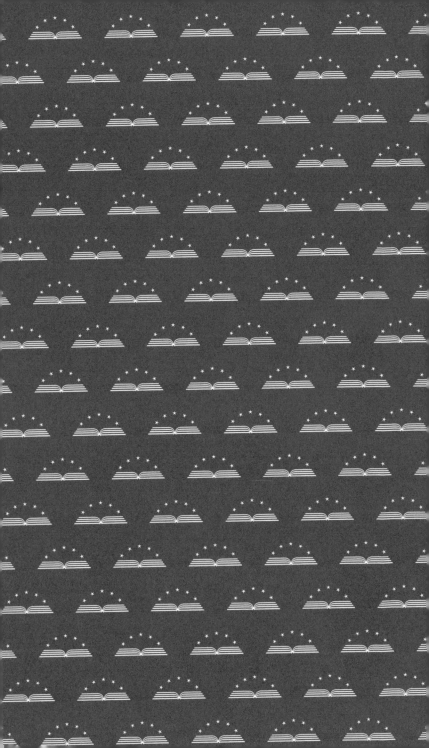